LADY JUSTICE

LADY JUSTICE

WOMEN, THE LAW,

=== *and the* ===

BATTLE TO SAVE AMERICA

Dahlia Lithwick

PENGUIN PRESS

NEW YORK

2022

PENGUIN PRESS
An imprint of Penguin Random House LLC
penguinrandomhouse.com

Copyright © 2022 by Dahlia Lithwick
Penguin Random House supports copyright. Copyright fuels creativity, encourages
diverse voices, promotes free speech, and creates a vibrant culture. Thank you
for buying an authorized edition of this book and for complying with copyright
laws by not reproducing, scanning, or distributing any part of it in any form
without permission. You are supporting writers and allowing Penguin
Random House to continue to publish books for every reader.

LIBRARY OF CONGRESS CATALOGING-IN-PUBLICATION DATA
ISBN 9780525561385 (hardcover)
ISBN 9780525561392 (ebook)

Printed in the United States of America
4th Printing

DESIGNED BY MEIGHAN CAVANAUGH

For Aaron, wherever we go, there we are,
thankfully together

For my parents—justice and loving-kindness
in perfect symmetry

CONTENTS

═══

INTRODUCTION

Freedom is a dream
Haunting as amber wine
Or worlds remembered out of time.
Not Eden's gate, but freedom
Lures us down a trail of skulls
Where men forever crush the dreamers—
Never the dream.

—PAULI MURRAY, *"Dark Testament"*

I'm not sure if my involvement in causes, benefits,
marches, and demonstrations has made a huge difference, but I know one thing: that involvement
has connected me with the good people: people
with the live hearts, the live eyes, the live heads.

—PETE SEEGER

I sometimes think of the Supreme Court oral arguments in *Whole Woman's Health v. Hellerstedt* on March 2, 2016, as the last truly great day for women and the legal system in America. There are, to be sure, many such glorious moments to choose from, both before and after Trump, but as a professional court-watcher, I had a front-row seat to this story, one that offered a sense that women in the United States had achieved some milestone that would never be reversed. The landmark abortion challenge represented the first time in American history that a historic abortion case was being heard by a Supreme Court with three female justices. Twenty-four years earlier, when the next momentous abortion case—*Planned Parenthood v. Casey*—had come before the Supreme Court, only one woman, Sandra Day O'Connor, sat on the bench. Go back a bit further and *Roe v. Wade*, the pathbreaking 1973 case that created a constitutional right to terminate a pregnancy, was argued before and decided by nine men and zero women. And when *Griswold v. Connecticut*, the lawsuit protecting the rights of married couples to buy and use birth control, was argued at the high court back in 1965, that bench comprised nine males so uneasy with the topic of contraception that at oral arguments nobody was brave enough even to name the birth control device being litigated. (As a result, the entire transcript from *Griswold*, argued fifty-one years before *Whole Woman's Health*, reads like an Abbott and Costello "Who's on First" sketch.) From that long-ago argument one may easily derive a general constitutional precept that nobody—not even well-meaning progressive male jurists and legislators—should be in the business of regulating birth control devices they are too freaked out to name.

Buried in that story is the truth about how legal decisions involving women, their salaries, their bodies, their educations, custody of their children, and their votes have been framed in American courtrooms until very recently: by husbands and fathers with good intentions and staggeringly low information. We lucked out. We got contraception and access to military schools, the right to our own credit cards, and all sorts of equal rights over the years. But it all felt different in 2016. Women now made up 50 percent of the law school population; they were partners at law firms, members of Congress, judges, professors, and three of them sat, with lifetime tenure, on the highest court in the land. Generations of women who had played by the rules, and changed American institutions and government, were poised to be a part of a genuinely equal polity. Sure, there were hiccups and setbacks. Although half of America's law students and lawyers were women, women made up only one-third of attorneys in private practice, 21 percent of equity partners, and 12 percent of managing partners, chairs, or CEOs of law firms. Hmm. Weird. Less than 5 percent of CEOs of Fortune 500 companies were women. And women made up only about 24 percent of Congress, 18 percent of governors, 29 percent of state legislators. So, okay, it wasn't perfect. But it was progressing. Equal pay was around the corner, better child-care and leave policies were barreling toward us, and as arguments progressed in *Whole Woman's Health*, it seemed distinctly possible that the last days of men telling women what to do with their freedom and their life choices and their family decisions, were dawning.

On that bright, freezing March morning, Ruth Bader Ginsburg, Sonia Sotomayor, and Elena Kagan tag-teamed their interrogation of Scott Keller—Texas's solicitor general—as he stutter-stepped through his justification of why, back in 2013, Texas had passed new requirements on clinics and physicians that would effectively close most abortion facilities and prevent women from terminating their pregnancies. These were onerous regulations. In rural areas, with clinics shuttered, women were forced to drive for days to access care. Whole swaths of Texas had no accessible clinics remaining at all. Poor women and women of color were hardest hit by the lack of facilities. They had to seek days off from work, sleep in their cars, return for repeat appointments. State lawmakers had argued that their sole interest in the new clinic laws was in protecting women's health, but women's well-being had declined catastrophically, and in court proceedings Texas could provide no evidence that improving health outcomes was the real reason for the regulations. Pressed on this question at oral argument, Solicitor General Keller could barely finish a sentence.

As the three women justices—deftly aided by Justice Stephen Breyer, the court's fourth feminist—took turns snacking on Texas's beleaguered lawyer, I witnessed for the first time in my sixteen-year career as a journalist something amazing: the rules of the Supreme Court road had shifted overnight. Court argument sessions are tightly controlled, highly formalized enterprises that haven't really changed much over two centuries, with the exception of COVID-era telephonic sessions. The nine justices sit at the same high bench next to the same spittoons (spittoons!), sipping from the same tall, silver milkshake cups they have been using for decades as lawyers make their formal arguments. But on that morning in 2016, the three women justices ignored the formal time limits, talking exuberantly over their flummoxed male colleagues. Justice Ruth Bader Ginsburg at one point essentially instructed the chief justice to add extra time to the clock for a female reproductive freedom advocate. And he complied. I described that day of three female justices and Justice Breyer going to town on counsel as a "four-car train of whoop ass." Not the usual controlled analysis from the staid justices. But what was exceptional and—at least in retrospect—heartbreaking that morning was that it afforded America a glimpse of what genuine gender parity or near parity might have meant for future women in powerful American legal institutions. It felt like the end of constitutionally sanctioned mansplaining. It felt, in a way, like the end of history.

That morning felt like nothing so much as an explosion of bottled-up judicial girl power that had been two centuries in the making. The 5–3 ruling that came down almost four months later upheld a woman's fundamental right to choose to end her pregnancy. That majority opinion, penned by Justice Breyer, asked courts and lawyers to puncture centuries of accumulated lies and stereotypes about fragile, confused women making bad choices in order to consider instead the actual ways in which women live their economic and moral lives. It was a constitutional breakthrough, written by a man who saw women as agents in full. At that moment, the country appeared inches away from leveraging the law to serve women's dignity and equality interests on a massive scale. Back in that spring of 2016, we really thought we could see gender equality from our back porches. And then it was gone. With the death of Justice Ginsburg in September 2020; the seating of three committed antichoice justices by Donald Trump in the years since *Whole Woman's Health*; and the reversal of Roe in June of 2022, that case will now likely stand as a high-water mark we may not soon see again in the courts, or in women's constitutional progress. It has become, at least for me, a marker of the end of history, but in completely the wrong direction. In a matter of weeks after *Whole Woman's Health* came down, constitutional history began to unravel quickly.

Every woman I know remembers what that summer before the 2016 election felt like. The GOP candidate for president who referenced Mexicans as rapists in launching his campaign. Four short months after *Whole Woman's Health* came down, we would all hear with our own ears the audio from *Access Hollywood* of the US Republican nominee for president boasting on camera that because he was "a star," he could "grab [women] by the pussy" without consequences. By November of 2016, we learned that the only consequence for such an admission would be a promotion to the Oval Office.

Every woman I know remembers precisely where she was when the 2016 election was called for Donald Trump. I was covering polling places in North Carolina that day, and it was dawning on me that the number of affronted women showing up in pantsuits to pull the lever for Hillary Clinton was underwhelming. Like so many of the women in this book, I spent election night comforting distraught kids and pounding bourbon. What had happened? How did it happen? Millions of people—millions of *women*—had voted for a man who had proven a thousand times over throughout the campaign that he thought women were best seen as the creamy offerings on a dessert cart. If we spoke up, pushed back, we were pigs, we were dogs, we were bleeding from the whatever. On the campaign trail, Trump expressly floated the idea of punishing women for terminating their pregnancies. How did we get here and how did it happen so quickly? Who, so many of us wondered, had voted for this man?

Yes, there was dancing in the streets in some quarters, but there were also hushed, horrified whispers over the phone all night. The day after the election I found myself on a dais, in a ballroom at a fancy hotel in Washington, DC, at a woefully poorly timed luncheon event celebrating women oral advocates at the Supreme Court. The tables were laid with white linen and sparkling crystal, and some of the young women lawyers, law clerks, and law students in the crowd sobbed openly. So did some of the speakers on the dais. So did *this* speaker on the dais. How could this event be happening? Hadn't history just ended? (Over the course of the next four years, as I covered the Mueller report and Michael Flynn and emoluments clause violations and Hatch Act violations and the slow implosion of the Justice Department, I met every Super Bowl, every Thanksgiving dinner, and every Presidents' Day White Sale with the same exact confusion: How could this event still be happening? Hadn't history just ended?)

But just as it seemed that women's progress was unraveling like a cheap sweater, something was rising up in its place. In response to what was happening at the top, extraordinary women were doing exceptional things everywhere else. There was the Women's March; there were armies of women phone banking; women's groups were teaching themselves about chattel slavery and systemic racism, about voting rights, about gender and power; women were creating circles, squares, and tetrahedrons of new kinds of activism. And in the midst of that, almost as if by unspoken mutual agreement, women lawyers were turning on a dime, upending their lives and their careers and their families to organize a new kind of resistance movement that would play out in courthouses, in statehouses, and in elections.

In the days and weeks before Donald Trump was inaugurated in January 2017, Sally Quillian Yates, the acting attorney general of the United States and highest-ranking official at the US Department of Justice (DOJ), had agreed to stay on as interim head of the DOJ. Yates was born and raised in Georgia in a family of lawyers. After almost three decades of public service as a prosecutor, she was well aware that she would be replaced by the new president at the first opportunity, because attorneys general serve at the pleasure of the president. But she had no idea she would immediately be fired for refusing to sign off on a travel ban she deemed rooted in religious intolerance. Yates had no notion she would be the first casualty in Donald Trump's war on the Constitution.

In New York City, at almost the same time, Becca Heller was a young lawyer who had co-founded the International Refugee Assistance Project (IRAP), an organization that had been working to help refugees fleeing intolerable conditions abroad to find lawyers to assist them with their asylum efforts in the United States. Humanitarian crises in Syria and around the world were already creating formidable challenges for the group. But Heller had no idea that she would, within mere days of Trump's inauguration, find herself on the front lines of what would become one of the biggest spontaneous public protests of the year—an uprising of citizens and lawyers swarming the nation's airports after Trump summarily banned immigration and refugees from Muslim-majority nations.

In New York City, Roberta Kaplan, a successful commercial litigator at Paul, Weiss, Rifkind, Wharton & Garrison, the tony white-shoe law firm, had no idea she'd soon be leaving her job to start a brand-new, woman-run litigation shop that would do large-scale pro bono social justice work. Kaplan, the winning lawyer in the pathbreaking 2013 marriage equality case, *United States v. Windsor*, had devoted twenty-five years to a big-city law practice. Little did she know when she marched in the first Women's March in January 2017, that within months she'd be in federal court in Virginia, suing Nazis who'd violently invaded Charlottesville and defending female whistleblowers in a series of #MeToo lawsuits. (Kaplan would later resign from Time's Up over a conflict about work she did for Governor Andrew Cuomo.) Kaplan would also come to represent E. Jean Carroll, a woman who alleged the president had raped her, and Mary Trump, the president's niece, who alleged that he and his siblings cheated her out of her inheritance.

In New York, Brigitte Amiri had planned to do big, impactful reproductive justice work for the ACLU after Hillary Clinton secured the presidency. She was looking forward to teaming up with the new administration to advance and secure women's contraceptive and abortion rights. She never expected to be thrust into the limelight when the Trump administration began to bar pregnant teen migrants from terminating their pregnancies. Vanita Gupta, formerly the head of the Justice Department's Civil Rights Division, was named president and chief executive of the Leadership Conference on Civil and Human Rights and found herself fighting against police brutality and immigration reforms and fighting to protect voting rights. Gupta had always thought of herself as a civil rights lawyer, not an organizer, but she would help helm several of the most important movements of the period—from marches protesting family separation policies to demands for social media reforms to voting rights. Women in Washington, DC, became the beating heart of an effort to eradicate sexual abuse and harassment in the judiciary, and, later, to oppose the nomination of accused sexual abuser Brett Kavanaugh to the Supreme Court. Anita Hill, who had leveled similar claims about Clarence Thomas decades earlier, would once again become the face and the voice of the urgent need to eradicate sexual predation in the workplace.

Stacey Abrams, who ran for and lost Georgia's governorship in a 2018 election marred by allegations of rampant voter suppression, reconstituted herself as a national voting rights juggernaut and modeled for millions of women, Black, Latino, and poor voters what it would take to organize, knock doors, and get out the vote in a presidential election year beset by a pandemic and vote suppression. In Texas, Nina Perales would spend years litigating against a different form of vote suppression, the race-based redistricting seeking to outrun demographic changes in America through gerrymandering and malapportionment. All of these names represent a fraction of the women on the front lines of the lawsuits, injunctions, organizing efforts, advocacy, and lobbying work seeking to fend off every conceivable assault on the environment, health care, unions, family separations, and more.

What exploded into existence in the days and weeks after Hillary Clinton lost the 2016 election was a small army of female lawyers with, perhaps not coincidentally, backgrounds similar to that of their preferred candidate. Like Clinton, they were women; like Clinton, they possessed law degrees; and like Clinton, they were simply unwilling to drift backward to a time when men made policy and women made dinner. Almost overnight that meant that armies of female lawyers and advocates—seemingly born for this precise moment—were galvanized and awakened before the Trump inauguration, and only deepened their engagement with the legal system in the weeks and months and years that followed. These women became equity partners in America's sprawling, pop-up resistance law firm, each seeking to preserve freedoms that were under daily assault for the four years in which Donald Trump assured us all that he himself was above the law, and also that the law could be bent to harm those who thwarted him. More than anything, this soaring women's legal resistance revealed, at least to me, that while we have all been waiting around despondently for Ruth Bader Ginsburg's next iteration to rescue us, the RBG 2.0s have been among us all along.

Two short years after Donald Trump left office, we face new headwinds that threaten to leave American women vulnerable in ways we could barely have imagined when *Whole Woman's Health* was argued. The Supreme Court is expanding gun rights, dismantling the power of agencies to protect the environment, and opening the door to state efforts to criminalize abortion, miscarriage, and contraception. The high court is also participating in efforts to stymie the vote. But women are not without legal and constitutional resources to fight back. Female lawyers know this fight intimately; they've been doing this work for decades. This is their playbook. This is the task ahead.

1

The Beginning

———

L ock her up!" "Lock her up!" "Lock her up!"
The crowds at Donald Trump's 2016 campaign rallies
would chant it about his opponent, Hillary Clinton. At the
Republican National Convention in 2016, in Cleveland, "Lock her up"
was the proposal on which delegates agreed most vocally and en-
thusiastically. Florida's governor, Rick Scott, New Jersey's governor,
Chris Christie, Trump's soon-to-be national security advisor Michael
Flynn, and Pam Bondi, the top law enforcement officer in the state of
Florida, each led screaming delegates in chants of "Lock her up." In a
subsequent presidential debate, the then candidate Trump warned
Clinton, "I'll tell you what. I didn't think I'd say this, but I'm going to
say it, and I hate to say it. But if I win, I am going to instruct my attorney general to get a special prosecutor to look into your situation."
Even years after Clinton lost the presidential election, Trump's attorney general, Jeff Sessions, gave a speech in 2018 to a group of mostly
male conservative high schoolers who gleefully chanted, "Lock her
up," as he smiled and chanted along.

If you're a woman who went to law school, or if you are a woman at all, or know one, or respect one, or if you are anyone with any conception of what the rule of law means, a rabid crowd screaming for the incarceration of a woman for imaginary "crimes" ranging from a terrorist attack in Benghazi, to the misuse of a private email server, to the management of a fictional pizza-parlor-based child-sex-slave ring is chilling. It is a threat about using the law—the apparatus that itself guarantees a woman's freedom and equality in America—to punish a woman for seeking elected office. This wasn't the garden-variety sexism that allowed men to chant "Iron my shirt" at Clinton campaign events. This was a threat to use the coercive force of state police power to lock up powerful females. It wasn't *Leave It to Beaver*. It was the Salem witch trials.

It was terrifying to watch it blossom and spread. It was terrifying when the language of "Lock her up" was invoked by Trump during the 2016 campaign to threaten "some form of punishment" for women who exercised their right to reproductive freedom. It was terrifying when the language of "Lock her up" was used against migrant women and girls. It was chilling when Trump led adoring crowds to chant "Lock her up" after Christine Blasey Ford accused his Supreme Court nominee of sexual assault. It was terrifying as campaign crowds in 2020 chanted "Lock her up" about Nancy Pelosi for "distracting" Trump during his State of the Union address, or when "Lock her up" morphed to "Send her back" as crowds would come to roar about Representative Ilhan Omar of Minnesota. "Lock her up"—as a prong of Make America Great Again—became a promise to weaponize the machinery of law to silence, threaten, and isolate women. In the end it didn't even matter whom the pronoun "her" referenced. For crowds who embraced it, it was a generalized promise that after centuries of women's diligent efforts at bending and shaping and coaxing the law into affording them equal protection and dignity, their gender itself could become a crime.

By the summer of 2022, this was no longer hypothetical or just rhetorical. Even before the Supreme Court issued a final abortion decision, states raced to criminalize the endangerment of fetal persons and fertilized embryos. Emergency rooms struggled over whether to admit patients experiencing miscarriages. Almost overnight, amid whispers that *Roe v. Wade* was no longer good law, women (and especially women of color) were being criminally charged for fetal endangerment and self-managed abortions. The capacity to bear life had suddenly turned the womb into a crime scene. "Lock her up" wasn't just a slogan anymore but a promise.

American women, including Hillary Clinton, Ilhan Omar, Christine Blasey Ford, and, yes, Pam Bondi, have a special relationship with the law. They're exceptionally good at it. The law rewards and elevates qualities that transcend force and brutality. And yet every woman I interviewed, even if she was a lawyer, a judge, or a law professor, heard in 2016's exuberant "Lock her up" the echoes of savagery, vigilantism, and abuse. It became a promise that the law was not going to protect us but that it could and would be used to punish. That meant that women in the age of Donald Trump, and in the years that followed, wouldn't simply have to fight to preserve the rule of law. They would have to fight to keep the law itself from being used against them.

The law has been used as a cudgel against women from time immemorial, and the greatest women pioneers in the law spent their lives doing battle against its personal constraints even as they went to war against its systems. Which brings me to Pauli Murray, the most important woman lawyer few people know about. I first learned of Murray just a few years ago, despite matriculation from law school, a clerkship for a federal appellate judge, and two decades of writing about the federal courts and constitutional law. Yet I never learned about Murray, one of the most visionary and effective race and gender equality lawyers of the twentieth century. How is that even possible?

Despite her (and if alive today, Murray might have preferred "their") importance, Pauli Murray was and is still not well known even among the women, especially white women, who revere trailblazing women lawyers like the "Notorious RBG" or Michelle Obama or Hillary Clinton. There are not, to my knowledge, a whole lot of mugs, fabric tote bags, or dissent collar earrings dedicated to Murray. There are no huge fan clubs and no comparisons to famous rappers, even though she deserves comparable legal superstar status. Her list of firsts was landscape altering: Murray helped co-found the National Organization for Women in 1966; organized sit-ins at segregated restaurants in Washington, DC, twenty years before the sit-ins began in Greensboro, North Carolina; and was arrested in Virginia for refusing to move to the back of the bus fifteen years before Rosa Parks.

Pauli Murray's activism was surpassed only by her legal vision and intellectual rigor. Her 1944 law school paper on the Thirteenth and Fourteenth Amendments was used in 1954 by the NAACP Legal Defense Fund to successfully litigate *Brown v. Board of Education* to desegregate public schools. But the NAACP did not mention her at the time, and she only found out years later. Murray's radical legal framework, set forth in a 1965 law review article co-authored with another lawyer, Mary Eastwood, was used (credited this time) to litigate a landmark gender equality case brought in 1971 by Ruth Bader Ginsburg at the ACLU's Women's Rights Project: a successful first effort to establish that the equal protection clause of the Fourteenth Amendment should apply to protect women's equal rights under the law. Murray was a queer, gender-nonconforming attorney so far ahead of the curve of modern constitutional history that it all but forgot she had been one of its principal designers.

Murray—great-granddaughter of slaves on one side and of wealthy southern slave owners on another—believed she was "one of nature's experiments; a girl who should have been a boy." Orphaned as a child after her mother died and her father was beaten to death by a white

guard with a baseball bat at Maryland's Crownsville Hospital for the
Negro Insane, where he had been committed, possibly for having had
typhoid fever, Murray taught herself to read at five, graduated from
high school at fifteen, and was denied attendance at her preferred college on the basis of her race, then denied attendance at Columbia
University in New York because of her sex. The University of North
Carolina, which her slaveholding ancestors had attended, turned her
away for being Black, but Harvard Law School wouldn't take her for
being a woman. But none of this would preclude Murray from becoming the only woman in her class at Howard University, where she
graduated first in the class of 1944 and served as its valedictorian. She
was the first African American to be awarded a doctorate in law from
Yale University. Her 746-page book, *States' Laws on Race and Color,*
a compendium of state segregation laws written for the Methodist
Church in 1950, was described by Thurgood Marshall as "the bible"
of *Brown v. Board of Education.* As a board member of the ACLU,
Murray wrote (with Dorothy Kenyon) the brief in *White v. Crook*
(1966), which led to the demise of the all-white, all-male jury system
in Alabama. Murray was a decades-long confidante of Eleanor Roo-
sevelt's, earned four advanced degrees, served as California's first Black
deputy attorney general in 1946, then served on President John F.
Kennedy's newly created President's Commission on the Status of
Women. To boot, Murray was an accomplished poet and memoirist.
I like to imagine Murray looking around today, spotting voting rights
activist Stacey Abrams, then thinking, "Romance novels! I could have
written romance novels too."

Murray lobbied almost single-handedly to ensure the word "sex"
was inserted into Title VII of the Civil Rights Act of 1964; then in
1971 she penned a letter to President Richard Nixon, suggesting herself for a seat on the US Supreme Court. The historian Susan Ware
has written, "It may be that when historians look back on twentieth-
century America, all roads will lead to Pauli Murray." Yet despite a

film about her that was released in 2021, that prediction has largely failed to come true. Few people have had as much impact on the modern legal system as Murray, yet somehow the law alone wasn't capacious enough to hold all that Murray was or wanted to be. After years of teaching law at Brandeis, and having finally secured tenure there, Murray resigned to enter New York's General Theological Seminary. In 1977, she became the first African American woman to be vested as an Episcopal priest. In 2012, twenty-seven years after her death, Murray was designated a saint by the Episcopal Church. In 2017, Yale University named a residential college for undergraduates for her.

Why does a book about women and the law open with someone nearly forgotten by both? And why does a book about women and the law open with someone who found both those categories so stifling as to be ultimately uninhabitable? Perhaps because while everyone has heard of the former Supreme Court justice Ruth Bader Ginsburg and her pioneering path through constitutional history, Murray's legal story strikes me as in fact more common, and maybe even more enduring, with its zigzagging trajectory, the wins and reversals and near obscurity. Throughout history, the women who strived to reshape legal regimes, whether from the inside or—as was far more frequently the case—from without, did precisely what Murray did: digging in, writing letters, learning the case law, getting over rejection, fighting bias in the profession, forming coalitions, building movements. This was sometimes a matter of personal ambition, and Murray was, to be sure, personally ambitious, but it was also a question of necessity, of persistence, of—as Murray would put it—"a dream / haunting as amber wine."

None of our legal and constitutional progress happened in a straight path from dark to light, although that is the narrative we favor. It is and has always been a chiaroscuro journey through a legal system designed chiefly by men, for men, for the principal purpose of advancing the lot of men. The histories of the women who, against those currents, chose to center their professional lives on the law "are likely to be stories of piecemeal progress and circumscribed success," as the feminist scholar Carol Sanger put it. And yet Murray's is a story of neither piecemeal progress nor circumscribed success. It's simply that others took credit for the progress, and many of the successes came only when Murray was no longer alive to witness them. That, too, may be a more authentic story about women in the legal system than the tales we tell about men. It is certainly the story of the women's legal resistance of the Trump years. It will not be the story of the years ahead.

It's not just that legal history represents a pendulum swinging back and forth between expansion and contraction of freedoms and rights, then, but that, like a mallard moving across a lake, you can always see men gliding effortlessly above the water while women work furiously just underneath the surface. This story, then, is of the women who dropped everything, changed course, took pay cuts, missed kids' recitals, and paddled furiously to protect constitutional democracy in the four years during which Donald Trump was president, from 2017 to 2021. And it opens with Pauli Murray, a hero who wasn't a hero, a star who wasn't a star, an elite so ultimately disappointed by elites that she turned for the last decade of her life to God and faith and public service. Murray carved much of the constitutional world in which we currently reside out of rough rock face with her bare fingers. That one lone woman could do all this was not because the world was smaller back then, or its problems less extravagant, but because so much needed to be done, and because whatever the world and country thought of her, Murray knew herself capable of doing the work. Congresswoman Eleanor Holmes Norton, in her introduction to Pauli Murray's autobiography *Song in a Weary Throat*, wrote that Murray "lived on the edge of history, seeming to pull it along with her."

Those are words we could use to describe the women who came before Murray, and also some of those you will meet in the pages of this book. And, like Murray, they have changed history nonetheless. These women lawyers, who fought to beat back the racism, sexism, transphobia, xenophobia, corruption, and casual violence that took root and flourished during the Trump presidency and that still thrive in the wake of his defeat in 2020, did it for the same reasons Murray did it: for the dream of a more democratic future. Through the dark and the light, Murray paved the way for Ruth Bader Ginsburg, who paved the way for the women in this book. Through the dark and the light, the subjects of this book are paving the way for our children.

As this book was headed to the printers, the Supreme Court voted to overturn *Roe v. Wade* in the summer of 2022. The majority opinion evinced broad solicitude for the rights of unborn babies and state legislators. The lives of pregnant people were all but invisible to Samuel Alito, writing for the majority, who cited with some delight a seventeenth-century jurist who approved witch-burnings. Even before that opinion was formally filed, and even as it faced redrafting, states raced to pass laws criminalizing abortion and allowed citizen vigilantes the power to enforce them. Emergency rooms turned away women who were miscarrying; a ten-year-old rape victim in Ohio had to cross state lines to terminate a pregnancy; clinics refused to treat women from states with abortion bans. Gone was the talk of helping pregnant women make better choices. In a flash, states were enacting versions of "Lock her up." The same women who'd spent four years beating back family separation policies and vote suppression would again be tasked with making women visible, ensuring their equality, and safeguarding their votes.

I maintain that there is a special relationship between women and the law, and while one is loath to essentialize, this may be because law is the most conventional way with which to effect radical change. Back when a prominent constitutional law professor learned that I was writing this book, he asked why I would waste time and credibility writing a "pink book about the law." But of course the law itself has always dictated what women could be or do or wish for. The law has always been a pink book, only one written by men. Over two decades spent covering the courts, I've come to believe that women have a deep connection to the justice system, the Constitution, and the project of equality, and that this relationship actually dates back centuries. It's just that it's been a secret love affair and one not always clocked by the men who wrote history. In the absence of access to brute power or brute money or, well, brute brutality, the law has long been the best ordering force to promote fairness and equality and dignity for women. Women, nonbinary people, the poor, immigrants, and male minorities and men of color in America live inside a split screen, a dual consciousness, eternally aware of how much we have secured and how quickly it can be snatched away.

Long before a woman was admitted to the practice, women were deeply enmeshed with the legal regime. And long before women had access to power, they had access to justice. That's why Portia gets all the best lines in *The Merchant of Venice*. It's why Pauli Murray figured out the desegregation strategy that would become *Brown v. Board of Education* for a law school paper years before it became a legal brief. Famous women lawyers are few and far between, even in literature. The biblical Deborah was a judge, although that term likely meant "warrior chieftain" more than dispassionate arbiter of legal outcomes. Shakespeare's Portia famously dressed up as a male attorney, ostensibly to deliver a stirring oration about the essential quality of mercy. But we should note for the sake of accuracy that Portia was in fact a gorgeous heiress, dressed up as a lawyer as part of her larger plot to snag a husband, thus rendering *The Merchant of Venice* the first *true* pink book about the law.

Women have known since the founding that lawyers would dictate their role in the Republic. Abigail Adams cautioned her husband, John, hard at work with the Continental Congress in 1776, to carve out a place for women. "And, by the way," she wrote to him, "in the new code of laws which I suppose it will be necessary for you to make,

I desire you would remember the ladies and be more generous and favorable to them than your ancestors. Do not put such unlimited power into the hands of the husbands. Remember, all men would be tyrants if they could." "Lock her up," in epistolary form.

In the United States, even after women had secured the right to attend law school or take the bar exam, they were still barred from the practice of law by dint of statute and stereotype. After Myra Bradwell took her quest to become a practicing attorney all the way to the US Supreme Court in 1873, that court upheld an Illinois law excluding women from licensure, with Justice Joseph Bradley famously writing in a concurrence that "civil law, as well as nature herself, has always recognized a wide difference in the respective spheres and destinies of man and woman. Man is, or should be, woman's protector and defender. The natural and proper timidity and delicacy which belongs to the female sex evidently unfits it for many of the occupations of civil life."

American women were actually granted access to the practice of medicine long before they were allowed to be lawyers, in part because doctoring seemed a natural outgrowth of a woman's innate caregiving function. Lawyering, on the other hand, was seen as rough-and-tumble men's work, but also as the gateway to real power. As Barbara J. Harris has written, "Female doctors could claim that their careers were natural extensions of women's nurturant, healing role in the home and that they protected feminine modesty by ministering to members of their own sex. By contrast, women lawyers were clearly intruding in the public domain explicitly reserved for men." In short, women were given access to the practice of medicine for the same reasons they were allowed to be nurses, teachers, nannies, and cooks. But to be allowed to tinker with the machinery of democracy, and governance itself, would have afforded them far too much access to systemic change. It's not an accident at all that in America, in the late nineteenth century, the women's suffrage movement worked intimately alongside the movement to admit women to the practice of law. As this book will show, winning lawsuits is a part of what women lawyers must do, but reshaping the law itself is the only way to enduring change.

Even without access to power or prestige, American women have been on the front lines of every civil rights battle, from abolition of slavery, to equal suffrage, to race and gender equality. But to be on the front lines at a time in which women finally helm law practices and civil rights projects and sit on the bench is what makes this a different story—and a new one. Women lawyers not only hacked a pathway through the destabilizing policies and programs of the Trump era but also set the stage for its demise. In the days around Trump's inauguration, as early as January 2017, women lawyers across the country, unknown to one another, were organizing to become the spine of the legal pushback against Trump. Women's anger by itself can become paralyzing and isolating. But something extraordinary happens when female anger and lawyering meet.

Beyond almost anything else, one central objective of Trump's opponents lay in a dogged refusal to accept and to normalize terrible injustice, and women lawyers retained a unique capacity to hang on to horror in the face of new outrages on an almost daily basis. Every woman in this book was derided as overreacting at some point. But the law gives us tools to chronicle and mark the slow erosion of norms and to demand accountability. The slow progress of the law works against the impulse to forget the past and move on. And in a nation that could make an art form of forgiving and forgetting, these lawsuits demanded remembrance and holding to account. Maintaining a baseline resting state of "hysteria" over four years is nearly impossible. But justice itself demands a refusal to normalize the abhorrent, and women appear to mind being dismissed as histrionic less than men do. Perhaps because after centuries of being told it's all in our heads, we've learned to smile and press on.

As Trump peopled his administration with white men—some of whom were later determined to be abusers—and the wealthy wives of white men, as he filled the federal bench with overwhelmingly white male judges, and as he named white men to be the bulk of his US attorneys, he happily consigned most of the women around him to shift dresses and kitten heels. As quickly as that happened, American women understood they would have to be louder, more visible, more engaged with politics, and more organized. That was the impetus for the Women's March that took place on January 21, 2017—the largest single day of protest in US history. And as the legal system became the mechanism by which the Trump family, foreign oligarchs, and wealthy donors enriched themselves, it quickly fell to women to protect the poor, the immigrants, the children, and the vulnerable who were either overtly targeted or merely left behind. Happily, the more invisible we became to the administration, the more visible we would become to one another. When the Trump presidency ultimately led to the horrors of January 6, 2021, it was, again, no accident that some of his staunchest loyalists to resign in protest were women, including his education secretary, Betsy DeVos; his transportation secretary, Elaine Chao; and Stephanie Grisham, the First Lady's chief of staff. At some point, the symmetry had become inescapable. Trump was an agent of violence when he assumed office and an agent of violence when he refused to depart. For many women, the violence, the lawlessness, was the breaking point.

I interviewed Justice Ruth Bader Ginsburg very shortly before the Supreme Court shut down for COVID in 2020, and she assured me she was only the second smartest woman in her class at Harvard Law School. For all the rock-star status she achieved, she didn't think she was special so much as diligent and stubborn. The women you will meet here are similarly special because of what they did and how they did it, but like RBG before them, they don't think they are extraordinary. But I do. These are just a select few examples of hundreds and thousands of women lawyers and activists who did similar things in different fields, and also different things in similar fields. I shine a light on their lawsuits and organizations and institutions because they looked around after Donald J. Trump was elected in 2016 and saw that many things needed doing and that they themselves were capable of doing them. They were assisted in this work by staff attorneys, interns, law clerks, law students, partners, volunteers, and more. For every woman who will be remembered for the work of resisting Trump and Trumpism in America, there will be thousands who are not remembered and many we forgot to remember.

The enduring lesson of the Trump years and beyond is that the law is a fragile arrangement of norms, suggestions, and rules. It is not, we learned, self-enforcing. Ignore a congressional subpoena and it seems nothing happens if the attorney general is in your pocket. Violate the Hatch Act and everyone might just shrug. Subpoenas are for suckers, and presidential pardons are for loyalists. The precariousness of such a system was, and indeed still is, revealed on a daily basis. Yet one of the reasons the law remains such a powerful force, even in a culture that rewards fame and brand identification, is that on its best days, the law really does see and honor everyone, or at least it strives to. You don't always win because you're rich or important. Despite the legal chaos of the four years of the Trump presidency, legal processes are scrupulously formal and demanding. Sloppiness, of work product or of thought, is lethal. As we will see, the administration lost time and again, even before sympathetic judges, because legal niceties were ignored. One of the reasons Trump eventually collapsed under the forces of law and democracy, in the courts and at the ballot box, is that nobody—not the president and not the wealthiest of the wealthy—can perpetually evade the rule of law in America. At least not yet. Not always, not for everyone, and maybe not forever, but legal accountability is still available and it's what we must still fight for. There is just one canonical text in a country that guarantees liberty and equality, despite differences in income, power, gender, and race. That text is the Bill of Rights. And somehow, for now, that was enough.

The law is a proving ground that rewards patience and induce-ment. It was from Justice Ginsburg, and her sister in the law Justice Sandra Day O'Connor, that we learned about the slow and strategic deployment of persuasion to bring about change on the courts them-selves. It was from them we learned that having a seat at the counsel table is a step toward having a seat on the bench, which is a step from achieving a seat on the highest court in the land. And it is from them we learned that power isn't always dramatic and furious; it can also be institutional and enduring.

Make no mistake. There were a good number of women lawyers who worked to implement some of the Trump era's most noxious imperatives—from family separation policies, to the rescission of De-ferred Action for Childhood Arrivals, to the ban on transgender ser-vice members. Indeed, since Trump has been sidelined, lady lawyers have served integral roles in bringing meritless challenges to the re-sults of the 2020 election; they have harassed nonpartisan election officials into retirement and helped foment the violent insurrection of January 2021. But just as there is no doubt that women played a crucial role in defeating Trumpism after 2016, women attorneys were essential to the story of women, Donald Trump, and the rule of law. Like Pauli Murray, they might not have been recognized. Like Mur-ray's, their work forms an invisible web of small actions, connections, awakenings, confrontations, and change that held the country together as others sought to tear it apart.

This, then, is why I open with Pauli Murray. Americans, as the feminist political philosopher Rebecca Solnit has observed, are some-times too apt to succumb to the "Great Man" theory of social change, even when that great man is a female. We spent too many of the Trump years believing that Robert Mueller, then Adam Schiff, then Jamie Raskin, and then someone else would single-handedly save us in a blaze of cowboyish heroism. But in so doing, we often lost track of the everyday heroes in our midst. As Solnit put it in her 2019 essay "When the Hero Is the Problem," "We like our lone and exceptional heroes, and the drama of violence and virtue of muscle, or at least that's what we get, over and over, and in the course of getting them we don't get much of a picture of how change happens and what our role in it might be, or how ordinary people matter."

Pauli Murray was, to be sure, the very opposite of "ordinary people." But even the lone hero theory of American social change opted to ignore her contributions, to valorize those who came along later, built on her work, and did things she had done years earlier. The fact of Murray's almost complete erasure from American constitutional and civil rights history suggests two things: not only that the "Great Man" theory of history and social change ignores all of the ways in which deep connection, listening, organizing, collective action, and storytelling can bring about widespread change, but also that such theories fail, in so many ways, to account even for the heroic and great individuals who really do, nearly single-handedly, rewire the world.

This is the story of the invisible web that binds these lawyers, not just to one another, but to a set of timeless constitutional values: dignity, equality, justice, law, truth, and reason. It's the story of strong women who stepped up, even though the practice of law typically rewards caution. It's the story of women who for the most part had grievous doubts about their own capabilities but who were willing to place boundless confidence in a legal system that would have excluded them just a few decades earlier. Some of them were terrified, and others were sanguine. Few of them could spare the time to workshop ideas or to consider what bold actions would do to their careers. Maybe it's also the story of what it takes for women to leap before they look: a net made of statutes and rules and conventions so weighty and substantial that it seemed as if it might just hold, despite everything.

In countries birthed in stories of princesses, kings, and wizards, all power resides in the powerful. But in a constitutional democracy, enduring power lies in the people who step into the fight. And by that yardstick, the women who stood up to defend the Constitution in the Trump era, and who remain in the fight for democracy and equality today, held the line with mundane petitions for certiorari and exhaustively formatted appendixes. When the framers of the Constitution conceived of a nation built on the core democratic values of freedom and equality, they couldn't have suspected that women would be at the heart of the fight to preserve them some two centuries later. Indeed, they were quite determined to ensure—Abigail Adams notwithstanding—that men had all the rights and women had the protection of men. But in some ways, the women who fought to preserve equality and justice and privacy and dignity in the Trump era were perfectly located to inherit the mantle of radical constitutionalism created by James Madison, Thomas Jefferson, and Benjamin Franklin. They tethered themselves to a system that managed to hold, under great strain.

These questions—of who is visible and who is seen, of who does the work and who is remembered for the work—are almost as central to a book on women and the law and the Trump era as the women themselves. I believe that cowboys are all well and good, but change doesn't result exclusively from the biographies of a Guy in a Hat Who Did a Thing. This book is thus ultimately less about celebrating the Great Men, or even the Great Women, from a time in which democracy faltered and almost fell, than about surfacing justice, which rises and falls on the shoulders of everyone and which must every day be bent by each of us toward the dignity and humanity of us all.

2

The First No

—————

Sally Yates:
The Government Lawyer

B y long-standing necessity or habit, the climactic scene in at least half of our greatest romantic movies takes place at an airport. From *Casablanca* to *Friends*, the departure gate is a dramatic proxy for wrenching goodbyes and heartfelt truths. But airports aren't just the modern-day symbol of romance and new beginnings, what wharves and piers were for passionate Victorian adventure-seekers. Airports are also the physical manifestation of Western liberty, freedom, human connection, and opportunity. What the Statue of Liberty once represented in New York Harbor now plays out daily at the baggage claim in LAX: immigrants and asylum seekers, climate and war refugees, students and teachers, lovers and families reunited amid hopes of a better life, equality, and dignity.

But that all changed, suddenly, a week into Donald Trump's presidency. On January 27, 2017, the newly inaugurated Trump signed into law an executive order banning entry into the United States by immigrants and refugees from Iran, Iraq, Libya, Somalia, Sudan, Syria, and Yemen. These are all countries with populations that were over-whelmingly (in most cases, more than 99 percent) Muslim. Other countries—including Saudi Arabia—that had in fact sent actual ter-rorists to do real harm to the United States on 9/11 were not on that list. There was no coherent explanation at the time for why these particular nations were selected or why others were omitted. And because the order was rushed out without proper vetting, or serious coordination between government agencies, the new rules somehow also barred entry by *any* non-US citizen from these countries, includ-ing students, visiting professors, tourists, and green card holders.

On formally signing the original executive order, President Trump was quite clear that it was intended for Muslim travelers. As he signed it, he stage-whispered, with a wink at the formal title, "Protecting the Nation from Foreign Terrorist Entry into the United States," saying, "We all know what that means." He also clarified what that meant on the day of the rollout by promising in a television interview that his administration would now give Christian refugees priority over Mus-lim refugees. Just in case there was somehow still any lingering con-fusion about whether this was indeed the long-touted "Muslim ban," Rudy Giuliani, a vice-chair of the president's transition team, hastily confirmed on another television hit that the executive order imple-mented the president's directive to "do" a "Muslim ban" "legally."

But behind the scenes at the White House, there were questions. Trump's acting attorney general at the time was Sally Quillian Yates, a thirty-year veteran of the Justice Department and a former US at-torney from Georgia. Born into a family of lawyers and Methodist ministers, Yates is an institutionalist's institutionalist. Her father was a judge on the Georgia Court of Appeals, and her father's father sat on the Georgia Supreme Court. Yates's sister is a talk show host for a conservative radio station in Alabama, and her husband is a lawyer who runs a school in Atlanta for children with speech, language, and learning disabilities. Yates once told *The New Yorker*'s Ryan Lizza about her own lineage as a pathbreaking American lady lawyer: Her paternal grandmother, Tabitha Quillian, was one of the first women to be admitted to the Georgia bar. In 1934, Quillian had been studying under another attorney, but without ever telling her husband. According to family lore, Yates's grandpa learned about it when he found her name in the newspaper. Yates told Lizza, "My grandfather turned to her and said, 'Look at that! There's another Tabitha Quillian who passed the bar.'"

"She would have been a heck of a lawyer. But women weren't hired as lawyers back then. It just wasn't done," Yates explained to *The Atlanta Journal-Constitution*. "So instead, she was a secretary, first to my grandfather, who was a lawyer, and then for my father and his brother and their practice." But, Yates noted, her grandmother didn't complain. "Interestingly, I don't remember my grandmother ever complaining about the fact that she was a secretary. Looking back on it, had I been her, I would have resented the heck out of it. I realized that tenacity counts for a lot. She became a lawyer without support systems. I thought to myself that if she did that, how hard could it be for me?"

Sally Yates faced a few obstacles of her own. In 1982, she graduated magna cum laude from the University of Georgia with a journalism degree, then attended the University of Georgia School of Law, graduating in 1986. She immediately went to work in private practice at King & Spalding, a big law firm in Atlanta. She didn't love big law. But at her firm, Yates tried her first pro bono, or unpaid, case in 1987. She represented Lovie Morrison Jones, an African American woman in her nineties whose land had been sold out from under her, without her knowledge, by a developer looking to build a subdivision. Jones hadn't registered the deed because she didn't trust the government. But the land had been given to her family, and Jones had worked it for years with the deed tucked away in her clothing. Yates pulled together a defense, prevailed at a jury trial, and was so transformed by the experience that she decided to move in her late twenties to a criminal position at the Justice Department. In 1989, Bob Barr, then the US attorney for the Northern District of Georgia and a staunch anti-Clinton Republican, gave her a job. As Yates later told *Recode Decode*'s Kara Swisher, "I didn't go for the right reasons. In fact, I wouldn't have hired myself later. I went because I wanted more hands-on experience, I wanted to try cases on my own. In big law firms, cases are staffed with a dozen people. . . . The immense responsibility you have at the Department of Justice, representing the people of the United States . . . you are responsible for seeking justice and equal justice in this country. So, I was totally unprepared for . . . how totally taken I would be with the mission."

It was very different when she started, she told Swisher: "Look, it was the late '80s when I started at the US Attorney's office in Atlanta. I wanted to go into the organized crime section, but they wouldn't put me in that section. The first assistant, which was the top career person there, thought that it was kind of too rough and tumble for a woman to go into organized crime—I know, I know, that's so patronizing—so he put me in the white-collar section, because he thought that I would not be tough enough." It was a long way from her grandmother in some ways, and in some ways not enough: "There weren't very many women on the criminal side. I suppose I was a tad aggressive, which I have learned with one of the US attorneys there, I remember going to a meeting and before we walked into this meeting, the US attorney looked at me and said, 'I really think that the agency would appreciate a more demure woman.'"

Ironically, compared with many of the other women attorneys in this book, Yates codes as pretty demure. She doesn't swear, she doesn't shout, and she isn't apt to lose her temper. She also talks about the rule of law and the DOJ as though she were in a Frank Capra movie, describing sacred beliefs and institutions she prizes right down to her bones.

As a US attorney with virtually no background in criminal law, Yates slowly racked up a raft of high-profile cases, including winning a corruption case against Atlanta's first African American council-man and signing the plea deal for a life sentence with Eric Rudolph, the Atlanta Olympics bomber. In a 2013 interview with *The Atlanta Journal-Constitution*, Yates recalled, "The Rudolph case was one of the most interesting cases I've ever done. One of the great lessons is that nobody is a success on their own. The case was an example of a whole lot of people coming together to try to solve that case."

In that interview, Yates took the time to surface the unsung teams that go into solving complex criminal cases: "I don't care how good a prosecutor you are. If you hadn't had really extraordinary FBI and ATF (Bureau of Alcohol, Tobacco, Firearms and Explosives) agents who were incredibly dedicated and worked day in and day out liter-ally for years, it wouldn't matter how good you are. Of all the cases I've done, that's the greatest example of the power of a team."

Yates also believed passionately—even romantically—in the idea of a nonpartisan Department of Justice. As she would put it to Swisher, "Until the Obama Administration, I was a career civil ser-vant, so you stay, regardless of administrations, and 99.9 percent of the people at the Department of Justice are career." In 2009, Barack Obama thus tapped Yates to be the US attorney for the Northern District of Georgia. She was confirmed unanimously. And when Eric Holder stepped down as Obama's attorney general in 2015, Yates was tagged to become the new deputy attorney general under Loretta Lynch. Even after Holder left the Department of Justice, Obama kept asking him, "What does Sally think?" In March 2015, her confirmation hearing quickly became a strange foreshadowing of what would happen after Obama left office.

Yates was grilled by Senate Republicans about her independence and her capacity to act as a check on President Obama, to whom she would have to answer. Indeed, it was the then senator Jeff Sessions—who would later become Trump's first attorney general—pressing Yates hardest in her hours-long hearing, about her capacity to stand up to a too-powerful president: "Do you think the attorney general has a responsibility to say no to the president if he asks for something that's improper?" Sessions urged. Yates replied that the deputy attorney general "has an obligation to follow the law and the Constitution, and to give their independent legal advice to the president." She was confirmed by a margin of 84–12. Senator Jeff Sessions, who would prove nearly incapable of standing up to President Trump when he became US attorney general in 2017, voted no.

I met Sally Yates in 2016, when she was heading up President Obama's efforts to reform American prisons, and she struck me as an archetype of a government attorney. She talks softly, with a slight southern drawl, and dresses in the conservative suits of buttoned-down lady lawyers. But she was, at the time, Obama's point person on prison reform at Justice, and she was spearheading what had become a remarkable coalition of right- and left-wing reformers trying to end over-incarceration in America. Even in the overheated final years of the Obama presidency, Yates had somehow brought together allies from the NAACP, the conservative Koch brothers, and US senators unlikely to agree on anything else, including Mike Lee (R-Utah) and Cory Booker (D-N.J.), to work together on mass sentencing reform and rehabilitation. Around the time of the 2016 election, Yates had created a model "school district" for federal inmates, offering education opportunities in literacy and high school diplomas. The year before, she had pushed the Bureau of Prisons to phase out the use of private prisons for federal inmates. She had also headed up Obama's clemency initiative, allowing the president to commute the sentences of thousands of low-level drug offenders before he left office.

Yates had not yet become a household name, but I thought to myself that she was the kind of lawyer's lawyer they'd stopped minting in the 1950s. Law before politics. No drama. No ego. Yates had made the quasi-radical act of challenging over-incarceration policies so conventional and pragmatic that it was hard to fight her on it. She'd assembled a coalition of improbable allies who all believed in ending over-incarceration and reforming a disastrous prison policy. I love dramatic lawyers, generally. But she had the gift of making radical top-down prison reform sound as if it were an obvious move that simply needed a push from serious people at the top.

After the 2016 election, the Trump administration asked Yates to stay on as acting attorney general after the inauguration, at which point Jeff Sessions, Trump's nominee for attorney general, could take over as soon as he was confirmed. That's a long-standing tradition to preserve continuity, and it should have been a brief and cordial stint. As Yates later put it to Kara Swisher, there's "a tradition for the No. 2 to stay until the new Attorney General is confirmed. There is this other tradition, and that is that nothing happens during that time, and you can just sort of stay the course, you keep the trains running. My chief of staff actually told me it would be so quiet there would be time for a lot of long, boozy lunches."

But, in the first weeks of 2017, Yates found herself in a quagmire of law and politics and national security. It started right after the inauguration with Trump's national security advisor, Michael Flynn. Within just days of the transfer of power from Obama to Trump, Yates already knew she had a massive counterintelligence problem in Flynn, and she needed to figure out how to bring it to the president's attention. Yates had learned that Flynn had talked on the phone to

Sergey Kislyak, the Russian ambassador, on December 29, 2016, the same day Obama had imposed sanctions on Russia for its interference in the 2016 election. The discussion between Flynn and Kislyak itself violated a federal law, the Logan Act, which bars private citizens from interfering in government negotiations. But Flynn also lied about it to the FBI. Then Vice President Mike Pence unknowingly repeated that lie, and then the White House press secretary, Sean Spicer, also unknowingly echoed the lie. As Yates later explained in her *Recode Decode* interview, this was no longer just a problem for the Trump administration:

> The investigation into Russian interference in the election had started during the Obama administration, and during the transition between the administrations it became a thing about whether Mike Flynn was essentially telling the Russians not to worry about the sanctions the Obama administration was imposing. . . . And nobody could really figure out why the Russians weren't reacting when we imposed the sanctions that we did. And we discovered, through some recordings we had access to, that in fact he had been talking to the Russian ambassador, and saying, colloquially, "don't worry about this, we're going to take care of this."

For Yates, the issue wasn't just that members of the new Trump administration were now falsely saying, "No, there was no discussion with the Russian ambassador," but that "they were getting more and more specific, and the Vice President even goes out and says, 'I talked to General Flynn and he told me they talked about Christmas greetings,' and downplaying it." This was, in other words, now a big fat national security, counterintelligence problem. As she put it, "One thing we did know was that we weren't the only ones who knew he'd been having these discussions with the Russian ambassador. The Russians obviously knew it as well. And he'd been out publicly providing false information about it, which creates a potential compromise. And you really don't want your national security advisor compromised with the Russians. It's not a good way to start." This counterintelligence problem, the fact that American officials can be manipulated by foreigners into doing things that were not in the United States' interests, was the seed of what would become the Mueller report.

In the simplest terms, having lied, then allowed others to lie, Mike Flynn became susceptible to Russian blackmail. Yates decided she needed to tell the White House that Flynn was exposed. The challenge was that in a brand-new administration she had no idea who knew what and at what level Flynn's lies had been condoned. If nothing else, she felt the vice president himself should know the information he was repeating was inaccurate. As she explained in a later interview, this was not an area in which she had vast experience. She checked with the CIA to figure out if the Russians would be interested in using Flynn's lies against him, and they confirmed that they were. In the end, as she put it, "the short straw came to me."

On January 26, 2017, Yates met with Trump's White House counsel, Don McGahn, to discuss Flynn's false statements. As she later testified, his response was perplexing. "Why does it matter to D.O.J. if one White House official lies to another White House official?" McGahn asked her, seemingly failing to understand that if Flynn lied to his bosses, and Russian officials knew it, they would use it against him. McGahn asked to see the underlying documents, and Yates promised to get them to him the following Monday. Yates later explained, "I expected that they would do something about it. I mean I call up the White House Counsel, Don McGahn, and tell him I have something vitally important and I need to talk to him about it right away and it can't be on the phone. We need to talk about this in a SCIF, in a secure place. . . . He saw me immediately. I told him what was going on. I went back the next day to answer some of his questions about it." Again, at that second meeting it felt to Yates that he was missing the point.

That Friday, January 27, Yates headed from the White House to her office at Justice, then straight to the airport, to fly back to Atlanta for a charity event for a camp for disabled kids. En route to her plane, she got a call from her deputy at the Justice Department, Matt Axelrod. "You're not going to believe this, but I just read online that the president has executed this travel ban," he told her. Nobody had consulted her at all. McGahn, whose office she'd just left, hadn't said a thing about it. None of the national security agencies had been consulted. The lawyers at the Office of Legal Counsel had been directed not to share it with her. Axelrod first learned of it on the *New York Times* website. And the acting attorney general of the United States had to look up the text of an executive order about Muslim travelers on her phone on the internet just like the rest of us.

Yates spent that charity event in the back of a ballroom in Atlanta on the phone with her team at Main Justice. As the first lawsuits challenging the travel ban were rushed into courts that same evening, she asked the government lawyers at DOJ to avoid taking any formal position yet on the constitutionality of the order, but she expressed two initial concerns. The first was that the ban seemed to target Muslims and give preferential treatment to Syrian Christians. This would violate the establishment clause of the First Amendment, which prohibits the state from favoring one religion over the others. The ban also seemed to Yates to raise due process questions about visa holders and legal permanent residents, who were being stripped of the legal status they had already acquired, without due process of the law.

Yates spent her weekend reading the briefs filed by travelers who'd been denied entry to the country and trying to determine for herself whether the ban was unconstitutional. As she told Swisher, "Look, the Justice Department is this incredibly hierarchical organization. Normally, for something of this import, lots of layers below have worked this all up. And there have been lots of memos done and it is all just still . . . There was no time for any of that stuff." Within seventy-two hours, her entire Justice Department would have to take a position on its constitutionality in court. Yates returned to her office at DOJ on Monday morning and convened a meeting to talk it over. She knew she would have to either defend the executive order in court or resign on the spot. And as she later explained to Lizza, "But here's the thing: resignation would have protected my own personal integrity, because I wouldn't have been part of this, but I believed, and I still think, that I had an obligation to also protect the integrity of the Department of Justice. And that meant that D.O.J. doesn't go into court on something as fundamental as religious freedom, making an argument about something that I was not convinced was grounded in truth." She added, "In fact, I thought, based on all the evidence I had, that it *was* based on religion. And then I thought back to Jim Crow laws, or literacy tests. Those didn't say that the purpose was to prevent African Americans from voting. But that's what the purpose was."

As Yates later told Swisher, "To defend it, it also became evident I was going to have to send Department of Justice lawyers in to argue that this travel ban had absolutely nothing to do with religion. Religion was completely irrelevant. And that's in the face of all the statements the president had made both on the campaign trail and after he had been elected. I didn't believe that that was a defense that was grounded in truth, and we were the Department of Justice." She added, "I don't think any lawyer should go in and be arguing something that's not grounded in truth, but I sure don't think the Department of Justice should be doing that."

Yates also thought back to her own confirmation hearing when senators pressed her on what she would do if ever a president asked her to do something unlawful or unconstitutional. Her answer had been that she would say no, not resign, but say no. Because Yates believed that the travel ban was rooted in religious animus, or hate for a religious group, the issue was particularly painful for her. She told Lizza, "This is a defining, founding principle of our country: religious freedom. How can the Department of Justice go in and defend something that so significantly undermines that, when we're not convinced it's true?" She heard opinions and canvassed her staff, but eventually, having heard their best arguments in support of the ban, she couldn't convince herself that it was constitutional or defensible.

The religion clauses of the First Amendment don't always get as much attention as their cousins that protect free speech, press freedoms, and freedom of assembly. Make no mistake, those are some *great* clauses, and we will talk more about them later. But the First Amendment protects religious freedom, and indeed the religion clauses lie at its very heart. One truly lovely theory of the First Amendment—articulated brilliantly by the former ACLU director Burt Neuborne—holds that its core protections (in sequential order) of religion, then free speech, then press, then free assembly, and finally the right to petition one's government, allow Americans to be truly free. Unless your religious conscience is protected, speech doesn't matter. Unless there is a free press, the right to assemble is ephemeral. Only when you have been guaranteed all these other core liberties can you feel free enough to seek redress. And all that really means is that the right to practice one's faith lies at the very heart of the constitutional freedoms.

But the two religion clauses can be tricky because they sometimes row in opposing directions, essentially providing, first, that Congress shall "make no law respecting an establishment of religion" and, second, that Congress cannot do anything "prohibiting the free exercise," or practice, of religious faith. These clauses can be in tension because, for all intents and purposes, Congress must allow every religion to remain unencumbered, but also cannot promote any one religion over another. So, for instance, if people of faith want to say Christian prayers before secular legislative meetings, or seek to erect massive crosses on public lands, these two clauses working in tandem often get a little pinchy. In sum, Americans are free to exercise their faith as they choose, but the government is *not* free to privilege or downgrade any one faith over another.

All this has led to centuries of contentious litigation over school prayer, school vouchers for parochial education, and sectarian religious displays on government land, among other heated controversies. These cases tend to be anxiety producing precisely because they often pit those who claim the United States is by definition a Christian country (or a "Judeo-Christian" country) against those who are members of minority faiths or are nonbelievers. But even though we can and do argue about this a lot in the courts, generally the president doesn't lay claim to overtly antireligious notions about minority faiths in public. By calling in his election campaign for a "total and complete shutdown" of the country's borders to Muslims, Trump forced that precise issue into the courts.

IN THE EARLIEST DAYS of the Trump administration, thousands of lawyers found themselves in a position similar to Yates's that weekend in late January, workshopping whether sloppy legal ideas could be rendered defensible in a courtroom. Many of them squinted their eyes and went on to offer up falsehoods and fabrications, pretexts and distractions. Over the next four years, Justice Department lawyers brazened their way through hearings about children in cages and bans on transgender service members and efforts to build a wall intended to brick in all of Mexico. In the summer of 2019, an entire team of DOJ lawyers litigating the Trump administration's effort to add a question about citizenship to the 2020 census, confronted with proven lies they had offered up, removed themselves from that case en masse. Lying to federal jurists had become too much for them. But very few DOJ lawyers have so publicly refused to do something unlawful or immoral. What made Yates different? And why didn't others follow where she had led?

YATES TOLD SWISHER in the fall of 2018 that it was pretty straightforward. "I loved the Department of Justice," she said. "I felt privileged every single day to be part of that institution. I believed in the mission. I believed in our responsibility. I had experienced firsthand how it felt for people in the community to count on us to be the ones who were administering justice." The institution itself, its mission, public trust in it, was a place she had dedicated thirty years to serving. "I had a really strong feeling and a really strong commitment to what I believe that institution is supposed to stand for. And I'll be damned if I'm going to abandon all that in the end and say that none of that matters, when that's actually *all* that matters, is what that institution is supposed to stand for."

So on Monday evening, January 30, 2017, Yates wrote up a statement in which she announced that she did not believe the executive order was "wise or just." As she explained, "At present, I am not convinced that the defense of the Executive Order is consistent with these responsibilities, nor am I convinced that the Executive Order is lawful." She ended her statement with the following: "For as long as I am the Acting Attorney General, the Department of Justice will not present arguments in defense of the Executive Order, unless and until I become convinced that it is appropriate to do so." Yates did this because she believed the First Amendment's prohibitions on religious discrimination precluded the singling out of Muslims for special abuses or the creation of special privileges for Christian refugees. When the courts almost immediately struck down the travel ban in the days and weeks following, Yates was vindicated, if unemployed. Subsequently, virtually every federal judge to hear the case made similar findings. The travel ban had to be reengineered not once but twice by Trump's Justice Department before, eventually, in 2018, in *Trump v. Hawaii*, the Supreme Court determined that it was within the president's discretion to pass a watered-down version. The four liberal justices dissented. In a separate dissent, Justice Sonia Sotomayor opened with the statement that "the United States of America is a Nation built upon the promise of religious liberty. Our Founders honored that core promise by embedding the principle of religious neutrality in the First Amendment. The court's decision today fails to safeguard that fundamental principle. It leaves undisturbed a policy first advertised openly and unequivocally as a 'total and complete shutdown of Muslims entering the United States' because the policy now masquerades behind a façade of national-security concerns." Justice Sotomayor went on to detail Trump's multiple statements and tweets insisting that he wanted a Muslim travel ban and explained that the executive order clearly ran afoul of the establishment clause.

That concern echoed the lofty solicitude for religious minorities first expressed by Sally Yates, who knew in January 2017 that she would be fired for writing as much. She was in her office four hours later when a letter from the White House was hand delivered to her. (She later learned they had tried to fire her via email, but it kept bouncing back, which she has likened to being broken up with via text.) In announcing her firing, the president wrote that Yates had "betrayed the Department of Justice by refusing to enforce a legal order." Democrats dubbed it the "Monday Night Massacre," calling back to that moment in the Watergate scandal in 1973 when Richard Nixon fired Special Prosecutor Archibald Cox and accepted the resignations of Attorney General Elliot Richardson and Deputy Attorney General William Ruckelshaus. Yates's replacement, Dana Boente, who was then the acting deputy attorney general, became the new acting AG. Yates cleaned out her desk and went home, but by the next morning she had become the first very public face of Trump's legal resisters. It mattered that her objections were *coming from inside the house*. She was the first and highest-profile person in the government to say no to the president and to lose her job for it.

Sally Yates had one other made-for-TV moment before mostly departing the public main stage. In May 2017, months after she was summarily fired, she was called on to testify before a subcommittee of the Senate Judiciary Committee about what happened in the early days of the Trump administration with Michael Flynn. That morning, Trump had, as was his wont, tweeted out a threat. "Ask Sally Yates, under oath, if she knows how classified information got into the newspapers soon after she explained it to W.H. Council," he wrote (misspelling "Counsel"). But the exchange that blew up on social media involved her determination that she could not support the first iteration of the president's Muslim ban. Senator Ted Cruz (R-Tex.) peered down at her in the witness chair and inquired whether Yates was familiar with 8 U.S.C. Section 1182, the section of the US Code related to the Immigration and Nationality Act. Yates's initial answer was that she was not, which allowed Cruz to make the mistake of condescending to her. He smirked and said that "it certainly is a relevant and not a terribly obscure statute" and then lavishly quoted from it: "By the express text of the statute, it says, quote, 'Whenever the president finds that entry of any alien or of any class of aliens into the United States would be detrimental to the interest of the United States, he may by proclamation, and for such period as he shall deem necessary, suspend the entry of all aliens or any class of aliens as immigrants or nonimmigrants, or impose on the entry of aliens any restrictions he may deem appropriate.' Would you agree that is broad statutory authorization?"

Yates listened politely and replied, "I would, and I am familiar with that." Cruz leaned back, certain he had created a viral kill shot for the ages. Until Yates added, "And I'm also familiar with an additional provision of the INA that says no person shall receive preference or be discriminated against an issuance of a visa because of race, nationality or place of birth, that I believe was promulgated after the statute that you just quoted."

That video went viral. As my *Slate* colleague Leon Neyfakh noted at the time, it was the Aaron Sorkin ending everyone had been longing for. The baseball writer Molly Knight tweeted, "In my darkest hours I will think of Sally Yates destroying Ted Cruz on national television, and it will sustain me." The blogger Yashar Ali posted the scene from *My Cousin Vinny* in which Marisa Tomei explains the difference between a 1964 Buick Skylark and a 1963 Pontiac Tempest. Sally Yates had become a household name for refusing to be the kind of lawyer the president wanted, the kind who first says yes and only then checks the relevant statute. There should have been thousands of her. But in the first few weeks, it meant a lot to have just the one.

YATES SHOWED US that the best government lawyers do it for the sake of the law itself, and not for personal glory or for some other guy's personal glory. The best government lawyers don't serve as yes-men ensuring that the president gets whatever the president wants. Attorneys must answer not just to the client but to the law itself, as abstract and old-fashioned as that may seem. In a 2013 interview with *The Atlanta Journal-Constitution*, Yates was asked about the advice she gave young lawyers. She explained that "the key to professional happiness and success is pursuing what is meaningful to you and pursuing it with a vengeance." She cautioned that you could score powerful, lucrative legal jobs and never feel satisfied with the work you do each day. "What I do is meaningful to me and has made a difference in the big scheme of things," she explained. "I realize that we're not doing Mother Teresa's work here at the US Attorney's Office, but I do think what we're doing makes a difference." When she recruits young lawyers to work for the government, Yates reminds them, "It's worth every penny you don't make. I know this sounds incredibly corny, but I absolutely believe it—the thrill that comes with saying that you represent the people of the United States, there's no greater honor that you can have as a lawyer."

Over time, other high-ranking Trump administration officials stood up for the rule of law, even if it meant losing their jobs, but not nearly as many as we might have expected. By the end of the Trump era, it was stunning how few of his appointees took the opportunity afforded by a spectacular and rousing public firing to state clearly that what was happening to the rule of law on Trump's watch was immoral. Most of them said yes, until they finally said no, up to and including his second attorney general, Bill Barr, who spent the summer of 2020 making false claims about vote fraud and stolen elections, then slunk away through the fire exit after telling the president that the 2020 election had not been stolen. That is how many lawyers chose to cut ties; some lobbed a few potshots, but few stood up to say loudly and clearly that no president is above the law. They papered themselves over with CYA letters to their confidential files, certain that would exculpate them from personal liability. Many of them have jobs in prestigious law firms and think tanks today. The Mueller report itself is replete with examples of high-ranking officials asked to break the law, or to lie about breaking the law, by the president. Not one of them publicly repudiated him.

In August 2019, Chuck Park resigned from the Foreign Service with a piece in *The Washington Post* conceding that the federal bureaucracy under Trump had become "the complacent state." Park noted, despairingly, that "among my colleagues at the State Department, I have met neither the unsung hero nor the cunning villain of Deep State lore. If the resistance does exist, it should be clear by this point that it has failed." What Park was bemoaning, toward the end, was the banality of government bureaucracy. But that complacency and normalizing had not yet calcified in the earliest weeks of the Trump era.

In retrospect, Sally Yates stands in stark contrast to the many, many government officials who left the Trump administration to profit off what they knew without really calling it out. Without fanfare or drama or a book deal or a CNN contributor spot, Yates defied the president a week after inauguration. In doing so, she herself became something of a cult figure and has garnered big crowds when she speaks or writes the occasional op-ed. She tweets occasionally, and in the 2018 elections famously rebuffed public pressure to run for elected office. In 2018, she returned to her old Atlanta law firm, King & Spalding, heading up their investigations practice. She lectures at Georgetown Law School. She's also used her newfound celebrity status to speak openly about her father's suicide in 1986 and the need to break the stigma that surrounds mental health and depression.

One of the things Yates came to deplore most over the course of the Trump era was how quickly everyone seemed to go numb. As she told Swisher in 2018, "It's not even a thing anymore when the president tweets some of this stuff or says it in speeches. We just kind of move on to the next thing. We can't even make it through a full twenty-four-hour news cycle." She added, "You know, if we get to the point that that's how people think our justice system works, at the risk of sounding melodramatic here, stuff starts falling apart." Her related concern was that there is no codified book called "The Rule of Law." The law is, instead, a network of interlocking norms and beliefs and conventions, and as it came under attack, so many people stood back expecting it to fight for itself. The two complaints are connected. Because we prefer to believe that the law is an unassailable cathedral, self-reinforcing and professionalized, whenever it is deployed to unlawful ends, we tell ourselves it's normal. If it comes into a courtroom with a suit and a briefcase, that must mean that the Rule of Law is at work. We forget to fight for it.

Women are sometimes better than men at recognizing that the law isn't an immutable, timeless cathedral and at recognizing that just because it travels with a yellow pad doesn't mean it's doing justice. We know that because until relatively recently, the law insisted that women couldn't have their own credit cards. The distance from Sally Yates's grandmother to Sally Yates isn't long enough to lock in illusions of perfection. That means if there's mold and dry rot in the castle walls, we sometimes smell it first. For four years Yates gave speech after speech urging audiences *not* to normalize a president willing to use the DOJ to punish enemies and reward friends, *not* to normalize legal ideas that are antithetical to freedom and dignity. In ballroom after ballroom, she urged people, particularly young people and young women, to continue to fight for the law itself, to speak up and say, as she often put it, "this isn't normal, this isn't what we stand for."

Perhaps more than anything else, then, to me Yates came to represent adults behaving like adults. Not winking and grinning, not wringing hands and hoping that someone else will step up. Not putting memos in confidential files that read, "I wasn't for *this*." And for Yates herself, inspiration has come from the young people who refused to stand by. In the fall of 2018, Yates described in an interview how even before her famous firing, she found hope in the young women entering government service. She spoke of finding herself at a Whole Foods in Washington, DC, on the day of the first Women's March, in which she had avoided participating because she was still the acting attorney general. "It was freezing," she said, "and all these young women were just pouring into the grocery store, because the Metro was overflowing, and they had signs and the hats, and I'm there with my security detail. And I just kind of wanted to watch for a while. And there were all these young women, who were comfortable in their own skin. They knew who they were, and what they believed in, and they weren't the least bit hesitant to say it out loud." For Yates, having spent the Trump years speaking at colleges and universities, rather than in government service, the fuel was, as she put it, "the young women who come up to me and tell me they had never thought about public service before. They really feel a calling to be a part of defining our country."

Young women don't always know it, but in dark times they really can serve as inspiration for the very same women who inspire them most. It's a poetic feedback loop, lit by the mutual hope that government can and should always work to protect dignity and equality, even as it sometimes exerts itself to do the very opposite.

3

The Airport Revolution

―――――

Becca Heller:
The Activist

onald Trump's executive order barring travel from majority-Muslim countries was born in chaos, by design. Moments after Trump signed it into law—late on a Friday afternoon—major airports across the country were melting down. For many people, word of the travel ban seeped out only as family members waiting for travelers from the affected countries learned they were being detained at airports. The homeland security secretary, John Kelly, later confirmed that he hadn't even seen the order until after the president signed it. The White House never asked his department for a legal review. (Odd, for a policy said to be rooted in urgent national security needs.) As we now know, Yates and her staff had also been deliberately roped out of the process. And no Customs and Border Protection (CBP) officials had seen the wording of the new rule before it went into effect; they were simply told in a conference call that evening to behave as though the ban were already in effect. The rollout of the travel ban electrified the rifts in the West Wing between traditional Republican Party bureaucrats like Chief of Staff Reince Priebus and the most nihilistic Trump loyalists like Steve Bannon and Stephen Miller—rifts that would stoke chaos throughout the administration— and left the cabinet and Congress scrambling to find out what the new executive order actually did.

In the hours following the launch of the order, uncertainty deluged the nation's airports as travelers abroad who had boarded their flights legally—some had sold all their worldly possessions to make the trip—found themselves denied entry to the United States. Green card holders, dual citizens, and travelers were being banned at customs. Noncitizen academics with work authorization who were returning to their teaching jobs at US colleges, foreign students coming back to campus after winter break, critically ill babies requiring urgent medical attention, and people who had long ago been cleared to join future spouses were all locked down for hours in detention at the US border without access to an attorney. Elderly immigrants with little English were impounded without proper food or medical care in the backrooms of major US airports. Others were forced to sign documents waiving their rights, then frog-marched back onto planes to be flown to foreign countries to which they had no connections, their passports and travel documents seized by US officials. Some of these people would become, in the words of one federal judge, "like Tom Hanks at the airport," in a wry reference to a 2004 film in which Hanks's character was trapped in permanent limbo, ambling between the Cinnabons and the Starbucks at a terminal he could never leave. These travelers had no papers, no local family, and nowhere to go. The US government had promised them lawful entry and then changed its mind without warning, in some cases, midflight.

Two such travelers, Tareq Aqel Mohammed Aziz and Ammar Aqel Mohammed Aziz, held legal American green cards. Both young men were refused entry to the United States at Dulles International Airport on Saturday. Their papers were confiscated at US customs, and they were flown back to Addis Ababa, Ethiopia. "Back" is of course a misnomer. They were from Yemen. Another stranded traveler was Hameed Khalid Darweesh, who had served for ten years as an interpreter for the US Army's 101st Airborne Division in Baghdad and Mosul in Iraq, and later as a contract engineer. As he would write after his ordeal, in *The Washington Post*, "When I was with my Army colleagues, we were brothers in arms. We lived together, ate together and looked out for each other. They treated me like a soldier alongside them, and we were all one unit." After his service, Darweesh became worried for his safety and that of his family when other former interpreters he had known were murdered. Insurgents were staking out his home. He contacted the International Refugee Assistance Project, a New York nonprofit that offers legal representation to people seeking refugee status. With the help of IRAP, Darweesh applied for a Special Immigrant Visa available to Iraqis who had helped US fighters in 2014. He waited three years, but his approved papers finally came through in January 2017, just before Trump's inauguration.

Darweesh and his family flew to John F. Kennedy International Airport, arriving at 5:45 Friday evening, January 27, 2017—one hour after the travel ban was signed. Over the course of their eleven-hour flight, the executive order had gone into effect. When he deplaned, he watched as his wife and three children cleared passport control and customs and disappeared into the arrivals terminal. But instead of being allowed to accompany them, Darweesh was taken to a back office, stripped of his passport and Special Immigrant Visa, then detained overnight—handcuffed at times—and barred from calling or meeting with his attorney, who was waiting in the arrivals area. Overnight, immigration officers forced Darweesh to empty his pockets, moved him to a different room in the airport, and told him he was being sent back to Iraq, where his life was in danger. Nobody would tell him where his family had gone. After nineteen hours, yet another officer approached and asked him a few questions, then apologized and told him they were just doing their duty and following an order. "Welcome to the United States, and thank you for serving our country," the officer said.

This wasn't just taking place in New York. In Philadelphia, two Syrian families were detained and then sent back, and more than a dozen people were being held in Chicago. Fifty other travelers were detained at Dallas Fort Worth. A recent Clemson PhD visiting her family in Tehran found herself stuck there. A Syrian family of six with valid visas was put on a plane back to Doha. Overall, the ACLU estimated up to two hundred people were being held, although the government was not releasing their names. The Department of Homeland Security (DHS) put out a statement after the chaos erupted, insisting that just a small fraction of passengers arriving in the United States that Saturday were "inconvenienced while enhanced security measures were implemented." The statement went on to add that "these individuals went through enhanced security screenings and are being processed for entry to the United States, consistent with our immigration laws and judicial orders."

While in custody, Darweesh and another traveler—Haider Sameer Abdulkhaleq Alshawi, the husband of an Iraqi woman who had worked for a US military contractor in Iraq who had received refugee status—would become the two named plaintiffs in the first major lawsuit filed to challenge the travel ban.

BECCA HELLER, the co-founder of the International Refugee Assistance Project, was only thirty-five when the travel ban thrust her and her organization into the public eye. If ever an attorney had been hydroponically raised, deep in an underground lab someplace, to be the polar opposite of Sally Yates, Becca Heller is that lawyer. She is a ferocious (and devotedly foulmouthed) advocate who uses the law instead of her bare knuckles, although it's clear that in another life she might have been a hell of a brawler. Heller is almost incapable of artifice and talks often of having to restrain herself from blurting out precisely what she is thinking. Her smile is vast, but like any tactician, she always appears to be thinking on two tracks at once. Even her hair feels like a metaphor; she's been going prematurely gray for years. Heller grew up in Piedmont, California, the daughter of a cardiologist and a teacher. A *New York Times* profile described her as having been voted "most likely to debate with a teacher" in school, and she almost failed to graduate from high school because she refused to abide by the school's physical education requirement. She does not suffer fools, or even the fool adjacent, gladly. She has the kind of rat-a-tat-tat machine-gun mind for tactics and strategy that would serve her well in wartime. And she leans hard on war metaphors when she talks.

Heller went to Dartmouth for college, where she became interested in international hunger and housing, then won a Fulbright scholarship to work on nutrition policy in Malawi. She then entered Yale Law School. Why law school? Heller told me, "I'd worked on a range of different issues throughout college and then in the two years after college, and I just felt like in every area I was working on, I would inevitably rub up against the ceiling of the law." As she explained it, she would be out participating in rallies and demonstrations at which it quickly became apparent that "everyone is freezing and we're in this circle and every single person in the circle would've cut out their left eye" to help, say, the mother of a wrongly incarcerated son, "and we were all, 'What can we do?' And she said, 'Well, are any of you a lawyer?' And nobody was." That, said Heller, was when she realized, "Ugh. I guess I've got to go to law school."

It wasn't clear to her that the act of obtaining a JD would help anyone. "I thought maybe if I went to law school, I would have a tool to break the ceiling or at least to hit the ceiling harder. And I was worried that I would go to law school and I would go $180,000 into debt and spend three years of my life and then discover, 'Oh, that's a powerful fucking ceiling.'"

While she was at Yale, Heller scored a summer internship in Israel, which wasn't working out, because she couldn't speak any Hebrew. As she explained, "The upshot was that I just didn't really have anything to do. And I really hate wasting my time, to basically a compulsive level, in part because life is really short." So after she ran out of *Mad Men* episodes ("there were only a couple of seasons then"), she began to follow news reports about Iraqi refugees stuck in Jordan. She made her way to Amman and began to interview refugees, just to hear their stories.

Heller had done enough work with refugees that she expected to find the same challenges in Jordan she'd found elsewhere: a lack of access to education, adequate medical care, housing. But what she found instead was that "every single one of the families I met with independently identified their primary need as essentially legal, which is that, the biggest problem you have as a refugee is that you can't claim the protection of any nation-state." Heller met with people who could not return to Iraq but couldn't stay in Jordan. "They had no legal status in Jordan, and so their only hope was to try to get referred by the United Nations to a third country and to try to get that country to essentially adopt them." But, she continued, "the legal process for that was so complex and bureaucratic and involved hundreds of pages of paperwork, all in English or sometimes for the third country in French or Dutch. You had to be interviewed a minimum of four times; the interviews could last up to seven hours. They were often through multiple interpreters, and sometimes through bulletproof glass. And at the end of this, they're making a decision on which your life literally depends."

She had no formal affiliation or organization or credentials, but Heller talked her way into meetings with the United Nations Refugee

Agency and the US embassy. But what haunted her was that, as she put it, "I just kept thinking, you know if I was going through an adjudication and my life were on the line, because I think of it as if you're on trial for the death penalty, right? Because if you lose, and you get sent back to Syria, it's a death sentence." These people most needed what defendants need in a death penalty case: lawyers.

"So," said Heller, "I went back to law school and tried to organize some type of legal representation for these folks." With her fellow Yale law student Jon Finer, Heller founded IRAP in 2008, originally in a bid to help Iraqi refugees resettle in the United States and other Western countries. Heller and Finer were—as she phrased it—"tooling around with these cases," and their supervising professor at Yale, Michael Wishnie, "called us into his office one day and he said, 'You guys aren't working on cases, are you?'"

"And we were pretty stupid, but not *completely* stupid, so we answered, 'Oh, Mike. What an interesting question. . . . Why do you ask?' And he said, 'Because that's illegal. It's called the unauthorized practice of law.'" So Heller and Finer had to find real lawyers to argue their cases. Their idea was simple. "We realized that these private firms were coming to Yale to recruit all the time. And so we decided we should turn around and recruit *them*. So we started reaching out to the firms and saying, 'Hey, do you want to get to know some Yale law students? If you agree to supervise us on these cases, it'll give you a hook into our class and into campus.'" That model scaled up beautifully. Law students scored the mentorship of supervising attorneys at prominent firms, while big firms got pro bono cases and eager top-tier law students. The firms covered the extra costs—expert witnesses, immunization costs—and asylum seekers were taken out of limbo. Why? Because, as Heller likes to remind people, "in the asylum context, the General Accounting Office has found that having a lawyer makes you 400 percent more likely to be given refugee status."

The little law shop initially conceived by two law stu

sist refugees represent their own legal interests grew and grew. By the time Heller graduated from Yale, IRAP had chapters at ten law schools, working with a few dozen different law firms. And nobody was more surprised than Heller. "For the first year we were doing this, I just kept trying to figure out, who else was doing this? I knew I didn't want to start a thing. I went to law school because I wanted to be a lawyer." But at some point during the summer of her second year at law school, Heller realized that nobody else *was* doing the thing. And during an internship, someone from the UN High Commissioner for Refugees (UNHCR) actually called her cell phone asking her to take on a case. "And I had this completely, almost irreconcilable response," says Heller. "On the one hand, I thought, 'Oh my gosh, UNHCR wants to refer cases to us.' But on the other hand, I thought, 'They don't have anyone *else* to call?'"

The second summer of law school is when most law students need to make the big decisions about future employment and scrabble for prestigious judicial clerkships. But Heller knew she was not going to clerk for a judge. "Clerking, I think, was never in the cards for me," she says, "on account of authority." That was also when she figured out that IRAP would be her future. By 2014, IRAP had two dozen law school chapters and attorneys from more than fifty law firms tackling an ever-expanding caseload. They opened offices in Jordan and Lebanon. She'd have been content with the shop they'd built, but the election of Trump changed the stakes. For one thing, Heller knew that Trump literally meant what he'd said during the 2016 election campaign about banning all Muslim travelers and refugees. She never thought it was just campaign talk. Immediately after the election, she says, "I went into this very warlike mentality, where I just started thinking in very militaristic metaphors: What weapons do we have, how do we deploy them, and what does it mean that we have this army of lawyers who wants to help refugees?"

Heller knew the January 2017 executive order was coming, two days before it was signed. "We were tipped off," she told me. "We were sent a screenshot of a computer monitor, I think in the White House, that had the text of the Muslim ban on it." And, added Heller, "our first thought was for our existing clients." So IRAP ran searches in their database to turn up anyone who had an imminent travel date. They contacted each of their legal teams, and on January 25 Heller sent out a mass email warning their lawyer foot soldiers what was to come: "Tell any clients who already have visas to board a plane for the United States. Get ready for the possibility that they will be detained upon landing." They also sent out letters to their clients through Viber and WhatsApp to present to US border officials, with their lawyers' phone numbers and a statement of their well-founded fears of returning to their home countries.

Tending to their clients with imminent travel dates was the first order of business, but two nights before the ban was signed, Heller was up late G-chatting with their policy director, Betsy Fisher, and both were expressing relief that one particular transgender refugee client had been met at the airport by one of the IRAP lawyers and allowed into the United States without incident. They were marveling that all the other refugees on that flight had also been lucky, because refugees are often slated to fly together in groups. Says Heller, "And then we had this moment of realization that at any given time when this thing comes down, there's going to be thousands and thousands of people in midair who had legal permission to enter when they took off. And no one knows what on earth their status is going to be when they land or what's going to happen to them at the airport." That was when it occurred to them that "this one lawyer at the airport is something that we need to replicate, basically all over the country, on a much larger scale."

It was eleven o'clock at night, on January 25, but Heller started calling everyone she knew, asking whether it made sense to deploy a handful of lawyers at every major airport. "We made this Google form that said, 'Where are you, where's your nearest airport, what hours can you go?' And we just sent it out to maybe two listservs." The lawyers on the list could have been tax attorneys or real estate lawyers, Heller didn't care. "It was a question of who we could deploy. It's not necessarily that they're providing legal services; they're just at this point bearing witness. . . . I just knew something fucked up was going to go down at the airport. We should have lawyers there to try to deal with it."

IRAP sent out the email blast on January 26, 2017, the Thursday morning before the executive order was signed. Within an hour and a half, sixteen hundred people had filled out the Google form and the website had crashed. The sign-up blasted through the immigrants' rights community, where any lawyers with information about who would be on planes and what their schedules might be could also weigh in.

And then, suddenly, on that same Thursday, everything hit pause. As Heller explained it, "I started getting calls on Thursday afternoon from the refugee advocacy community saying, 'There's word that you're mobilizing a bunch of lawyers to go to airports. You need to tell them to stand down.'" These groups had been given assurances from the State Department that any travelers who already had legal permission of any kind to enter would be allowed to enter. Heller froze, unsure whether to call off her troops. As she remembered it, this might ultimately be one of the most gendered parts of her story: "I get a series of calls from people I know and largely respect in the refugee advocacy community saying call off the dogs. They're worried that they had all these assurances and if you have all these lawyers there, it's going to provoke the government." Heller is young, she's female, she's an inveterate rule breaker. But all these older establishment lawyers are telling her that she's overreacting. "So," she continued, "I have this crisis of . . . not conscience, but a crisis of hubris, this anxiety moment about trying to weigh how much of this is my own ego, and also thinking I know better. . . . I think a man would have been just like, fuck you guys, the lawyers are going." She wavered, in part because she thought the insiders getting promises from other insiders knew better. And she wavered because she convinced herself that when women step out of line, it must be egoism driving them.

So Heller ended up calling off all her volunteer lawyers, with the knowledge that they could still be activated instantly if needed. They would stand down but be ready if things went sideways. They divided up the twelve major US airports among their staff, with each staff member responsible for one airport, and two lawyers they knew personally hanging out at the airports just in case. At 4:30 eastern time on Friday afternoon, January 27, the executive order was announced, virtually identical to the screenshot from earlier in the week. This was the order Sally Yates was reading about from news reports. Becca Heller was surprised. She'd believed that the most blatantly unconstitutional provisions would have been lawyered out before the signing. She also knew they had clients, including Darweesh, scheduled to arrive in New York at 7:30 p.m. She put her baby daughter, Anna, to bed and waited.

Heller soon got the call that Darweesh's wife and children had been allowed into the arrivals terminal but that he himself had been detained. At 11:00 that night, two agents from Customs and Border Protection approached his wife and children as they waited anxiously in the arrivals hall and asked them to voluntarily come back into the customs area to join Darweesh, who was in detention. Jonathan Polonsky, with the law firm Kilpatrick Townsend, who was the family's lawyer alongside an IRAP attorney, asked the CBP agent whether this was a request or an order. Told it was merely a request, Polonsky and IRAP put the Darweeshes into a cab and got them to a hotel. Their father and husband remained in custody somewhere in the airport.

Mark Doss, Darweesh's IRAP attorney, arrived at JFK after CBP had moved Darweesh and Alshawi in handcuffs from Terminal 1, which had shut down for the night, to Terminal 4. Doss tried to make his way back to the customs area, but a CBP officer barred his way. "Who is the person we need to talk to?" Doss asked a CBP official, still trying to get access to his client and attempting to comprehend the chain of command.

"Mr. President . . . Call Mr. Trump," said the officer.

So much for calling off the dogs. The government was now detaining lawful visa holders and giving no information about what they were doing with them or why; this is what the immigration groups had been told would not happen. "Everyone at IRAP went into action," Heller said. "We activated the lawyers, we had points of contact for each airport, we had NGO points of contact for each airport, we started putting together habeas templates. My first litigation phone call was to Justin Cox of the National Immigration Law Center in Atlanta."

Heller was already beyond the place where she had operated at IRAP. "And I said, 'Turns out they're holding people, I know the name of one, what do we file?' And Justin said, 'We file a habeas petition.' And I said, 'Great, how do we do that?' Because I'm not a lawyer." (She's a lawyer.) Then Heller and her team called Mike Wishnie—the same Yale law professor who'd once told her and Jon Finer they probably shouldn't practice law without first taking the bar. And Wishnie had the audacious idea of filing something called a class-action habeas suit. "Since nobody had any idea of how many people were being held, the suit could be filed on behalf of all of them," explained Heller. Coalition members and law students debated: Filing a class action would protect the unknown Muslim travelers trapped without lawyers in the skies. But it might also mean that Darweesh and Alshawi would not get instant relief. Wishnie contacted the American Civil Liberties Union (ACLU) for help. Then the lawyers and students stayed up all night that Friday drafting the pleadings. They knew they needed to file before any international flights could take off early Saturday, which was when detained travelers would begin to be deported on morning flights. So, at 5:33 that Saturday morning, IRAP, the ACLU, and the other groups filed a habeas corpus petition on behalf of Darweesh and Alshawi and a motion to certify a nationwide class. The petition was filed in a federal court in New York. *Darweesh v. Trump* would become the first lawsuit challenging the Muslim ban.

THE TERM "HABEAS CORPUS" sounds obscure and lofty, but at its simplest it's the name for an ancient right of any persons in detention to be brought before a judge to show there's some lawful basis for that detention. The dream team behind the Darweesh suit included attorneys from the ACLU, IRAP, the National Immigration Law Center, and Yale Law School's legal services clinic, demanding government accountability for the seizure. These lawyers would appear in court just over twenty-four hours after the men were detained, and thanks to organizing by groups like Heller's, random attorneys around the country made their way to airports to do the same. Not surprisingly, some of these first heroes of the Trump resistance were the legal nerds. In the days following, as I reported out the story, I was being directed over and over to lawyers who had taken it upon themselves to drive to airports—lawyers with no background in immigration law, people who were just showing up to find a way to bear witness. A story by Reeves Wiedeman in *New York* magazine crunched the numbers: in response to a call earlier in the week by IRAP, three thousand lawyers had volunteered in just four hours. "By midafternoon a stream of lawyers, some with immigration experience, others from big corporate firms in the city, had begun arriving at JFK. (Women make up just 35 percent of all lawyers, but 60 percent of public-interest attorneys are women, and the numbers seemed to reflect that.)" Reporting suggested that about a hundred lawyers were deployed at the four terminals at Kennedy airport.

But as astounding as this reality on the ground was, the other great

American story lay in the massive *public* reaction to the travel ban. Because while the lawyers were hastily drafting court petitions and lining up in airports to help, the other thing that happened that weekend can only be described as a big unscripted constitutional flashmob. It was breathtaking: the Boston Tea Party at luggage carousels and parking lots. The crowds kept swelling, and by 6:00 p.m. on Friday, January 27, there were thousands massed outside JFK communicating by way of human microphone. Even before the journalists and politicians showed up, the cabdrivers, with their union, the New York Taxi Workers Alliance, had demanded an hourlong work stoppage for drivers serving the airport. The organizers at JFK announced another protest slated to happen the next day in Battery Park. Thirty thousand people turned up. The American people themselves showed up, disorganized but purposeful.

As Eli Rosenberg of *The New York Times* put it, of the scene on Saturday at JFK, "By the end of the day, the scattershot group had swelled to an enormous crowd. They filled the sidewalks outside the terminal and packed three stories of a parking garage across the street, a mass of people driven by emotion to this far-flung corner of the city, singing, chanting and unfurling banners." By 3:00 p.m. Saturday, crowds that had hastily organized themselves on Facebook were gathered at JFK and chanting, "No hate, no fear, immigrants are welcome here." Folks watching online were moved to march on Trump Tower or the White House or to stand in huge crowds on the sidewalks outside airports. At San Francisco International Airport, this swelling crowd of protesters chanted at immigration officials to "let the lawyers in." In Philadelphia and Chicago and Houston, at Washington Dulles and Seattle-Tacoma, crowds asked for nothing more than this: let these lawyers speak to their clients. These were real people, showing up with blankets and snacks and hastily Sharpied signs, demanding constitutional rights for travelers trapped in limbo. It was a scene that could have embodied the fondest constitutional hopes of the framers:

lawful protest to demand legal redress for unlawful government detention. And the attorneys, accustomed to being the butt of jokes that
often include the words "bottom of the ocean," were delighted to be
celebrated like heroes. Back at JFK, attorneys were hunched on the
floor over their laptops, filing emergency habeas petitions on behalf of
anyone they knew to be detained in a back room.

This "Airport Revolution," as I've come to think of it, was one of
the first mass uprisings of the Trump era, and parts of it were—
not unlike the Women's March that took place just days before—
spearheaded and organized by a lot of women who were angry and
itching to act. In some sense, both movements were animated by the
same feeling: America had elected a serial misogynist and xenophobe,
and the outrage around that needed to be expressed publicly. But the
lawyers, particularly the female lawyers, turning up at airports that
first weekend seemed also to be responding to a call to *do* something,
to show up. This would become a through line as groups of women
who had no prior experience with political organizing gathered over
four long years to register voters, or to phone their representatives, or
to march against racialized police violence. As Jennifer Rubin put it in
her 2021 book, *Resistance: How Women Saved Democracy from Donald Trump*, one change after 2016 was that women came to understand that "politics was no longer about what *other* people did." The
same, I would submit, was true of women lawyers. Dozens of them
described to me the ways in which Trumpism forced them to break
from their focus on family law, antitrust, trusts and estates work to do
democracy work because, to paraphrase Becca Heller, they realized
that "They don't have anyone else to call." Which could just as well
have been the alternative title for this book.

HELLER HERSELF finally made her way to JFK at about 2:00 a.m. on
Saturday, less than twelve hours after the Muslim ban went into

effect. Television and social media were broadcasting images of family members at airports begging to see their loved ones. Heller hadn't really grasped what was happening on the ground, because her voice mail and email had crashed and she'd been on conference calls with lawyers all night. "I didn't know there were protests," she said. "So when I actually got to JFK and there were thousands of people outside, I said, 'Who the fuck are all these people and what are they doing here?' That was my first impression, that we'd organized maybe a hundred lawyers to be here, but who are these people and why are they outside?"

Heller told me these civilian protests were largely spontaneous. Someone connected her with Daniel Altschuler from Make the Road Action, a group that empowers immigrant communities, who was a better organizer than she was. "I had forgotten a coat," Heller told me. "I was also wearing jeans with a hole in it and a hoodie because it just didn't occur to me that any of it would be televised." Heller was trying to give press interviews and track the protests, and for part of the day she was attached to a *New York Times* reporter solely because she was using his computer to power her dead phone battery. She was hardly an expert in any of it. "There was this dude, whose name I forget, who was doing a really good job organizing people. And I remember thinking that I should try to recruit him to come work at IRAP. So I pulled him aside at one point and I said, 'Hey, where do you work now?' And he said, 'Oh, I'm a consultant at McKinsey.' And I said, 'Oh, do you like it there?' And he said, 'Oh yeah, I love it.' And I went, 'All right, forget it, great job.'"

"But people were self-organizing," she added, still sounding dazed at the way it came together. "This is what a movement looks like." Heller says that someone from Mayor Bill de Blasio's office realized that the best way to figure out the names of detained travelers—names necessary to file a habeas petition—would be to canvass the families waiting at the arrival gates at JFK. So they created signs in the languages from the banned countries that said, ARE YOU WAITING FOR SOMEONE WHO HASN'T COME OUT? They held up signs saying, DO YOU NEED A LAWYER? in Pushtu and Arabic and other languages, then blasted that suggestion out to IRAP lawyers at airports nationwide. A lawyer from a prominent Manhattan law firm realized there was a diner, called Central Diner, inside Terminal 4, and she somehow negotiated with the management to co-opt it into a makeshift law office where attorneys could interview client families.

Darweesh was released early Saturday afternoon after almost nineteen hours in detention. He emerged from the JFK terminal with Congresswoman Nydia Velázquez and Congressman Jerrold Nadler, who'd spent the morning trying to negotiate his freedom. According to an account in *New York* magazine, "The first thing he asked, putting his hands behind his back as if they were being restrained, was, 'Why did this happen to me?' He couldn't stop crying." When he was able to speak to reporters, one of them asked Darweesh if he was angry. "No, because I have these people," he said, holding on to his attorney's shoulder. "This is America."

That Saturday night, January 28, 2017, I marveled in a column for *Slate* that lawyers could become American superheroes overnight. "Today, the lawyers joined the fight. Donald Trump has no idea how terrifying a blue book and a Lexis password can be. He's about to find out," I wrote. But Heller was quick to point out that what really killed the first travel ban, long before any judicial action had been taken, was democracy itself. "I take comfort from the fact that it didn't take a court to defeat the first executive order," she said. "The lawsuit that we won, it didn't defeat the order; it just said people couldn't be detained and deported under it. . . . What defeated the order was people showing the fuck up." The Trump administration walked back the worst parts of the travel ban almost immediately, and, as Heller says, "they didn't roll back the first executive order in response to a court order or a congressional inquiry review, or anything like that. They rolled it back on their own, because democracy scared the shit out of them. Because it turns out that what democracy looks like is chaos at the airports." After years of marching, it's easy to forget that marching itself is protected First Amendment activity. It is democracy hitting asphalt.

Of course, what was happening that weekend in courtrooms around the country was as important as the mass protests. The first emergency hearing happened at 7:30 on Saturday evening, January 28, in a Brooklyn courtroom. The lawyers, seeking an emergency hearing, had simply called the courthouse, which was closed for the weekend, and somebody had picked up. They requested and were granted a hearing that night. The courtroom was packed to capacity, while a massive crowd converged on Cadman Plaza outside. The federal district judge Ann Donnelly, who happened to be the duty judge that weekend, presided as protesters shouted outside.

Donnelly, a former federal prosecutor who had once prosecuted a Tyco executive convicted in 2005 for looting almost $100 million from the company, took the bench. The ACLU took the position that the Muslim ban violated the Constitution's due process and equal protection clauses—the same issues Yates had flagged that weekend. The class of plaintiffs still included Darweesh, and the Trump administration's lawyers tried to argue that the ACLU's case was now moot because the two named plaintiffs—Darweesh and Alshawi—were no longer in government custody. But there were many others still being detained, and in her courtroom, Judge Donnelly worried about all the travelers who hadn't been granted special waivers and were still being denied entry.

In Washington, DC, that night, Trump administration officials were headed out in black tie and ballgowns to the Alfalfa Club dinner, a swanky event for the DC elite. But in Brooklyn, standing before Judge Donnelly, ACLU lawyer Lee Gelernt was making a furious case against the slapdash order. He explained that these detainees posed no risk to the United States: "It's not as if these people weren't vetted; they were just caught in transit." As he argued, his team was monitoring the airports. Gelernt was thus able to tell the judge, in real time, at about 8:00 p.m., "We just got word that the government is threatening to put someone on a plane at 9:20." He added that this particular detainee at JFK was Syrian, part of the group of detainees he represented, and was about to be sent back to a war zone while the hearing was happening.

Judge Donnelly then turned to the government attorneys: "Apparently, there is somebody who they're putting on a plane—what do you think about that—back to Syria? Irreparable harm?" She asked Susan Riley, a civil lawyer who worked in the Brooklyn US Attorney's Office, whether the Trump administration could assure her these people who were about to be deported would not suffer irreparable harm as a result of being sent away. Riley didn't know: "This has unfolded with such speed that we haven't had any opportunity to address any of the issues, the legal issues of the status of anyone who may be at the airport." Donnelly was frustrated. "Our own government presumably approved their entry to the country," she said, then asked Riley, "If they had come in two days ago, we wouldn't be here. Am I right?" Donnelly then asked how many people the government was detaining. Riley replied that "the government does not have sufficient information to answer."

"That's exactly why I'm going to grant" the ACLU's request, replied Donnelly, announcing from the bench, "The stay is granted." She signed the order at 9:00 p.m.—twenty minutes before the Syrian traveler at Kennedy airport would have been returned to the war-torn country. Gelernt asked the administration for a list of those who were still being held at airports. "We don't know. People are coming in all the time," replied Riley. Donnelly ordered that such a list be generated, warning the government that if there was anyone else "who is in danger of being removed, I direct you to communicate that we have a stay." Nobody was being flown out that night. "I am directing the government to stop removal if there is someone right now in danger of being removed," Donnelly repeated. "No one is to be removed in this class."

This very first judicial order had come down just before 9:00 on Saturday night, January 28, just over twenty-four hours after the travel ban had gone into effect. Donnelly signed her emergency order, writing that refugees and travelers with valid visas being detained at US airports could not be sent back to their home countries. She ordered the Trump administration to refrain from deporting previously approved refugees as well as "approved holders of valid immigrant and non-immigrant visas and other individuals . . . legally authorized to enter the United States" from the targeted countries. Enforcing Trump's order by sending the travelers home could cause them "irreparable harm," she wrote. Her order applied nationwide, not just to the travelers arriving at JFK. It didn't grant entry to these travelers or those who followed, but it did keep them from being packed onto flights and shipped back to countries where their lives were in danger or countries to which they had no connections.

A crowd of at least a thousand New Yorkers had gathered outside the courthouse. They erupted in cheers when Donnelly's ruling was announced by Gelernt and the ACLU's Anthony Romero on the courthouse steps as people waved signs and shouted, "Thank you!" while someone played a trombone. It was by no means over. Lawyers at airports showed screenshots of Donnelly's injunction to immigration officials on their smartphones. Not every government official was moved to comply. The Yale professors Muneer Ahmad and Mike Wishnie fought for an Iranian Fulbright scholar on a plane at JFK that night who was being returned to Iran after the order came down. They were negotiating with the government as the flight was taxiing down the runway. One of their first-year law students, brand new to their legal clinic, got a call through to the Port Authority of New York and the New Jersey police, finally reaching a supervisor to call the control tower and turn the flight around.

Judge Donnelly was the first in a long string of judges who would look at Trump's travel ban and call it what it was—a hasty order that didn't account for the pain it caused immigrants, travelers, and refugees. Indeed, it bears mentioning that of the first judges to declare the travel ban unconstitutional in the last days of January 2017, most were women. A few minutes after Judge Donnelly entered her order, a veteran judge in the Eastern District of Virginia, Leonie Brinkema, issued another temporary restraining order (TRO), granting all permanent legal residents detained at Dulles airport access to lawyers and blocking any petitioners from being removed. At 1:51 a.m. eastern time, two federal judges in Boston, Allison Burroughs and Judith Dein, imposed a seven-day restraining order pausing the executive order. And early Sunday morning in the Western District of Washington, the US district judge Thomas Zilly issued another order halting any deportations. Four of those first five judges were women, all in that first twenty-four hours.

Researchers have been studying the data on women judges for several decades, trying to ascertain whether women make different kinds of judicial decisions from men. The bulk of this research suggests that having women on the bench leads to different results in cases that have to do with gender; that when appellate judges sit together on three-judge panels, a single woman can impact the opinions of her male colleagues on cases about gender discrimination or sexual harassment. (I have always loved these studies insofar as they seem to suggest that feminism is contagious and that men are susceptible to catching it.) There is less data to support the idea that women have a uniquely feminine judicial voice or viewpoint on all legal questions. Justice Sandra Day O'Connor famously rejected the notion that women judge from a uniquely female perspective, while Justice Sonia Sotomayor famously embraced it. As an empirical matter, it may not be statistically relevant that so many women judges enjoined the travel ban in the early hours, any more than it is statistically relevant that so many female attorneys showed up at airports as volunteers. But it certainly dovetails with the big rise in women's activism and engagement generally in the Trump years. Maybe the most important thing to be said of that four-out-of-five statistic is that it speaks volumes about the ways in which, in recent decades, America managed to seat record numbers of new female judges and credential record numbers of new women lawyers. At minimum, we can say it matters that even a randomly selected pool of jurists could reflect a better gender balance on the federal bench. At the end of his presidency, Trump's federal judicial nominees were 76 percent male (Barack Obama's judicial nominees were 58 percent male). Those numbers matter whether or not women, or people of color, bring different "viewpoints" to the bench. They matter because for courts to be legitimate, they must look like the country itself.

In a call with reporters two days after the first travel ban was pushed out, senior administration officials insisted that the rollout had been a "massive success story in terms of implementation on every single level." The president insisted, "It's not a Muslim ban, but we're totally prepared. . . . It's working out very nicely. You see it at the airports, you see it all over. It's working very nicely."

A week after a raft of emergency restraining orders were entered in New York, Virginia, Massachusetts, and California courts, the long, slow slog of nationwide legal challenges began. Various states, led by their own attorneys general, filed lawsuits, first in Washington State, then in Virginia. Briefs and responses were filed, hearings were docketed across the country, and lawyers were cooperating and coordinating strategies and legal theories. And the Trump Justice Department was having an increasingly difficult time justifying the president's shambolic order. Over that first week, the scope of the travel ban had already been narrowed to reflect both pushback from the courts and concessions from the administration: Green card holders from the seven affected countries were now to be allowed into the United States. DHS amended its opinion to allow dual citizens with passports from countries other than the seven listed to be admitted. Detainees were now being given access to counsel.

Over a two-year period, travel ban lawsuits would ping back and forth from the federal trial courts to the federal appeals courts. Every time the Trump administration suffered a loss, the president would tweet out invective at the judges and unspool yet another version of the ban. In March 2017, the administration announced it was withdrawing the original order and implementing a new one. In September 2017, a *third* version was unfurled. In no sense could the new versions have been said to cure the religious animus that infected the original Muslim ban. But they managed to mask it and softened some of the worst aspects of the first iteration. In a way, the courts were doing just what courts are meant to do—constraining and checking the executive branch. Both the Ninth and the Fourth Circuit Courts of Appeals eventually struck down even this 3.0 version of the ban. It went on to the highest court in the land.

In the spring of 2018, all eyes were on the US Supreme Court, where oral arguments over the final version of the Trump travel ban were being heard. On the last day of the term in June 2018, the court handed down its decision in *Trump v. Hawaii*. By a 5–4 margin, the justices upheld the final version of the travel ban. Chief Justice John Roberts, writing for the five justices in the majority, determined that despite Trump's anti-Muslim rhetoric, the government had demonstrated "a sufficient national security justification" for the September 2017 Proclamation, which had replaced the original executive order, to survive. At times striking an almost rueful tone, Roberts wrote that "the issue before us is not whether to denounce the statements. It is instead the significance of those statements in reviewing a Presidential directive, neutral on its face, addressing a matter within the core of executive responsibility. In doing so, we must consider not only the statements of a particular President, but also the authority of the Presidency itself." President Trump had won one of the few major cases of his presidency. He would cite this victory and the vast executive powers the court had granted him in February 2019, when he declared a state of emergency on the southern border.

Becca Heller told me it isn't an accident that the first spontaneous mass uprising of the Trump era happened at US airports. It's the same lesson she learned about asylum seekers more than a decade earlier: "I think it's about the inevitability of human movement, the push of human flow; this is both where their fear comes from and why, ultimately, their xenophobic program is doomed to fail." Humans move; climate change and global instability make that inevitable. The problem of refugees and asylum seekers would prove to be one of the central humanitarian failures of the Trump era—made manifest in family separation policies at the border and the declaration of a national emergency to fund a border wall Congress had already refused to pay for.

As for Becca Heller, IRAP went on to file one lawsuit after another, in a fight that seemed to lurch onward in ever-changing forms. She was the recipient of a MacArthur Genius Grant in the fall of 2018, some of which she used to pay off her law school loans. She told me that at one point in the midst of the great Airport Revolution of 2017, she got a call from her mother. "It was maybe Sunday," she said, "so three days of no sleep and my mom called to ask how I was doing, and I said—and I do like dark humor—'Oh, I'm living the first line of my obituary.'" She paused. "I thought I was kidding. And now I'm worried that I wasn't."

Heller also told me that whatever she felt throughout that time, she didn't feel angry. "To be angry is to become like them," she said. "I have a kid now. I don't want to live in a place where I'm that angry.

I had to find some other psychological framework from which to fight this." She added, "Resistance, by definition, means you're losing. And you don't have to be okay with losing. But you can't let losing set you back. You had to understand that for the next four years or eight years or whatever it is, we're all in damage mitigation mode. And that if you were winning, it wouldn't be called resistance; it would be called tyranny."

Heller isn't sentimental or starry-eyed about the courts and the law. She says she never really fetishized either, which sets her apart from some of the other women in this book: "I didn't go to law school because I had a deep respect for the courts and the rule of law. I think a lot of the law is completely ridiculous. The law says a lot of really horrible things, and historically has said a lot of really horrible things, and it has been used in a lot of really horrible ways. But, I think, sometimes you can use it to achieve good things. I mean, to me, getting a law degree is just about using the master's tools to destroy the master's house." So many of the women I met over the Trump years expressed this ambivalence. The American legal system was fundamentally a machine built to privilege propertied white men. But it's the only thing going, and you work with what you have.

Heller also captured that ambivalence as a woman who graduated from law school a generation after Sally Yates. We have come so far and sometimes it seems nothing has changed. "I have not personally experienced very much gender discrimination," she told me, "in part because my personality has a lot of what you would call 'masculine traits.' I'm very loud, very assertive. I don't scare easily." But Heller also recalls that the moment she decided to start her own litigation shop at IRAP came during one of the Muslim ban lawsuits, "in a conference room with some very high-powered and very allegedly open-minded liberal litigators, and they were almost all men." The team was doing a practice oral argument, "and every time I talked, it was like I hadn't spoken." This was not, she observes, because she is a quiet person.

As she described it, the session "got to the point literally where I said something. And then someone else in a position of a lot of power said exactly the same thing right after me, and I lost my cool." She told him, "I literally just said that." She described the room going silent and getting "five texts all at once from other people in the room saying, 'We heard you say it.'" But for her, the problem was that "nobody said shit out loud." Justice Ruth Bader Ginsburg frequently described having precisely the same experience as a law faculty member and on into her time on the Supreme Court—that she would make a comment that would be met with silence, and when the same words were shared by a male colleague, the room would respond with "great idea, let's discuss it."

Heller decided on the spot: "I want my own litigation shop. . . . I want a female litigation director." Her doubts about the law and the courts extend, by the way, to litigation itself. As she explains, "I just think this whole idea of litigation—that truth is best arrived at by two people taking diametrically opposed positions and fighting it out—is such a stupidly masculine way to arrive at consensus." But again, this is the world in which she must operate, and so as she said, "I decided to build a litigation shop that involves people who recognize the stupidity of the system, but will still use it to fight in the ways we need it as a tool, but won't let ego affect their decisions." As she noted, they have brought some huge cases and so far won every single one of them. Speaking from the vantage of someone who learned a lot about gender and law and power, at a very young age and on the job, Heller conceded the following: "The gender thing, I've realized, is not what happens when I speak up . . . but what happens in my own head."

Becca Heller sits uncomfortably beside some of the women in this book who remained ardent institutionalists despite recognizing that the law could be distorted and manipulated. And yet like Pauli Murray, she proves that even a woman with grievous doubts about the American legal system can leverage that system to benefit everyone.

And if doing your level best with what's out there isn't sometimes a defining theme of American womanhood, I'm not sure what is.

Heller walked into the first week of the Trump era as a very young attorney with a complicated coalition of immigration lawyers and a strong foreboding about what was about to happen. She had a plan, a set of committed volunteers, and the conviction that she should be listening to that little voice in her head as if she were a man. Before Trump was elected, we liked to believe that the attorneys could just magic up answers, and while they did so, everyone else could pop up some buttery snacks and wait and watch. Becca Heller and the Airport Revolution are proof that constitutional democracy isn't just for spectators and it certainly isn't just for attorneys. (Heller doesn't care much for attorneys, anyhow.) There was something about ordinary people showing up, and the handful of activists who engineered it, that still feels like the end of a rom-com. And there's something about the images of those spontaneous crowds that still undoes us, perhaps because four years later it would be mirrored by elections activists on the ground in Georgia doing the very same thing. Becca Heller likes to credit chaotic democracy for brushing back the xenophobia and fear of the Muslim ban. Me, I like to credit chaotic democracy for saving chaotic democracy itself.

4

Charlottesville Nazis

Robbie Kaplan:
The Big Firm Litigator

The first time Nazis marched in Charlottesville, Virginia, was May 13, 2017. Charlottesville is a small city. As Professor Richard Schragger of the University of Virginia School of Law put it in a 2018 law review article, "It has a population of approximately 47,000 residents; it occupies a territory of about 10 square miles. The Charlottesville 'downtown' is about eight square blocks. The city has a part-time city council and mayor, a professional city manager, a city attorney and an assistant city attorney. The Charlottesville police department has 127 officers." When you walk down Charlottesville's bricked-in downtown mall, you will see fifteen people you know, whether you want to see them or not. It is—as my husband was advised when we first moved there in 2000—not a smart town to pick if you really want to cheat on your wife.

This blue college town in the heart of a central Virginia that was quickly turning purple was deliberately selected for the first torchlit white supremacy rally of the Trump era. The attraction was ostensibly a raging dispute over Confederate war monuments in the city's parks that had started a year and a half earlier when a local high school student launched a petition to have them removed. Residents were dialed up to 12 over the city council's decision to sell and remove these monuments in 2017. Richard Spencer, a white supremacist who claims to have popularized the term "alt-right" and who led chants of "Hail Trump, hail our people, hail victory!" at a 2016 postelection celebration of the new president in Washington, DC, was a graduate of the University of Virginia. So was Jason Kessler, a local white supremacist who became the point person for the march organizers. Nor is it immaterial that UVA is housed in Charlottesville, that it was known as "the Harvard of the Confederacy," and that the town still lies pinned under the shadow of Monticello, home of Thomas Jefferson—the progenitor of constitutional democracy, yes, but also the casual promoter of both slavery and the flagrant sexual exploitation of Black women's bodies.

It was never really about the monuments. The statues at issue in Charlottesville were not even monuments from the Civil War. The Confederate statues we were debating were not actually erected until 1924, part of an unsparing campaign to push African American residents out of Vinegar Hill—a vibrant Black neighborhood—in a show of white dominance and supremacy at the height of Jim Crow. And yet, theoretically in defense of these monuments, in May 2017, a few dozen Nazis (who prefer to be called the "alt-right," or "white supremacists," but they do like to wear Nazi insignias and chant Nazi slogans) gathered beneath the statue of Robert E. Lee on horseback, brandishing some of Walmart's finest tiki torches and candles. Richard Spencer, who led the torchlit spectacle through Lee Park as attendees chanted "You will not replace us" and "Blood and soil" (or the original version, "Blut und Boden"), insisted that the flickering torches were not intended to evoke Klan marches and that the chants weren't meant to echo Nazi rallies; it was all simply "a beautiful aesthetic" and "kind of mystical." They chanted for a few minutes, filmed themselves heroically in the manner of Leni Riefenstahl, and then dispersed.

Those few moments were long enough for the videos to rocket around the world and long enough to plant an emotional bruise on Charlottesville that still hasn't quite healed all these years later. I know, because I had been living in Charlottesville for seventeen years when the white supremacist marchers first made their way to this town in which they didn't live, to fight over monuments about which they didn't care, to make a troll-ey point about white people and their "replacement" by Jews and nonwhites. The city was hardly a case study in diversity and inclusion; the long history of segregation still informed every part of the town's racialized education, housing, and policing disparities. But the white supremacist rally proved to be salt in a wound for a community that believed itself progressive.

Soon after the first march, the local organizer Jason Kessler sought a permit for a far bigger and more ambitious rally in August. On July 8, 2017, the KKK decided to get in on the white supremacy action, and about fifty of the Loyal White Knights of the Ku Klux Klan, headquartered in North Carolina, gathered at Justice Park, many in hoods and waving Confederate flags, all escorted by police in riot gear. Hundreds of local counterdemonstrators showed up in protest (I was one of them), and the Klansmen themselves offered conflicting media statements about whether they were there to support the Civil War monuments or simply to protest "the ongoing cultural genocide . . . of white Americans," as one explained to the press. When counterprotesters failed to disperse quickly enough, the police tear-gassed them, which added fuel to the burgeoning narrative that the local cops were there to protect and coddle white supremacists while gassing antiracist counterprotesters.

That long summer of 2017 also featured a visit from the Proud Boys, yet another white supremacist group that also fetishizes white

dominance, male bonding, and Gap khakis. Locals struggling to understand why the city was rapidly becoming Disneyland for Nazis
were split as to whether the best strategy was to face them down in
bars and fight or stay home and ignore the juvenile attention seeking.
We were also dealing with the growing anticipation of the so-called
Unite the Right rally, slated for August 12, which promised to be—
according to Spencer and the other organizers, including the Traditionalist Worker Party's co-founder Matthew Heimbach and other
white supremacist leaders—the biggest white nationalist rally in modern history. Kessler had received his permit. Signage for the rally featured prominent Nazi symbols. Participating groups would include the
National Policy Institute, the neo-Confederate League of the South,
neo-Nazi groups, and the Traditionalist Worker Party groups as well as
Vanguard America and the National Socialist Movement. The former
KKK Grand Wizard David Duke would attend as part of the who's
who of white pride and racial intolerance.

To repeat: It was never about Civil War monuments or southern
dignity or states' rights or the erasure of white history. It was about
white fury and violent white ethno-nationalism, and that was fueled
by Donald Trump's endless claims about Mexican rapists and Muslim terrorists. During the 2016 campaign Trump had initially refused
to condemn David Duke, retweeted a Twitter account called White-
GenocideTM, and persistently derided refugees and immigrants. It
needn't reflect a causal connection that after Trump won the election,
white supremacists like Spencer celebrated the presence in the White
House of someone whom he believed shared his vision of "peaceful
ethnic cleansing" and his loathing of the *Lügenpresse*, the Nazi word
for the media.

IT's HARD TO REFLECT on the Trump presidency without taking
into account the ways in which it proved a challenge for defenders of

free speech. From accusations about "fake news" and claims about censorship and deplatforming, Trump's great gift lay in recasting First Amendment liberties as weapons to be used against other institutions. The framing of the Charlottesville alt-right rally as protected speech and protest was of a piece with that larger move.

The First Amendment prevents Congress from "abridging the freedom of speech, or of the press; or the right of the people peaceably to assemble." In a sense, then, it celebrates this quintessentially American value—the right to talk smack—and is the most apt liberty to inflame the modern era, with debates over "cancel culture" and mandatory donor disclosure and doxing dominating every policy question we face. The current Supreme Court turns out to be the most speech-protective court in American history. That means that in recent decades it's used the idea of protecting free speech to, just for starters, kill sweeping efforts to limit campaign contributions. It's barred states from posting even truthful signs in reproductive health clinics. The court has used speech rights to make it harder for unions to collect member dues and organize. It is perhaps fitting in its own way that virtually any sort of conduct that can be recast as "free speech" is permissible in a country where nobody ever seems to stop talking.

The free speech clauses are also among the most widely misunderstood. Every time someone insults someone else on cable news, then faces repercussions, people start to hoot and holler about the death of the First Amendment. But of course the First Amendment applies only to government censorship and not to every censor or sponsor or employer. And the First Amendment also doesn't render any of us immune from the public or economic consequences of doing and saying stupid or hateful things. More than any other category error, the mistaken notion that the First Amendment allows any American to say anything, anywhere with impunity is among the most pervasive. That said, there are not a lot of Supreme Court free speech cases featuring people we admire greatly. A vast array of sketchy pornographers, overheated rabble-rousers, and notable bigots and bigmouths have given their names to the body of cases that protect free speech rights for the rest of us.

The Chicago suburb of Skokie, Illinois, had a population of about 70,000 people in 1977, of whom approximately 45,500 were Jewish. Between 5,000 and 7,000 of those Jews had survived the concentration camps of the Holocaust, which is precisely why the Nazi Party of America chose Skokie for their symbolic hate march in May 1977. The thirty to fifty demonstrators planned to wear Nazi uniforms and swastikas, but organizers made clear that they had no intention of threatening or harming anyone. When it became clear that thousands of counterprotesters would come out in response to the march—and that some kind of violence might ensue—a federal district court enjoined the wearing of Nazi uniforms or swastikas in the parade or the distribution of pamphlets that might incite hate. Both the Illinois appeals court and the Illinois Supreme Court refused to lift the injunction. The case came up to the US Supreme Court in the spring of 1977.

In a per curiam, or unsigned, opinion authored by Justice John Paul Stevens, the high court found that the lower courts in Illinois should have imposed stricter procedural safeguards before allowing the injunction to remain in place and then sent the case back to the lower courts for another look. It was a technical solution, yes, but the substance of that *Skokie* ruling has come to stand for the broader legal proposition that the constitutional bar for banning—in advance—a parade or a march is exceedingly high and that courts must be extraordinarily deferential to the free speech interests asserted by protesters. The court battle over the Nazi marchers in Skokie went up and down the court system for fifteen months, until the final march was indeed allowed to take place, but relocated to Chicago, on June 24, 1978, at which point *The New York Times* estimated that two thousand counterprotesters "drowned out" the twenty Nazis, and the *Chi-*

cago Tribune snickered that the whole march "sputtered to an unspectacular end after 10 minutes." It was one of the most underwhelming
displays of Nazi pride in recorded history.

But the Skokie litigation roiled the ACLU, which had tapped a Jewish attorney—David Goldberger—to defend Frank Collin, the leader
of the Nazi Party. Hundreds of ACLU members resigned from the
group in protest. The case stood for both Jews and civil libertarians as
a high-water mark for the principle, articulated by Noam Chomsky,
that "if we don't believe in freedom of expression for people we des-
pise, we don't believe in it at all."

For decades the Skokie story stood as a testament to the idea that
allowing hateful and bigoted speakers to have their forum, so they
could be drowned out by right-thinking speech in the bright sun-
light, was the obvious solution to the free speech dilemma. Sad Nazis
marching to the cartoonish *womp womp* of sad trombones for dumb
ideas was the physical manifestation of the notional defense of the
marketplace of ideas and its power to sort good speech from bad.

All through the long summer of 2017, at every dinner party and
barbecue and visit to the pool (which had been for whites only just a
few decades earlier), when I was asked my opinion about free speech
and the plans for August 12, my answer was twofold: One, that *Skokie*
was the reason the Nazis had to be allowed to march. And two, that
the police and the city would protect us. I was ultimately wrong on
both counts.

IN THE DAYS LEADING UP to the Unite the Right rally, when it
became clear that hundreds of white supremacists, many of whom
planned to wear military garb and shields and carry repurposed flagpoles and sprays, and some of whom intended to bear arms, were
coming to protest, a legal scuffle ensued between the march organizers and the city. The town abruptly announced that the permit for

the march would be approved only if the event could be moved to a larger park, far from the monuments in a crowded downtown square. Kessler, the local organizer, supported by the ACLU, then sued the City of Charlottesville on free speech grounds; he argued the protest had to be near the monuments. A federal trial court judge agreed. The march would take place at the cramped downtown parks, where the disputed statues stood, and the Nazis made various promises about how they would conduct themselves honorably.

Local residents made hasty decisions about whether to join the counterprotests—which might turn violent—stay home, or attend antiracist rallies at alternate venues. I joked wryly that each of the three rabbis in the lone synagogue in town picked one of the options: rally for justice, basement, or head downtown prepared for conflict, and families divvied themselves up to follow the rabbi of their choosing. We sat quietly in the Black churches and listened to women who had grown up forbidden to cut through the "white" parks as they described their fear of the local police and worried for the fates of their grandsons if they protested the Nazis out in the city parks.

We knew days in advance that a dangerous march would happen on the UVA campus on August 11. We knew because leaked internet plans and chats were already in circulation showing that this was not to be a peaceful white pride march. We knew there would be guns carried and that plans were surfacing about physical conflict with counterprotesters. My then twelve-year-old son, summing up what would become my mantra for the remainder of the furor over the march—if not for the Trump era more broadly—sadly told me on August 10 that if we engaged with the Nazis, we would lose, and if we ignored them, we would also lose. He was correct on both scores, and the lingering question of how to deal with bigots who feed off the outrage they engender seems like the defining question of our lifetimes.

By the morning of August 11, it was clear this was no longer a free speech problem, even for those who had persuaded themselves otherwise. I woke up that day to the buzzing of drones overhead, street closures, sirens, helicopters, and the news that armed white supremacists were rolling in from out of town, arriving at the tiny local airport, checking into hotels. David Duke was reportedly staying at one of the finest resorts in town. An armed white supremacist, Chris Cantwell, was briefly detained by the police for having a gun in the parking lot outside Walmart, presumably as he stocked up on tiki torches. The police, noting that "open carry is legal in Virginia," quickly let him go. Suddenly, in a town where you knew everyone and couldn't even *attempt* to cheat on your spouse, everyone looked like a stranger and a threat.

As the local journalist Hawes Spencer described it for *The New York Times* that night, and later, in his 2018 book, *Summer of Hate*, on Friday evening, August 11, in an unannounced parade preceding the Unite the Right rally, "several hundred torch-bearing men and women marched on the main quadrangle of the University of Virginia's grounds, shouting, 'You will not replace us,' and 'Jews will not replace us.' They walked around the Rotunda, the university's signature building, and to a statue of Thomas Jefferson, where a group of counterprotesters were gathered, and a brawl ensued." The twisting line of torchlit white supremacists should not have been allowed to carry an open flame on campus. A student RA ended up hiding a group of Black students in a nearby basement. White supremacists were shouting "Hail Trump!" and "Into the ovens" and threatening to put counterprotesters into camps.

Nazis began to punch counterprotesters and to hit them with torches. As UVA's best-known faculty member, the political commentator Larry Sabato, who was present on campus that evening, would later say, campus police "gathered on the Rotunda steps in a line of about ten and did nothing." In the melee, UVA students protesting the Nazis had lighter fluid thrown on them and were pepper sprayed as lit torches were thrown in the air. Up the street, community members of various faiths who had gathered at a prayer vigil held in St. Paul's Memorial Church were not allowed to leave the building. At Congregation Beth Israel, the primary synagogue in town and my own synagogue for seventeen years, Torah scrolls salvaged from the Holocaust had to be spirited away to congregants' homes. Trust me here: none of it feels much like a movie when it's happening on the streets and parks where your toddlers learned to walk.

But Friday night was of course nothing compared with the events of Saturday, August 12. Virginia's governor, Terry McAuliffe, declared a state of emergency and called out the national guard just before the rally was set to start at noon. Hundreds of Nazis armed with shields, Mace, body armor, clubs, flagpoles, rocket launchers, and semiautomatic weapons marched through the park, in violation of their prior agreement to enter only through a single entrance. They swarmed in from all sides, and protesters and counterprotesters could not be differentiated by law enforcement. White supremacists hurled insults—calling counterprotesters fat but promising that "we'd still do you" and threatening to put one African American woman on the "first f—— boat home." Counterprotesters were assaulted and beaten, sometimes in sight of the police. An African American man, DeAndre Harris, was brutally beaten by Nazis dressed in military tactical gear in a local parking garage. And the law enforcement response was—as a comprehensive report undertaken later would show—minimal, as officers stood by, untrained and unprepared for what was occurring. School crossing guards had been conscripted into active duty. A police helicopter crashed, killing two officers inside. And of course David Duke offered up triumphal speeches in the park, assuring his cheering fans, "This represents a turning point for the people of this country. We are determined to take our country back. We are going to fulfill the promises of Donald Trump, and that's what we believed in. That's why we voted for Donald Trump, because he said he's going to take our country back."

Armed militiamen patrolled, in unreadable insignias, claiming they were keeping the peace, but who could know what they were protecting? Drones buzzed endlessly overhead. In interviews with faith leaders from several houses of worship, I was told that to the extent anyone was protecting local counterprotesters that day, it was members of antifa, the loose amalgam of antifascists who showed up at white supremacist events. The city, the cops, and the state were overwhelmed. It was an invasion.

That afternoon, a Dodge Challenger driven by James Alex Fields Jr., a white supremacist who had traveled all the way from Ohio to participate in Unite the Right, struck a group of counterprotesters with his car and killed Heather Heyer, a thirty-two-year-old paralegal and social justice protester, who died from blunt force injury to the chest. Nineteen others were injured in that attack, including Marcus Martin, a friend of Heyer's who was hit by the car as he pushed his fiancée out of its way. His leg was ruined. Martin, whose red sneakers can be seen in the iconic footage from that day, was captured for all time, upended and flying through the air from the force of Fields's car, in a Pulitzer Prize–winning image of the attack.

The trauma didn't end on August 12. Community members were stalked online by Nazi sympathizers, egged on by the neo-Nazi website *The Daily Stormer*. African American neighborhoods were terrorized for days after the rally. Locals who had spoken to the press were doxed. Vans parked outside the synagogue, keeping watch. But what could be done? Fields had been arrested and charged with murder. Kessler attempted to give a press conference and was shouted down, then punched by a counterprotester. Activists and antiracist protesters helped track down the identities and whereabouts of several Nazis by crowdsourcing images online. The community was shattered, and it wasn't initially clear that anyone who had planned the rally would be brought to justice in any meaningful way. The Justice Department, which would ordinarily investigate the event as racial violence directed at minority communities, stood by silently as the president refused to condemn the white supremacists. The police, the courts, the university, the city, and the state had all let Charlottesville down, as had the federal government, and years later social justice activists argued that systemic racism was and is the reason for the near-total breakdown of government and institutions that day.

ROBBIE KAPLAN CALLED ME at home in Charlottesville on August 14 from her office in Manhattan. She had an idea for a lawsuit. She just needed some plaintiffs. Kaplan had made a name for herself in legal circles as a powerhouse commercial litigator at Manhattan's Paul, Weiss, Rifkind, Wharton & Garrison—one of those fancy-name law firms that most young attorneys would kill to work for. A profile in *The Washington Post* from 2021 describes her as a "'traditionalist,' in pearls, pumps and, pre-coronavirus, superior blond highlights." But the nonlegal world also got to know Kaplan when she went to the Supreme Court in 2013, representing Edie Windsor, the eighty-three-year-old widow who successfully challenged the Defense of Marriage Act. Kaplan surprised a whole lot of court-watchers, myself included, when she prevailed in Edie's case, in part because she wasn't one of a very rarefied group of (mostly male, mostly white) specialty appellate litigators who argue the bulk of the cases at the high court. Even in the *Windsor* case, Kaplan was an outsider in every way: a Jewish, gay, brash commercial litigator from New York City, arguing a towering constitutional case at the highest court in the land.

Windsor had been slammed with more than $350,000 in federal estate taxes after her wife, Thea Spyer, died in 2009. Had Spyer been her husband, no such penalty would have been exacted. Because while the State of New York recognized their same-sex marriage, the federal government did not, as a result of the Defense of Marriage Act, a federal statute that barred the government from recognizing gay marriages for the purposes of many federal benefits. Windsor started calling around to find a lawyer. As she was later fond of saying, unlike the other big law firms and lawyers who ignored her calls, "Robbie Kaplan knew there was no wrong time for justice." In 2006, Kaplan had lost a big ACLU suit she'd filed on behalf of thirteen couples who sued New York State seeking the right to marry. Undaunted by the loss, she was raring to try again. So, on behalf of Edie Windsor, Kaplan sued the federal government, claiming that Section 3 of DOMA was unconstitutional. The Supreme Court agreed. Windsor's victory in 2013 would become the stepping-stone to the Supreme Court's landmark *Obergefell v. Hodges* decision in 2015, finding a constitutional right to marriage equality throughout America.

Kaplan, who is in her mid-fifties, doesn't come across as "scary smart" until she opens her mouth. That's when you see her doing three-dimensional jujitsu that can't always be followed by even a seasoned legal reporter. Kaplan says she knew she'd be a lawyer before she could talk. Actually, she says she knew she would be an attorney because there seemingly *was* no time before she could talk. Growing up in Cleveland in the 1970s, she was family famous because of her proclivity for the loud talking, early and often. When her grandmother Belle implored tiny Robbie to just please stop yapping for fifteen minutes, she replied, "I can't, Grandma. I'm a big talker." She was two. By twelve, she knew she was headed to New York City to become an attorney, because, as she said, "at some point I realized, if you got paid to talk as a lawyer, then that's the career for me." She graduated from Harvard in 1988 and Columbia Law School in 1991. She knew she was gay for a long time before she finally allowed herself to kiss a girl at age twenty-four.

Kaplan's life was altered forever when she took time off after a year as a young associate at Paul, Weiss to clerk for Judith Kaye, at the time the chief judge of the New York Court of Appeals. It was 1994, gay marriage was a distant dream, and Judge Kaye was hearing an adoption case that included claims by same-sex couples seeking to adopt their partner's child. Working on that case as a clerk, Kaplan began to see how law could drive large-scale social change. She returned to Paul, Weiss, working under Martin London, a legendary litigator, on complex commercial cases. "I loved litigating," she said. "I loved the ethos of the place, that we always did it at the very highest level. I loved that it was this incredible group of incredibly smart people and all that really mattered was, are you really, really smart? And are you funny? And Marty London, who was just a tremendous lawyer, was the epitome of that." She worked on big corporate corruption cases including a massive suit involving a Japanese executive who lost a billion dollars through rogue copper trading, as well as complex litigation involving WorldCom and AIG. She made partner in 1998 at age thirty-one. She was, in London's words, smashing a "concrete ceiling" as opposed to just a glass one.

Kaplan met her partner, Rachel Lavine, the following year. They were married in 2005 in Toronto, where same-sex marriage was already legal. Their son, Jacob, was born in 2006, but Kaplan was not allowed to carry him out of the hospital when he was released after a bout of jaundice. Rachel was the only "mother" listed under the hospital's regulations. Kaplan agreed to take Windsor's case, as she relates in her memoir, *Then Comes Marriage: United States v. Windsor and the Defeat of DOMA*, because both she and Edie were gay women, they both married in Toronto before it became legal to marry in the United States, and, improbably enough, Kaplan had actually heard about Edie Windsor eighteen years earlier.

One of the ways Kaplan's fundamentally conservative worldview manifested itself was that she was in the closet until her law school graduation. When she finally came out to her parents at age twenty-five in 1991, her mother was devastated. She walked up to a wall and began banging her head, repeatedly, in dismay. "Which she has apologized for over and over again," Kaplan says. But she experienced a fairly serious bout of depression. She met with a therapist named Thea Spyer, who mentioned her own same-sex relationship as she counseled Kaplan. Thea Spyer was referring to her lifelong partner, Edie Windsor.

As Kaplan stood to present Edie's case before the nine justices in 2013, one of the things she said about the antigay hostility legislated into the Defense of Marriage Act was that "times can blind." She referenced that phrase—penned a few years earlier in an opinion by Justice Anthony Kennedy—in part as a strategic effort to win Kennedy over to her view, which is just savvy lawyering. But she also deployed his phrase as a clarion moral call: our times themselves can blind us to what is right and wrong.

Kaplan was worried about what was happening to the country even before November 2016. She was in Ohio doing campaign events for Hillary Clinton and recalled that "as we drove from Kenyon to Oberlin, there were no superhighways; it was all rural roads. And I remember doing that drive and seeing Confederate flag after Confederate flag. And being in shock. Because I grew up in Ohio, and especially in Oberlin, which was the seat of the Underground Railroad, and thinking to myself, we're in deep trouble. Ohio was *not* part of the Confederacy." Kaplan had been hoping for a job in a Hillary Clinton Justice Department postelection. Trump's victory put an end to that. So immediately after inauguration weekend, she started talking about creating her own firm. The vision, she said, was "to have this really high-end commercial practice that would have this very strong dedication to public interest and pro bono." That summer of 2017, she launched Kaplan Hecker & Fink, her own boutique firm, almost unheard of in the world of female corporate attorneys. The model combines commercial litigation with progressive public-interest practice. She started out with three lawyers, working out of a borrowed barn, looking for cases related to Trump business practices.

The day after Heather Heyer's death on the streets of Charlottesville in August 2017, Donald Trump made a brief public statement in which he said "we condemn in the strongest possible terms this egregious display of hatred, bigotry and violence on many sides, on many sides." That made no sense. A police affidavit detailing who was planning to show up at the Unite the Right rally listed roughly 250 to 500 Klansmen and more than 150 "Alt-Knights," an offshoot of the Proud Boys. The neo-Nazi Andrew Anglin had posted on *The Daily Stormer* on August 8, 2017, what the purpose of Unite the Right would be:

> Although the rally was initially planned in support of the Lee Monument, which the Jew Mayor and his Negroid Deputy have marked for destruction, it has become something much bigger than that. It is now an historic rally, which will serve as a rallying point and battle cry for the rising Alt-Right movement.

"Blood and soil" had nothing to do with Civil War statues, and claims about violent antifa counterprotesters were deflections. The violence and terror were the object, and it was performed in plain sight. Posters for the rally were styled to look like Nazi propaganda and featured every white supremacist who was looking for a star turn on white supremacist Twitter. The public reaction to Trump's equivocating was furious, including from members of his own cabinet. He attempted to walk it back in a scripted public correction but then immediately made the now-infamous observation "You had some very bad people in that group, but you also had people that were very fine people, on both sides." In later years, he would claim that the alt-right provocateurs were just peacefully protesting the war monuments on the night of August 11. Those were the people with the torchlights chanting "Jews will not replace us" and gassing students with pepper spray.

There were no fine people on the White supremacist side of the Charlottesville invasion, but for a time it appeared that nothing would be done to correct that public record. Robbie Kaplan was stunned. Her fledgling team were still working on folding chairs in an office they'd occupied only five days earlier, when August 12 unfolded on TV in front of them. "We were working on card tables, and Charlottesville happened, and I said, okay, let's watch the press conference during lunch. Huge mistake." Why? "Because a couple of the paralegals started crying. I watched it and I thought to myself immediately that something needed to be done. That I very much doubted that with Jeff Sessions as the attorney general he would focus on it as a broad-based conspiracy, the way I thought it needed to be focused. And I thought back to this case involving this website called the Nuremberg Files, and why can't that be the strategy here?" She called me at home in Charlottesville and asked if it made sense to come down and meet some people.

Not forty-eight hours later, Kaplan and a small team of litigators arrived in Charlottesville, set up a makeshift office in the borrowed conference room at a legal aid office, and started to interview potential plaintiffs. First, they got a walking tour of the town and the places in which private tragedies had unfolded: the statues, the African American neighborhoods, the narrow street where the car ramming had occurred. Then they began interviewing victims. Kaplan said, "People kept coming in and out, and I was probably less sensitive than I should have been. I've learned to have very thick skin. And at the end, we were driving to the airport and the team was crying, bawling in the car. And I said, 'Buck it up, guys. We've gotta do this case. The time for crying is over.'"

What she proposed to do, she explained, as she recruited victims of August 11 and 12, some of whom were still badly injured and some of whom were still being harassed online by white supremacists, was to figure out who planned and executed the Charlottesville attacks and, almost as urgent, who was funding them. Kaplan, backed by Integrity First for America, a nonprofit that finances civil rights and abuse-of-power litigation, realized she was going to need another big gun and so she contacted another veteran super-litigator, Karen Dunn. Dunn is a partner at Paul, Weiss and a former federal prosecutor in Virginia who'd once served as communications director for Senator Hillary Clinton and as associate counsel to Barack Obama. Dunn had worked with the owner of Washington, DC's Comet Ping Pong pizza parlor after a North Carolina gunman walked into the crowded restaurant and fired off three rounds with a semiautomatic rifle because he believed a debunked internet conspiracy theory about child slavery taking place in its basement. (There was no basement.) Watching Dunn cross-examine a witness is the heady stuff of *Perry Mason*.

Kaplan said, "I brought Karen in, because I knew she'd been involved in Pizzagate, representing the guy who owned the pizza parlor. She had a lot of expertise in this intersection between the First Amendment and violent threats. I'd admired her for a long time. I admired the practice she'd built for herself at Boies Schiller. But I didn't know her. And so I just called her out of the blue and said, 'Hey, Robbie Kaplan. How'd you like to sue some Nazis with me?'" Dunn's response proved prescient. She told Kaplan, "Yes, as long as I have security. I have three kids and I need security."

KAPLAN'S LEGAL THEORY was inspired by a lawsuit that had been brought in the 1990s by two legends from the law firm Paul, Weiss— Maria Vullo and Martin London—who'd sued an antiabortion website that posted photos of abortion providers with their home addresses and other identifying information. The website also included a legend: "Black font (working); Greyed-out Name (wounded); Strikethrough (fatality)." While the case, *Planned Parenthood v. American Coalition of Life Activists*, never went to the Supreme Court and thus is not national precedent, a lower federal court determined that websites that encouraged readers to take violent action constituted an unprotected "true threat." That suit prevailed in the Ninth Circuit Court of Appeals in 2002, on the theory that free speech stops when incitement to violence begins. As that appeals court noted, finding for Planned Parenthood, which had brought the suit, "being listed on a Nuremberg Files scorecard for abortion providers impliedly threatened physicians with being next on a hit list." So Dunn and Kaplan proceeded on the legal theory that the twenty-five white supremacist leaders and organizers who came to Charlottesville on August 11 and 12 intended to incite racial and religious violence and had planned for just that. As their legal vehicle, they relied on a post–Civil War statute known as the Ku Klux Klan Act of 1871, passed to protect newly freed slaves from mob violence. The Klan Act makes it illegal to conspire to deprive any person or class of people of their rights in a manner that is racially motivated. A 1983 amendment to the Klan Act allows victims of such terrorism to sue for money damages. The theory of the case was that these groups conspired for months to commit racially motivated violence, which meant this was a lawsuit not about radical speech and political parades but about elaborate plans by multiple conspirators to commit racial violence.

In October 2017, Kaplan and Dunn filed their suit on behalf of eleven Charlottesville residents injured in the Unite the Right rally, either as student counterprotesters on the evening of August 11 or in the violence of the next day. Four of their plaintiffs were injured by James Alex Fields Jr.'s lethal car ramming, including Marcus Martin. Elizabeth Sines, the lead plaintiff, a law student in 2017, witnessed both the Friday night march across campus, with its torches and chants, and the car ramming the crowd of protesters the next day. "The trauma will never go away," Sines told *The New York Times* in 2019. "Among other things, I will always be on high alert when I'm in a large crowd and I'll always have nightmares—of the car attack, of torchlight rallies. I'll be scared forever. But the events from that weekend have reaffirmed for me how important it is to show up."

Among the twenty-five named defendants were Richard Spencer; the rally organizer Jason Kessler; Christopher Cantwell; the *Daily Stormer* founder, Andrew Anglin; and James Alex Fields. Also named were the groups Identity Evropa, Traditionalist Worker Party, League of the South, and several KKK groups whose members attended.

But in the weeks after Charlottesville, African Americans were still being terrorized by white supremacists in vans, and menacing white vans were still parked outside the synagogue. Meeting with traumatized witnesses who were certain they were still being followed and stalked by white supremacists communicating online was proving terrifying. Julie Fink is the managing partner at Kaplan Hecker & Fink, and she was one of the lawyers who went down to Charlottesville in the days after August 12 to help interview potential plaintiffs. She'd worked with Kaplan on the Edie Windsor case and came over with her when Kaplan founded her own firm in 2017. "I think Robbie is affected differently," she told me. "Things that make me feel sad and scared, I think they make her feel like 'we're going to fix it.'"

Fink said when they got to Charlottesville, they immediately understood that the average New Yorker might find it hard to appreciate what had just taken place. "Just being there, you realize how small it is. And you can't picture what it's like to open your door and see someone, you know, ten feet from you with a semiautomatic weapon and a Nazi flag. I couldn't have really imagined what that fear would've been like." In a borrowed conference room, they were hearing from the furious African American community, Fink said. "'We had these text messages,' they said. 'We went into the city council. We told them, They're coming here to kill us, and they're coming here to hurt us. And we told them this was going to happen, and nobody did anything.'" These Black citizens had been terrorized, said Fink, "just feeling like there's nowhere you can go, and sitting in a park and hearing, whether it's true or not, that a group of people were going to African American neighborhoods. It was all so close."

And that is precisely what it felt like, that whole summer of 2017, where you were afraid to make eye contact with anyone on the streets and when every T-shirt and every tattoo was suddenly a threat and my own sons ran home from the local sprinkler park because a man with a huge swastika tattoo was suddenly hanging out shirtless in the water. My husband, braving a trip to the downtown mall to support the counterprotesters on the night the Proud Boys were commandeering local bars, was gravely advised by my elder son, then fourteen, to "bring a knife." Whatever it was that was happening those weeks prefigured what would eventually happen at the Capitol on January 6, 2021, when your town is suddenly unrecognizable to you and your entire country feels cracked in two.

Fink said that feeling was everywhere the week after August 12: "That was the other thing about being in Charlottesville, it was like, 'This isn't over.' They were afraid that they were going to be hacked. They were afraid of talking in public. They were afraid of anyone knowing that they were communicating about it. They were afraid for their families. Their families were still being targeted."

The complaint in *Sines v. Kessler* reads like no legal document I had ever seen. The ninety-six-page pleading, filed in a federal district court in Virginia, is a documentarian's dream, replete with all the tweets, messages, and graphic photos that capture in pointillist detail both the premeditated planning of and the ongoing online delight in an event that terrorized a small city. Judge Norman Moon, the federal district court judge overseeing the lawsuit, noted that the filing's length was "pushing the limits" of federal filing requirements, before he allowed it.

As the complaint explains, "Under the pretext of a 'rally,' which they termed 'Unite the Right,' Defendants spent months carefully coordinating their efforts, on the internet and in person. They exhorted each other: 'If you want to defend the South and Western civilization from the Jew and his dark-skinned allies, be at Charlottesville on

12 August,' and, 'Next stop: Charlottesville, VA. Final stop: Ausch-
witz.' In countless posts on their own websites and social media, Defendants and their co-conspirators promised that there would be
violence in Charlottesville, and violence there was. What the planners
of the rally later claimed was protected free speech was, according to the
complaint, a conspiracy to commit and to encourage others to commit
racial violence."

What Kaplan and Dunn really wanted to put out into the public
sphere was online evidence of thousands of messages posted on an
invitation-only online platform called Discord. These messages showed
that whatever this event was intended to be, *Skokie* it was not. The
complaint scooped up messages and posts that chortled, "I'm ready to
crack skulls" and "If you don't have a flame thrower you're wrong"
and "Bringing women to a protest/rally where we expect violence
is fucking retarded . . . even if you aren't expecting violence you
should prepare for it." They alleged that Christopher Cantwell had
"encourage[d]" his own followers "to carry a concealed firearm." Organizers told attendees that there would be "money and a legal team
set aside for" arrestees. Chillingly, they also used their internet chats
to coordinate transportation and to debate whether car ramming was
legal. One posted, "Is it legal to run over protestors blocking road-
ways?"

Kaplan and Dunn also showed in their filing that the organizers
were celebrating Fields's murder of Heyer, with one writing, "Dirty
apes playing in the street gotta learn the hard way #Charlottesville."
Christopher Cantwell told a *Vice* reporter, "I'd say it was worth it.
Nobody on our side died . . . none of our people killed anybody
unjustly . . . our rivals are just a bunch of stupid animals who don't
pay attention that couldn't just get out of the way of the car." For Kaplan and Dunn, a Justice Department with a robust concern for civil
rights in the face of lethal white supremacist violence would have
brought this suit. The Trump administration had in fact done the

opposite: rolling back government efforts to track and prevent white domestic terrorism, even though it was resurgent, and minimizing the massive rise in race-based murders and hate crimes.

How did they divide the workload? Says Kaplan, "In the motion to dismiss, Karen did the constitutional issues and I did the statutory issues. We're a great team. We're very, very different. Their motions to dismiss were not very serious and I was, 'Oh, I'll just spend a day or two getting ready.' And Karen was, 'Oh my God, I'm devoting all week.' So she guilted me and I spent all week in the large conference room, getting ready for the motion. Which she was right about. She's kind of cautious. And I'm maybe not so much. I'm more like, 'Hey, what about this? What about that?' And she'll suck me back when she needs to."

Some of the white supremacist defendants were represented by James E. Kolenich, a civil rights attorney from Cincinnati who told *The Cincinnati Enquirer* that he took the case "to oppose Jewish influence in society" and because "white people are the chosen people in the New Testament." How do you do your job as a lawyer when you're a Jew sitting at a table next to a Holocaust denier? Kaplan asked. "When we argued that motion to dismiss, I'm having this, you remember the scene in *Animal House* where there's the devil and the angel? And this guy's trying to talk to me, and that's how I looked. Okay, what do I do? Do I make chitchat with this guy? Or do I just sit and ignore him? And I decided to make chitchat with the guy." She laughed. "Karen Dunn, of course, sat at the table and had nothing to do with anyone. . . . Just completely ignoring everyone. And then I'm chatting with this guy about LeBron James—talking about the Cavs, and how incredibly surreal is this?" She shook her head. "Life is fricking complicated."

The various defendants attempted to have the lawsuit dismissed, arguing that all their planning was just protected free speech. In Kessler's motion to dismiss, he contended that the entire suit was intended to "intimidate, silence, financially damage, or generally harass defendants." Chris Cantwell argued that remarks from his "Nazi themed entertainment program" were being misconstrued. It's a decent defense. The First Amendment generally protects even the most inflammatory speech, and the courts have carved out very limited exceptions, allowing that only the kinds of speech "directed at inciting or producing imminent lawless action" or "likely to incite or produce such action" may not be protected in the Charlottesville context. As Kaplan and Dunn saw it, it's not the controversial speech at issue; it's the conspiracy to use racial violence. And while the Klan Act has rarely been used in the modern era to enforce civil rights, in 1971 the court ruled that two white men in Mississippi had violated the act by conspiring to deprive a group of Black men of their civil rights by beating and intimidating them with weapons. The KKK Act was dusted off again after the January 6 riots at the Capitol and used in a host of civil suits alleging a conspiracy among Donald Trump, his lawyers, and his political allies to prevent Congress from certifying the Electoral College's findings in the 2020 election, a conspiracy that ended in violence and death.

In July 2018, in a sixty-two-page ruling, Judge Norman Moon allowed the case to go forward to trial, finding that "Plaintiffs have, for the most part, adequately alleged that Defendants formed a conspiracy to hurt black and Jewish individuals, and their supporters, because of their race at the August 11th and 12th events." As to their free speech claims, Judge Moon wrote, "Just as the Supreme Court has recognized that cross burnings are often intimidating, the torchlight march and the violence directed at Plaintiffs and other counterprotesters at the foot of the Thomas Jefferson statue, was likewise intimidating 'in the constitutionally proscribable sense of the word.'" The case went to trial in October 2021.

The real effect of the *Sines v. Kessler* suit transcended the litigation itself, however: Kaplan and Dunn were hoping pretrial discovery would smoke out connections between the various far-right groups and their sources of financing. The team obtained millions and millions of messages to reconstruct how the August 12 events came to be.

And the defendants fared badly under the heavy succession of losses and costs. Both Anglin and Spencer loudly distanced themselves from a failed effort to celebrate Unite the Right's anniversary in August 2018. (The 2.0 rally lasted under an hour, and only thirty bedraggled Nazis showed up, much like the Skokie rally relocated to Chicago back in 1978.) In January 2019, Nathan Damigo, another defendant and founder of the white nationalist group Identity Evropa, filed for bankruptcy. James Fields Jr. was sentenced in July 2019 to life in prison plus 419 years for killing Heather Heyer. Matthew Heimbach was arrested in a trailer park brawl with other members of his neo-Nazi group, and Richard Spencer canceled a speaking tour. Emails released as part of the suit show organizers calling Jason Kessler, the local leader of the event, "stupid and weird." Kessler was caught on video live broadcasting white supremacy while his father scolded him. It seemed a rather apt symbol for the story of white nationalism as largely a sad product of too many years spent living as an adult in your parents' basement. The defendants have been reduced to crowdsourcing online to pay their attorneys' fees.

In July 2019, the lawyer James Kolenich refused to further represent two prominent clients, Chris Cantwell and Robert "Azzmador" Ray. Cantwell in July had threatened violence against Kaplan on the messaging platform Telegram: "After this stupid kike whore loses this fraudulent lawsuit, we're going to have a lot of fucking fun with her." In a filing withdrawing from representation, Kolenich wrote that "Mr. Cantwell has rendered Attorney's continued representation of him unreasonably difficult, has created a conflict of interest between himself and Attorney's other clients, and has engaged in conduct Attorneys consider 'repugnant or imprudent.'" Cantwell was convicted and sentenced to forty-one months in prison in 2020 for extortion and rape threats against another white supremacist's wife. The defendants refused to turn over documents and filed frivolous motions. Innumerable cell phones were dropped in toilets.

Some of the white supremacists didn't have lawyers or funds to pay them. The trial was delayed repeatedly due to their obstruction and then because of COVID. Kaplan and Dunn spent the bulk of that time watching the defendants fail to comply with subpoenas and other discovery requests. In a sense, that contempt for the courts, the judge, and the very processes of the rule of law mirrors the contempt that allowed them to plan and realize the violent events of August 2017. They delayed, evaded, and confounded this litigation. In Cantwell's case, he continued inciting followers to violence toward Kaplan and the victims from behind his keyboard as the litigation played out. The problem with nihilists is that the guardrails of the legal system do not contain them. Contempt motions don't stop them. Told to quit inciting their online followers to harm opposing counsel, they doubled down. Kaplan and Dunn were left fighting on two fronts: proving their case in court and forcing the defendants to comply with the basic tenets of the legal process. Nihilists, in their dreamworld of race wars and violent glory, ultimately do nothing but hide out and tweet. But just because they are silly, and small, and infighting doesn't mean the white supremacists are powerless.

Fink told me that people were always very much mistaken when they imagined that Charlottesville 2017 could never happen again. "One of the things I felt when I was in Charlottesville was 'My God, there is a race war happening,'" she said. "Across the country, under the surface of all the things that we all do and take for granted every day, are the things that I don't know about. Or that I hadn't known about before." The events of January 6, 2021, proved that none of what happened in Charlottesville was contained there. For anyone who has lived through these white supremacist events, it's clear that this is an emboldened movement. Said Fink, "There are people like

Chris Cantwell who devote their lives to promoting violence and racist ideas. . . . There's a group of people, many of whom were in Charlottesville, who spend all their time and their lives combating what they see as this really dangerous group in the country. And the rest of us are just going about our business."

There is some solace in doing this work through the courts, as opposed to placing one's body on the streets, acknowledged Fink. "This battle with people who are white supremacists and neo-Nazis, it's their life, and vice versa. And now we're in it, but I think we're in it in a slightly different way. I think that there's some safety that comes with being in a court. We're doing this with a process that's different than people who get doxed and have people driving outside their house or leaving things on their porch." Years later, when I told people that I felt bad for personally failing to take to the streets to protect the antiracist counterprotesters who stood up to white supremacists on August 12, I included the story about frantic calls to my big brother while I sobbed that there were Nazis parked on my sleepy residential street, and how I should have been out there slashing tires and punching fascists. Alex was very direct in the manner of big brothers everywhere. "You're a little bit slow and a little bit fat," he soothed, on the morning of the Nazi march. "You just write about it."

Kaplan's superpower must be her confidence. Because she presents as relentlessly bubbly and cheerful, the "big talker" of her own toddlerhood, it's easy to forget what constant death threats by anonymous men with millions of followers would do to most of the rest of us. As Julie Fink put it, "The thing about Robbie is she's fearless and she's the most effective person I know. So we had a dinner here on a Tuesday where we talked about Charlottesville. We all said, 'Let's do something.' And three days later we're in Charlottesville. And within two months, we have co-counsel, funding, a lawsuit, and plaintiffs." When the death threats came, Kaplan swallowed hard and moved on. Fink mused, "I don't know if Robbie genuinely *is* fearless or if she is just really good at putting her fear to the side. Or if she used to have fear, but just doesn't anymore. Even just having had the experience of losing the New York marriage case, and then a few years later being like, 'Yeah, I'll bring a defense of marriage case.' That takes just an incredible amount of bravery, and a lot of people don't have the confidence that goes hand in hand with bravery."

Immediately after Donald Trump was elected, Robbie Kaplan started her own little law firm, co-founded the Time's Up Legal Defense Fund, which supports women filing sexual harassment cases, and began serving as chair of the Time's Up organization. She resigned from Time's Up in August 2021 amid reports that she had been one of several lawyers involved in some of the then governor Andrew Cuomo's efforts to discredit women for sexually harassing them. Kaplan sued Trump and his family for defrauding participants in ACN, a multilevel marketing company promoted on *The Celebrity Apprentice.* She represents Mary Trump, Donald Trump's niece, in a suit claiming that Donald Trump and his siblings deprived her of an inheritance worth millions of dollars. She represented the journalist E. Jean Carroll, who is suing Trump for defamation because after she claimed that he raped her a quarter century ago in a Bergdorf Goodman dressing room, he denounced her as "totally lying." And as Carroll told *The Washington Post* in 2021, she brought her suit "for all the women in the country who have been harassed or assaulted by powerful men, and feel helpless to do anything about it." Pressed on why she is willing to be someone who does something, Carroll replied, "I don't have to be brave . . . [b]ecause Robbie Kaplan is brave for me."

I asked Kaplan recently whether she would have stayed at her old firm if she'd been a man, and she said, "Probably." She has been wildly successful in a world of legal advocacy still dominated by men, but while she has an uncanny gift for optimism and perpetual motion, she isn't blinkered to the ways in which this is a game that still gives points and benefits to male litigators. "Look," she said, "gender's a part of everything I do." She added, "I remember when I was a young law-yer going into court with Marty London, and I don't even remem-ber what the case was. And Marty walks into the courthouse, walks into the courtroom, and the conversation is, 'So, Mr. London, how's the fishing been?' And, 'What bait have you been using lately?' And, 'How's your boat?'" This is how men have spoken to men in American courtrooms since the founding. Added Kaplan, "And I remember thinking to myself, 'Damn, but this will never happen to me. This is so . . . in one sense it's so unfair, and in another sense it's so cool. . . . That Marty London gets treated this way. . . .' So I now get treated that way."

She added, "I don't have conversations with judges about my boats or anything. But because of my reputation or whatever, what I've done, I now get that extra degree of, what's the word I want? Cama-raderie." Kaplan is of a generation of women that went to good law schools, scored good clerkships, got recruited at the best firms, and assumed that the arc of the gender universe was bending toward equal-ity. She was and will ever be busy. But in a way that is emblematic of so many women activists and organizers, after the shock of revanch-ist misogyny that came with the Trump election, she just tripled her output.

Kaplan was also at pains to clarify that she is the furthest possible thing from a wild-eyed radical. As she told *The Washington Post* in 2021, "I'd never been a burn-down-the-ramparts sort of person. I believed in working in institutions." The reason she was such a rabid warrior for and believer in marriage equality was itself fundamentally conservative: "Living a life very much on the margins didn't appeal to me. I really wanted to have kids. I really wanted to be part of the Jewish community. I really wanted to have a career. All of this would have been unavailable in the world I grew up in."

Kaplan also believes that not everyone doing public-interest work needs to work in public-interest firms. Her own firm, at a moment when the entire legal profession is struggling to build a better business model, is proof, she believes, that there's a market for what she's attempting to do. "One thing I tell young law students now, when they ask, is that the legal profession has undergone really substantial change, at least with respect to litigation. That what people do in large firms is very different today than what they did when I started. They write interoffice memos, and if you really want to learn to stand up in court, and have the full 360-degree skills you need to be a great litigator, you should think about a different kind of place." She's trying to build that kind of place.

Anyone who really saw what happened in Charlottesville in 2017 was unsurprised by the riot at the US Capitol in January 2021. Nothing about the latter was unfamiliar: not the Nazi-curious cosplay or the claims that it was protected speech and protest activity, or the casual violence and property destruction. The claims that the violent rioters and looters were the real victims were also to be expected. Least surprising of all was the failure of law enforcement to anticipate and prepare for a violent riot that was planned in plain sight for weeks. White supremacist violence has been on the rise for decades, documented by the FBI and organizations that track the activities of hate groups, yet often justified or minimized as juvenile foolishness or "boys will be boys."

Sines v. Kessler went to trial in the fall of 2021. As plaintiffs testified to harrowing injury and trauma, defendants' online communications in the run-up to the rally were read to the jury. "I would go to the ends of the earth to secure a future for my people," Kessler wrote to Spencer around the same time. "This is war." In another communication, he assured Spencer, "We're raising an army my liege. . . . For free speech, but the cracking of skulls if it comes to it." "I'm willing to risk a lot for our cause, including violence and incarceration, many in my audience would follow me there too," Cantwell wrote to Spencer a week before the gathering, "but I want to coordinate and make sure it's worth it to our cause." The white supremacists defended themselves by dropping the n-word, repeatedly using the word "Kike," and questioning one another about their favorite Holocaust jokes. They insisted their speech was unconnected to the violent and lethal events of the rally.

On November 23, 2021, after a four-week trial featuring thirty-six witnesses, the Charlottesville jury unanimously found that all twenty-four defendants and defendant groups had engaged in a conspiracy to commit violence and intimidation to deprive minorities and their supporters of their civil rights under Virginia law. They deadlocked on the two federal conspiracy charges. The nine plaintiffs were awarded $26 million in damages. After the verdict, Richard Spencer said he had no hope for the future of the alt-right, a movement he'd not only named but helped create. "That's long dead and gone in my opinion," he said. "It's buried."

Kaplan likes to tell the story of how truly easy it is to go numb, slowly and invisibly, during times of genuine evil. Her wife, Rachel, is related by marriage to Siegmund Warburg, a prominent German Jewish businessman who once famously said, of the Nazis in 1930, "Once they are in government they will immediately become, first, more sensible and, secondly, once again less popular." That claim still haunts her. Kaplan thinks constantly of Warburg and how easy it is to explain away and minimize events that are profoundly evil, even when we should know better. She lives with the risk of constant threats to herself, her firm, and her family. But still she maintains that putting naked, senseless, violent hate on trial, with the attendant chaos, delay, and danger, offered a once-in-a-lifetime chance at a moral reckoning in a country that at times seems to have fallen into a deep slumber on questions about violence, hate, and what America really represents.

Abortion at the Border

Brigitte Amiri:
The Litigator

I n the fall of 2017, a fight over abortion, religious conscience, and the actions of government officials became the next marquee controversy over the Trump administration's new worldview, in which religion and law became frequently interchangeable. It was a story told most commonly through the aperture of Margaret Atwood's dystopic novel *The Handmaid's Tale*. And the comparison was not inapt. Brigitte Amiri knows all about this strange dystopian metastory, because, well, she litigated it. In fact, the Trump Justice Department tried (unsuccessfully, as it turned out) to ruin her professional career for prevailing in a constitutional challenge to it.

"Jane Doe" was the name given by the courts to a seventeen-year-old unaccompanied immigrant who fled her home, and parental abuse, in Central America, crossing the US-Mexico border in September 2017. Jane was detained and taken into custody by the Office of Refugee Resettlement (ORR), then placed in a government-funded shelter in South Texas, operated under a contract with the Trump administration's Department of Homeland Security. While she awaited immigration proceedings, Jane found out she was pregnant. She immediately asked for an abortion; she was nine weeks pregnant at the time. Texas has a parental consent requirement, meaning that minors need a judicial bypass from a judge in order to terminate a pregnancy, if they cannot get consent from their parents. Texas judges are not, as a rule, great fans of granting abortion waivers to pregnant teenage girls.

Jane went to state court with Marie Christine Cortez, an attorney from Jane's Due Process, a nonprofit organization that offers pregnant minors in Texas legal assistance. She also had an appointed guardian ad litem, Rochelle Garza, to advocate for her. A state judge granted Jane permission to terminate her pregnancy on September 25, 2017, and the procedure was scheduled for September 28, toward the end of her first trimester. No government money would have gone toward the procedure; Jane had rides to and from the clinic. At that point, the shelter that contracted with ORR, an office within the US Department of Health and Human Services (HHS), quite literally needed only to open the door to the facility and allow her out for a few hours. But Scott Lloyd would not allow it.

And who is Scott Lloyd? In 2017, Donald Trump placed him in charge of ORR, which has custody over all immigrants under age eighteen who come to the United States without parents. Lloyd got this position even though his professional experience in the area of refugees and resettlement was nonexistent. As *Politico* noted in 2018, "[Lloyd's] predecessor, Robert Carey, who led the office during the last two years of the Obama administration, had decades of experience managing refugees' issues, including 15 years in resettlement and migration at the International Rescue Committee." Lloyd had none. What Lloyd *did* have was many years' experience crusading against reproductive freedom. In fact, Lloyd's main professional qualification for heading up ORR was a lengthy career in antiabortion activism, including service as a lawyer for the Knights of Columbus, where his writings included claims that abortion and contraception were the same things and that women should be denied access to both. As an attorney in George W. Bush's Department of Health and Human Services, Lloyd had co-authored a "conscience rule," allowing religious health-care workers to deny abortions, contraception, or any other care they opposed on moral grounds. So while he knew virtually nothing about refugees and asylum, Scott Lloyd knew a whole lot about abortion, or at least his opinions about it.

Under both the George W. Bush and the Barack Obama administrations, ORR had largely permitted undocumented teens to have abortions, so long as they had secured private funding. Both administrations were also required, under a federal consent decree, to give minors access to emergency health care and family planning services. The threat of sexual violence is pervasive for migrants and asylum seekers journeying to the United States, and the need for such services can be acute. The ACLU had been investigating a Bush-era policy that permitted Catholic shelters receiving HHS funding to opt out of providing abortion access to unaccompanied immigrant minors. As they probed the problem, the ACLU discovered that some religiously affiliated shelters were kicking minors out for requesting abortions. They ended up suing the Obama administration in 2016, demanding that shelters permit these minors access to abortion under both US constitutional law and the *Flores* settlement—a court-mandated promise that unaccompanied immigrant minors have access to routine and emergency medical care, including family planning services. That suit was already working its way through the system when Scott Lloyd took over at ORR.

In March 2017, Lloyd put a new policy into effect, banning shelters that contract with the government from helping any pregnant migrants to obtain abortions and decreeing that these shelters could not take "any action that facilitates" abortions for unaccompanied minors, including "scheduling appointments, transportation, or other arrangement," without "direction and approval" from Lloyd personally. He further ordered that ORR's shelters provide only "pregnancy services and life-affirming options counseling" and "not be supporting abortion services pre- or post-release."

"The unborn child is a child [in] our care," Lloyd wrote in an email to all of the shelters, seemingly forgetting that the refugee herself was also a child in his care. In other emails, Lloyd told shelters not to let young women meet with attorneys regarding termination—or to allow them to go before judges to receive judicial bypasses. In one email, he opined that "often these girls start to regret abortion," and after speaking directly with one teenage girl in a Texas detention center, he wrote, "If this comes up, we need to connect her with resources for psychological and/or religious counseling."

In the fall of 2017, Lloyd's new ORR policy began to offer pregnant migrants seeking to terminate pregnancies only the names of approved "crisis pregnancy centers," or CPCs, that provide exclusively antiabortion "counseling." This meant that, back in Texas, Jane Doe was required to visit a religiously affiliated CPC to undergo "counseling" urging her to continue the pregnancy. She was forced to watch an ultrasound of her fetus. She told her lawyers that the staff at the "clinic"—because she had been told that it was a clinic—prayed over her. A staff member at the CPC also called Doe's mother, over her objections, and told her Jane was pregnant, a clear violation of state confidentiality laws. Despite all that counseling, Jane claimed she still wanted to terminate her pregnancy. As her lawyers struggled to get Jane into a clinic to do that, workers at her shelter put her under constant one-on-one supervision and barred her from any physical activity, forcing her to sit on a bench while the other teen residents exercised.

Rochelle Garza was appointed by the court to represent Jane in her state proceedings. Garza's name became the name of the massive class-action lawsuit—*Garza v. Hargan*—that eventually became the ACLU's challenge to the entire ORR pregnant migrant policy. In an interview with *New York* magazine's Cristian Farias in 2018, Garza explained that she had become a lawyer in order "to be an advocate for people and people who are vulnerable. And she's vulnerable." Garza added, "I told her many times, '*Eres muy fuerte. Tienes un caracter muy fuerte*,'" and later mused, "I don't know if I would've been as strong if I were in her position."

Brigitte Amiri, deputy director of the ACLU's Reproductive Freedom Project, was called in when it became clear that the Texas team would need someone to handle what was becoming a lawsuit with major national implications. Amiri looks like what Audrey Hepburn would be if she'd become a reproductive rights litigator. With doe eyes and sweeping bangs, and age forty-four at the time of the lawsuits, Amiri initially wanted to be a dancer, and you can still see it when she's at a lectern before a panel of judges. Amiri is unerringly controlled, in courtrooms, in depositions, and in interviews. In the corner of her New York office, she has hung a print that reads, "Nolite te bastardes carborundorum." That's from Margaret Atwood's *The Handmaid's Tale*, Latin roughly translated to mean "don't let the bastards grind you down."

"I'm the daughter of an Iranian immigrant," Amiri said. "My father came here in the 1960s, pursuing the American dream. He worked a bunch of odd jobs before he went to a liberal arts college in the Midwest, where he met my mom, who grew up in a small farming community in mid-state Illinois. They moved to Ann Arbor, Michigan, where my dad opened a Persian rug store. And that's where my sister and I grew up." Amiri's dad was raised Muslim but brought up his daughters without religion. Even though she was only a small child at the time, she remembers that even in liberal, tolerant Ann Arbor during the Iranian hostage crisis in 1979 the family suffered harassment, including bomb threats and hate mail.

"The rug store is called the Persian House of Imports, and we were known in the community as being from Iran, and I remember the fear my family felt during that period," she told me. Amiri credits her mother with her own childhood political activism. "My mom took us to political rallies. She was trying to get the ERA ratified. She was a stay-at-home mom, and that was something she'd agreed to in marrying my father, which was also this interesting dichotomy because my dad expected my mom to stay home, based on cultural norms, but expected my sister and me to be successful and not depend on anyone." Amiri added that her career in justice might have started unnaturally early: "When I was in fifth grade, and the crossing guards were assigned to certain posts, I noticed that a boy was always assigned to put up the flag, and guard the parking lot, and a girl never was. I got together a petition of people saying, 'That's not fair. You can't treat boys and girls differently, and we should get that post too.' And I won." She paused for a beat. "Also I think there was chocolate milk associated with that post."

Her parents divorced when she was fifteen, and by then Amiri was babysitting for a nurse who worked at a Planned Parenthood. She added, "I was somewhat of a rebellious teenager, and it was also a way to channel that, because I could see how upset people got about abortion and how they were using abortion to control women, and this was a way to channel my own rebelliousness into this fight." She quickly realized there was systemic work to do on women's rights advocacy when she started attending college at DePaul University, a Catholic school. "I tried to start a pro-choice group on campus, and that was squashed by the administration, so that was kind of an early first lesson for me in terms of organizing and fighting back." Amiri then began writing columns and doing advocacy, and her professors urged her not to apply to law school if it would mean becoming what she calls "a corporate clone." Her advisors instead steered her toward a dedicated public-interest program at Northeastern Law School with a coop rotation program, mixing internships with classwork, so she would graduate with a full year of legal experience. "I was the first generation to go to college, and being able to have those jobs during law school allowed me to prove myself. I didn't graduate from a fancy law school. I didn't do a clerkship. I didn't know anyone who was a lawyer before I went to law school."

Amiri ended up taking a position at the Center for Reproductive Rights, then at South Brooklyn Legal Services, doing foreclosure prevention for low-income homeowners. In 2005, she got her dream job, the position she currently holds at the ACLU. Even prior to the 2016 election, Amiri had a long and storied history fighting for abortion access in states seeking to restrict it, fighting for Medicaid expansion, and bird-dogging the Obama administration's ORR policy around pregnant migrant teens. She was involved in complex litigation over the Affordable Care Act's contraception mandate. And had Hillary Clinton won in 2016, Amiri would have found herself on a very different career path: "I firmly believe that the job of every public-interest lawyer is to put herself out of a job. I felt like we were going to get one step closer to that; moving to a place where abortion wasn't so restricted, and where the Hyde Amendment didn't prohibit low-income people from having coverage for abortion." In 2016, reproductive rights groups had also just secured a huge victory at the Supreme Court with the *Whole Woman's Health v. Hellerstedt* decision: "And suddenly we weren't just banging our heads against the wall anymore, and even this Supreme Court was not going to allow restrictions that served no medical benefit, and created obstacles. We were going to be in this bold era in terms of being able to challenge restrictions."

That was Amiri's plan, but on election night 2016 her mandate changed very quickly: "I remember, I just burst into tears, and I said to my husband, 'I am already so tired from doing this for so long. And we were on the precipice of real change, and I don't know how I'm going to have the energy to keep doing this, but I also know that there's no way I can't.'" She took a deep breath. "So even though I know it's going to be a hundred times harder, I know that I have to keep doing it because it's really kind of the only thing I know how to do."

Amiri didn't go to marches, she said. She skipped the 2017 Women's March because she had a young baby at home. "Look, I think that people should take to the streets, absolutely, but part of it is just also thinking about where my own reserves lie, and so part of me feels like I work a lot, and it's a weekend, and I want to be with my kid and my family. I think about the work that I do and I'm not sure that my extra body on the street is really going to matter. I have to pick and choose how I'm going to spend my time to be most effective in the job that I do."

In 1973, the US Supreme Court handed down a 7–2 opinion in *Roe v. Wade*. And the American public has been in a heated civil war over women's bodies ever since. This one issue—abortion—has been at the heart of every Supreme Court confirmation hearing for decades, either explicitly or by way of secret signals and codes. Abortion providers have been gunned down, clinics have been closed, and state legislatures with the highest maternal death rates have passed laws that make it all but impossible to terminate a pregnancy there. As of June 2022, *Roe v. Wade* is overturned, and in half the states, abortion is illegal or soon will be. The death of Ruth Bader Ginsburg in September 2020 and her replacement with Amy Coney Barrett just days before the 2021 election changed everything. But long before *Roe* was struck down, it had been whittled away for poor women who were barred by the Hyde Amendment from financing a termination, and in states that operated with a single clinic, and for those in jurisdictions like Texas that functionally ended all abortion after six weeks in September 2021. Long before the words "*Roe v. Wade* is overturned" were printed in a Court opinion, for women across the country, an abortion had become functionally impossible to procure. For many it will be a crime.

In 1992, in *Planned Parenthood v. Casey*, the Supreme Court—in a plurality opinion jointly authored by Sandra Day O'Connor, Anthony Kennedy, and David Souter—introduced a new test, replacing *Roe*'s rigid trimester structure. They determined in *Casey* that states could regulate pre-viability abortions so long as they do not place an "undue burden" on a woman's right to choose to end her pregnancy. Working out what does and does not constitute an "undue burden"—defined in *Casey* as placing a "substantial obstacle" between a woman and termination—became a boom industry in state legislative backrooms. States were enacting laws demanding waiting periods, medically unnecessary ultrasounds, and medically incorrect warnings and regulating clinics out of existence, all under claims that they were not banning abortion so much as helping mothers make better choices. But in 2016, in *Whole Woman's Health v. Hellerstedt*, the high court reaffirmed that while states could enact rules to protect maternal health, they could not pass pretextual regulations that served no legitimate ends beyond shuttering clinics. The majority in *Whole Woman's Health* empowered judges to look closely at the arguments advanced by states about maternal health and best medical practices, then tasked the courts with "an independent constitutional duty to review factual findings where constitutional rights are at stake."

This launched a new bitter fight in the five-decade war over the right to choose. Conservative outrage over the result in *Whole Woman's Health* no doubt aided and abetted the Senate majority leader Mitch McConnell's unprecedented blockade of a vote for Merrick Garland, Barack Obama's pick for a seat on the Supreme Court. Garland would likely have become a sixth vote for upholding *Roe*, and a fifth even after Ginsburg died. The result in *Whole Woman's Health* also probably helped ambivalent evangelical voters show up for Donald Trump, a newly pro-life, serial philanderer and alleged sexual predator, in the 2016 election. Trump claimed at one point in his campaign that women who had abortions should suffer "some form of punishment" and campaigned on the explicit promise that he would seat only antiabortion justices on the high court. He even published a list of his candidates for that seat. It all worked out for him; with the court balanced on a razor's edge and a chance to grab the seat vacated by Antonin Scalia's death, exit polls showed that Trump won a higher percentage of white evangelical voters than either Mitt Romney or George W. Bush, garnering 81 percent to Hillary Clinton's 16 percent. White Catholics also went all in for Trump, by margins of 60 as compared to Clinton's 37 percent. For many, overturning *Roe* was a critical factor in their vote for president, and in exchange they would tolerate even Donald Trump as chief executive.

Tony Perkins, who helms the anti-LGBTQ group Family Research Council, summed up Trump's 2016 electoral strategy one day after the 2016 election: "First, he chose a pro-life conservative running mate, he did not try to weaken the party's platform, and he laid out a list of potential justices that he said are pro-life. We've never had a Republican nominee do this. And I think he basically closed the deal in the last debate when he went into late-term abortion in the first 15 minutes." By seating Neil Gorsuch, then Brett Kavanaugh, and then Amy Coney Barrett at the high court in just four years in office, and by seeding the lower federal courts with dozens of judges whose records on abortion are unapologetically anti-*Roe*, Trump cemented his legacy as the most antiabortion US president ever to have made serial hush-money payments to extramarital lovers.

States emboldened by Trump's rapid reshaping of the federal judiciary scrambled to enact abortion regulations that would deliberately violate the core holdings of *Roe*, *Casey*, and *Whole Woman's Health*. Confident that they would win at the newly configured Roberts Court, state legislatures raced to pass so-called personhood bills, fetal heartbeat bills, six-week abortion bans, eight-week abortion bans, eighteen-week abortion bans, "trigger" laws, fetal remains laws, and the kinds of TRAP, or Targeted Regulation of Abortion Providers, laws identical to those struck down in 2016 in *Whole Woman's Health*. None of this was a surprise. In the spring of 2019, after Brett Kavanaugh was confirmed and *Roe* appeared doomed, Georgia, Ohio, Mississippi, and Missouri passed what were, by design, unconstitutional bans. The state of Alabama went one further, banning *all* abortions with virtually no exceptions, and certainly none for rape and incest. Mississippi's fifteen-week ban, in which the state explicitly asked that *Roe* be overturned, was upheld by a 6–3 vote in June 2022. These purposefully unconstitutional laws were intended as invitations to the Supreme Court, with Brett Kavanaugh as the fifth vote and Amy Coney Barrett as the sixth, to end *Roe* for all time. That invitation was accepted with alacrity.

But it wasn't just individual states gunning for reproductive rights, and it wasn't just the courts. The Trump administration itself was behind moves to defund Planned Parenthood; allow employers to deny contraception to employees; and double down on overheated rhetoric describing abortion, as Trump did in a 2019 tweet, as "executing babies AFTER birth." Efforts to pack the federal courts on this issue have led to the wholesale sidelining of Senate rules and norms and resulted in the seating of lifetime appointees to the federal bench, including Judge James Ho, who wrote that he deplored abortion as a "moral tragedy." These judges, some of whom are in their thirties and forties, will sit on the bench long after our grandchildren have begun to vote. And our grandchildren may grow up in an America in which only wealthy women, and pregnant people only in blue states, can terminate a pregnancy. That was the point.

To be sure, reasonable people can differ about when human life begins. Reasonable people might also differ about whether morality steeped in religious dogma and doctrine should color public policy in an ostensibly secular country. But the stealth battleground in the reproductive rights debate in America has migrated in recent years to a fight about whether religious actors can be forced to act against their conscience when faced with a neutral law or policy that troubles them. Whether it was ambulance drivers refusing to treat AIDS patients for religious reasons, pharmacists refusing to fill prescriptions for the morning-after pill, or a for-profit corporation—a chain of craft stores named Hobby Lobby—refusing to allow workers access to statutorily guaranteed birth control, religious conscience claims have become the sword with which individuals claiming religious liberty could dismantle laws and rulings that protect civil equality. As the Yale Law School professors Reva Siegel and Douglas NeJaime have put it, "After failing to prohibit abortion and same-sex marriage, conservatives have sought to create religious exemptions from laws that protect the right to abortion or same-sex marriage." As hospital ownership became consolidated nationally, and with religious hospitals declining to permit abortions, these religious conscience claims work to limit patient access to basic medical care. Faith-based foster care and adoption agencies may refuse to place children with same-sex or Jewish parents for religious reasons. Religious exemptions to the COVID vaccine have proliferated nationwide. In that spirit, even before Trump was elected, faith-based shelters for teen immigrants were declining to participate in lawful termination of pregnancies.

AMIRI WAS WORKING ON AN ACLU lawsuit attempting to keep the last abortion clinic in Kentucky open, when she got a phone call from Susan Hayes, at Jane's Due Process, in September 2017. According to Amiri, Hayes told her, "We have a minor who is in the Rio Grande valley matched with one of our volunteer attorneys there, who has taken her to get her bypass, so she can consent to an abortion on her own. But ORR is now telling her she needs to go to a crisis pregnancy center to be counseled and that they have to tell her parents in her home country." Soon Hayes called back to say the government was now prohibiting Jane from leaving the shelter for *any* abortion-related appointment, even the twenty-four-hour mandatory counseling session required under Texas law. Amiri quickly called the Justice Department. "I said, 'You can't do this,' and they said, 'Well, that is what our client wants.' And I said, 'Well, then you won't be surprised when we sue you.'"

Amiri got in touch with Rochelle Garza, the guardian ad litem appointed for Jane, and Christine Cortez, the attorney ad litem appointed to protect her interests. She talked to Jane on the phone and got a declaration from her. "And I remember thinking," she told me, "I'm going to go home, put my kid to bed, and write the temporary restraining order papers. This is an easy case. You can't ban abortion." She laughed. "We thought we'd be in and out of court, like that." The ACLU first tried to attach the Jane Doe complaint to their ongoing California case challenging ORR policies at shelters, but the judge felt it was the wrong venue. And the clock was still ticking down for Jane. "Jane at this point is nine weeks pregnant," Amiri said. These dates matter because terminating a pregnancy becomes more medically complicated the longer you wait and because in Texas abortion was generally illegal at twenty weeks. So Amiri filed an emergency petition in a DC federal court in October 2017. "I'm not sure I've ever seen a federal district court judge so angry at any party as she was at the government," said Amiri of Judge Tanya Chutkan, who oversaw that case. "She immediately understood why this was outrageous, that effectively they were holding Jane against her will, preventing her from accessing an abortion. She granted a temporary restraining order later that day, after the hearing."

Judge Chutkan ordered HHS to allow Jane to leave the shelter for her procedure on either the twentieth or the twenty-first of the month and instructed them not to interfere with her further. But the Justice Department still refused to permit Jane to leave the shelter. It appealed Chutkan's order to the federal appeals court in Washington, DC. At this point, the various arms of the ACLU legal team began to wrap tighter around the litigation. Asked about her own immigration law background, Amiri smiled. "I have none," she said, waving to the corridor. "I'm going down the hall," where the ACLU's immigrants' rights team sits. "It's now a huge team," said Amiri, "my colleague Meagan Burrows, down the hall, and Jen Dalven, who's my boss, and Art Spitzer and Scott Michelman in DC, and we got the emergency papers to the court of appeals. And we're writing the briefs in the middle of the night, trading things off. I wake up early; Art stays up late at night, getting four hours of sleep."

The DC Circuit Court of Appeals agreed to hear the case on a fast track. So on October 19, Amiri got a call from the clerk, asking if she could come down to DC the next day to argue before a three-judge panel on the court of appeals. "I keep a suit on the back of my office door. I have a bunch of random uncomfortable shoes down here," Amiri said, pointing under her desk. She decided to go straight from her New York office. "I go get a free T-shirt from the closet. I decided I'm going to buy toiletries and underwear when I get to Union Station at the drugstore and Victoria's Secret, respectively." She checked herself into a Washington hotel, then called Rochelle and Christine and started preparing. There was going to be real-time audio of the oral argument, still a rarity at many federal appellate courts. There wasn't even time for a moot court practice session before her argument.

The panel Amiri drew for oral argument in *Garza v. Hargan* consisted of three appellate judges: Karen LeCraft Henderson, Patricia Millett, and Brett Kavanaugh. Attorney Catherine Dorsey, representing the Justice Department, opened by telling the court that the government was "not preventing, blocking, or imposing any obstacle on Ms. Doe pursuant of an abortion here, such that it could constitute an undue burden within the meaning of *Casey*. The Government has not put any obstacle in her path; rather the Government is refusing to facilitate an abortion, which it is permitted to do in furtherance of its legitimate interest in promoting childbirth." The government wasn't impeding her, it said; it just wouldn't help her.

Judge Kavanaugh pressed Dorsey on how it could be true that if Jane were an adult in a federal prison, she would have a constitutional right to abortion under *Roe v. Wade*, but not as an immigrant minor. Dorsey replied that "Ms. Doe has the option of voluntary departure" to her home country. Later in the argument Dorsey would be asked whether Jane's home country allowed abortion. She conceded that it did not. Dorsey explained to the court that adult migrants in ICE detention can obtain an abortion but minors cannot because HHS has an interest in promoting "the best interests of the child," which is, presumably, to give birth in every single case. Judge Kavanaugh asked how many pregnant minors were currently in ORR custody. Dorsey did not know. Judge Millett asked how it was possible that ORR would be "facilitating" an abortion given that Jane is "in the custody of a grantee who has no opposition to letting her go, other than . . . the Government's threat to take away funding if they let her go have the abortion." Dorsey acknowledged that the shelter needed only to do the paperwork to transfer her and provide care for her post-procedure. Millett was confused: "So the one health care they're not willing to do is for abortion. They'd be willing to do anything if she were to continue the pregnancy and do all this facilitation if she were to continue the pregnancy?" Dorsey repeated that the government had an interest in promoting childbirth. Millett: "You've already had a judicial bypass that says she can make this decision herself, not her custodian. She's got a *guardian ad litem* that agrees. And your position is that the facilitating would be ORR saying okay we're going to let you exercise your choice."

Then it was Brigitte Amiri's turn at the lectern. "May it please the court. Good morning," she opened. "Since 1973 the Supreme Court has held that the Government may not ban abortion. By refusing to transport J.D. for an abortion, or refusing to allow anyone to transport J.D., including the shelter or her guardian ad litem, the Government is violating well established Supreme Court Precedent." Judge Kavanaugh pressed her on why a sponsor couldn't be found for Jane. Giving custody of Doe from the government to a sponsor would prevent the shelter from facilitating an abortion and thus allow the court to avoid making a ruling on an undocumented minor's right to an abortion in federal custody. Amiri replied that the government had been unsuccessfully seeking a sponsor for six weeks already, that one attempt to locate a sponsor had already fallen through, and that finding a sponsor could take months.

Judge Millett asked why the federal government didn't have an interest in helping unaccompanied minors make decisions that are safe and appropriate for them. Amiri replied, "Your Honor, they do have the requirement to act in the best interest of minors. And I will say that they are not doing that with respect to J.D., when she has made a decision to have an abortion. She has a judicial bypass from a state court judge. What they are actually doing is supplanting their decision about what J.D. should do with her pregnancy and that is not acting in her best interest and that is actually veto power over J.D.'s abortion decision." Judge Kavanaugh pressed her on why having a sponsor, another adult to talk to, wouldn't help Jane make a better, more informed decision. Amiri reiterated that Jane already had a judicial bypass, plus a guardian ad litem, plus an attorney ad litem for emotional support. She added that Scott Lloyd had gone to another minor in a shelter, personally "to talk to her about her pregnancy and, I believe, unfairly pressure her to carry her pregnancy to term."

Amiri answered questions about the government's facilitation argument: "Defendants really only need to step aside. This idea that

somehow they have to approve the abortion by filling out some paperwork is completely unpersuasive. Really all that has to happen is that
the Office of Refugee Resettlement needs to make a phone call to the
shelter and say that the shelter may now transport the minor or that
the guardian may do so."

Later Amiri said this: "People asked me about this later, about appear-
ing in front of Judge Kavanaugh. It was a very respectful exchange. He
asked pressing questions of the government about why adults in ICE
detention would be allowed access to abortion. . . . So, I'm not leaving
that argument thinking, 'That Judge Kavanaugh, he hates abortion
and he's going to rule against us.'" Amiri closed her arguments before
that appellate panel by focusing on Jane Doe: "What we're talking
about here is an unaccompanied immigrant minor, seventeen years
old, pregnant, who has been forced to remain pregnant against her
will for three weeks because the Government has blocked her abortion decision. Every day she remains pregnant takes a toll on her physical and emotional health." Jane had waited three weeks since a Texas
judge had granted permission to proceed, and that, said Amiri, has
already been "three weeks too long. And balancing her harm compared to the Government's making a phone call, it's quite easy here."
The court transcript shows the proceedings concluded at 11:34 a.m.
Amiri got on a train back to New York. That evening the panel issued
its decision.

Judges Henderson and Kavanaugh had vacated the lower court's
abortion order. They took the "compromise position"—proffered at
the oral arguments by Kavanaugh—that Jane should stay in limbo for
eleven more days as the state tried to locate a sponsor, something it
had not been able to do for weeks. The new order set a new deadline
of October 31, stating that if Jane couldn't find a sponsor by then, the
litigation could start up again. By that point Jane would be starting
her entire case again at seventeen-plus weeks. The usually temperate
judge Patricia Millett dissented with this sober observation: "There are

no winners in cases like these. But there sure are losers. As of today, J.D. has already been forced by the government to continue an unwanted pregnancy for almost four weeks, and now, as a result of this order, must continue to carry that pregnancy for multiple more weeks." Millett wrote that the government's conduct constituted "not just a 'substantial obstacle' [but] a full-on, unqualified denial of and flat prohibition on [Jane's] right to make her own reproductive choice." It was, she wrote, "an astonishing power grab, and it flies in the teeth of decades of Supreme Court precedent preserving and protecting the fundamental right of a woman to make an informed choice whether to continue a pregnancy at this early stage."

For Amiri, the loss was devastating: "As soon as I got off the train, I was doing day-care pickup or after-school pickup, and we got the decision, and I'm on the sidewalk in tears." At that point, the press had started paying attention. "And so I'm also fielding press calls, and the *Washington Post* reporter who'd been following me says, 'Oh, congratulations.' I'm like, 'No, no, no.' They kept saying, 'Well, yeah, but in ten days . . .' But I'm saying 'No, no, no, no.' We had to explain that it's not as if Judge Kavanaugh's ruling said that in ten days Jane can get the abortion if they can't find a sponsor. He was saying we'd have to start our case all over again." As Amiri had put it to me at that time, this was a government that respects the autonomy of women only if they make the one theological decision favored by the government. "For the Trump administration, what Jane needs only matters if it lines up with their extreme antiabortion agenda. If she wanted to remain pregnant or go to a fake clinic—they'd be all too happy to 're-spect' her decision."

Amiri paused. "So that was Friday. I went home and had a glass of wine and collapsed into a puddle. And then the next day we started again, getting our petition for rehearing papers ready. I think we filed them on Sunday. That night the court called for a response, eleven hours later, in the middle of the night, from the government. We got the decision from the en banc court." If a federal appeals court wants to revisit any three-judge panel's decision, they may do so sitting as a larger panel; it's called a rehearing "en banc," from the French, meaning "on the bench." In Jane's case, again acting at light speed, with the entire DC Circuit sitting to rehear the matter, the court voted by a 6–3 margin to reverse the Kavanaugh ruling and allow Jane to terminate her pregnancy. Judge Kavanaugh penned a bitter dissent in which he argued that the government had a genuine interest in not "facilitating" abortion, then condemned the majority for finding that "unlawful immigrant minors have a right to immediate abortion on demand." By ruling in favor of Jane Doe, he wrote, the court had strayed from precedent "holding that the Government has permissible interests in favoring fetal life, protecting the best interests of a minor, and refraining from facilitating abortion." In his nine-page dissenting opinion, Kavanaugh actually used the words "abortion-on-demand" three times. That's not a phrase with any legal meaning, but it is, and has long been, a talking point for antichoice activists. He was, it would seem, dissenting in part and auditioning in part.

The ACLU had won, again, but it was still an uphill battle to get Jane her procedure. All the clinic dates Amiri had sought in the original TRO application had expired. They needed new deadlines. Texas doctors were available on limited days, and there was a need to perform another mandatory counseling session, by the same physician who would perform the procedure, before termination could occur. Getting counseling plus a date for the procedure became an elaborate jigsaw puzzle. Amy Hagstrom Miller is CEO and founder of Whole Woman's Health—the clinics that had prevailed at the Supreme Court in the summer of 2016, which ended the pretextual laws Texas had passed in order to shutter women's health facilities. It was at one of her Texas clinics that Jane had originally been seen and had her ultrasound, and that was where the procedure needed to be rescheduled. It was a clinic, she notes, that barely survived Texas's efforts to close all the clinics in 2016. "It's a miracle that clinic was even open," said Hagstrom Miller. "After the delay happened, we were starting to, what we call, 'chase the weeks' because not all of the physicians who go to that clinic are trained into the second trimester. And when she first came to us, she was in the first trimester. But after the delays, we were left with just one provider we could bring in to see her. She just barely made that limit." She added, "And this clinic only has a provider three days a week."

Said Amiri, "So after we got the good decision from the en banc court, we had to go back to the district court to get a new TRO saying that Jane could go as soon as a doctor was available, or as soon as the clinic was available to see her." On October 24, the lower court judge, Tanya Chutkan, entered another order, again preventing ORR from interfering with Jane's procedure and specifying that her termination now needed to happen "promptly and without delay."

"As soon as we got that," Amiri said, "Rochelle called the shelter and said, 'Okay, take her now. Take her now for her counseling.' And they dragged their feet, and they dragged their feet, and that's when I sent an email to the DOJ and the shelter saying, 'If you don't take her right now, we are going back to the court and saying that you are in contempt.'" And on Jane's side? Said Amiri, "They were saying, 'We've got to get the van ready.' And 'we've got to figure out if there's a driver to take her.' So by the time they were on the road, the clinic calls us and says, 'We can't stay. At this point, we can't . . . it's too late.'"

The ACLU team decided to find out whether the doctor who had originally counseled Jane, back on October 19, would be willing to perform the procedure the next day, on October 25. "That night I spent on my couch so as not to wake up my husband, with my computer and my phone by my head, until 1:00 in the morning, trying to figure out whether this was actually going to work and whether the shelter was going to actually do it. I was woken up by a phone call from Rochelle and Christine at, like, 5:00 my time, 4:00 their time, and they said, 'We're at the clinic. Jane's here. The clinic staff is here. They let us in.' And I just burst into tears because at that moment it was going to happen."

Amy Hagstrom Miller took up the story from there: "We were constantly in communication about, for this specific patient, trying to set up a doctor who could meet her needs on a day that she could get out. The doctor, with less than twelve hours' notice, left at four in the morning in order to get to the clinic. We got the patient in before sunrise, under the cover of dark, basically. And I remember when the doctor landed in the community, the patient and the staff were all in the clinic, and everybody in the whole clinic, including the patient, cheered. . . . The staff went in, in the middle of the night, and it was completed before ten o'clock in the morning." She added, "I actually spoke to her, because I had to because of what she had been through and to tell her what her persistence and her bravery represented to all of us; that was really profound." In the days before her procedure, Jane did an interview with *Vice News*. She said she wasn't ready at seventeen to be a mother. "I want to get to the place I want to go," she said, "and, if God allows it, study, to study and get ahead. I want to be a doctor."

Hagstrom Miller added this: "There's this narrative about Jane, a hopeful narrative, which is what she experienced, right? She experienced the United States like we want people to experience the United States. She left a country where she wouldn't have had access to abortion and came here seeking a better life for herself and a better future for herself, and she got it." She stopped, then said, "Do you know how many more people are in detention that need those services and that care that we're not able to provide it for [them]? That's heartbreaking to know that we don't know who they are, or they might not know how to get to us, because it took so much to be able to advocate for this one person. And the thank-you that she had for us was so profound and it was so humbling. But we were all, 'No, no, don't, no, don't. Thank you for all that you've taught us.'"

The Justice Department believed Jane would get mandatory counseling on the morning of October 25 and have the procedure October 26. The night before, the ACLU had received an email from DOJ asking about the new timing. Amiri said she'd let them know, assuming their interests were about logistics and transportation. I asked Amiri if she has any regrets. "No, I don't. I don't have any regrets. I've obviously thought a lot about this, but no. I had no obligation to tell them anything affirmative; we had a court order saying that Jane could get the abortion as soon as the abortion was available. We did not ever tell them that we would let them know when she was going to the clinic, other than for transportation purposes."

In an unprecedented move nine days after Jane got her abortion, the US solicitor general Noel Francisco filed an appeal at the US Supreme Court seeking that the en banc panel decision of the DC Circuit Court of Appeals be wiped off the books so it would not impact any future Jane Does. Francisco further asked the Supreme Court to sanction the ACLU attorneys, including Amiri, for failing to notify them of Jane's scheduled abortion. The DOJ asked the Supreme Court to force Doe's lawyers to "show cause why disciplinary action should not be taken" against the ACLU—either by the court itself or by the state bars in the states in which they practiced—for "material misrepresentations and omissions" designed to thwart an appeal.

"It felt like a punch in the stomach," Amiri said. "I didn't actually think they could take my law license. But, look, I've always aspired to argue in the Supreme Court someday. And so I thought, could there be Supreme Court discipline? And also, my reputation, you know? I'm a good midwestern girl, and nobody has ever accused me of anything unethical in my whole life. And so it's also just 'Me? They're accusing me of *this*?' I felt sick, I think, probably for the first few days. After I processed it, I was just pissed." She was lucky, she said, that the ACLU stood behind her, as did leading members of the Supreme Court bar, including prominent lawyers who supported her, but it was part of an ongoing pattern of Trump's Justice Department, which was going after litigation shops and deporting leaders of immigrant rights groups.

"This was retaliation against people who dared to stand up against government, who dared to win," Amiri said. "Lawyers who are doing their job." She added, "I remember a conversation I had with my dad where I said, 'This is something that would happen in Iran. This is something that happens in an oppressive regime. This is not what happens in the United States of America.'" This also felt like another version of "Lock her up," a call for disciplinary action against a woman lawyer who had helped another woman fight for a constitutionally protected right. She hadn't just beaten the Trump administration; she'd embarrassed them. The counterpunch seemed designed to punish her for using her law license to do that.

Ultimately, Amiri said she started to think of the solicitor general's attack as a "badge of honor." She said her boss, Jennifer Dalven, still tells her, "They're upset they got beat by girls." It was hard not to see Jane and her team of women lawyers, along with a woman judge in DC, as doing battle with Scott Lloyd and a Justice Department that seemed hell-bent on claiming that the only real and lasting injury in this litigation would be to an inanimate facility and an inanimate government body that didn't want to have "caused" an abortion. That a teenage girl was suffering seemed immaterial. For so many women lawyers involved in the case, and for women following the lawsuit in horror, the notion that teenagers in government custody could be held hostage in facilities designed to protect them and forced to bear children was the stuff of nightmares. It was both heartening and horrifying that Jane was passed along a chain of female lawyers, judges, and reproductive rights activists and providers in order to circumvent a man insisting that he would be "complicit" by doing nothing at all. A modicum of imagination, if not actual empathy, would reveal that Scott Lloyd and ORR were not the victims here. It should not be the case that imagination or empathy is the province of females, but in this case the asymmetry was staggering.

In the meantime, as they tried to tag Amiri for misconduct, it became clear that Justice Department lawyers had also been untruthful in arguing before the DC Circuit that they would never restrict abortions in cases of rape. Internal ORR documents revealed that Lloyd had done precisely that, in December 2017, in a case involving another migrant teen, known as Jane Poe, whose abortion he had also blocked. In subsequent Jane Poe litigation, there emerged a letter from Lloyd saying that abortion would not be in that teen's best interest, even though she had been raped and was suicidal. Lloyd denied her abortion request, he said, because it would result in the "ultimate destruction of another human being." It was finally being said explicitly: there was no case under which he would have permitted a termination, not ever.

The Supreme Court eventually dismissed the request to sanction Amiri, but it took almost six months of closed-door conferences before they decided to do so, suggesting that at least some of the justices were considering it. For Amiri it meant six whole months of just "waiting every Monday for the orders and clicking 'refresh' to see what's going to happen." On June 4, 2018, the justices did grant the DOJ petition to wipe the *Garza* case off the books.

While the en banc opinion in *Garza* is no longer precedent, the ACLU filed a separate class action in January 2018 seeking to protect all of the young migrants in ORR shelters. Amiri said that finding the teen girls to make up that class was enormously challenging: "We knew there were other young women out there, but we didn't know how to get to them. There are shelters all across the country, and we were trying to get out the word to immigration attorneys, but there's no systematic way of getting the word out and no entry point. And then I got, via snail mail, an envelope with my name misspelled, and it was in pencil, and there was a letter in there with enough accurate information to find what then became known as Jane Poe and then Jane Roe. And there was no indication of who this came from, and I will never know."

In March 2018, Judge Chutkan, the same district court judge who'd ruled for Jane Doe, barred DHS from denying any immigrants in federal custody access to abortion services. She also certified the ACLU's class-action lawsuit such that every similarly situated Jane now had legal status and access to relief. At the time of Jane Doe's case, HHS reported there were thirty-eight other pregnant girls in ORR custody. It wasn't until September 2020, three years after Jane Doe was able to terminate her own pregnancy, that the Trump administration finally issued a new policy clarifying that ORR and ORR-funded shelters may not block or interfere with unaccompanied immigrant minors' access to reproductive health care, including abortion. Only then did the ACLU drop their class action on behalf of hundreds of other Janes.

"There is some book by John Irving," said Amiri, "where one of the characters is practicing a basketball layup over and over again, and he doesn't know why he's practicing that layup, necessarily. And then he's in Vietnam, and there's a bomb, and he's in this school with these kids and he has to throw these kids out the window. And he realizes that this thing that he's been practicing over and over again? This was the moment. This was it. I'm incredibly proud that this was the case I was able to lead, drawing from all those ten years. And the confluence of all the legal planes: I'd done prisoners' access to abortion claims; I'd done cases about parental involvement. The only case about a law forcing people to go to crisis pregnancy centers as a condition of getting an abortion is a law in South Dakota that I'm challenging with Planned Parenthood. So doctrinally, you have this confluence of all of these issues I'd worked on for years."

And of course this brings us back to Scott Lloyd, who had been practicing his own layups for years, which involved denying women their constitutional rights. Amiri was finally able to depose him as a part of the litigation over other Janes in his custody. In his first deposition, taken in December 2017, Lloyd admitted under oath that he had considered forcing a pregnant minor in his care, who had already taken the first pill in a medication abortion, to attempt a controversial and medically unsupported "abortion reversal" in order to "save the life of the baby." In another deposition, taken in February 2018, Lloyd told Amiri he didn't actually know whether childbirth was safer than abortion—it is not—and when she asked him whether he believed abortion involved "destruction of human life," he replied that this was "objective fact." Amiri was thunderstruck. From the transcript:

> AMIRI: "That's objective?"
>
> LLOYD: "Um-hum."
>
> AMIRI: "You believe everyone, regardless of their belief systems, believes that abortion is the destruction of human life?"
>
> LLOYD: "Well, it's not just in my mind. . . . I think the objective facts are that it involves the destruction of a human life. How people internalize every element is a different question."

Lloyd further said under oath that he believed abortion was a sin and that he had conducted no real literature review before writing his memo claiming that women who have abortions "experience it as a devastating trauma." He claimed he had taken that view based on reading information provided by his staff as well as "stuff" he found "on the internet" indicating "an increased likelihood of self-harm, suicide, that sort of thing." There is no medical evidence whatsoever supporting these claims.

Lloyd's most stunning admission in this same deposition involved Jane Poe, the minor to whom he had denied access to an abortion in 2017, even though her pregnancy was the result of a rape. The DOJ had promised the DC appeals court that this would never happen. But it had happened. And Lloyd had written in an ORR memo that compelling minors to carry to term was in their "best interest"—even in cases where they were likely to self-harm. Asked by Amiri about Jane Poe, Lloyd replied that she had "claimed to have been raped."

The ongoing ACLU lawsuit would come to reveal that Lloyd had dedicated an outsize share of his professional time to calling, visiting, and otherwise micromanaging the teen migrants in ORR custody. A FOIA request showed that Lloyd had been keeping meticulous track of the menstrual cycles of those girls and that this continued long after he had been ordered by a court to stop blocking young women seeking to terminate their pregnancies. The *Handmaid's Tale* designation was finally truly apt; these young women were being held hostage by the US government and forced to continue unwanted pregnancies while one man monitored their fertility as part of his self-assigned "job."

It would later become clear that Lloyd was also at least partly responsible for the federal government's catastrophic inability to keep proper track of thousands of immigrant children separated from their parents at the border pursuant to the Trump administration's "zero tolerance" policy, announced by the administration during the spring and summer of 2018. Lloyd would testify, in February 2019, that he had failed to alert HHS officials about the dangers of family separation, even though he had been warned in explicit detail by a subordinate of the mental health catastrophe that would follow. Although his office was in charge of the thousands of children separated from their parents, Lloyd had told his staff to stop keeping spreadsheets. His eventual review of the case files of separated families was so slow that his boss, Secretary of Health and Human Services Alex Azar, had to eventually undertake it himself. In lawsuits, federal judges ordered

ORR to remove migrant children from facilities—one located south of Houston and another in Virginia—when allegations surfaced that staff had administered psychotropic drugs in the Texas shelter and that migrant teens had been beaten and stripped naked at the Virginia facility. But Lloyd dutifully kept his spreadsheets of teen girls' periods.

Amy Hagstrom Miller said that as a person of faith herself, Lloyd's conduct was shocking. "It makes me shudder that he was using that position to further his own personal beliefs, and the tracking of the menstrual cycles is absolutely terrifying. Especially that they're losing track of actual people and actual children, yet they have a spreadsheet for when people are getting their periods, it just speaks so loudly to this notion of women as vessels." Hagstrom Miller added that it was only days after her case, *Whole Woman's Health*, was decided at the Supreme Court in 2016 that state legislators "pivoted from the health and safety framework and from the notion that the state really cared about women and families and started to talk about women as 'hosts.'"

As Hannah Levintova at *Mother Jones* noted in 2019, "Three federal courts have rebuked Lloyd [in 2018] for making policy decisions based on his personal beliefs—what one judge called his 'flight of whimsy.'" In July 2018, he was quietly removed from any formal official oversight of the office, and in November 2018 he was redeployed just as quietly from head of ORR to HHS's Center for Faith and Opportunity Initiatives, to focus on outreach to faith communities. One month later he published a novel, called *The Undergraduate*, based on his own essay about his life in college. His protagonist, William Ferguson, has a girlfriend who becomes pregnant and has an abortion, which leads Will to rekindle his Catholic faith. The narrator tells his priest, "I paid for the abortion of my baby, which . . . would mean that I have helped commit murder . . . of my own child. I can't think of anything a person can do that is worse than that." The ellipses are his.

The redemption, well, Lloyd forced that on all the rest of us. In May 2019, Lloyd quietly left the Trump administration once and for all.

Amiri was frustrated that a man with a personal mission to save all women from his *own* collegiate abortion regrets was given responsibility for thousands of vulnerable minors. "It was absolutely deliberate," she said. "It was absolutely based on his personal opposition to abortion. He came in knowing that he was going to use his power to do this, and that was probably the *only* thing he cared about, given all of the kids he lost after they were separated from their families."

The sudden flurry of press attention and TV hits at the time was also new to Amiri, even as a seasoned litigator. Interviewed a year later, she said, of the weeks around the *Garza* case, "I couldn't quite figure out the size of it, and also I'm not sure what to compare it to. I've got these other cases that may get to the Supreme Court about whether *Roe* should be overturned. That case was part of this larger narrative of where we are right now on abortion rights. I really felt like this was the canary in the coal mine. So yes, this was the most attention that the press has paid to a case of mine." But, she added, the case was also part of a mass effort that never stops. "There's so much other stuff going on that's important in this country too."

Brigitte Amiri is not unlike the millions of us who allowed ourselves to believe, after the Supreme Court reaffirmed the core holding of *Roe* in its *Whole Woman's Health* decision in 2016, that we were on the brink of something akin to the end of America's abortion wars. For so many of us that one big, big win in the courts signaled that we could move past the artifice of paternalistic state claims about tragic little women who need help making hard decisions and pretextual policies that had no purpose beyond terrorizing vulnerable pregnant people and shuttering clinics. We had hoped that we could instead begin the genuinely imperative work of rolling back the Hyde Amendment, improving maternal and infant health outcomes, and reducing the shame and stigma around reproductive choice. Like Amiri, we watched in horror as the newly transformed courts set back the clock on abortion rights, sidelined the pregnant and their physicians, and bolstered the religious claims of the few over the rights of an entire nation. In the few years after 2016, this attack moved rapidly from banning abortion to undermining the rights to contraception, in vitro fertilization, and surrogacy. In 2021, we watched the second most populous state in the nation ban abortion after six weeks as a newly conservative Supreme Court stood by, winking. And Amiri has stayed in the fight as history speeds backward on women's freedoms. She's a living embodiment of that sign that became familiar after the first Women's March: I CAN'T BELIEVE I'M STILL PROTESTING THIS SHIT.

One of the lessons I took from the case about migrant teens at the border is that you can win, and even win big, in the courts and still face immense backsliding if you aren't doing mass political organizing at the same time. As Amiri put it to me, "I think that courts are incredibly important, and they have stopped a lot of bad stuff from happening, but I think that if people think that the courts are going to be the place that will save us, we will be complacent about all the other work." The Trump years offered us a lot of trials to watch as theater. When the travel ban was argued in telephonic form at the Ninth Circuit Court of Appeals, listeners tuned in en masse. Trump's first impeachment trial featured gripping televised testimony by steely women like Fiona Hill, one of Trump's top Russia advisors, and his former ambassador to Ukraine, Marie Yovanovitch. I almost find myself missing those blockbuster proceedings, as morality plays if nothing else. Covering the highs and lows of the lawsuits challenging cruel Trump policies like those prohibiting migrant teens from exercising bodily autonomy was very satisfying work and made for good journalism. But it was always only half the story.

One of the things lawyers can do is win trials, including big symbolic trials like so many of the signature wins of the Trump years. An extensive review undertaken by the Institute for Policy Integrity at

the New York University School of Law showed the Trump administration's win rate at about 17 percent in federal courts, in the summer of 2019. The usual win rate for the government stands at about
70 percent. Why all the losses? Shambolic, hasty legal work, indefen-
sible new rules, attempts to fast-track lawsuits that ended up back-
firing, failures to comply with basic administrative demands of the
federal Administrative Procedure Act. Trump's own tweets and statements had been the basis for adverse rulings in multiple lawsuits. But
as was the case with the travel ban, bad policies can be cured, and
legal losses can net out to eventual wins. Amiri was candid about the
fact that litigation can take you only so far: "I am a litigator, so of
course I have to say that the courts are important. But this is where I
do my work."

This is where the organizers and the policy people step in, and as
Amiri said, "I am not an organizer. I am not that kind of activist." As
we will soon see, extraordinary women were stepping into the big policy work around gender rights, immigration policy, voting rights, court
reform, and so many other matters. Ultimately, they worked hand in
glove with the litigators doing battle in the courtroom, ensuring that
legal wins became policy victories and vice versa. Amiri was drawn to
litigation because it is tightly controlled and rule bound and rewards
preparation. (She is, I always recall, trained as a dancer.) For so many
women who have thrived in the law, the predictability and structure
are a draw. Play by the rules and you can prevail. But Amiri cautions
that the two-front war—lawsuits and organizing—is imperative. "I
spend my days doing this work and writing briefs," she told me. "But
organizing and movement work reinforce each other, and they become
the safety nets for each other. Regardless of the changes, I will continue to do this work because this is kind of the only thing I know how
to do. And I also really love it. I love being a lawyer. I love being a litigator. I love being in court, and I love the structured conflict, and I
love the fight for my clients and for what is right." For the women who

went to law school to master the fine art of structured conflict, the Trump years were a proving ground. For others, the chaos required a move to large-scale organizing; entire systems would need to be restructured. The law would light their way as well.

Just a few months after Jane Doe's abortion, Brett Kavanaugh, who had been left off President Trump's various Supreme Court short lists, found himself at the very top of a new one. Many viewed his angry dissent in the *Garza* case, with his references to "abortion-on-demand," as part of his tryout for the high court. Kavanaugh would be very quickly tapped to replace the retiring justice Anthony Kennedy, for whom he clerked, less than a year later. "The whole Kavanaugh thing was just, you know, surreal," said Amiri. "That this was his only abortion case, and now he might be the fifth vote to overturn or undermine *Roe*." While Jane Doe and Jane Roe and Amiri all won their lawsuits, the elevation of Kavanaugh, and later of Amy Coney Barrett, to the Supreme Court became the surest threat to the viability of *Roe v. Wade* in our lifetimes. Ultimately, Amiri and Jane won the abortion battle, but with his dissent, Kavanaugh positioned himself to win the war.

By the summer of 2022, Donald Trump's three appointments to the US Supreme Court—Neil Gorsuch, Kavanaugh, and Barrett—would help forge a new majority willing to find that *Roe v. Wade* was "egregiously wrong from the start," and needed to be overturned. The issue of abortion would be "returned to the states" as lawmakers floated introducing a federal abortion ban and Oklahoma banned abortion, all before the Supreme Court even issued a final ruling in the case, *Dobbs v. Jackson Women's Health Organization*, that was leaked before it was released. IVF, surrogacy, and birth control became suspect incursions on "fetal personhood." And the Supreme Court abandoned its earlier language around protecting mothers in order to green-light a state-by-state assault on pregnant people and their physicians and those who would "aid and abet" or counsel them. Most Americans on reading the Dobbs opinion professed themselves shocked to learn that a fifty-year-old constitutional protection could simply disappear overnight. We believed Roe had been engraved in stone. And yet everything that had happened in those migrant shelters in Texas signposted the truth: for many women in America, the right to control their own body was always merely a paper right, dependent on geography, income, race, and the courts. It could be taken away by judges in due time. In 2022, it was.

The Civil Rights Lawyer

Vanita Gupta:
The Insider-Outsider

V anita Gupta has litigated a *lot* of cases. She's indisputably gifted at it. But from her perch as CEO and president of the storied Leadership Conference on Civil and Human Rights—a coalition of two hundred of America's most prominent civil and human rights organizations—she became, first and foremost, an organizer in response to the legal challenges of the years from 2016 to 2020. And nobody was more surprised by that turn of events than Gupta, who had spent most of her professional life on the outside, pounding on the doors of the American justice system and demanding a seat at the table for minorities, for the poor, and for women.

"To me, this moment, more than litigation, is about organizing. Organizing and power," she told me in an interview in 2019 when she was still at the helm of the Leadership Conference. It was Gupta who really helped me understand that so much of democracy is won and lost in the blur of big, impersonal systems. So many of the most salient battles in recent years involved neutral-sounding changes to questions on the census form or seemingly invisible tweaks to the way mail-in ballots were delivered. Yes, lawsuits were a part of bolstering systems of democracy, but so was democracy itself. So Gupta became, in a sense, a systems wrangler over those four years, and it was a strange fit for someone who had trained as an attorney, then spent years in the trenches doing litigation.

"As a person who has litigated her whole life," Gupta explained in an interview that took place before the 2020 election, "what history will say about this moment is that in the face of layers and layers of challenges for vulnerable people, there was a very broad base of people who never saw themselves as activists before. And litigation itself doesn't mean power. It is important. It can be the backstop. But in a lot of ways, what litigators had failed to do is build power, and a public will, for the kind of country we want to be."

Born in Philadelphia to parents who were Indian immigrants, Gupta—who is just over five feet tall and pulls off "having style" more ably than any attorney I know—lived for much of her childhood in England, where her father worked as a business manager for a multinational company. She recalls sitting at a McDonald's in London at age four as skinheads, throwing French fries at her family, shouted, "Pakis, go home." And as she told *Rolling Stone* in 2019, "There was a series of incidents like that that made me acutely aware that my family was always going to be seen as an outsider in a certain way." By the time she was in high school, back in the United States, Gupta was already thinking about racial inequality in legal systems and "otherness."

"I became an activist in high school," she told *Glamour* magazine in 2020. "There are no lawyers in my family, but I went to law school focused on what was happening in our criminal justice system." Gupta went to Yale as an undergraduate and then on to New York University for law school, graduating in 2001. She had spent two years before law school working on youth violence prevention, and as she explained, "I

was seeing young Black and brown kids getting funneled into the criminal justice system. I was just distraught about the dehumanization of
so many of our children, and at a really early age, I realized this was one
of the greatest civil rights travesties of our time." All this was evident
to her even in the mid-1990s. So she went to law school "with a keen
sense that I wanted to focus on justice reform issues and racial equality." Years later she tells me, "It didn't even feel like making a choice; it
just felt like the path I was on."

Immediately following graduation, Gupta took a job at the NAACP
Legal Defense and Educational Fund, and within three weeks of her
arrival, she had become obsessed with a legal travesty in Tulia, Texas,
that she learned about from a TV documentary. As part of an undercover drug sting in Tulia in 1999, the local law enforcement system
had arrested and convicted more than 12 percent of the town's Black
population—all based on the uncorroborated testimony of a single
white undercover cop who had a history of using racist language and
of profoundly troubled policing decisions. Forty-six people—of whom
forty were Black—were arrested. Local media was ecstatic. The day
after the raid, *The Tulia Herald* feted Tulia's law enforcement with the
headline TULIA'S STREETS CLEARED OF GARBAGE.

The alleged conspirators included young mothers and a hog farmer,
and of course the "raids" turned up almost no actual evidence of
drugs or money. The arresting officer wore no wire and had no backup.
Testifying at trial, he claimed to have recorded names, dates, and
other pertinent facts about his mass of drug buys by writing all relevant information on his leg. The defendants, all poor, had court-
appointed lawyers who conducted no investigations. Many had been
persuaded to plead guilty. The resulting prison sentences would have
seen some of them die in jail. One defendant was sentenced to 341
years.

By the time the twenty-six-year-old Gupta got herself down to
Tulia, most of the defendants had already lost on appeal without

lawyers. Gupta pledged that the Legal Defense Fund would represent all of them, bought a suitcase at a local Walmart that she filled with their case files, then returned to New York to organize a sprawling team of pro bono attorneys from across the country. She went back to Tulia as lead counsel for the appeals and filed her first petition in an action that would essentially put the local law enforcement system on trial.

In 2002, Nate Blakeslee of the *Texas Tribune*, followed by the *New York Times* columnist Bob Herbert, helped publicize the Tulia travesty in a series of scorching columns that drew instant national outrage. And when even Texas media began to realize that the much-heralded arrests and convictions had become evidence of a national policing and courts scandal, Gupta worked with state news organizations to tell the story of mass systemic failure. That media attention put new pressure on the Texas appeals courts. After two years of relentless investigations and court filings, Gupta's team was able to discredit the uncorroborated testimony of the one officer on the case, had the lawsuits taken away from a biased judge, and entered into a mass settlement. On August 22, 2003, Texas's governor Rick Perry granted full pardons to almost all of the defendants. Gupta then helped negotiate a $6 million settlement on behalf of them all. As she would later write of the Tulia litigation, in a 2005 law review article, this conclusion hardly represented a "win":

> To those who hold the Tulia victory as a symbol of a justice system that works, I say that my clients who spent four years in prison on bogus charges did not have a system that worked. And our victory came at enormous cost—both in terms of human anguish and real resources. It is a rare case that can glean as many resources as Tulia did. That it took so much time and money to right what was a fairly blatant injustice while individuals suffered is not a symbol of a machine at

work, but instead of a broken system that needs to be, and can be, fixed where there is political will to do so.

That proved prescient with respect to the years and years of police shootings and criminal injustices for Black and brown Americans that would follow. As long as two decades ago, Tulia, in Gupta's mind, was not just a high-profile criminal defense case. It was a vehicle for a desperately needed public conversation about a badly broken and racially tainted criminal justice system. As she told me years later, "I had poured my whole life into these [Tulia] cases, into representing these men and women, and I had become really close to the families. But when they got out of prison, which was a huge deal, it felt like a Band-Aid, because it was against the backdrop of laws and policies that were all going in one direction at the time."

For Gupta, the problem lay in massive, faceless institutions that were supposed to bring about justice but were instead perpetuating its opposite. After that, Gupta turned her attention to other aspects of the American criminal justice system that produced gross racial disparities, focusing on the war on drugs, the for-profit prison industry, increasing police militarization, and an asset forfeiture system that financially rewards law enforcement for predatory policing. In 2006, Gupta took a job at the American Civil Liberties Union, where she served as a staff attorney with its Racial Justice Program. There, she won a landmark settlement on behalf of immigrant children and became deputy legal director and director of its Center for Justice, with an eye toward policy change on a large scale. As she explained to me years later, "I went to the ACLU out of recognition that litigation was an important but limited tool. I wanted to work somewhere where I could actually begin to change laws." She admits, "I didn't know how to do that. I'd been trained in law school to file cases and how to represent people. I had to convince the ACLU to launch the campaign to end mass incarceration. But the ACLU had resources, they had a communications department, they had affiliate power, so I was really trying to leverage all of that for broader systemic change."

At the ACLU, Gupta worked to build collaboration between law enforcement entities, advocates, and elected officials to repair the criminal justice system in ways that could garner bipartisan support. She directed the ACLU's National Campaign to End Mass Incarceration. She sued the Bush administration in 2007, winning a landmark settlement on behalf of immigrant children detained in a privately run prison in Texas. As with other criminal justice issues, Gupta was calling out the failures of mass incarceration long before it showed up on the national radar. In a newspaper editorial she penned in 2013 for *The New York Times*, Gupta explained that the American carceral system is a bipartisan problem that demands bipartisan solutions. "I am not naïve," she wrote, "about the challenge, or of the needs of crime victims." In that piece, she explained that in 1992, as she was finishing high school, her own seventy-one-year-old paternal grandmother was murdered in a house robbery in Sahibabad, India. "The killing remains unsolved, and the anguish it caused my family will never fade away. But in America, our criminal justice system has too often focused on vengeance and punishment (and racial suspicion) rather than on crime prevention, restitution for victims and the social and economic reintegration of released prisoners into our communities so that they do not turn to crime again." Gupta was and is careful to lay blame for the buildup of our prison-industrial complex on a "bipartisan process that unfolded over decades," but argued that through unlikely political alliances, the political process could stop over-incarceration. Litigation should be the vitally important backstop.

In 2014, Gupta was floored to receive a phone call from Attorney General Eric Holder's office, wanting to discuss the possibility of having her head up his Justice Department's Civil Rights Division. "I had

spent my whole life suing the government, so I never thought that anyone in the government would put me in that position," she told *Rolling
Stone* in 2019. Gupta was thirty-nine when she assumed stewardship
of the Civil Rights Division, famously dubbed the "crown jewel" of the
Justice Department. It was the Civil Rights Division that had done the
work of desegregating schools following 1954's *Brown v. Board of Education*, and the Civil Rights Division that had spearheaded big police
reforms at the LAPD following the 1991 beating of Rodney King by
police officers. Gupta arrived in government at a crucible moment for
Black Lives Matter protests, police misconduct, and a series of brutal
police killings of unarmed African American men. In a way, the work
she did inside DOJ felt not dissimilar to what she had done at the
ACLU, as she explains: "When I went to DOJ, it was of course enforcement based, but at DOJ you have a mantle and a bully pulpit that
allows you through the course of litigation to use your platform as a
big megaphone about what was happening."

The change wasn't just the platform, though. It was moving to the
inside. "I had sued the government my entire life before I went into
the Justice Department," she tells me, "and that was my first time
ever being on the inside, but I got to see where the levers of power
were. Suddenly I was able to enforce the law to address these long-
standing problems I had worked on for most of my career: the criminalization of poverty, and policing and racial justice." Gupta joined
the Obama Justice Department in the fall of 2014, only nine weeks
after Michael Brown was killed by a police officer in Ferguson, Missouri. Brown had been shot shortly after a police officer killed Eric
Garner in New York. She was at the helm when DOJ released its massive report on the Ferguson Police Department and court system, a
report ultimately finding, among other things, that residents of some
Black neighborhoods around Ferguson had become "potential offenders and sources of revenue" for the cops and the courts. At the same
time, the report would explain why no federal civil rights charges

would be filed against the officer who shot Brown. Gupta wanted to use the report to talk—as she had done after Tulia—about race and policing and justice, and to connect the Ferguson Police Department, their asset forfeiture practices, and local court systems to the racial bias infecting and inflaming everything that had happened *after* Ferguson. Yet despite her extensive work on civil rights issues, Gupta managed to forge an unusual set of relationships with law enforcement leaders, police chiefs, and the Fraternal Order of Police, whose input she sought as the Justice Department tried to develop its best practices around policing.

Gupta told me on my podcast in the summer of 2020 that "the policing issues were the most central kind of issues that I dealt with at the Justice Department every week that I was there." DOJ was enforcing fifteen consent decrees in police departments across the country on her watch. She took heat from all sides over the mixed conclusions in the Ferguson report, but she also became adept at working with constituencies—in law enforcement, drug policy, and prisons—with whom she had once differed about virtually everything. As she explains in an interview, "I was at the Justice Department when we released the Ferguson Police Department report, and it was a really big deal. We had never done that. For a lot of people it was an indictment of the criminal justice system coming from the very office that upholds the machinery of law enforcement." Gupta was raising questions about government from inside government, but, as she tells me, "I was really comfortable with those inherent contradictions because I do believe ultimately in institutions." Gupta, like so many women lawyers, and even groups that seek change, is conservative in some ways. "I mean, look at the organizations I've worked with—they're all decades old," she tells me. "I believe in the power of institutions while recognizing how unequal and unjust they have been in people's lives. That struggle to make them more just and inclusive is something I've spent my whole life trying to do."

At a time in which it still appeared possible to reach bipartisan policy conclusions about changes to the police and justice systems, Gupta's DOJ work on criminal justice reform thrilled progressives and impressed conservatives, including Grover Norquist, founder and president of Americans for Tax Reform, and David Keene, a former president of the National Rifle Association. Immediately after the Ferguson investigation, Gupta had to turn to Baltimore when Freddie Gray died in police custody, again working with community leaders, local residents, and the Fraternal Order of Police in the investigation. In addition to overseeing fifteen major consent decrees that had the Justice Department monitoring city police policy reforms, Gupta worked at DOJ to achieve reforms in voting rights, housing, education, hate crime legislation, LGBTQ rights, human trafficking, disability rights, predatory lending, and voting. In a 2020 interview, she conceded that her work at DOJ was just a start: "I served a president and two attorneys general who were leaning forward into police reform, criminal justice reform, LGBTQ rights, and voting rights. But it was never enough, and it never felt like enough."

GUPTA LEFT THE JUSTICE DEPARTMENT just forty-eight hours before Donald Trump was to be sworn in, heartbroken it hadn't been enough and that the work still wasn't even close to being done. In a *New Yorker* profile of her last day at the Civil Rights Division, Gupta said goodbye to the entire staff of the division—700 employees, including 383 lawyers—then teared up as she told her team, who would now be reporting to the Jeff Sessions Justice Department, "Good luck, keep the faith, and keep fighting." That profile ended with her stuffing newspaper accounts of her work with the Baltimore Police Department and a pair of high heels into a bag, stepping into an elevator, and saying, "Goodbye, D.O.J."

The Civil Rights Division under Jeff Sessions and later under

Trump's second attorney general, William Barr, would busy itself rolling back the consent decrees—legal instruments that force institutions to reform their practices—as well as reversing itself on voting rights, affirmative action, and other Obama practices. As Gupta told me in an episode of my podcast after George Floyd was killed in 2020, the Trump Justice Department "had not opened a single pattern and practice investigation into a police department except on one with a very narrow issue out of Springfield, Massachusetts." She also noted that Barr had recently said in a speech that if Americans criticized the police, they may not receive police protection.

Instead of protecting immigrants, prisoners, and LGBTQ Americans, the Trump Justice Department would deprioritize civil rights enforcement. DOJ abruptly changed sides in voting rights cases, representing those who would constrict the franchise over those seeking to vote. In 2019, a *Vice* investigation found that the Civil Rights Division under Sessions and Barr had initiated 60 percent fewer cases over civil rights violations during the first two years of the Trump administration than during the Obama years and 50 percent fewer than under George W. Bush. Despite the surge in hate crimes after Trump was elected, the Justice Department's hate crimes prosecutions fell by about 20 percent compared with the Obama administration. The Trump administration slashed the division's staff and budget as well. It had become a shell of its former self.

But Gupta had come to believe that restoring trust between police and communities could not be achieved by DOJ pattern and practices investigations alone. She wanted to tackle another big invisible system, what she characterized as the "hyper criminalization in this country, not new, not started in the last few years, but that we've been saddled with over the last fifty years." She wanted to think about why "legislatures had increasingly criminalized mental health, substance use disorders, and other social problems and why we have placed those problems at the feet of police and expected them to solve for them with one tool—the criminal justice system. We did this while disinvesting from education, jobs, public housing, and healthcare."

Had Hillary Clinton won the 2016 election, Gupta would likely have become the Senate-confirmed head of the Civil Rights Division. But after that election, Gupta says, "I could have gone somewhere and put my head down and litigated at a big law firm," but it was the intractable, invisible systems that drew her still. "I wanted the ability to protect civil rights in this moment and also to figure out how you build power at the state and local level for the kinds of things you ultimately want to see federally. These attacks on civil rights and democracy kept me in public service. I just didn't think that litigation was going to be enough to protect our democracy."

If women are, as I've argued, particularly adept at the practice of law, it almost goes without saying that they are also uniquely gifted at strategizing, organizing, and activating. It was a foundational lesson of the fight for democracy from day one, and thus not an accident, that women in leadership roles were so focused and effective as well. At the Leadership Conference, Gupta turned to the big-picture work of strategizing, coordinating, messaging, and mobilizing her partner organizations to push back against the persistent efforts to attack civil rights. It was this daily, grinding work of advocacy, organizing, and showing up that mattered to Gupta, as much as the successful litigation. "What we have seen," she explained to me in an interview before the 2020 election, "was a weaponization of democratic institutions, from the census, to voting rights, to the courts." The scale of the assault was massive, she said, "and while litigation has been a really important backstop, to me, the power of this moment and what history will say about this moment is that in the midst of relentless, layered otherness, there is a very broad base of people who never saw themselves as 'others' before who now understand that we're in a fight to save the soul of our country."

That seemed an essential piece of the puzzle to me, the reaction
of people "who never saw themselves as others" to being told that
they no longer had a place in America. Gupta gave voice to so many
women who expressed the sense that 2016 awakened them to the
fact that maybe all the progress they believed themselves to have
achieved was illusory, that maybe the whole American dream thing
really was something that could be snatched away. For Gupta, the
work of collecting all those feeling invisible and left behind became
the work. It was bigger than legal change; it was about a much broader
project of building enduring political power. The courtroom victories,
the protection and promotion of individual rights carved out in the
Warren Court era, were vital. But they are not, in isolation, enough.
As she explained, the lesson of the decades before 2016 was that "we
had resorted to sometimes moral strategies in litigation, believing the
kind of groundwork we were laying in the courts is going to carry the
day in terms of rights." But as we learned, nothing achieved—even in
the courts—was immutable. "I think that we're in a moment," she
told me, "where we're reckoning with the fact that the other side, for
forty years, had an advantage because they have been fairly single-
minded and disciplined around understanding the importance of winning hearts and minds with simple messages; with organizing for the
long haul; with scenario planning for the long haul; and we've been
able to take things for granted in a way that today we are not able to,
and it's been a real crisis and wake-up call."

And perhaps because women never fully possessed this kind of broad
political power, or hadn't become used to it, or taken it for granted,
women were quickest to see it sliding out of their reach. Gupta quickly
recognized that it was women who were racing to construct, join, and
collaborate in organizing, and she told me she could see that women
understood this lesson absolutely intuitively. "I think that on a lot of
these issues, women are leading the way, or they are leading organizations that are changing tactics. They're leading mass protests, leading

long-term planning, and not just the touchy-feely stuff, but, for instance, thinking about what a long-term campaign to protect our courts could look like." To go, overnight, from a top government position in the United States to a world of threats to "Lock her up" is a visceral, primal reckoning. As a woman and as an attorney, Gupta recognized that law would never be an end in itself unless it was lashed to power.

Gupta became one leader of a massive pro-democracy movement helmed by women of color, many of whom were stepping into prominent, public-facing roles for the first time in their lives. She emphasizes that while she is grateful for the mentorship and support of those who blazed a trail before her, in the trenches of the four years from 2016 to 2020, her peers opened her eyes to what young, new, minority leadership could be. Gupta said in an interview in 2020, "In just the last few years, I have gotten a lot of guidance from other leaders, and particularly from other women-of-color leaders, some of whom are newer leaders in the movement. That kind of community of support has been essential to me."

When she took on the historic role of the first woman, and first Indian American, to helm the Leadership Conference in June 2017, Gupta, forty-two at the time, helped turn the organization into a strategic hub of the resistance. Founded in 1950 as the Leadership Conference on Civil Rights by three civil rights leaders—A. Philip Randolph, head of the Brotherhood of Sleeping Car Porters; Roy Wilkins of the NAACP; and Arnold Aronson, a leader of the National Jewish Community Relations Advisory Council—the Conference took as its animating principle the idea that the struggle for civil rights in America could be achieved only through coalitions working together across narrow parochial self-interests. Known as the lobbying arm of the civil rights movement, the Leadership Conference has weighed in on behalf of every major civil rights law since its founding, supplementing the marches and sit-ins of the civil rights era to ensure the passage of the Civil Rights Act of 1957, the Civil Rights

Act of 1960, the Civil Rights Act of 1964, the Voting Rights Act
(VRA) of 1965, and the Fair Housing Act of 1968. What began as a
coalition of thirty civil and human rights organizations at its founding
has grown to more than two hundred groups today, and the fight to
protect civil rights now sweeps in women's rights, LGBTQ rights,
immigrants' rights, workers' rights, and disability rights.

What Gupta did at the Leadership Conference required coordinating all these disparate groups who might be duplicating efforts, or
pulling in opposing directions, to focus and work together, often very
quickly and in tandem with multiple lawsuits and public actions. Asked
what she did all day in the years she worked there, she had a lawyerly
answer: "It depends." She elaborated: "Sometimes I'm on the Hill in
meetings pushing leadership to do something. Sometimes I'm talking
on the phone with leaders around making sure that we're unified. . . .
Sometimes I'm giving a speech and I'm running back to meet with a
coalition principal about a campaign they're working on or doing a
media interview around the census and making sure that our public
messaging is out there. . . . It's all policy organizing, communications,
activism." She stopped to concede, "Yeah, but I am not reading briefs
anymore."

Gupta brought her background in police reform to the Leadership
Conference to build what she described as "a policing program that
could, in the void of a Justice Department that focused on these issues and the communities most in contact with the police, actually
be a resource for continuing the conversation around justice reform."
After George Floyd's murder, the Leadership Conference brought
together more than 430 organizations to support a platform for what
Congress could do immediately to reform policing and to build back
community trust.

The Trump administration's family separation policy at the border
was another example, says Gupta, of an almost spontaneous explosion of coalitions and reformers coming together. "We were all learning

about what the Trump administration was doing in the summer of 2018. And there were groups coming together to organize," she told me. And women were everywhere. What became the massive Families Belong Together rallies in June 2018 were spearheaded, says Gupta, by women: herself, Representative Pramila Jayapal, Anna Galland from MoveOn, Ai-jen Poo and Jess Morales Rocketto from the National Domestic Workers Alliance, and Lorella Praeli, the ACLU's director of immigration policy and campaigns. Ultimately, in seven hundred cities across the country, marchers gathered, including—according to estimates from the organizers—thirty-five thousand demonstrators in ninety-six-degree weather in front of the White House, thirty thousand participants in New York, sixty thousand in Chicago, and more than seventy thousand in Los Angeles.

In an interview after those rallies, Gupta reflected that when it comes to power and powerlessness, gender was surely part of the story, her own and that of the other organizers. "It didn't have to be women, but in that moment, recognizing our own powerlessness and a complete lack of power in Congress, and the majority of Congress having abdicated any oversight of the president, we just weren't going to allow this outward assumption of powerlessness to rule the day." To her mind, those rallies protesting family separation at the border were "*our* show of power," and that happened in seven hundred cities around the country. "In the towns where fifteen people came, but that was fifteen people out of seven hundred in their town . . . that was also power." This was women and people of color leading a movement that said that even if they were not represented in the government or the courts or the administration, they would not be silent or invisible. That was a sea change for so many people, most especially for women, and to Gupta it meant "we had to be so much more creative than we've ever been, building power and sustaining power in this moment, and the key is going to be organizing, organizing, organizing."

Gupta told me that there's a sloppy tendency to think of law and

legislation as somehow manly and purposive and to dismiss organizing and coalition building as soft and fuzzy. Recall that Sarah Palin got
a big laugh by snarking at Obama as a community organizer in her
2008 RNC speech, when she said of her own professional background,
"I guess a small-town mayor is sort of like a community organizer, except that you have actual responsibilities." Gupta disagrees that building coalitions and creating movements represent a form of soft power,
but at the same time she told me that women are intuitively naturals
at organizing: "I feel like sometimes organizing can feel very touchy-
feely and that people forget the power of just showing up. And it's
relational. I just think that so many women have experienced that on
a very personal level. . . . It takes admitting to some feelings of weak-
ness, until you can find a relationship and build coalitions with others
who are like-minded regardless of party or background." One paradox
about power, also taught to me by Gupta and the groups she worked
with, was that vulnerability—the admission that one felt powerless
and unrepresented and all alone—was a gateway to organizing. Ask
any woman who found her way to a book group or an online voter
registration group, and she'll tell you that feeling isolated and unseen
was the key to finding a community.

The Leadership Conference gathered its allies again to oppose the
addition of an untested citizenship question to the 2020 census—a
question that was likely to significantly depress minority participation
in the census, which would, in turn, have resulted in fewer resources
and fewer congressional seats allocated to minority districts. Eventually, the US Supreme Court in June 2019 agreed that the question
could not be added to the census, but the litigation alone, the subject
of another chapter, wasn't the whole story. Gupta told me later that
while the lawsuits were raging, groups were at work behind the scenes.
"The litigation is just one piece," she told me. "Litigation is a tactic of
resistance. But in a much bigger way, it also required organizing people in the most vulnerable communities in the country and trying to

build a narrative about building the country we deserve, and to recognize that no community and no individual can be rendered invisible by their government."

As a journalist, I have covered many, many lawsuits, including those in this book. But we sometimes get so caught up in the drama of a courtroom that we miss the bigger shifts and trends. "Look, the media covers litigation," Gupta conceded to me. "And I believe in the importance of litigation, but I know firsthand that it isn't the thing that builds power. And to rely on doing whack-a-mole litigation case by case, without recognizing the importance of building a communications effort, and building an organizing effort, at the root of social change, I just think, has not served us well." Gupta was one of the first lawyers I interviewed who pointedly mentioned that after Trump seated more than two hundred lifetime-appointed judges to the federal bench and appointed what would turn out to be one-third of the current Supreme Court, the prospect of running to court was starting to look like a solution that came with new problems. That's why the composition of the courts themselves became the issue on which she fought harder than most.

Social justice advocates are historically extremely good, Gupta told me, at fighting on individual ideas. "We fight in silos," she explained, "we fight issues. We build campaigns around that." It meant they could win on climate and win on marriage equality and win on prison reform but somehow lose on democracy itself. For Gupta, the revelation of the years between 2016 and 2020 was that siloed campaigns were not sufficient. "As a leader," she told me, "I came in this moment, and we prioritized democracy, and for us that was the fair and accurate count in the census. It was voting rights. It was the courts. Because we see that without those institutions, and without really fighting for them, everything else that we care about basically falls." In the face of attacks on civil rights from the administration, civil rights lawyers were hyper-focused on lawsuits because they were good stories. But as the administration lost case after case, it became clear that entire systems needed repair. As Gupta told me bluntly at the time, "I find it incredibly frustrating when organizations are pouring money into issue-based fights that rely on the health of institutions and see the work of repairing those institutions as ugly, or political, or messy."

For decades, the Leadership Conference had reviewed and evaluated the records of judicial nominees, and throughout the Trump administration they had opposed just 13 percent of the nominees put forward. But because of the crucial role courts have played on questions of civil rights and rule of law, the Leadership Conference had prioritized a thorough review of Judge Brett Kavanaugh even before Dr. Christine Blasey Ford came forward with allegations that he had sexually assaulted her at a high school party. Groups allied with Gupta couldn't understand why the Leadership Conference was fighting over a nomination that couldn't be won. Indeed, many reproductive rights groups had determined to oppose placing Kavanaugh in Anthony Kennedy's seat simply because his record was so clearly opposed to those rights, as his tussle over migrant teens at the border had confirmed. As Ilyse Hogue, then at the helm of NARAL, would later tell Jennifer Rubin, even some progressive donors were skittish about opposing Kavanaugh. Without the Senate votes to scupper the nomination, why even fight? But fight they did, even before Dr. Ford came forward. And long after Kavanaugh was confirmed, Hogue would point to the women who organized to oppose him as a watershed moment. Women turned up. They were furious. As she later told Rubin, "Even in the face of a devastating loss, we had built something resilient. . . . Those women showed up again in the midterms and it proved to be a game changer."

A year after those hearings, Gupta co-wrote an op-ed with Fatima Goss Graves, president and CEO of the National Women's Law Center, reminding female voters that the energy women had brought to the Kavanaugh fight needed to fuel their opposition to the largely white, male, conservative judges who represented the bulk of Trump's judicial nominations. That organizing, that anger, the amassing of power, and, once again, the refusal to play nice and forget and just move along were the weapons in that larger fight.

The Kavanaugh nomination was a watershed moment for millions of women, and it became a template for raising understanding of institutions, including the federal judiciary, that don't surface as big issues and don't penetrate the public consciousness. I used to joke for years that when I wrote articles about the composition of the federal courts, only my dad read them. But that's not quite right. I don't think even he read them. The Kavanaugh confirmation was a lesson in why this rush to fill the courts mattered; that you could win every lawsuit but still lose the courts. For Gupta, "the success in filling these seats was galvanizing."

Of that day in 2018, when Dr. Ford testified about being assaulted, so many of us who sat in the hearing room felt something I have since heard from hundreds of women. They believed her. They saw her. And when Kavanaugh began to shout, they started to feel the prickling of genuine fear. Some sheathed violence or threat of it was in that room. And watching Dr. Ford testify, followed by Kavanaugh's angry response, changed everything, both because Brett Kavanaugh would take a seat on the Supreme Court as Trump followers chanted "Lock her up" about his accuser, and because we all saw something in that dynamic we had recognized in our own lives. The blue wave election in 2018 became the redemption. Yet still we kept hearing that it was energizing the Republican men in ways that would throw the midterm election.

Gupta took a lesson from all the pushback around Kavanaugh, she told me. "We were getting criticized for fighting. When actually, for women, that rage women felt, and the anger, had provable impact in activating women." In the end, she and other leaders decided that there was value in speaking out even among perceptions of inevitability. "There was so much energy among women that it wasn't in the power of any leader or organization to quell or direct. This was so much bigger than any single organization."

This is all, in a way, a refutation of the "Great Man" movie about legal change, in which one lone advocate moves mountains with a seminal lawsuit. But Gupta, who moved mountains in Tulia, Texas, instead focused on entrenched systems that don't grab headlines or buckle under even the most impactful lawsuits. Perhaps no more entrenched system exists than the machinery of voting, and one of Gupta's first priorities when she came to the Leadership Conference became just that. Long before Donald Trump the man began to insist that the 2020 election had been stolen from him, various states were trying to make it harder for people of color, the poor, students, and those who lived in cities to vote. They did so with a raft of gerrymanders, new voter-ID laws, and voter purges, all rooted in persistent false claims about vote fraud and illegal voting. Gupta presciently told me that the politicization of voting rights would become the next battleground. She testified in support of H.R. 1, which became the first bill passed when Democrats recaptured Congress in the blue wave of 2018. That bill is a set of comprehensive anticorruption, anti-vote-suppression, and pro-democracy reforms. In congressional testimony before the Judiciary Committee supporting that legislation in January 2019, Gupta noted that the Trump administration never filed a single Voting Rights Act case, but stood silently by in the face of myriad efforts to erect barriers to the ballot box for communities of color. She concluded her testimony by saying that "voting, and the ability to participate in democracy, is a racial justice issue. It is a civil rights issue." This, too, would become a defining issue around the 2020 election.

In the summer of 2020, after the killings of George Floyd and Ahmaud Arbery and Tony McDade, as Americans took to the streets to

protest racialized policing and vigilante law enforcement, Gupta worked
to help shape yet another major federal bill—the Justice in Policing
Act—testifying in both the House of Representatives and the Senate in
one week. When it comes to the types of changes she is seeking, Gupta
can be purposefully misread to sound like a radical. Senator Ted Cruz
(R-Tex.) tried to characterize her as seeking to "explicitly, unequivocally, with no wiggle room" support "abolishing the police," a claim
that has been debunked multiple times by FactCheck.org.

These accusations tend to come from some of the same people who
voted against certifying the presidential election results in January
2021 and who continued to parrot debunked claims about the election results. It's hard, bordering on impossible, to envision Gupta as
someone who seeks to destroy government institutions, but it's even
more absurd when it comes from those who actively participated in
just such an effort.

"There are some who think I'm a conservative because I still believe in the systems, but I do," Gupta insists. "I don't know what it
looks like to tear it all down. You can't just be resisting all the time.
You can't critique everything and have a dismantle paradigm without
offering some kind of forward-looking vision. . . . I'm a pragmatic
idealist. It's why I worked across the political spectrum when I was at
ACLU."

That's the paradox inside that greater paradox, and it helps explain why women were quick to take up the legal battles against
Trump. Gupta spent the bulk of her legal career making common
cause with police leadership, prison reformers, big business interests,
and other constituencies that seemingly had nothing in common.
That's why every major national law enforcement organization supported her nomination to be associate attorney general under Merrick Garland in 2021. Put aside the undisputed facts that she is a
woman of color descended from immigrant parents, and Gupta would
have emerged as one of the most small-c conservative reformers of

the Trump era, because, as she explained to me in an interview, the institutions of a democratic society are only as robust as our willingness to battle for them. "If everyone just becomes cynical, we lose. That's how we lose."

Gupta doesn't seek to prop up institutions merely so that they may serve the communities she cares about. She genuinely wants to restore public faith in first principles she echoes from Sally Yates: an independent Justice Department; a fair and accurate census; one person, one vote; and the rule of law. And that requires trust in the government. Part of the reason democracy is still under threat, she says, is apathy. "It is low voter turnout. It is the belief that government doesn't do enough and why trust a state that hasn't given us meaningful change in our lives?" It is why she once gently scolded me for writing that even after the challengers won big in the census case, Trump's DOJ would merely find another way to suppress minority participation in the census. In her speeches, Gupta warns frequently that "despair is the enemy of justice," and also that "a feeling of complacency is the enemy of justice." She says that in hard times, hope itself "is a discipline because you have to keep working every day. But yet, I also think that if we don't find hope as a discipline, it's a self-fulfilling problem." That, then, is the paradox for Gupta the organizer and the so-called radical. She believes in institutions and in slow reform from the inside out. "These institutions," she said, "have never worked for women and they have historically excluded women and people of color, but the struggle is to make them work."

The law is fundamentally both the cause of and the solution to women's equality battles in America. As Gupta put it, "If you come to the law with a certain premise or perspective, you understand that it's always been a source of oppression, but also why it's so important to be used to push for change and transformation in this country." Her career has straddled both sides of that paradox. "I started out as a criminal justice reformer, and I used the law to defend people who stood accused before the government," she explained. "And understanding that all of these things can be true at once, which is that you're using the system to seek change while recognizing the gross injustice of the system itself, that's a paradox I've become really comfortable with."

"Law," she conceded, "has often been a source of oppression, and yet civil rights advocates have relied on the rule of law to be able to end segregation, to be able to ensure integrated schools, to expand civil rights protections to vulnerable communities, and we have been fighting the fight for a long, long time, and it just didn't start in recent years." Making peace with the fact that these institutions of democracy "were never perfect so we're going to continue to fight for them while recognizing the inherent contradiction" requires, in her mind, that we "draw on this larger historical arc and situate all of us in something bigger."

For Gupta, straddling the line between working from within and without "is something I think I do every day; doing the inside-outside thing. I've always been an inside-outside player. And even when I was inside, I was an inside-outside player. I was an ACLU lawyer coming in to head up the Civil Rights Division, and there weren't that many people with my background on the inside." Even Gupta concedes that she can get "institutionalized." As she fights from within systems, she says, "I do recognize, now, the importance of being pushed and of big ideas, and it can be really uncomfortable, because there is a generational thing. I think young folks now have big ideas and they are tired of the status quo, but that's why you see organizing around voting rights and Dreamers, because they say, 'We don't care that it's always been like this.' And I love that. Because I succumb to the idea that 'you can't change that, people have tried and failed.'"

Women working to bolster institutions that have marginalized women for decades defies logic, right? But it was Gupta, years ago, who first reminded me that public faith in the institutions of democracy can be ephemeral, it can be shaken, and when it's lost, it cannot always be restored. "I think to wholesale dismiss institutions," she told me, "is to ignore the role they have in our lives and to hope that somebody else is going to take care of that. And just, I don't think we have that privilege."

One big shift she has seen in recent years was "women working on the inside too. That has produced a lot of change, and people of color becoming a part of these institutions and being seen as legitimate voices, pushing for change." Even if it was not evident to everyone, that made a difference, "if you only have people on the outside—that's an important role to play—but the reality is, you won't win just through outside agitation." In part because activist women have long been discouraged from being too wild, too hysterical, and too radical, working inside institutions gives some measure of cover. As she explained, "As women who are trained to express ourselves through the machinery of institutions, there's protocol and polite behavior that we are instructed to use, because otherwise, if we're screaming, people will just stop listening to us." It's unfair, sure. The double standard persists, she said, "and you cannot imagine a woman displaying that kind of behavior and having anyone listen to her."

"It's not *even* a double standard," Gupta added. "It's existing in different universes." Gupta and I both appeared on the same television show the night Dr. Ford testified. Years later, I still recall screwing on my game face to talk about it dispassionately, because that is what we do.

This is a book about women who sometimes occupy dual worlds, and Gupta's is a consummate story of being a huge success in American legal circles but never quite belonging. Her sense of being an outsider, not simply to American institutions, but to America itself, is uncomfortable but also galvanizing. It's no accident that so many of the defining legal challenges of the Trump years were to notions of citizenship, residency, access to the ballot, and belonging. This is the "othering" Gupta recalled as a lesson from her own childhood, because the years after 2016 required recalibrating basic issues of who belongs in the United States and who doesn't. It was, says Gupta, most fundamentally an era of "trying to redefine who deserves to be in this country and who is an American. It goes to the census, it goes to voting rights, it goes to the deliberate effort to change how districts are going to get drawn, who gets to be counted, who doesn't, who's inside, who isn't."

Gupta has spent her whole life on that seam, in the most personal ways. "I've had folks throw these taunts of 'go back to your home, you're not from here.'" What has been most painful about recent years, about the mainstreaming of white supremacy, and about efforts to overturn the 2020 election is just that, for her, that which was unimaginable became true, and "now we've seen what the failure of our imagination can yield." The work ahead is to shore up the institutions and democratic norms so that in the future they can protect those who have been most vulnerable. In her view "these are not abstract principles." This is about power and democracy itself.

Toni Morrison argues that the critical function of racism was always distraction. Racism "keeps you from doing your work," she has said. "It keeps you explaining, over and over again, your reason for being." Vanita Gupta refuses to allow the distractions of racism, misogyny, xenophobia, and nihilism to stand in the way of the work, her dream of large-scale structural reform that values invisible communities in full. If women plus law equals change, Gupta keeps proving, from the outside in and also from the inside out, then women plus law plus organizing equals power.

7

#MeToo

The Kozinski Accusers

I started law school in the fall of 1992, the year after Anita Hill testified about allegations of sexual harassment against then Supreme Court nominee Clarence Thomas, who had once been her supervisor at the Equal Employment Opportunity Commission (EEOC). I watched every minute of her testimony and of Judge Thomas's. Like so many other women, I applied to law school believing that an all-male Senate Judiciary Committee asking insulting and pornographic questions of a credible witness was not really America doing its finest work to resolve a factual employment dispute. The dialogue from that hearing doesn't age well. "You testified this morning," Senator Arlen Specter (R-Pa.) said, "that the most embarrassing question involved—this is not too bad—women's large breasts. That is a word we use all the time. That was the most embarrassing aspect of what Judge Thomas had said to you." Senator Howell Heflin (D-Ala.) offered this: "Now, in trying to determine whether you are telling falsehoods or not, I have got to determine what your motivation might be. Are you a scorned woman?"

I also watched what happened when the Judiciary Committee— controlled by Democrats and chaired by Joe Biden—elevated the Senate's clubby norms of "civility" and "decorum" over its obligation to unearth the truth. In 1992, I witnessed the so-called Year of the Woman that swept women into the Senate and onto congressional committees after Hill testified, which became another stutter step both toward and away from the project of eradicating harassment and bias in the government and in the law. I also started school that fall in the full knowledge that had Sandra Day O'Connor not already been seated at the Supreme Court, I probably would not have applied to law school at all. As one empirical study after another has shown, it's vital for young women and people of color to see other women and people of color in positions of authority in order to imagine someday seeking such jobs for themselves.

I graduated from law school in 1996. (I took off a semester in the middle to try to understand what I was doing there. I never quite figured it out.) I had never intended to clerk for a judge, but I was offered a last-minute opportunity to clerk for Procter R. Hug, then the chief judge of the US Court of Appeals for the Ninth Circuit. Judicial clerkships, especially on the federal appeals courts, were and still are pretty much the golden ticket in the world of post-law-school employment, the Super Bowl ring to an already lucrative and gratifying legal life. At the nation's elite law schools, these yearlong apprenticeships with judges can be the launchpad for a clerkship with an even *more* powerful judge and—if one plays one's cards just exactly right—a clerkship at the Supreme Court.

Once upon a time, law clerks were essentially just clerks— apprentice readers and opinion drafters for overworked judges. Today, clerking for a so-called feeder judge—the prominent appeals court judges who serve as the almost exclusive pipeline to Supreme Court clerkships—not only gets you in the door at the high court, it also affords access to the highest echelons of the legal academy and practice. The last time I checked, former Supreme Court law clerks were being offered a cool $400,000 signing bonus at tony DC law firms, following their year of clerking at the court.

But that's not all. Of the nine current justices at the Supreme Court, six of them—Brett Kavanaugh, Neil Gorsuch, Amy Coney Barrett, Elena Kagan, John Roberts, and Ketanji Brown Jackson—all clerked at the same court on which they sit today. It is no exaggeration to say that elite federal clerkships, right or wrong, are the coin of the realm at elite law schools, where the impulse to compete for absolutely anything just because there's a competition afoot can be particularly acute.

The lesson law clerks quickly internalize is that they can and should put up with just about anything, at least for a year. In my case, I learned to shut up about something for several decades.

ONE LEGENDARY FEEDER JUDGE was Alex Kozinski, the former chief judge of the West Coast–based Ninth Circuit Court of Appeals. From 2007 to 2017—just for instance—twelve out of the forty clerks for the former Supreme Court justice Anthony Kennedy had previously clerked for Kozinski. So successful was Kozinski in placing his former clerks in coveted seats at the high court that Brett Kavanaugh, who had clerked for Kozinski in 1991 and then later, at Kozinski's suggestion, for Anthony Kennedy at the Supreme Court in 1993, eventually secured a Supreme Court seat himself. Subsequent reporting by *The Washington Post*'s Ruth Marcus revealed that when Kennedy gave up his seat, he expressly asked Donald Trump to put Judge Kavanaugh into it. This of course is how powerful systems operate.

Over the course of several years, Kozinski and Kavanaugh were tasked with helping select clerks for Justice Kennedy. Heady stuff, to be a kingmaker at that level. You are quite literally picking once and future justices. It probably won't surprise you to learn that of the top feeder judges to the Supreme Court, virtually all are white men. It probably also won't surprise you to hear that male clerks outnumber female clerks two to one at that court and that—as of the most recent study, done in 2018 by the Supreme Court reporter Tony Mauro—"since 2005, 85% of all Supreme Court law clerks have been white." Women, representing 50 percent of law school graduates, still constitute a third of all Supreme Court clerks.

This, too, should surprise nobody. As of August 2019, 73 percent of all sitting federal judges were men.

Alex Kozinski was universally acknowledged as an enfant terrible of the federal appellate bench. He served for thirty-two years, having been appointed in 1985 by Ronald Reagan. Kozinski was born in Romania in 1950, left for the United States at twelve, and had a reputation on the courts as a big, colorful personality. He was appointed to the Ninth Circuit at the age of thirty-five, making him, at the time, the youngest appeals court judge since William Howard Taft. That record has changed: in late November 2020, the Senate confirmed a thirty-three-year-old woman to a lifetime appellate judgeship. The Trump nominee had taken part in only two one-day trials in her career, both conducted while she was an intern.

Ironically, because the same thing would happen to Kavanaugh, back in 1985, having just approved Kozinski's nomination, the Senate Judiciary Committee reopened his confirmation hearing after former Kozinski employees charged him with "sadistic" and "abusive" behavior. As with Kavanaugh, it went nowhere: Kozinski was confirmed to the Ninth Circuit nonetheless. Kozinski's charm is that he's a showman on a court built upon the fundamental principle that if everyone is wearing a black robe, nobody can differentiate one person from the next. As a federal appellate judge in 1996, Kozinski famously shared in *Slate* an account of visiting a Malibu pajama and lingerie party with his law clerk. In 2004, he sent a link to a video of himself bungee jumping in an email to *Underneath Their Robes,* an irreverent blog about the federal judiciary. Years before his elevation to the bench he'd appeared on the TV show *The Dating Game,* where he planted a massive surprise kiss on the contestant who picked him to be her date.

Kozinski's judicial opinions were also spectacular performance art. While universally acknowledged to be brilliantly written, they were readable, accessible, and edgy. In a Second Amendment opinion, he tartly observed that "it is wrong to use some constitutional provisions as springboards for major social change while treating others like senile relatives to be cooped up in a nursing home until they quit annoying us." In one famous appeal, over a trademark dispute between the toy company Mattel and the company that produced the 1997 song "Barbie Girl," Kozinski famously wrote that "the parties are advised to chill." And in a 2014 dissent, he raised the possibility of a return to the firing squad as a means of capital punishment, musing, "Sure, firing squads can be messy, but if we are willing to carry out executions, we should not shield ourselves from the reality that we are shedding human blood. If we, as a society, cannot stomach the splatter from an execution carried out by firing squad, then we shouldn't be carrying out executions at all."

And, as the charges raised at his 1985 hearing suggested, he was also a notoriously demanding boss. In a 2004 profile of the judge in *Legal Affairs,* the legal journalist Emily Bazelon wrote,

> The downside of clerking for Kozinski is that he owns you. The hours are 9:30 a.m. to 1:30 a.m., with Friday nights and some Saturday nights off. There have been clerks who have been chewed up and spit out by the pressure. "He goes around telling clerks 'You're the gold medal clerk, you're the silver medal, you're the bronze medal,'" one professor said. "You subordinate yourself to him and maybe he gets you to the Supreme Court. It's a Faustian bargain."

But even when he publicly and lustily went after a former Supreme Court clerk, Eddie Lazarus, for writing a tell-all Supreme Court book called *Closed Chambers*, or made appellate advocates cry in court, there seemed to be a tacit agreement on the federal bench that it was all just "Alex being Alex."

In 2001, Kozinski and another judge jerry-rigged an internet security system the federal courts had erected in the wake of a review of the court's use of bandwidth after it was determined that judges were downloading porn on government servers. Nearly 4 percent of the sites visited had included imagery of sexual abuse. The work-around allowed hackers to breach the court's security. The then director of the Administrative Office of the US Courts described the results as promoting "the unfettered ability of all judges and court employees to illegally download pornography and view it in federal courts."

It gets better. From 2007 to 2014, Kozinski served as chief judge of the Ninth Circuit. In 2008, Scott Glover of the *Los Angeles Times* revealed that the judge and his son had maintained a publicly accessible website that contained pornographic images and material. It included images of "naked women on all fours painted to look like cows and a video of a half-dressed man cavorting with a sexually aroused farm animal."

Kozinski told the *Los Angeles Times* he thought the video was "funny." He contended that the website was intended to be private and that various other people had contributed posts to it. Later that same year, Glover reported that Kozinski had maintained an email list to send out crude and dirty jokes and emails to former clerks, journalists, and lawyers. In 2009, after a lengthy internal judicial investigation requested by Judge Kozinski, an eleven-judge panel of the Judicial Council of the Third Circuit handed down its findings on Kozinski's alleged judicial misconduct. They declined to impose sanctions, determining that his "acknowledgment of responsibility together with other corrective action, his apology, and our admonishment, combined with

the public dissemination of this opinion, properly conclude this proceeding."

The formal review determined that Kozinski and his son had merely
been careless in allowing the private server to be publicly accessible on
the internet, that Kozinski didn't personally maintain it, and that he
had cured the problem by removing the explicit material. Kozinski testified that he "does not visit and has no interest in pornographic websites," according to the final report. As the investigative reporter Lise
Olsen pointed out in her 2021 book, *Code of Silence*, the Third Circuit
review lasted nine months, and "other than Kozinski himself, it wasn't
clear how many witnesses were interviewed." After he was cleared, the
Los Angeles–based attorney Cyrus Sanai, who had been complaining about the judge for years, wrote, "In a judicial misconduct proceeding brought by Alex Kozinski against Alex Kozinski, the sole witness
for the prosecution and defense was Alex Kozinski. Not surprisingly,
Alex Kozinski was largely vindicated."

In December 2017, two women, Heidi Bond and Emily Murphy,
and four other unnamed former clerks and externs of Kozinski's came
forward to Matt Zapotosky of *The Washington Post* alleging inappropriate sexual conduct and misconduct, including asking them to view
porn in his chambers. Bond, who had gone on to clerk at the Supreme
Court after she clerked for Kozinski on the Ninth Circuit in 2006,
had left the law to become a successful romance novelist, publishing
under the name Courtney Milan. The same day *The Washington Post*
reported her story, she posted her firsthand account to her own website. This is part of what she wrote about her clerkship in 2006–2007:

> "Heidi, honey," the Judge said one day, when he'd beeped me
> into his office alone, "you're the computer clerk. I need your
> opinion on something." . . . This time, the thing he needed an
> opinion on was a set of pictures. He pulled them up from
> where he had saved them—a private server, run by his son,

that he used as a massive external hard drive. Those pictures showed a handful of naked college-age people supposedly at a party where other people were clothed and drinking beer. In one of those photos, a man and a woman were sitting naked on a couch. "I don't think your co-clerks would be interested in this," he said. "Do you think this is photoshopped?" At the time, I didn't know what to say. I remember thinking that I didn't want to be there, not without my co-clerks. It would have felt entirely different if my co-clerks—both male—were present; it would have felt like I was being treated as one of the guys. . . . I remember feeling like the sounds of the cars passing were very loud. I remember wanting to be so small I could disappear. "Yes," I said. "It's photoshopped." "Does this kind of thing turn you on?" he asked.

Bond's account went on to recount multiple episodes in which the judge showed her porn, as well as his "knock chart," a "typed piece of paper listing all the girls that he and his friends had banged while they were in college." She recalled the ways in which Kozinski took control of her time, what she read, and then—having trashed her—demanded to know whether she still loved him.

It had been ten years, but for Bond, who had tried in vain to find some mechanism to report the misconduct to the federal judiciary, the trauma still lingered. On her blog that day, she wrote,

> If someone controls when you eat, when you sleep, what you dream, they control who you love, too. I said it and I told myself it was true, because it is easier to feel love than to tell yourself that you must lie for your own protection. It took me years afterward to understand that the relief I felt at the absence of pain was not love. It was not anything like love.

The other person willing to use her real name in that *Washington Post* article was Emily Murphy. She had just started clerking for a different judge on the Ninth Circuit in 2012 when, as she later told the *Post*, Kozinski "approached her when she was talking with a group of other clerks at a reception at a San Francisco hotel. The group had been discussing training regimens, and Murphy said she commented that the gym in the 9th Circuit courthouse was nice because other people were seldom there." According to Murphy and two others who corroborated her account, Kozinski said that "if that were the case, she should work out naked. Those in the group tried to change the subject, Murphy and the others present said, but the judge kept steering the conversation toward the idea of Murphy exercising without clothes." As Murphy said in the interview, "It wasn't just clear that he was imagining me naked, he was trying to invite other people—my professional colleagues—to do so as well. That was what was humiliating about it."

The other four women who spoke to the *Post* did not provide their names. One said the judge had asked her to watch porn in his chambers, but she never reported it for fear of retaliation. "I was afraid," the former clerk said. "I mean, who would I tell? Who do you even tell? Who do you go to?"

The night that story, and Heidi Bond's personal blog account, posted, I received it in a text from at least seven people. Most of them knew that I had kept my own secrets about the judge for two decades. My first impulse was to cry, which I did, and then I went out to dinner with my husband and sons. Then I waited for the famous judge to step down or apologize to the women who had come forward.

But that wasn't what happened. Kozinski's first public comment to *The Washington Post* was a blanket denial: "I have been a judge for 35 years and during that time have had over 500 employees in my chambers. I treat all of my employees as family and work very closely with

most of them. I would never intentionally do anything to offend anyone, and it is regrettable that a handful have been offended by something I may have said or done."

After the initial *Washington Post* story was published, Kozinski went
on the offense, telling the *Los Angeles Times*, "I don't remember ever
showing pornographic material to my clerks," then went further: "If
this is all they are able to dredge up after 35 years, I am not too worried." He finished with a set of disconnected thoughts meant to em-
barrass Bond. After she had left the legal profession, he said, Bond
sent him an email asking if he wanted an audio version of one of her
novels. Kozinski described it as a romance novel with one chapter con-
taining "very torrid sex." He told the *L.A. Times* he wished Heidi Bond
had said something to him if she was offended by his behavior, although he admitted that he had used "salty language" on occasion,
saying again that he treated his law clerks "like family."

Of course, Kozinski had no real reason to worry about these revelations. Federal judges serve for life once they are nominated and confirmed. They can be impeached for bad behavior, but extensive reviews,
including one undertaken in 2018 by CNN's Joan Biskupic, have ana-
lyzed the approximately five thousand judicial orders related to accusations of judicial misconduct and the results are maddening. "The judiciary
itself is hiding the depth of the problem of misconduct by judges," the
CNN survey concluded. Impeachment virtually never happens; thousands of complaints about judicial misconduct are never investigated or
resolved.

In the very worst circumstances, judges accused of misconduct are
allowed to step down voluntarily, at which point their investigations
are closed, but they continue to collect a lifetime pension. As Biskupic
put it in 2018, "The abuse women have suffered in the nation's courthouses has been a largely untold story. And its system for complaints—
where judges police fellow judges—is a world so closely controlled and
cloaked in secrecy that it defies public scrutiny." Headlines continue

to expose state and federal judges accused of abuse, harassment, and worse. Two sitting Supreme Court justices have been credibly accused of harassment and assault in episodes that have never been thoroughly investigated or adjudicated beyond background checks and a Senate hearing.

I spent that weekend after the first *Washington Post* story broke on the phone with two close friends, with whom I had shared my own stories about Judge Kozinski years earlier. I talked to my friend, the journalist Rebecca Traister, who had reported extensively on #MeToo at *New York* magazine. I talked to another former Kozinski clerk who lived near me in Brooklyn. Then I sent emails to the best email addresses I could find for Emily Murphy, who is a law professor now, and to Heidi Bond. My husband and I talked to my two sons, who were twelve and fourteen at the time, about what I should do. I no longer felt as though I could wait for someone else to step up.

What haunted me then, and what still haunts me, was the sense that if, in 1996, I had reported what I knew, Heidi Bond and Emily Murphy and the women who followed might never have had to endure what they did. (Emily Murphy, before going on the record with *The Washington Post*, wrote to the students in her contracts class at UC Hastings that she was coming forward based on her "professional obligation to do whatever I can to make the legal profession better for the next generation.") For years I told myself and a handful of friends that if Kozinski was ever elevated to the Supreme Court, that would be my time to come forward. That would be—we would learn—Christine Blasey Ford's calculus as well.

Over that weekend several other women reported, mostly via Twitter, on what was an open secret among federal judicial clerks: Kozinski was a well-known menace toward women, especially young ones. Joanna Grossman, now a law professor at Southern Methodist University, tweeted, "When I clerked on the Ninth Circuit, Kozinski sent a memo to all the judges suggesting that a rule prohibiting female attorneys from wearing push-up bras would be more effective than the newly convened Gender Bias Task Force. His disrespect for women is legendary." Alexandra Brodsky, a civil rights attorney, tweeted that as a student at Yale, "Everyone knew, and women didn't apply to clerk for Judge Kozinski despite his prestige and connections to the Supreme Court. I always felt the men who took their places were traitors." Nancy Rapoport, special counsel to the president of UNLV, wrote, "I view his statement to the *Los Angeles Times* as a challenge; hence, this post to add to the other voices." She said that when she was a clerk, Kozinski invited her to have drinks with him and his clerks, then showed up alone and asked her, "What do single girls in San Francisco do for sex?"

The piece I wrote about the judge for *Slate* was fact-checked multiple times over several days. My friends, two former co-clerks, and my husband all corroborated my account of what had happened years earlier. So did Richard Hasen, a law professor at UC Irvine, who had witnessed another awkward encounter between me and the judge at a conference only a few months earlier and had been so discomfited by it that he'd sought me out afterward.

My editors reached out to Judge Kozinski and to the Ninth Circuit for comment. These were the first lines of the story I published, five days after *The Washington Post* ran its first piece about Judge Kozinski:

> The first time I met Alex Kozinski was in 1996. I was clerking for the chief judge of the 9th U.S. Circuit Court of Appeals, and there was an orientation for new clerks in San Francisco. One of my co-clerks and I were introduced to the already legendary, lifetime-tenured young judge at a reception, and we talked for a while. I cannot recall what we talked about. I remember only feeling quite small and very dirty. Without my prompting, my former co-clerk described this interaction in an email to me this week. "He completely ignored me and ap-

peared to be undressing you with his eyes," he wrote. "I had never seen anyone ogle another person like that and still have not seen anything like it. Was so uncomfortable to watch, and I wasn't even the subject of the stare."

The first time I spoke to Judge Kozinski on the phone came weeks later, when I called his chambers late at night. Our judge had a sitting in the same city as Judge Kozinski, and I had made plans with one of Kozinski's then-clerks, an old college friend, to meet late at night for a drink. When I called his chambers, Judge Kozinski himself answered the phone. I introduced myself and asked to speak to his clerk, explaining that we had plans to meet up. The judge asked where I was. I said I was in my hotel room. Then he said, "What are you wearing?"

In the hours before my piece went live, I was preparing to deliver a keynote speech in Florida. I stood outside the entrance to an urgent care clinic, next to my hotel, reasonably convinced that I was experiencing a heart attack. I had managed over an almost twenty-year career in legal journalism to write with a kind of wry, dispassionate scrim between me and my subjects. I'd been allowed to meet Supreme Court justices and to attend fancy parties and had done my fair share of junkets and prestigious events, some of them sitting next to Judge Kozinski himself, largely because I understood the drill: men were men, "Alex was Alex," none of this was really harming anyone, and clerks needed to toughen up and live with it, even when it included sly jokes and lewd touching and looking at porn. I'd kept my own Kozinski story to myself for more than two decades, not just because I knew that drill and had benefited professionally from that drill, but because the very nature of "open secrets," it seems, is that everyone understands that keeping secrets is part of the bargain.

My older son took me by surprise the morning of my keynote/

urgent care/Florida episode as I debated whether to get an EKG or find the banquet hall I was scheduled to address. He's surely the less likely to get sentimental of my two sons, but he called on my cell just moments before the Kozinski article went live online as I hovered in the parking lot. "Mom," he said, "I just wanted to tell you that I know this is really hard for you, and I know you never like to be the story, but sometimes in order for other people to tell their stories, you really do have to tell yours."

I pulled it together and gave my speech. As audience members at the event learned that my story had just posted, someone asked how I was feeling. I parroted back the line I had once heard from Becca Heller: "I'm afraid I've just written the first line of my obituary."

The reaction to my piece was not precisely what I had intended. Twitter was briefly abuzz with the news that Dahlia Lithwick just #MeTooed Alex Kozinski. But that had never been my primary intention. My piece was about complicity and power and open secrets and bystanders. I was furious with myself and humiliated by my own willingness to cover for the bad behavior of powerful men, and I had done it to protect my own career.

I had watched the reporting that fall, around #MeToo and Harvey Weinstein and other untouchable men, and I understood the dynamic in which I had participated. In my article that day I had tried to write a long meditation on why virtually everybody I knew in the federal courts and in the legal academy and throughout the wide world of law clerks, so many of whom had known that this particular lifetime appointee was wildly sexually inappropriate, never said or did anything. It was, for me, a story about secrets and authority and silence. It was also a story about perfectly closed power systems in which there are no opportunities for redress and only terrible professional consequences for speaking out. I found myself thinking about how I'd failed both Bond and Murphy that night when I wrote,

I am also thinking about those who opted not to apply for clerkships with him, sidestepping an opportunity to get within close range of a coveted Supreme Court clerkship. Like others who have now come forward, I had told young female law students absolutely not to clerk for him. I am thinking about the hundreds of plaintiffs in the discrimination and harassment suits he heard in the years he was on the bench. I am thinking of all the ways in which "open secrets" become their own spheres of truth, in which the idea that "everybody knew" something awful absolved all of us of the burden of doing anything. The former Kozinski and 9th Circuit clerks I've spoken to in recent days feel heartsick, as I do, that for the sake of our own careers and professional legitimacy we continued to go to the dinners and moderate the panels, all the while hoping this story would break someday and we'd be off the hook.

Everybody knew, I wrote, and I still believe that to be true. But I didn't blame them the way I blamed myself for my own moral cowardice:

This story really shouldn't be about me. I never worked for Kozinski, and even though his behavior affected me, my future never depended on him. But here is the part that does implicate me: When a prominent journalist with a national platform chooses—year after year—not to report on an open secret, or agrees to slouch through yet another dinner or panel or cocktail party, how can it only be about the victims and the harassers? Because really, if you can't tell a man to back off when you're 50 and at the peak of your journalistic power, who is ever going to do it? Back in the '90s, it was too early to report what I knew, what we all knew. And now it is too late.

As my friend Rebecca Traister has put it, "the stink got on me anyway. I was implicated. We all are, our professional contributions weighed on scales of fuckability and willingness to go along, to be good sports, to not be humorless scolds or office gorgons."

In the days following its publication, I was the beneficiary of a tsunami of support, largely building on what my son had said to me first: This was painful, but necessary. I got kind notes from judges on the Ninth Circuit and from academic friends in law schools. Robbie Kaplan and Karen Dunn, working on the early days of the Charlottesville Nazi litigation, both offered to represent any of the Kozinski victims pro bono after it was announced that he had retained Susan Estrich as counsel.

Within a few short days of my own piece, nine *more* women came forward to *The Washington Post*'s Matt Zapotosky, bringing the total number of women alleging inappropriate sexual behavior to at least fifteen. One had been a law student in 2016 when the judge deliberately touched her breast, purporting to be pushing a lapel to see a name tag. Another, Christine O. C. Miller, a former US Court of Federal Claims judge, said Kozinski had "grabbed and squeezed each of her breasts as the two drove back from an event in Baltimore in the mid-1980s."

Leah Litman, then a law professor at the University of California at Irvine, came forward in that follow-up story in *The Washington Post*. She opted to use her name when she realized that most of the accusers had remained anonymous. She described being at a dinner before a July panel at which "Kozinski talked of having just had sex and pinched her side and her leg, just above the knee, with his thumb and middle finger." Litman would later describe to the investigative reporter Lise Olsen that he had been "rubbing his hand on her bare knee, under the table, while describing how he kept *Playboy* in his chambers so his clerks could learn to write well." A former Kozinski clerk told the *Post* that Kozinski, in chambers, showed her an "open-legged image of a male figure that was naked." Every one of those reports was corroborated by contemporaneous witnesses or people who had been told.

Nobody had done anything because nobody had believed that anything would or could change.

An investigation was promptly opened into Kozinski's behavior, and all three of his clerks for that year abruptly quit without public comment, leaving the judge without staff. Susan Estrich, Kozinski's lawyer, released a new statement in which he said, "Many of the things that are being said about me are simply not true, but I deeply regret that my unusual sense of humor caused offense or made anyone uncomfortable. I have always treated my male and female law clerks the same."

Judge Kozinski stepped down on December 18, 2017, just ten days after the initial reports had surfaced. "I cannot be an effective judge and simultaneously fight this battle," Kozinski, then sixty-seven, said in a statement distributed by the Ninth Circuit Court of Appeals. "Nor would such a battle be good for my beloved federal judiciary." He added the closest thing he had ever offered to an apology. "I've always had a broad sense of humor and a candid way of speaking to both male and female law clerks alike," he wrote. "In doing so, I may not have been mindful enough of the special challenges and pressures that women face in the workplace. It grieves me to learn that I caused any of my clerks to feel uncomfortable; this was never my intent. For this I sincerely apologize." The apology encompassed only his own former clerks, not Litman, Murphy, Grossman, myself, or most of the other accusers. The apology suggested that it was okay to show explicit porn to law clerks, as long as you treated the males and females "alike."

The Second Circuit Judicial Council announced that it would not continue its investigation. Because the judge had now stepped down, it lacked "authority to do anything more." By statute the machinery of judicial misconduct review does not apply to former judges. That meant there would never be a factual record or conclusive findings about whether the allegations were true. As Lise Olsen later reported, the complaint against Kozinski was dismissed in February 2018, in an order that made it clear no investigation had taken place.

TWO PROBLEMS CONTINUED TO BE confounding in the months and years that followed this episode, both of which have changed the way I think about sexual impropriety in the workplace. Redemption was the first. A prominent California attorney at a private law firm, Kathy Ku, was another of Kozinski's former clerks who had been shown porn and belittled. She, too, had risked her professional reputation—she practiced in the federal courts—to come forward. Ku wrote in *The Washington Post* in January 2018, a few weeks after Kozinski's resignation, "With his immediate retirement, it appears that he has essentially shut down the federal judiciary's investigation of his conduct and deflected further revelations in the press. That allows him to disappear, quietly receiving his pension, until the outrage dies down. It allows him a greater chance at redemption." Ku, a superb lawyer who was thinking in terms of legal processes and investigations, cautioned that "in a few years, we may see an attempt at quiet reemergence—not on the federal bench, but perhaps through a law school teaching appointment or in the realm of private dispute resolution."

She was right. Within six months, Kozinski was writing editorials and giving radio interviews in which nobody in an editorial position saw fit to mention that he wasn't just a "retired" federal judge. In 2018, he published a tribute to Justice Anthony Kennedy on his retirement. He was back before his own court as an advocate soon after.

That leads us to the second problem: the complete absence of factual determination of what actually happened. Because there had been no formal adjudication of any of the claims, when Leah Litman, Emily Murphy, and Kathy Ku, in cooperation with other victims and advocates, went to write an op-ed in *The New York Times*, complaining that there had been no reckoning and that it was not yet time for the triumphant comeback that seems to follow every harasser, the editors made them change the language. Even though more than fifteen women had "alleged" sexual misconduct, it had never been proven, so "alleged" it remained. As Litman, Murphy, Ku, and other complainants noted in their op-ed, the other vexing problem was the complicity of bystanders: "Sexual harassment often persists because third parties are silently complicit in it. #MeToo requires some retrospection from people who are not harassers themselves."

Kathy Ku had also tackled the problem of bystanders who failed to come forward in her own *Washington Post* article, noting that without any formal findings it was not only the harasser who was let off the hook but also every single witness. "In the absence of an official inquiry," she wrote, "few additional targets of, or witnesses to, Kozinski's transgressions are likely to speak publicly. They may not want to be seen as piling on. They may think that the moment to speak is over. Or they may have concerns about repercussions in their careers."

As seems to have been the pattern, the lion's share of the responsibility fell on the handful of women who risked professional and reputational harms in speaking out first. "In writing this piece," warned Ku, "I'm the first and only former Kozinski clerk still in private practice to go on the record, by name, with allegations against the judge. And it's not something I do eagerly. The pressures to remain silent can be overwhelming."

One of the enduring lessons several years later is about who bears the heaviest burden of telling the truth and why so many do it alone. I believe there were literally hundreds of people who knew about Judge Kozinski. Some of them still seek me out at speeches, years later, to confirm—off the record—what they knew. In the earliest days of the reporting, only one man stepped forward to put his own name in the record. UC Irvine's Richard Hasen was one of the few men who would come to publicly corroborate both my story and Leah Litman's. One of Heidi Bond's co-clerks tweeted a sentence about how her story explained how miserable she had been throughout the clerkship. Others retweeted her story without comment. I received literally dozens of emails from women and men in the days and weeks after my piece was published, saying, "Of course we all knew about Kozinski." Virtually none of them ever went on the record. Many wished to thank the original accusers for going public—jeopardizing their own academic or legal careers—so that nobody else would have to.

In the wake of the revelations about Alex Kozinski, Chief Justice John Roberts noted in his 2017 year-end report on the state of the judiciary, that "recent months have illuminated the depth of the problem of sexual harassment in the workplace, and events in the past few weeks have made clear that the judicial branch is not immune." He ordered the judiciary to conduct "a careful evaluation of whether its standards of conduct and its procedures for investigating and correcting inappropriate behavior are adequate to ensure an exemplary workplace for every judge and every court employee."

Following extensive review, the federal judiciary amended its Code of Conduct to include in its definition of misconduct engaging in "unwanted, offensive, or abusive sexual conduct." The courts added more training and streamlined reporting of misconduct, but most of the critics who have spent years trying to reform the judicial branch felt the solutions were patchy and insufficient. The problem transcends reporting and discipline. It demands huge shifts in the way we think about power, secrecy, and loyalty.

It also demands consistency. Senator Chuck Grassley, the Iowa Republican who chaired the Judiciary Committee at the time, held a hearing in June 2018 in which he celebrated Heidi Bond and Emily Murphy for their bravery, denounced Kozinski's conduct, and faulted the judiciary's working group report for "kicking the can down the road." A few months later, Grassley would chair the confirmation hearings for the former Kozinski clerk and advisor Brett Kavanaugh.

Of course, when Judge Brett Kavanaugh was asked during his confirmation process about his close association with Kozinski, he denied witnessing or even knowing about any improper behavior. The legal journalist Irin Carmon, writing in September 2018, summarized the professional ties between the two men:

> Until recently, the two were part of an elite group that preinterviewed law students for clerkships with Justice Anthony Kennedy, whom Kavanaugh seeks to replace. The two men sat on panels together; on one at the Federalist Society, *Politico* reported, Kavanaugh "praised a 1991 article Kozinski wrote about judicial clerkship selection, titled 'Confessions of a Bad Apple.'" He even hired Kozinski's son to clerk for him. Bill Burck, the lawyer who is charged with deciding which of Kavanaugh's documents get publicly released, is a former Kozinski clerk who represented the judge after the accusations.

Reporting revealed that Kavanaugh had phoned Kozinski when the stories about him first surfaced, because he was worried about the judge's mental health. At Kavanaugh's confirmation hearing in September 2018, Senator Orrin Hatch of Utah asked him about the listserv of friends, former law clerks, colleagues, and journalists to whom Kozinski had for years distributed crude material. Kavanaugh told Hatch, "I don't remember anything like that, Senator." Hatch then asked, "Did you know anything about these allegations?" "Nothing." "OK. Before they became public last year?" "No. . . . It was a gut punch for me."

It was hard to believe. Senator Mazie Hirono of Hawaii tried to understand how Kavanaugh could have known absolutely nothing about the open secret around his mentor. His response was to deflect, insisting that the judges who worked in California should have been the whistle-blowers. "No, Senator," Kavanaugh said emphatically. "And I worked in Washington, DC. There were 10 judges in the courthouse with him in Pasadena, prominent federal judges in the courthouse with him. Who worked side by side with him day after day while he was Chief Judge in the Ninth Circuit."

That was of course correct, but also wholly unresponsive. Hirono pressed again: "To be clear, while this kind of behavior on the part of Judge Kozinski was going on for 30 years—it was an open secret—you saw nothing, you heard nothing, and you obviously said nothing. Judge Kavanaugh, do you believe the women who recently came forward to accuse Judge Kozinski of this kind of behavior?" Kavanaugh's reply: "I have no reason not to believe them, Senator."

What does it mean, to claim to believe women and yet despite a years-long relationship with the accused claim ignorance of what is widely known? In February 2020, just weeks before the country locked down for the coronavirus pandemic, Olivia Warren, who had clerked for one of Kozinski's closest friends, Stephen R. Reinhardt, a civil rights legend on the Ninth Circuit who died in 2018, testified before a congressional committee that Reinhardt "routinely and frequently" sexually harassed her and other female clerks. Over the course of her clerkship, which lasted from 2017 to 2018, Reinhardt—a prominent feeder judge for liberal Supreme Court justices—would, among other things, speculate—sometimes in front of other employees—that Warren's husband "must either lack a penis, or not be able to get an erection," because she was so unattractive. As she testified under oath, "There may have been a day in which I was not harassed. But I cannot remember one after searching my memory."

Like Bond, Warren testified that she felt impelled to keep her experience secret because she was "scared of offending the judge and alienating his powerful network of clerks, scared of ending my legal career before it had even begun, scared that the judge would exact revenge on me." And like Bond, she couldn't manage to figure out how to file a complaint, or whom to tell, in the federal judicial machinery, although she did report to members of the Harvard Law School administration, where she had graduated. Leah Litman, one of the Kozinski accusers from 2017 and now an assistant professor at the University of Michigan Law School, corroborated one part of Warren's testimony on Twitter, acknowledging that Judge Reinhardt had publicly confronted and insulted her about her accusations against his dear friend Kozinski.

Litman, who has become one of the most powerful voices demanding change and accountability both in the legal profession and on the judiciary, confirmed on Twitter that while many former Reinhardt clerks would later express support for Warren, the number of people who would confirm it would be minimal. That proved true. A letter signed by more than seventy former Reinhardt clerks affirmed both that the signatories "believe the clerk's testimony" and that some of them "experienced or witnessed conduct in chambers that we would call sexist, workplace bullying or mistreatment," and others did not, but that most were "shocked" by Warren's allegations.

But being told you are believed and also that nobody plans to do anything about it is not justice. Christine Blasey Ford, in a 2021 podcast with Anita Hill, disputed the utility of telling victims of sexual harassment and abuse that you "believe" them. As she explained, when you tell someone your name, the correct response isn't usually "I believe you." Presumably, the reason we constructed a legal system is so that whether or not we "believe" someone is not the relevant inquiry.

"Even though a lot of people on Twitter will express support for you when you come forward with an accusation like this, a lot of people—including very powerful and admired people—will be angry with you," Leah Litman tweeted, after Warren testified. "They will demean you and undermine you in ways you can see and ways you cannot. That is part of why it is not fair to say it is the responsibility of the person who is subject to harassment to do something about it."

I testified alongside Warren at that House Judiciary Committee hearing in 2020, meeting her for the first time that morning. I knew nothing specific about the Reinhardt claims—although I had heard clerks allude to sexism and bullying about him for years—but I wanted to support Liv Warren, and also to try to make the point I had tried to make two years earlier about the need for reform in the judicial system. My testimony amplified what I had written in 2017:

> Rightly or wrongly, the legal profession is among the most conservative and risk-averse of any modern profession, and the impulse to look away, downplay, secret-keep, and justify is stronger among attorneys than any group I know. In addition to helping judges figure out how best to police themselves, we need to create a culture of bystanders willing to step up and report abuse, and to defend victims, even if at some personal and professional cost. We entrust the judicial branch with the sole power and authority to adjudicate complicated matters every day; finding out what has happened in a given chambers and why should not be an impossible task. The only cure I know for "open secrets" and suggestions that young lawyers might benefit from abusive hazing is transparency and sunlight. The alternative—whisper campaigns and summary dismissals—doesn't only hurt individual victims, but also slowly undermines the judiciary as a whole.

I first met Judge Reinhardt in person at a conference early in the first decade of the twenty-first century in Washington, DC, where we were both speaking. He stepped into an elevator with me and my toddler son, and when the judge asked my son's name, he said, "Jack" (which is not his real name). So Judge Reinhardt called my son Jack all weekend, and I didn't correct him. *That's* how difficult it is to talk back to a federal judge with a lifetime appointment. Just as Liv Warren was crushed that her former judge's comments about her attractiveness and her husband's anatomy were now preserved forever in the *Congressional Record* of 2020, I was of course mortified to learn that her testimony included Judge Reinhardt's snarking to his assembled law clerks, after I wrote about Judge Kozinski, "No one has ever ogled Dahlia Lithwick."

Nobody wants to be adjudicated a silly, ugly little girl in the pages of the *Congressional Record,* and certainly not by a lion of the progressive legal movement who had only ever been kind to me. But as Warren explained in a law review article published in 2021, this endless, exhausting work of bearing witness is at least theoretically important because "there is virtue in screaming into the face of deafening indifference, if only because the sound of my voice reminds me that I have not yet succumbed to it."

Leah Litman and Deeva Shah, both of whom have dedicated years of their professional lives to understanding #MeToo in the judiciary, wrote a law review article in 2020 in which they argued that the entire legal profession needs to take individual responsibility for sexual harassment in the courts. This would, they wrote, require a massive shift across the legal academy and law firms and among attorneys. In the face of collective silence and tacit relief that others have spoken up, Litman and Shah argued,

> When we delegate the issue of harassment to a small number of committed individuals, we also force those individuals into a box. They become people who are known or expected to speak out about harassment, which minimizes the force of their statements. That identity minimizes their work in other areas, since they become known as individuals focused on harassment and workplace misconduct, rather than for their other professional accomplishments.

Like so many of the women mentioned in this chapter, I find myself called on routinely to brief judges, law students, lawmakers, lawyers' groups, and women's groups about how #MeToo has both succeeded and failed in the federal judiciary. I sometimes note ruefully that I may major in the law and the courts, but I have come to minor in #MeToo. The women in this chapter have become friends and advisors and sounding boards, but all of them would likely tell you that all of this extracurricular, unpaid work takes time and energy and focus from their own career advancement and their families and their personal goals.

And unerringly, at almost every speech and panel, someone in the audience sidles up to whisper a story about a judge who abused clerks, or staff, or court personnel, and when I ask them to put it on the record, they demur. As Litman and Shah noted, the people who have done the most rigorous and systemic thinking about the culture of silence in the legal profession are law students, who have their own careers and plans to which they should be attending. And as the two conclude,

> Problems of collective action are notoriously difficult to solve. If everyone has some stake in the problem, then the affected, interested group is so large that it can be difficult to coordinate that group to do anything. A large group may also limit individual group members' feelings of personal responsibility. If everyone is part of or contributes to a problem, then our own role may seem insignificant, which makes it easier for us to sit on the sidelines. But that means harassment will continue.

As VANITA GUPTA NOTED, it borders on impossible to rely on the very same justice system that has caused so much inequality to also remedy it. By the same token it seems too fanciful to hope that a judicial branch that has turned a blind eye to abuse in its ranks can either cure itself or provide just rulings for women.

And yet with few exceptions, it's been women lawyers, academics, and judges who have dedicated years to trying to reform the judicial system. It has probably not escaped your notice by now that while women lawyers were at the forefront of beating back Trumpism, they were almost alone in their attempts to root out sexual harassment and abuse in the judiciary. If women are going to use the law to make change, they require equal access to opportunities for clerkships, judgeships, and power. And if women are virtually alone in reforming the legal system, it appears, yet again, that they are still doing service work while men are advancing.

Anita Hill has been talking about the need for systemic reforms, process reforms, and broad cultural reforms since her own experience before the Judiciary Committee in 1991. She has no illusions that a handful of high-profile cases will change workplaces in which most predators operate with impunity and most accusers remain too terrified to speak up. "What we want to make sure is that it doesn't stop with just a few high-profile cases," she told NPR in September 2020, when a broad survey of the entertainment industry revealed that 64 percent of those surveyed did not believe that a person who was found to have harassed a subordinate would be held accountable. "We know that there are problems throughout workplaces, and we want to make sure that everybody, whatever their position is, can count on being heard," she added. Hill's focus has always been lawyerly and sweeping: entire processes need to change, and the role of bystanders must change, before any one system can begin to fix itself.

This is why the voice that echoes in my head throughout every new cycle of #MeToo is that of the journalist Irin Carmon, who was accepting a Mirror Award in 2018, bestowed by the Newhouse School at Syracuse University on reporters investigating sexual misconduct. Carmon was being honored alongside the *Washington Post* reporter

Amy Brittain for their piece on the television host Charlie Rose's conduct at CBS and that network's plodding and ineffectual response. At New York's Cipriani 42nd Street, in a roomful of journalists, lawyers, pundits, and CBS employees, Carmon told the assembled crowd,

> There's a temptation to think the last few months have been about individual men, that it was about a handful of bad apples and if we get rid of them it will end the cycle of harassment and abuse. But it's not true. The stories that we have been doing are about a system. The system has lawyers and a good reputation. It has publicists. It has a perfectly reasonable explanation about what happened. It has powerful friends that will ask if it's really worth ruining the career of a good man based on what one woman says, what four women say, what 35 women say. Indeed, the system is sitting in this room. Some more than others. The system is still powerful men getting stories killed that I believe will one day see the light of day.

I learned from Heidi Bond, Emily Murphy, and the other #MeToo accusers that a system of justice is only really as robust as one's ability to access it. Bond spent years trying to figure out how to bring a harassment complaint before the federal judiciary, questioning her own commitments to judge/clerk secrecy and circumnavigating the byzantine reporting rules. Similarly, Liv Warren couldn't find a channel to report what she knew, what everyone who worked with her knew. In their October 2021 podcast together, as part of the series *Because of Anita*, Christine Blasey Ford and Anita Hill tried to explain how intolerable it is to want to bring information—Dr. Ford called it "data"—to a system that has no mechanism with which to receive it. In the end, Ford brought her complaint about Brett Kavanaugh to her own member of Congress. But even then, she was subject to disbelief and disdain for somehow reporting it in the wrong way.

If even women like Bond, like Anita Hill, and like myself, who understand the shape of the legal system, can't always find the front door, there is something wrong that transcends formal equality. Systems, including legal systems, cannot change if they have been set up to thwart change and if they allow men to rocket from the outside to the inside by way of secret dirty email threads, advancement opportunities, and a vault in which "open secrets" can go to die. So many women who believed that the United States had achieved a measure of equality by 2016 quickly came to understand that if you can't even access the system, you cannot begin to repair it, and maybe that is why no book about women and the law should confine itself to the rock-star litigators and advocates and organizers. In one sense, women, nonbinary people, and other minorities are still on the outside looking in.

Their work is as essential as it is often invisible.

ONE CODA TO MY OWN experience in both writing about and reporting out the misconduct allegations around Kozinski in 2017: in the days after I wrote my article, and immediately after a host of other accusers came forward and Judge Kozinski stepped down, I lived in fear of being bankrupted or run out of journalism, and even of personal threats of retribution. The internet, as you might have heard, is unkind. I imagined sources in the judiciary, colleagues in the press, former clerks, all melting away from me. In those days, I was in near-daily phone contact with the first two Kozinski accusers who had gone on the record: Emily Murphy and Heidi Bond. We were all feeling raw, and exposed, and collectively couldn't shake the sense that we were indeed living out those first lines of our respective obituaries. I had received a kind email from Anita Hill, and I asked Emily and Heidi whether it would be helpful to try to wrangle a conference call with her. Professor Hill agreed immediately. So I arranged a call between Emily in San Francisco, Heidi in Colorado, Professor Hill from her office at Brandeis University, and myself at the magazine's bureau in Brooklyn.

At the last minute I asked my then fourteen-year-old son—who had been my ballast when I was having my wholly fanciful cardiac event only the week before—to come sit with me in our *Slate* conference room. I had shown him the footage, from twenty-six years earlier, of Professor Hill's testimony before the Senate Judiciary Committee. He was uncharacteristically quiet. After Heidi, Emily, and Professor Hill had all dialed into the call, I asked if it was okay if my son listened in and explained that he, too, had had a hard, sad week and that he had been my lifeline on what had felt like my very worst day.

Professor Hill asked me to put him on the line for a moment, and I did. He leaned into the speakerphone, and she thanked him and told him she genuinely believed young men like him would someday make a difference. I cried because I have literally no choice but to believe that is true.

#HerToo

—————

Christine Blasey Ford
and Anita Hill

When I first started covering the US Supreme Court, it was 1999 and I had never been inside the building. Most of the daily press corps have a somewhat obstructed view of the nine justices, and on crowded days, the reporters in the back rows have no view at all. Eventually, one developed keen voice recognition skills, but in the big-ticket cases, you relied on someone from the press office who would flash the number of fingers corresponding to the seniority of whichever justice was speaking. "Four fingers! Four! Scalia!" Until fairly recently, like 2004, if you perused an oral argument transcript, the name of the justice speaking went unmentioned; the transcript used "Question" interchangeably for every member. The justices are, after all, fungible and oracular, nine brains in a vat of constitutional understanding, mechanically calling balls and strikes.

The whole media setup at SCOTUS was always slightly ludicrous: reporters are prohibited from recording the oral arguments; we were permitted to take one pen and one notepad into the chamber. (My favorite true story was the time the federal marshal took my copy of Kafka's *The Trial* from me as I entered the room, my patient explanation of "irony" having fallen on deaf ears.) Everything about the way we covered the court felt feudal to me: the byzantine accreditation rules for the media; the way we were marched into the chamber and then seated in rows in the precise order of prestige and importance (at my peak I was the seventeenth most important Supreme Court correspondent in the room). The justices almost never gave interviews, and the Public Information Office appeared largely to exist in order to say no to interview requests. Unlike other government institutions, the arrangement is respectful and deferential, and press coverage inclines to courtly reverence and scholarly explication of doctrine. Even with all the beholdenness and the Patty Hearst syndrome, I always knew from day one that I had the best job in journalism.

This is the story about why in 2018 I quit the court, and it, too, has a place in a book about women and the law. For years I told people the Supreme Court press corps featured so many prizewinning female journalists because it was an ideal beat for women. The corps is unfailingly well prepared, steeped in case law, and—as I have remarked more than once—tends to cover the institution as though the Constitution were alive and the justices were dead. No gossip, no opinion, no muckraking. That was the province of the political reporters and bloggers outside the building. Supreme Court reporters largely had evenings and weekends and summers, unless a justice died, which is good for work-life arrangements, and this is, for the most part, not a beat that demands clawing through dumpsters for scoops or meeting with sunglasses-wearing sources in grimy DC bars. We covered affirmative action, abortion, and voting and gun rights. The justices were incidental to all that. In many ways, then, we in the press corps colluded a bit with the members of the high court to tell the story of a prophetic and nonpartisan court that neutrally "applied the law" using scientific interpretive principles.

I was lucky enough to be in the room for oral arguments in *Bush v. Gore* and to have a front-row seat—not really, I was after all ranked seventeenth—to historic arguments and decision announcements in seminal cases like *Obergefell v. Hodges*, finding a right to marriage equality in the Constitution, and *District of Columbia v. Heller*, finding a right to own firearms in the home. I groused at what I believed to be some of the "bad" decisions—like *Heller*—and I celebrated the "good" ones, like the 2016 abortion case, *Whole Woman's Health*. But even if I always understood that the court could be partisan, and ideological and political, I never doubted that it was in fact a court. I write this knowing that I began to cover the court only a few years after a television audience of more than twenty million had watched as Anita Hill, a young Black law professor, testified before the Senate Judiciary Committee about sexual harassment she said she experienced while working for the nominee Clarence Thomas at the Equal Employment Opportunity Commission. For one generation of women, after that point the court had already stopped being a court.

The Thomas hearings left an indelible impression on me, as they did on millions of us. It's part of why I went to law school. Thomas famously and furiously denied Hill's meticulous claims, characterizing the entire process as a "high-tech lynching for uppity blacks." By the time I started to cover the court, Thomas had gone famously silent throughout oral arguments and was writing lone dissents that put him further to the ideological right than even Justice Antonin Scalia, the court's conservative firebrand. At that time, Thomas was dissenting alone, with a coherent if radical view of race, gender, criminal law, and the role of government. Thirty years later, Thomas still sits on the US Supreme Court, and his ideas are ascendant. It is no exaggeration to say that, effective 2022, this is the Clarence Thomas Court. Thirty years later, Professor Hill teaches social policy, law, and gender, sexuality, and women's studies at Brandeis University. People like to say that they believed her all along.

Watching Joe Biden secure the presidency in 2020 was complicated for a lot of American women, in no small part because of what had happened, on his watch, to Anita Hill back in 1991. As Jill Abramson and Jane Mayer reported expansively in their 1994 book, *Strange Justice*, the then senator Biden controlled the process of the Clarence Thomas hearings in the Senate Judiciary Committee, and for millions of women who watched those hearings play out, that process was clearly flawed and indeed abusive. Republican members of the Senate set out to trash and discredit Hill. Senator Alan Simpson, a Republican from Wyoming, ranting about "this sexual harassment crap," ominously threatened, "I really am getting stuff over the transom about Professor Hill. . . . I've got letters hanging out of my pocket. I've got faxes. I've got statements from Tulsa saying: 'Watch out for this woman.'" Orrin Hatch, the Republican senator from Utah, portrayed her as a sexual deviant who had lifted scenes from *The Exorcist* to produce false claims about Thomas. Hatch also insisted that anyone who could produce allegations "so graphic and so crude and so outrageous" as Hill's was "not a person" but a "psychopathic sex fiend or pervert."

It all had the desired effect. Polls taken at the time showed that after the hearings only 29 percent of Americans believed Hill, because the prevailing sense was that if her charges were true, she should have made them back when the alleged sexual harassment happened. But when the "Year of the Woman" that followed pushed women into Congress and onto the Judiciary Committee, public opinion started to change around an employment problem that nobody had quite understood, much less named. We started to think differently about work and power and reporting and why we don't report. And for many American women, the Anita Hill testimony came to stand as a quasi-

legal, faux-neutral process of fact-finding that was itself the mechanism for further abuse. Powerful men had created a powerful system
that looked as if it were ferreting out truth but was instead destroying
a woman's life and reputation while making no effort to reach reasoned conclusions.

Biden's Democratic colleagues in the Senate later confirmed to
Abramson and Mayer that he had been flat-out outgunned and out-
maneuvered by Senate Republicans waging scorched-earth warfare.
Biden, an institutionalist and lifelong believer in bipartisanship and
due process, had struggled to be fair to both sides. Cynthia Hogan,
one of the lawyers on Biden's Senate staff during the confirmation
hearings, later told *The Washington Post*, "We got really politically out-
played by the Republicans. . . . They came with a purpose, and that
purpose was to destroy Anita Hill." Exhaustive reporting eventually
revealed that the process Biden had put in place was inadequate and
that it failed Hill entirely. As Elise Viebeck concluded in *The Washington Post* in 2019, "Biden failed to use the powers afforded to Senate
committee chairmen to conduct a judicious and thorough inquiry into
Hill's allegations. He did not give full consideration to witnesses whose
allegations seemed to corroborate her testimony or curb the attacks
and innuendo leveled at her during the hearing." Three other women
were standing by to testify with stories similar to Hill's, but they were
never called. They were allowed only to submit depositions or written
statements to the record at the last minute, which nobody credited.
Hill was isolated and left vulnerable, which led to what was essentially
a he said/she said contest in which facts didn't matter nearly so much
as the subjective opinions of the viewer. In 2018, a new generation of
American women would have the chance to witness that history repeating itself.

The way Hill tells the story, when she returned to her law school in
1991, after her Senate testimony, she'd intended to take a few weeks
to answer the stack of letters she'd received from victims of sexual

harassment in her absence. When I first interviewed her, back in 2014, she put it this way: "Initially, I thought I would just go back and do what I do: commercial law and contracts. But within months I was getting so many requests that it just felt that there was a sincere effort for people to understand sexual harassment." At the time, she told me she gave it two years. "[Twenty-three] years later," she would tell me back in 2014, "I say to people I *do* know how to count. There just seem to be so many layers to the problem that we're still trying to address them."

For Professor Hill, even with the watershed awakening of the #MeToo movement, institutional progress on workplace sexual harassment, bullying, and abuse happens in stutter steps. Progress is invariably followed by backlash. Yet Hill has never stopped publishing, speaking, advocating, teaching, and giving interviews, because she understands that two steps forward, one step back, is still vastly preferable to one step forward, ten steps closer to *The Handmaid's Tale*.

Hill has made this point time and time again over the years, and we never quite seem to hear her: The illusion of a neutral fact-finding process that obscures actual fact-finding is vastly worse than having no process at all. As Hill told *The Washington Post* in 2017, her hearing was a "trial that lacked all of the protections of a trial." As she noted at the time, among its many basic procedural flaws was this: "Even if somebody had been sitting at the table with me, you couldn't object, nobody could speak but me. . . . [I]t was worse than being put on trial because in a trial you've got legal protections." The problem, then and now, was that there was no actual system in place to test the credibility of Hill's or Thomas's claims. We relied on spectacle and our own subjective feelings and public performance—dignified in Hill's case and rageful in Thomas's—to decide for ourselves whom to believe. That is—not to put too fine a point on it—how we once determined whether one was a witch or if the earth was round. It's why we have evolved to an understanding of truth and due process that demands competing claims be tested by neutral fact finders and sub-jected to coherent procedural rules.

If you watched the Brett Kavanaugh confirmation hearings in Sep-tember 2018, it was plain that there was no neutral fact finder and no agreed-upon procedural rules. One of Kavanaugh's accusers (another was never called) sat at a table and politely told the truth as she re-called it. Then Kavanaugh was allowed to scream his refutation and insult those who questioned him. Whatever fact-finding that occurred "backstage" was never revealed. Groundhog Day, separated by twenty-seven years.

Not too long after Senator Chuck Grassley held his hearing on sex-ual abuse in the judiciary, holding forth on how appalling it was that federal judges accused of wrongdoing could retire with their full fed-eral pensions intact, he would convene the confirmation hearing for Brett Kavanaugh. Justice Anthony Kennedy, a stalwart conservative on the high court who had inherited the role of its "swing justice" after Sandra Day O'Connor stepped down, was a reliable conservative vote on executive power, criminal justice, policing, and guns, but he had proven unpredictably centrist in a handful of areas, including affirma-tive action, gay rights, the rights of juvenile criminal defendants, and of course abortion. The instant Kennedy announced his retirement, it was clear that unlike the replacement of Justice Antonin Scalia with Neil Gorsuch in 2017, this would be a watershed appointment. Trump's next appointee could swing the court to the far right for a genera-tion.

Kavanaugh, as we have seen, auditioned to get onto Trump's short list with his opinion in the appeal of a pregnant migrant teen at the border. He'd worked on the Bush team—along with John Roberts and Amy Coney Barrett—in the case that became *Bush v. Gore* in 2000. He also worked under Ken Starr on the Bill Clinton impeachment report, ultimately drafting a memo that excoriated Clinton for his immorality and urged sexually graphic questions to be asked of the president including "If Monica Lewinsky said you inserted a cigar into her vagina, while you were in the Oval Office area, would she be lying?" and "If Monica Lewinsky says that you had phone sex with her on approximately 15 occasions, would she be lying?" Kavanaugh had also reportedly been less than completely candid with the Senate Judiciary Committee in answers about his work in the Bush administration during his confirmation hearings for the federal appeals court in 2006.

But Justice Kennedy wanted Kavanaugh, and so did the president. His hearings should have been straightforward, but as the summer of 2018 progressed, reporters began to hear rumors that a #MeToo story was bubbling connected to Judge Kavanaugh. On September 14, *The New Yorker*'s Jane Mayer and Ronan Farrow reported that Senate Democrats had received an anonymous allegation from a woman claiming that Kavanaugh, as a high school student, had "held her down, and . . . attempted to force himself on her" at a house party in Maryland in 1982. Two days later, that woman, Christine Blasey Ford, came forward and confirmed her allegation on the record. Shortly after, another accuser, Deborah Ramirez, a Yale undergraduate classmate of Kavanaugh's, alleged publicly that he had exposed himself to her while drunk. A third came forward with claims that did not seem credible at the time.

For the women who had come forward a few months earlier with claims about his former mentor Kozinski, Kavanaugh's insistence that he never saw anything or knew anything was doubly destabilizing. As Heidi Bond would later write in *Slate*, the only way Kavanaugh could have been completely unaware of his former boss and colleague's fondness for porn and dirty jokes in chambers "would be if he had amnesia about the clerkship in its entirety." As Kavanaugh told a group of students in 2014 about his law school years, they had a motto around the school's drinking culture: "What happens on the bus stays on the bus." Having buried the investigation into Kozinski, the Judiciary

Committee had ensured that we would never know what happened in those chambers, or on the bus.

Christine Blasey Ford, a professor of psychology with a deep understanding of neurobiology, would come to say under oath before the Judiciary Committee that Kavanaugh attempted to rape her at a party while they were both teenagers. In her opening testimony, she said of Kavanaugh's friend Mark Judge, who was also drunk and in the room, "Mark was urging Brett on, although at times he told Brett to stop. A couple of times I made eye contact with Mark and thought he might try to help me, but he did not." Judge, having authored a book in 1997 about his youthful blackout drinking that included a character named "Bart O'Kavanaugh" who "puked in someone's car" and "passed out on his way back from a party," wasn't called to participate in the inquiry. One of Judge's former girlfriends, Elizabeth Rasor, told *The New Yorker* that he had "told her ashamedly of an incident that involved him and other boys taking turns having sex with a drunk woman." In a letter to the committee, Judge claimed to recall nothing at all of the events and declined to speak publicly because "as a recovering alcoholic and a cancer survivor, I have struggled with depression and anxiety. As a result, I avoid public speaking." Judge would spend the hearing holed up at a friend's beach house in Delaware.

In *The Education of Brett Kavanaugh*, the 2019 account by Robin Pogrebin and Kate Kelly, the two *New York Times* reporters combed through all available evidence, including reports ignored by the FBI, and arrived at their conclusion that Kavanaugh was a student partier and an athlete who drank too much. (He scored his big break clerking for Judge Alex Kozinski when the law professor who recommended him described him as a "good student" and not a "great one," but added, "I got to know his character from basketball.") The authors found no smoking gun but ultimately concluded that both Ford and Ramirez were credible and were likely mistreated by Kavanaugh as teenagers.

Their conclusion was also that over the next thirty-five years he became a better person and a mentor to young women.

When Dr. Ford came forward in the summer of 2018, Professor Hill wrote a measured and lawyerly opinion piece in *The New York Times*, suggesting the types of formal mechanisms and protocols the Judiciary Committee might adopt in order to do a better job with the upcoming hearing than it had done with hers. As she pointed out, the stakes were as high as they had been in 1991: "The integrity of the court, the country's commitment to addressing sexual violence as a matter of public interest, and the lives of the two principal witnesses who will be testifying hang in the balance." The Republican-controlled Senate instead opted to cull from the worst elements of the Thomas-Hill debacle while adding a few procedural measures that would make it yet worse.

When the Kavanaugh hearings opened, there had been no neutral outside investigation of Dr. Ford's claims, and the proceedings themselves were truncated and rushed. Many Democratic activists fretted privately, as Vanita Gupta has indicated, that the battle was unwinnable in the Republican-controlled Senate and would engender an electoral backlash in the midterms. Women's groups, knowing that the Republicans would not defect on Kavanaugh's nomination, elected to press ahead with their opposition.

Republican senators, all eleven of them men, were too afraid to attack Dr. Ford personally, and thus had hired Rachel Mitchell, an Arizona sex crimes prosecutor, to question the witness. Mitchell did so from a small table positioned below their dais. Mitchell spent little time on the alleged assault, trying to catch Ford out on matters that would impugn her credibility, such as that she's traveled on airplanes despite her fear of flying. Ford—a white, PhD-educated mother of two from Palo Alto—testified haltingly, politely, over four hours, in a voice so tiny she was difficult to hear. "Indelible in the hippocampus is the laughter, the uproarious laughter between the two," she said, describing the memory of Kavanaugh and Judge mocking her.

Eventually, the Republican Judiciary Committee chairman, Grassley, cut Mitchell's questioning of Brett Kavanaugh shortly after his testimony had begun, at which point the men on the committee retook control and ignored her. The committee's Republican majority also declined to give a public hearing to Ramirez, who had come forward to report an incident of inappropriate sexual touching that she alleged had happened at Yale, or to her many classmates seeking to corroborate her story. One thing that had changed since the Thomas hearings? The presence of several extraordinary women lawyers on the Democrats' side of the hearing, including Senators Kamala Harris, Amy Klobuchar, and Mazie Hirono. In her allotted time, Senator Klobuchar asked Kavanaugh a question about whether he had ever had so much to drink that he couldn't recall what happened. Kavanaugh's response was to demand whether Klobuchar had a drinking problem herself. Rock, meet bottom.

Because no meaningful independent investigation had been conducted and key witnesses with material information were never asked to testify, the fact-finding part of the hearing turned on whom you liked better. After the hearing, the limited FBI investigation—extended for a few additional days in a feint toward bipartisanship and a stated desire to get to the bottom of the competing claims—was controlled by the same entities that wanted Kavanaugh seated. Multiple witnesses with material evidence left messages for the FBI that went unreturned. Twenty witnesses wishing to speak about the Ramirez allegations were not contacted. Kavanaugh used the lack of certainty both to proclaim that he had been exculpated and to threaten revenge on the groups and individuals who had supported Dr. Ford during his testimony at the hearings. He was swiftly confirmed and sworn in. Kavanaugh was fifty-three at the time. He will likely serve for thirty years or more.

I was in the Senate chamber when both Dr. Ford and Judge Kavanaugh testified. There were a small number of journalists present, and after Dr. Ford was done with her testimony, the consensus was that

she was completely credible and poised. "This is a disaster for the Republicans," said Fox News's Chris Wallace in the break between the
two witnesses. When Kavanaugh began to slam his binder and shout
that the proceeding was all about Democrats seeking "revenge on
behalf of the Clintons" and promising the Democratic senators, "You
sowed the wind for decades to come," one of my sons texted me from
his high school classroom to ask whether I was perfectly safe in a room
with someone who appeared unstable. I texted back that the nominee
was being shouty to impress the shouty president. That I was of course
perfectly safe in that room. And of course, after that, none of us would
be perfectly safe at all.

The public polling following the Kavanaugh hearing revealed at
least one sea change from 1991. According to Kelly and Pogrebin, after
the hearings, the majority of voters polled by the research firm Perry-
Undem believed Kavanaugh had lied about his actions as a teenager.
Forty-nine percent of respondents had an unfavorable impression of
him, as compared with the 29 percent who had a favorable one. Thirty-
five percent said the Senate did the right thing by confirming him;
41 percent disagreed. Public opinion polling, to be sure, does not represent truth. But public understanding about the nuance of memory,
reporting, power, and gender had at least come a long way since the
Thomas confirmation. Before the vote on Kavanaugh could be held, a
woman, Ana Maria Archila, confronted Arizona senator Jeff Flake in
an elevator. She had herself remained silent about a sexual assault that
had happened more than thirty years earlier. "This is not tolerable,"
Archila told Flake as the television cameras rolled. "You have children
in your family. Think about them."

In her opening statement, Dr. Ford had described why she'd been
unwilling to go public earlier with her high school memories. "I believed that if I came forward, my voice would be drowned out by a
chorus" of powerful political men who would say anything to protect
her alleged attacker. After the hearing it was clear that she had been

prescient. "Judge Kavanaugh showed America exactly why I nominated him," tweeted President Trump. Kavanaugh's outrage, the open threats, the insults hurled at committee Democrats, was all perfect comeuppance for #MeToo as a movement. As Adam Serwer would write in *The Atlantic*, "Those who chanted 'Lock her up!' for more than two years have rediscovered the principle that people are innocent until proved guilty."

With Trump and Kavanaugh claiming that he'd been formally vindicated, it was time for the death threats and intimidation against Dr. Ford to begin. At a rally in October in Mississippi, President Trump said that the enduring lesson of #MeToo was that "it's a very scary time for young men in America when you can be guilty of something you may not be guilty of." He began mocking Dr. Ford about her lack of a detailed memory of events. "'How did you get home?' 'I don't remember'"—he whispered in a baby girl voice—"'How'd you get there?' 'I don't remember'" (same baby girl voice). The crowd roared, "Lock her up, lock her up." Only days earlier the president had been quoted saying he found Dr. Ford's testimony "very credible."

But public opinion polling is also not a truth-seeking process. And that is where we persist in misapprehending what #MeToo had hoped to achieve. We might have witnessed a culture shift between the spectacle of public testimony of Anita Hill and Christine Blasey Ford around who should be believed and why, but the factual inquiry as to what actually happens between men and women in allegedly abusive situations still remained suspended in time, sealed in amber, along with the big shoulder pads and the shabby insults of 1991. The legal philosopher Martha Nussbaum has written in *Citadels of Pride: Sexual Abuse, Accountability, and Reconciliation* that the failure to scaffold the #MeToo movement with legal processes and checks has meant that competing forces roam around demanding punishment, without a mechanism for assessing or even understanding the crime. "#MeToo has helped win accountability," she writes. "But the fact that so much of the #MeToo movement is social rather than legal creates a problem: how to secure justice and protect equal dignity when punishment is meted out not by impartial legal institutions but by shaming and stigmatization."

Dr. Ford and Professor Hill created social change. But where was the law? When shaming and reputational and professional stigma are meted out following performative investigations—investigations that feature the theater of cross-examination and testimony under oath—it creates the false impression that fact-finding has occurred when it has not. Those who persistently demanded that Judge Kavanaugh receive "due process" didn't understand that he wasn't being deprived of any rights; he was interviewing for a job. And those who believed that confirmation hearing represented "due process" failed to understand that what they had watched was a TV show that passed itself off as a legal event. *That* is the real danger Hill has tried to warn about since 1991. Processes that pretend to be about truth but that are in fact about obscuring truth under the levers of power and access to power victimize both accusers and victims. And that part—the actual process—is what needs to change.

Dr. Ford lives with the outcome to this day. She has moved her family multiple times and contends with the trauma of threats of violence. One year after the confirmation hearings, Hill told *The New York Times* that one of the central problems with the Senate's confirmation process for Kavanaugh was that "they should've had a process in place for receiving complaints. They had none." In a podcast done in 2021, Ford told Hill that even after she decided to come forward, she couldn't figure out "who I was supposed to call, who I was supposed to contact." She added that there's no HR department in government, and nobody to contact as a citizen, that she had friends suggesting she needed an attorney. But "I didn't see why I needed an attorney because I didn't think I had done anything wrong." Both Ford and Hill pointed out that nobody had told them the investigation would stop at their testimony, that no other evidence would be assessed.

Hill, as a lawyer and professor, worries about the public perception of the court, an institution that relies wholly upon public acceptance for its continued legitimacy. As she told me in an interview, "Can you imagine that we are putting judges on the bench—not just on the Supreme Court, but on the trial court benches, on the courts of appeals benches—who may in fact have complaints against them, but where people are not able to come forward because they don't have a system to come forward in?" In part, that is because a tranche of judicial ethics complaints filed against Kavanaugh were dismissed by a federal court in 2019, after he was sworn in at the Supreme Court. The Committee on Judicial Conduct and Disability of the Judicial Conference of the United States determined that as soon as Kavanaugh was elevated to the high court, it had no jurisdiction to probe "complaints against a judge who has resigned his or her judicial office and thereafter been confirmed as a Justice of the Supreme Court." In plain English? Nobody has jurisdiction to investigate a sitting justice. That is precisely why Hill advocated for a thorough investigation beforehand.

On October 5, 2018, Susan Collins, the Republican senator from Maine, was conscripted because of her gender to offer a perfectly incoherent explanation for why she would be voting to confirm Brett Kavanaugh. While she found Dr. Ford's testimony to be "sincere, painful, and compelling" and while she insisted that she did "believe that she is a survivor of a sexual assault and that this trauma has upended her life," she concluded that the lack of "corroborating evidence" meant Kavanaugh was off the hook. She said that although "this is not a criminal trial, and I do not believe that claims such as these need to be proved beyond a reasonable doubt," she also wanted to be on record as someone who believed the "#MeToo movement is real." Collins said,

"It matters. It is needed" and that "rape and sexual assault are less likely to be reported to the police than other forms of assault" and that "we must listen to survivors, and every day we must seek to stop the criminal behavior that has hurt so many." Then she sided with Kavanaugh. Lost somewhere in this hour-long speech, to which logic had clearly gone to die horribly, was any theory of how one could believe the accuser, and also the accused, and also all the witnesses, and also all women, and also in the rule of law. There was no standard of proof, there was no way to learn what had happened, and nobody had bothered to try. As compared with the male senators who had once derided Anita Hill as a sex-obsessed erotomaniac, Collins's performance was, in one sense, progress. But the implication that one should believe all women without ever finding out what had happened to them showcased the stalled-out discourse of #MeToo. The culture has boldly moved from shaming the accuser before discounting her to feeling sorry for the accuser before discounting her. Baby steps.

IN 2019, AFTER PRESIDENTIAL CANDIDATE Joe Biden telephoned her to apologize for the way the 1991 Senate Judiciary Committee had handled the process for the Thomas hearings, Anita Hill again insisted that none of this was a matter of personal forgiveness and that it couldn't be corrected by expressions of empathy for her pain. The problem was, as it always has been, a deficient mechanism for discovering the truth. Writing once again for *The New York Times*, Hill argued that in America, formal systems for reporting, investigating, and redressing sexual harassment and abuse continue to be inadequate. "After Dr. Blasey's courageous testimony, many saw the callous and ham-handed approach of Senator Charles Grassley of Iowa, the committee's chairman, as a replay of the Thomas hearings," she wrote. "Even worse, a new generation was forced to conclude that politics trumped a basic and essential expectation: that claims of sexual abuse would be taken seriously."

If you are a person who believes that in a shape-shifting world, words, facts, and law matter, and that they matter most particularly to women and vulnerable communities that rely on the rule of law to vindicate their rights, the Thomas and Kavanaugh hearings are in fact worse than no process at all. They are show trials, with foreordained outcomes, that give the imprimatur of a legal inquiry, with none of its guarantees. The threat of "Lock her up"—so chilling to women who heard it hurled at Hillary Clinton, Nancy Pelosi, and Christine Blasey Ford—is the threat that what *looks* like law will become the mechanism for undoing the law. For the millions of American women who witnessed Ford's testimony and Kavanaugh's response, the icy realization that male entitlement, threats, and fury could still outrun and overmaster the truth, even in a process that purported to surface the truth, was another earthquake in the Trump years. Law or the trappings of law could be used to silence and sideline women. That isn't a fight about equality; it's a fear of retribution.

When Biden apologized for Hill's pain, he performed a version of the dance that now passes for legal conclusions. Due process is for men; women can mostly just hope for sympathy. In a 2021 podcast conversation between Hill and Ford, Hill noted that the solution here is not for the next #MeToo victim to walk headlong into the wood chipper and then the next one after that. "I reject the idea that it will change if more women step up, I disagree. We need better processes and systems." Neither Hill nor Ford wants to be told they were credible and to move on. Both just wanted to ensure that suspected sexual harassers and abusers are not the ultimate arbiters of what is lawful and what is not. Claims of sexual abuse remain dead serious, and our systems to redress them are not working. Among other things, Hill cited a recent survey by the Department of Defense showing that sexual harassment and assault in the military rose by 38 percent from 2016 to 2018, and CDC reports that one in three women and one in four men will experience sexual violence during their lifetimes. According to the EEOC, claims of sexual harassment increased by more than 12 percent from 2017 to 2018. While the world focused once again, for a fleeting moment, on an individual woman's pain, Hill called not for a revolution but for better machinery for testing what happened: she is not saying that all women tell the truth or that all men are predators. What she calls for is hardly radical: the kind of system we use to redress every other harm we deem to be a social ill.

Professor Hill is a systems person, a process person, a small-bore structures person. Like so many of the women in this book, she is one of the most conservative radicals you will ever come across. As a result of her own brush with the Senate Judiciary Committee, Hill has been tapped to work on #MeToo issues on multiple commissions on workplace equality and sexual abuse. She's written multiple books, including an autobiography, and has been the subject of a major documentary as well as a Hollywood film. Still, what seems to excite her most is a high-octane discussion of arcane reporting and investigatory systems. Hill hardly believes that the law alone can right this balance between women's pain and accountability. It's just that it's *her* solution. "Part of the reason I think the processes and systems alone can't get us there," she told me in an interview, "is because I think the processes and systems are in such bad shape." But even when the law is functioning correctly, it's always going to be in a footrace against the larger culture. "For me," she says, "I always go back to things like, think the South, in Mississippi in the 1960s, where there were these breakthrough moments in the law. . . . And it was *almost* as though this was what's going to change things. But then there was the culture. And it's a strong, invisible force. The law is much more visible. It has buildings. It has courthouses. It's got lawyers; it's got parties, plaintiffs and defendants. But these cultural things are just so enormous. And they are often invisible in the way that they interact with the law."

In Anita Hill's view, the law alone can't make change. Even during her own hearings, she told me, although Title VII had been a part of the Civil Rights Act of 1964, "even late in 1991, people had no idea that sexual harassment was a real thing that you could actually sue someone for. Something was happening to interfere. And it wasn't as though there hadn't been cases. There *were* cases. But there hadn't been a culture that actually even talked about those cases." There was a law, but nobody believed it. She told me, "When I was teaching employment law in the '80s, there were three cases in the casebook that I was using. In this huge, thick casebook on employment law, there were *three* blurbs of cases on sexual harassment." And this, she said, was after the 1970s, after the gender theorist Catharine Mac-Kinnon "had woken us all up to it. There was still, even the people who were talking about the very area of law that it sits in, were not talking about it."

And why is that? Hill believes it's "largely because we just don't value women's experiences."

There is formal equality. That is the thing Ruth Bader Ginsburg started her career pushing for: women should be allowed to serve on juries; they should be able to inherit property; they should be allowed to serve in the military and own credit cards. But what Hill is contemplating is something beyond what she imagined even when she started law school in the 1970s. "We find ourselves further behind because we are, every day, learning how far behind we were," she told me. "I graduated from law school in 1980. And it was a decade in which a record number of women became law students. I think by the end of the '60s . . . something like 7 to 8 percent of law students were women. And by the end of the '70s, that number was up to maybe a third or so." She told me that if you looked around, even then, "you thought things look pretty good, like you're a little bit off on this trajectory. But then when you get to the '90s and even today, and you realize, hey, those women, they're not in positions of power. There's stagnation in terms of careers."

For Anita Hill, looking back, the stagnation was in some sense a failure of legal imagination: "I think the law framed a success as 'will women be hired in a position? So, hey, you got hired, there you go. That's it.' The law didn't necessarily count on pay discrimination or pregnancy discrimination; even in 1964, when the framing started, it didn't count on sexual harassment." For Hill, the real reason women cannot seem to catch up is that "we didn't even know what equality *was*. We thought it was as the law had framed it."

For the millions of American women who watched the Kavanaugh hearings in dismay, for the protesters in the Senate chamber in 2018, dressed up in the bloodred gowns and white hats of Margaret Atwood's *Handmaid's Tale*, the feeling was that we were all moving backward to an America in which women had no control over their own bodies, or to a dystopian future in which their autonomy and dignity would forever be determined by powerful men. In September 2021, after Amy Coney Barrett became the third Donald Trump appointee on the Supreme Court, and a six-justice supermajority appeared ready to strike down *Roe v. Wade*, Texas passed a novel law, known as SB 8 but widely referred to as a "bounty" system. Abortions after six weeks would be banned, but the ban would be enforced not by courts or other state officers. Civil suits against abortion providers, their staffs, and anyone who "aids and abets" those providers, such as Lyft drivers or mental health counselors, would result in at least $10,000 rewards to any citizen, anywhere, deputized to bring suit. All private enforcement was removed from the state and put into the hands of vigilantes. Suddenly Uber drivers, high school counselors, and insurance companies could be subject to multiple civil lawsuits, forced to pay out the bounties again and again. The day after the law went into effect, by a 5–4 margin, and in an unsigned one-paragraph order, the Supreme Court refused to enjoin it, citing "complex and novel" procedural problems.

The day the law went into effect, all abortions after six weeks effectively stopped. Victims of rape, incest, and violence must either travel out of state to terminate pregnancies or carry to term. The State of Texas had nullified *Roe v. Wade*, and the Supreme Court had ratified it. In December 2021, after formal briefing and arguments in the same case, the court allowed the law to stand again. Brett Kavanaugh and Amy Coney Barrett, voting with the majority, may feel great sympathy for these women, but it seems their hands were tied. That is how reproductive freedom ended for 10 percent of the women of childbearing age in America, through cowardice dressed up as sympathy—the same legal outcome Susan Collins showed for Christine Blasey Ford. Sympathy, empathy, "I believe you," and "she seemed very credible" are not legal outcomes. They are cold comfort intended to mollify you as actual power slips away.

What Brett Kavanaugh would do to women's freedom and equality was not in doubt during his confirmation hearings; his record was clear. The added insult—that nobody would ever investigate the claims against him—was almost beyond bearing. For weeks and then months after he was installed at the Supreme Court, I stopped attending oral arguments. I would pretend to have a cold or tell my editors that I was working on something else. At some point, it became clear to me that I couldn't go back into the building, couldn't pretend that something about the confirmation hearing had "cleared" him, and couldn't pretend that he hadn't threatened at that hearing that anyone who had opposed him would "reap the whirlwind." As conventional and respectful as I had always been about the norms of civility at the court, the idea that, like Thomas, Kavanaugh was now cleansed of any allegations because a majority of the Senate declined to evaluate them wasn't just a failure of law or process. It was gaslighting.

In October 2019, a year after the hearings, I finally wrote an article explaining why I would no longer cover the Supreme Court from inside the building. It was a brutal and public breakup. I explained that "my job as a Supreme Court reporter used to be to explain and translate the institution to people locked out of its daily proceedings" and that this project had been "swathed in black robes and velvet curtains, in polite questions, and case names and at least the appearance that this was all cool science, as opposed to blood sport."

I noted that, a year later, polling had shifted in Kavanaugh's favor, the other justices had welcomed him, and he was being feted in Washington. Indeed, because his vote mattered so much now, I wrote, "the game is forgiveness and forgetting, in service of long-term tactical appeasement." Two years later, Kavanaugh is the median vote at the court, the swing vote poised between two camps of four. Chief Justice John Roberts is now considered a liberal. Every brief is written to appeal to Kavanaugh; oral arguments are pitched to his preferences. He is the most powerful jurist on the court and it's in everyone's interest to pretend that Christine Blasey Ford never happened, that he is a champion of women's equality, and that whatever that was in 2018 is well and truly behind us. As I wrote at the time, "That is the problem with power: It incentivizes forgiveness and forgetting. . . . The problem with power is that there is no speaking truth to it when it holds all the cards."

I loved my job beyond words. I believed in the courts beyond all things. But as I also confessed one year after the confirmation hearing,

> It is not my job to decide if Brett Kavanaugh is guilty. It's impossible for me to do so with incomplete information, and with no process for testing competing facts. But it's certainly not my job to exonerate him because it's good for his career, or for mine, or for the future of an independent judiciary. Picking up an oar to help America get over its sins without

allowing for truth, apology, or reconciliation has not generally been good for the pursuit of justice.

I was at pains to praise my colleagues in the press corps, who remain the most talented journalists I know. But I no longer felt I could cover the court without also giving cover to a system that erased women. As I concluded in that piece, "There isn't a lot of power in my failing to show up to do my job, but there is a teaspoon of power in refusing to normalize that which was simply wrong, and which continues to be wrong."

For me, as I would later put it in an anthology about the Kavanaugh hearings, every one of us who sat in the room as Dr. Ford testified and found her credible and pretended that the confirmation process has worked had failed her. "Indelible in the hippocampus," I wrote, "is that we sat there listening, and practicing reasoned 'both sides' journalism, and going on television, and all of us believed her. And it didn't matter." This issue—of how long you stay inside a system that no longer serves justice and perhaps produces the simulacrum of justice—was an animating theme for me during the Trump years. I was constantly frustrated by the tension between those who walked away from collapsing institutions and those who remained to try to mitigate the damage. For myself, I felt that the country had betrayed Dr. Ford and her testimony, and there was a connection between the paternalism that led us to pity her, and yet step over her, and the paternalism of a legal system that would increasingly treat all women the same way.

In an interview years later, I asked Anita Hill whether and when it was appropriate to give up on the legal system, to walk away and claim that it was a force for more harm than good. So many of the women in this book shrugged and told me that the law is an imperfect solution at best, but Anita Hill recoiled when I suggested as much: "Without law it's chaos, right? Because we will lose. We will lose with chaos. We will always lose." Perhaps more than anyone else she articulated the special relationship that exists by necessity between vulnerable communities and the legal system. "Chaos," she told me, "allows for behavior you could not anticipate. With institutions, if you understand an institution, you know how things work. They may not work perfectly for you, but you know how they work. Chaos, you don't know how it works, and it's survival of the fittest. And people can really act on their worst instincts. That may be true, to some extent, in institutions. But there is something that you can navigate."

Women have a special relationship with the law, because the next best alternative is violence. Women have a special relationship with the justice system, Hill believes, because it is something we can navigate. But for the law, she told me, January 6, 2021, the day on which rioters stormed the US Capitol seeking to halt the certification of the 2020 presidential election, "could have been passed off as just like any other day in the White House or in the Capitol." So we rely upon the law, she explained, because without it we have far less. And perhaps because we are so vulnerable to its failures, we tend to be especially vigilant, maybe even hypervigilant, when it feels as if it were sliding away.

Hill spoke for so many women lawyers I have interviewed when she told me about giving a talk, "probably in the '90s," about the court system and civil rights and how the Supreme Court was procedurally making access to class-action suits and punitive damages less and less accessible. "And this young white man," she said, "on a college campus stepped up and he said, 'Aren't you just being a little paranoid? You act as though the sky is falling.' I thought about it. I said, 'Well, here's the list. You can tell me when the sky is falling.'" She said she thought about that for a couple of days until she realized, as she told me, "it wasn't just that the sky wasn't falling for him. It was because we don't live under the same sky." For Hill, that was when she came to understand that she wasn't paranoid; she simply resided in another world.

"And you don't have to know these things. But my very survival relies on me knowing these things."

When SB 8 went into effect in Texas, an awful lot of people told me that my coverage sounded "paranoid" and "hysterical" and overheated and slightly insane. And I realized that much like the 6–3 conservative supermajority that now controls the court, they simply don't live under the same sky. Hill's formulation—that we don't all live under the same sky—is an elegant encapsulation of what the Trump era, the COVID pandemic, and the #MeToo movement unpeeled for millions of women who believed that the American system of justice was forever chugging along on its own steam to a more perfect, just union: that despite claims of fundamental and foundational equality and access to justice, the sky was cloudless and blue for many Americans from 2016 onward, and for many others it wasn't just bucketing down endless suffering and misery, but they were also being told, over and over again, that they weren't actually getting wet.

So many of the women I interviewed for this book mentioned moments in recent years in which, despite their credentials, their impressive law degrees and achievements, their invitations to speak in crowded ballrooms with lush flower arrangements and table linens, they found themselves surrounded by progressive allies telling them to calm down, take a beat, or see the big picture. It often came from a place of seemingly genuine concern. The impulse was simply to warn them that their overreaction was somehow intemperate, or premature, or counterproductive to progressive objectives. The problem was that it was almost unerringly directed toward women by men, who found themselves living under a different sky. For Hill, it looked and sounded something like this: "I was at an event and it was a big thing, and all the people, at least that I knew, were liberals." She says the year was 2018 or 2019. She told the crowd, "'I used to feel we are going to be okay, as long as we have the court . . . but we're losing the court.' And afterward there was another speaker, a historian. And he said, 'Oh, we've had times this bad before. . . . We'll get through this.' And the organizer came up to me and said, 'Well, I hope you're feeling better after listening to that speech.' And I said that the speaker was a southerner and he has learned to serve his cold water warm." The mirror image of telling a woman you believe her is telling her she is being hysterical. Being told you are believed without consequences being levied is neither justice nor power. And that is the real problem when women's pain is substituted for actual justice. Pain seems to have a sell-by date. Justice does not.

Almost every woman in this book has described screaming in secret, melting down in the privacy of elevators and bathrooms, being told to calm down because the sky isn't really falling. I think one reason we all turned to law as a stabilizing force is that it was, as Hill put it, navigable, and it presents as neutral and rational even when you are screaming on the inside. And especially for women who are taught to suppress emotion, grief, pain, and trauma to appear more credible, the double insult of being told you are hysterical as you evince perfect control is beyond imagining. So where do women who feel scorching, lethal rage put all that scorching, lethal rage? Citing the work of Rebecca Traister and Brittney Cooper, who have written about women and anger, Anita Hill told me that "the best way to express it is how we've learned to talk about issues, especially as lawyers. That's what we do. We know this can be effective. We have enough history with that to say it can effectively change things by making really strong arguments." But she added, "I think we all have rage in us, and I think we all express it differently."

When I asked her where she had stuffed her rage during her perfectly controlled testimony in 1991, she replied that when she thought back on that testimony, "as contained as it appeared to be, it was an outrageous thing to do. And it was outrageous as a woman. It was outrageous as a Black woman. It was outrageous. And I think we are all in some ways exercising our rage at different times in different ways. But I think we all feel it. And I also think that sometimes our very presence is outrageous. And the fact that we even say *anything* is a sign of resistance." This was Olivia Warren's testimony as well: "screaming into the face of deafening indifference, if only because the sound of my voice reminds me that I have not yet succumbed to it."

That was the motivation for my own refusal to return to the Supreme Court; a male editor I knew once referred to it as my "little boycott." A reminder that I had not succumbed to it. For Anita Hill, and for so many of the women lawyers who have grave doubts about the justice system and the current Supreme Court, the real work to achieve enduring justice for women requires a recalibration of both the machinery of justice itself and a culture that can accept the outrageousness of women's voices. And maybe, above all, what drew so many women to the law was the possibility of being outrageous together. For all the flaws of the legal system, of the court system, and even of the #MeToo movement, it helped us find our way to one another, and on the very worst days that was enough. When women marched against Donald Trump in 2017, or protested against Brett Kavanaugh's confirmation and then family separation in 2018, or organized to get out the vote in 2020, what they were doing was fundamentally justice work and fundamentally outrageous. And that is of course why it is always met with the blowback, the rape threats, the personal hate and intimidation. That is why the chant is always "Lock her up."

For Anita Hill, the question is, "Can we push at the moment in which we have the eyes of the public on us? Can we push far enough that we can withstand the backlash?" So why do we do it? Why did *she* do it and why did Dr. Ford do it? Why do we continue to demand that the next woman do it and the women who follow? Why does the woman who is now believed by the great majority of Americans to have told the truth in 1991 still maintain that it was worthwhile, even as the man she accused of sexually harassing her sits in a life-tenured position at the US Supreme Court, deciding cases that shape the lives of every woman in America? Asked for the two thousandth time to explain why it was all worth it, Anita Hill told me this: "What would I be doing if I didn't? If I were holding my tongue and keeping silent?"

She then quoted Leon Higginbotham, a prominent federal circuit judge who had championed Hill at the time of the confirmation fight. "I think at one point, I might have been complaining, 'Why did I have to tell these people in these rooms what's wrong?' And he said, 'Just think about where we would be if nobody was doing it. And think about how you would feel if you walked away and you didn't even try.' So here we go."

ELECTIONS PART 1

Voting Georgia 2018

Stacey Abrams:
The Game Changer

Nobody would have guessed that one of the most transformational political figures of the Trump years would be Stacey Abrams, a Black female tax lawyer, voting rights activist/litigator, and organizer who is also a romance novelist and who ran for governor of Georgia in 2018. Had Abrams prevailed in that election, she would have become the nation's first female African American governor and likely gone on to become a household name in politics. But Abrams lost that race and is now easily one of the most recognizable thinkers and activists in the country. That's a testament both to her prodigious skills as a voting rights organizer and to the reality that, by 2018, the prospect of free and fair elections had already become visibly diminished. Abrams put a voice to the proposition that without serious nationwide remediation of the barriers Georgia voters had faced in her own governor's race, democracy itself was in trouble. Abrams—who'd served as minority leader in Georgia's state legislature for six and a half years without serious political blowback—would soon become one of the most vocal and effective messengers about the centrality of voting rights to every other freedom. Abrams had identified and cracked the problem of free and fair elections, and she did it before most of us were aware that this was a crisis.

Stacey Abrams was born in Madison, Wisconsin, in 1973 and raised in Gulfport, Mississippi, the second of six children. In 1989, when she was fifteen, her parents decided to attend Methodist divinity school and enrolled at Emory University's Candler School of Theology in Atlanta. Her parents would both eventually become Methodist ministers. In 1991, Abrams—as valedictorian of her high school class—was invited to meet the governor of Georgia. As she told CBS News in 2021,

> My parents and I arrived on the MARTA bus, because we didn't have a car. We go up the driveway of the governor's mansion. We get to the guard gate, and the guard stops us and tells us we don't belong there, that it's a private event. My dad says, "No, this is my daughter, Stacey. We have an invitation." But the guard doesn't ask for my invitation that my mom has. And I remember watching him watch the bus pull off. . . . And if my mother had not had my arm in a death grip, I would have been back on that bus. I think two things happened that day. One, they were not going to let me be denied this honor that I'd achieved. But two, I think they wanted me to see my responsibility is to not let someone else tell me who I am and where I belong.

Abrams was a voracious reader, and she constantly watched PBS, in part because it was one of only two channels her family's TV got. She has said that her father was an original feminist role model for her, because he unhesitatingly told people that his wife was the smartest woman he knew. As a student, Abrams excelled. She was always in advanced studies, though she frequently found herself the only Black student in her classes. She read encyclopedias and dictionaries because her mother routinely directed her to look things up. In 1991, Abrams headed to Spelman College, a historically Black women's university, where she was elected student government president, which she came to credit with her first lessons in fundraising and the allocation of funds. At Spelman, she majored in interdisciplinary studies (political science, economics, and sociology) and minored in theater. Abrams went on to earn a master's degree in public policy from the University of Texas, then entered Yale Law School, where she opted for a career in tax law. She told *The Washington Post* that she became a tax lawyer because after a stint working in the mayor's office, she realized that if she wanted to be a public servant, she needed to learn how the entire system worked.

It was at Yale that she started writing romance novels under the pseudonym Selena Montgomery. In 2021, Abrams told *Essence* that she was always, first and foremost, a writer: "The writing. I've been writing as long as I can remember. I learned to read when I was very young. I learned to write soon thereafter and I love telling stories." She has always connected her writing to her politics and to her interest in government, and swims as easily in popular culture references as she does in lofty political theory. While Abrams has told interviewers that she isn't a "glad-hander" and that she is perfectly happy to sit in silence, she emphatically believes that political leadership demands a certain amount of vulnerability, goofiness, and lack of pretension. In a 2020 interview with *New York* magazine's Rebecca Traister, Abrams explained why a recent tweet about *Buffy the Vampire Slayer* is central to how she thinks about leadership: "It's important that we enjoy what it means to live in a free society and to have these moments of respite.

But it's also an organizing tool. If you can meet people where they are, and they want to be with you when you get there, that helps a lot." For Abrams, the lofty, prophetic hectoring will backfire. "If we enter this work chastising, lecturing, and hectoring," she told Traister, "you might get a few people to do something in that moment to get you to shut up, but you're never going to convert them or convince them that it's worth doing again."

Abrams said she wants people to "see the normalness" of activism and political engagement, and if they see that "normalness can be profound in how their lives get better, then they're going to be more willing to risk showing up and standing in that line and being rained on and being yelled at by some guy in a truck who's telling them to go home. They're going to be more willing if they think that they're in this together, as opposed to they're being sort of led to do this by people who think they're too important to show up." For the millions of women who launched themselves into organizing and knocking on doors and marching after 2016, what Abrams was naming here was the way in which you could sweep activism into your everyday life, with Facebook groups, wine-tasting circles, or Etsy projects. Politics needed to become a thing you did while you drove to work and were on the sidelines at the school play.

Abrams isn't just a prolific writer. She's also a meticulous researcher. "I'm the daughter of a research librarian," Abrams told CBS News in 2021. "I grew up not only writing but learning how to research, learning how to dive in and think strategically about how to learn new things." And what Abrams had been researching for years was how to expand the electorate in ways that would allow Georgia, a state that hadn't gone for a Democrat since Bill Clinton in 1992, to turn blue. *New York* magazine's Traister described her as having "one of the most detailed-oriented, forward-looking, compulsively organized brains in politics."

In 2006, Abrams won a seat as a Democrat in the Georgia Assembly, going on to become the first female minority leader of her party. What she came to understand was that between redistricting and vote dilution, something massive needed to be done to reverse a tide that led to a Republican sweep of state offices in 2010. So she put together a twenty-one-page PowerPoint diagnosing the challenges facing Georgia Democrats and laying out what would have to happen if state Democrats wanted to recalibrate power by 2020. Abrams then took that PowerPoint on the road, first to her caucus and then to potential big donors around the country, and her pitch was, as she says now, straightforward: "Please pay attention to Georgia. We are not the South that you remember. We've got some real opportunities, and we need you to pay attention." Abrams wanted people to understand that more than half a million Black Georgians were not registered to vote. Her big idea was simply to "register and civically engage the rising electorate in our state."

Abrams traveled to New York and to California and to Washington, DC, as a slightly audacious minority leader in a southern state that shouldn't be written off, and she told potential donors that she had a plan, that they should pay attention, and that she would be back to ask for their money. Back in 2012, as she later told Traister, "people were skeptical but willing to meet with me because they'd never had a minority leader from a Southern chamber come to them and say, 'Give me your money.'"

Abrams identified a host of groups on the ground doing important work, but it was all work that needed to scale up. She gathered a fleet of disparate entities that were organizing voters: the Georgia Coalition for the People's Agenda; the Concerned Black Clergy of Metropolitan Atlanta; the Georgia Association of Latino Elected Officials; the Asian American Advocacy Fund; and Helen Kim Ho of Asian Americans Advancing Justice-Atlanta. They reached out to churches, NAACP chapters, historically Black Greek letter organizations, looping in Black communities that were underfunded in South Georgia or gerrymandered so as to be invisible in white districts. In 2012, after state Republicans had drawn districts that seemed guaranteed to give them a supermajority in the election cycle, Abrams, who had raised more than $300,000 in support of Democratic candidates, funded get-out-the-vote strategies that included canvassing teams and volunteer networks instead of TV and radio ads. In that election, the Democrats improbably held on to four redistricted seats.

After the 2012 election, donors were suddenly interested. Abrams had initially launched the New Georgia Project to help Georgia's vulnerable residents enroll for health-care coverage under the Affordable Care Act. But she was also seeing that no legislative or policy solutions could be counted on if the electoral power of Georgia Democrats was being hollowed out by the teaspoonful. In 2013, while serving in the Georgia state legislature, Abrams had figured out why state Democrats were being crushed electorally, even as demographics suggested they should have been winning. Despite the country itself, and particularly the South, becoming more diverse almost by the hour, state Republicans were locking in their own electoral power, creating supermajorities that controlled every aspect of state government. Women, young people, and people of color were engaged and interested in local and national politics, but oddly they were less and less represented in office. In the presidential elections of 2008 and 2012, Black women famously had the highest voter-participation rates of any demographic group but were still the least likely to hold elected positions. What Abrams intuited over a decade ago was that if you could get out the vote in numbers that could counter and even exceed red state efforts to suppress the vote, you might claw back power, at least in some key races, and start to win elections. Giving up on the South, on minority voters, or on places that skewed Republican was handing over power that would soon be leveraged to become permanent. Her formula would prove to be the silver bullet that defeated Trump in

2020 and flipped the two Georgia Senate seats, and thus the US Senate, blue in the first days of 2021.

The problem Abrams named before it had a name was actually also the oldest problem on record: racialized vote suppression. America had, after all, been founded on the premise that voting would be exceptionally easy if you were white and wealthy and male, whereas it would be challenging, if not impossible, if you were not. As Justice Elena Kagan characterized it in her dissent in *Brnovich v. Democratic National Committee*, the 2021 case that would shrink the power of the Voting Rights Act to fight race-based voting requirements, "Democratic ideals in America got off to a glorious start; democratic practice not so much." While the Declaration of Independence made lofty promises about "deriving [its] just powers from the consent of the governed," for at least a hundred years, consent was necessary only from white men. African Americans, Native Americans, women, and all those who didn't hold property were presumed to just float along in the slipstream of liberty.

After the Civil War, the Fifteenth Amendment held out at least the hope of meaningful new representation: "The right of citizens of the United States to vote shall not be denied or abridged by the United States or by any State on account of race, color, or previous condition of servitude." But again, Black Americans ran headlong into what Kagan called the "not so much." Despite the formal legal regime, in actual practice poll taxes, understanding clauses, literacy tests, lynch mobs, and intimidation made voting a right on paper and a life-threatening proposition all over the South. In 1867, after the Civil War, more than 65 percent of newly enfranchised Blacks had registered to vote in Mississippi. That number stood at 4.3 percent in 1955. As Kagan noted, again dissenting in *Brnovich*, "By 1965, only 27% of black Georgians, 19% of black Alabamians, and 7%—yes, 7%—of black Mississippians were registered to vote." Many of the practices that kept

Blacks, Hispanics, and Native Americans out of the voting booth were neutral sounding on their face. And on March 7, 1965, when civil rights protesters—among them a young John Lewis—were beaten bloody on the Edmund Pettus Bridge as a horrified nation watched, President Lyndon B. Johnson asked for and received a piece of legislation to "help rid the Nation of racial discrimination in every aspect of the electoral process and thereby insure the right of all to vote." Johnson signed the Voting Rights Act into law in August 1965.

The VRA was the landmark legislation guaranteeing that the right to choose one's elected representative would be protected from racist Jim Crow policies. Among other things, Section 5 of the VRA made it harder for states with long histories of racist voting practices to enact new racist voting practices by requiring "preclearance"—a green light from the Justice Department or a federal court—before any new voting rules could go into effect. It worked. As Kagan points out in *Brnovich,* "In the five years after the statute's passage, almost as many African Americans registered to vote in six Southern States as in the entire century before 1965."

The VRA was designed to address legislative sneakiness that came dressed in sheep's clothing. In his 1965 address on the Voting Rights Act, President Johnson put it this way: "The harsh fact is that in many places in this country, men and women are kept from voting simply because they are Negroes. Every device of which human ingenuity is capable has been used to deny this right." Well, maybe not *every* device. Because even after the VRA was passed, we were discovering that there were plenty of new and ingenious ways to impede minority ballots so long as you didn't come out and say what you were doing.

In a Senate Judiciary Committee report on the 1982 Amendments to the Voting Rights Act, the problem, post-1965, was laid out explicitly: "Following the dramatic rise in registration, a broad array of vote dilution schemes were employed to cancel the impact of the new black vote. Elective posts were made appointive; election boundaries were gerrymandered; majority runoffs were instituted to prevent victories under a prior plurality system. . . . The ingenuity of such schemes seems endless. Their common purpose and effect has been to offset the gains made at the ballot box under the Act." This was Lee Atwater's classic formulation of the southern strategy as applied to racialized voting practices, a primer on how to be racist without sounding racist: "You start out in 1954 by saying, 'N——, n——, n——.' By 1968 you can't say 'n——'—that hurts you, backfires. So you say stuff like, uh, forced busing, states' rights, and all that stuff." The new voting rules, like forced busing and states' rights, would achieve the effects of suppressing minority voting without the overt language.

In 2013 in *Shelby County v. Holder*, under cover of "states' rights and all that stuff," the Supreme Court hacked out the heart of Section 5 of the Voting Rights Act. Chief Justice John Roberts, writing for five justices, soothed himself that racialized voting problems were long past in America. And his evidence for that proposition lay in the fact that fewer racist voting laws were in effect. To be sure, doing away with preclearance because preclearance prevented racist voting practices didn't mean that racism was over. In 2006, a near-bipartisan Congress had reviewed evidence of racial discrimination and reauthorized the preclearance formula for the VRA for another twenty-five years because they knew it was still working.

That's because it was still working. As Justice Ruth Bader Ginsburg noted in her dissent in *Shelby County*, between the 1982 amendments and the 2006 reauthorizations of the Voting Rights Act, the Department of Justice had blocked more than seven hundred proposed changes to voting laws because they were racially discriminatory. That could have at least plausibly reflected the fact that preclearance was effective and not that it was superfluous. As Ginsburg then tartly— and notoriously—observed in her dissent, "Throwing out preclearance when it has worked and is continuing to work to stop discriminatory changes is like throwing away your umbrella in a rainstorm because you are not getting wet."

But in Roberts's view, by 2013 "things have changed dramatically," and Section 5 of the VRA violated the "principle of equal [state] sovereignty" and also offended states' "dignity." The dignity of the minority voters struggling to vote in those states wasn't materially important. The majority opinion required that the stigma suffered by states that had participated in America's racist voting history be removed, and this could only be done by tacitly allowing the states to reinstate racist voting laws. Those states were delighted to accept the invitation. *Shelby County* instantly released nine states—Alabama, Alaska, Arizona, Georgia, Louisiana, Mississippi, South Carolina, Texas, and Virginia, along with various other jurisdictions—from supervision under the preclearance formula; they were now free to enact voting rules as they liked. Within twenty-four hours of the Supreme Court's ruling, Texas was passing one of the strictest voter-ID laws in the country, a law that had failed preclearance. That Texas voter-ID law was eventually deemed to have left 600,000 African Americans and Latinos without the requisite ID needed to vote.

Despite constitutional amendments, voting laws, and court oversight, states with Republican governors fell all over themselves to make elections hardest for the very people who were making America what it had long promised to be: an actual democracy. Texas, Georgia, and Florida went on a spree. Alabama got drunk. North Carolina danced on the bar. It doesn't much matter which tactic they used. Strict new voter identification laws, challenging new registration requirements, closing minority polling places, purges of the voter rolls. It was open season, and any old trick that could shave a few points off election results was in play.

Just two days after *Shelby County* came down, the mayor of Pasadena, Texas, proposed changing the structure of the city council elections to dilute the number of Latino seats. His candor was refreshing. He explained that it could be done "because the Justice Department can no longer tell us what to do." But it wasn't just Texas. Alabama tried to close thirty-one DMV offices, many in majority-Black counties, after instituting new photo-ID rules. A few weeks after *Shelby*, North Carolina passed the strictest voter suppression law in the country, eliminating same-day registration and out-of-precinct voting and reducing early voting, including souls-to-the-polls drives that traditionally aided Black voting on Sundays. (That law was eventually deemed by a federal appeals court to have targeted "African Americans with almost surgical precision.") Georgia? Check. Florida? Also check. *Vice* reported in 2018 that "in the years following the *Shelby* decision, jurisdictions once subject to federal supervision shut down, on average, almost 20 percent more polling stations per capita than jurisdictions in the rest of the country."

As Ari Berman, the voting rights columnist at *The Nation*, would explain after *Shelby County* came down, the 2016 election was to be "the first in 50 years without the full protections of the act." Unsurprisingly, he went on, "fourteen states had new voting restrictions in effect in 2016, including strict voter ID laws, fewer opportunities for early voting and reductions in the number of polling places. These restrictions depressed turnout in key states like Wisconsin, particularly among black voters." Maybe the bluntest way to put it is this: In the face of demographic changes that were turning red states purple and purple states blue, it was manifestly easier to make voting harder or impossible for the kinds of voters who tend to pull the lever for Democrats than to moderate an increasingly conservative GOP agenda to attract their votes. Cookie-cutter laws were being passed all over Republican-controlled states that would, in the aggregate, ensure that some votes would once again be more equal than others.

Stacey Abrams calls all of this "Jim Crow in a suit and tie." It's vote suppression under cover of "election integrity" that makes it vastly harder to vote if you are poor or Black or a student or Latino or disabled. And long before Donald Trump promised that he would *only* accept the results of the 2016 election if he won (and then later revealed that he would *never* accept the results of the 2020 election because he had lost), false claims that busloads of foreigners were voting in state elections were being used to justify laws that made voting more difficult for everyone. Republican legislators were making it harder to vote with false claims that dead people, Mickey Mouse, the heavyweight boxer Joe Frazier (dead since 2011), and Marxist agitators were voting multiple times at the same precincts.

It was Stacey Abrams who more than fifteen years ago recognized that this burgeoning impulse—to undermine the legitimacy of certain (read: minority) voters, in certain (read: minority) jurisdictions, with claims that certain (read: minority) populations were cheating in elections—needed to be countered by an equal and opposite imperative. That imperative was that more people should vote and that unless every ballot is valued and counted equally, democracy itself is in peril. After her 2018 election run, Abrams became both the voice and the symbol of that proposition.

Abrams unfailingly references herself as just another avatar, someone who merely represents a legion of extraordinary Black female elected officials, voting rights advocates, and community organizers on the ground who are all working together to register new populations and to get out the vote. That claim understates the extent to which she was also the architect of a strategy that would become a juggernaut in the face of efforts to limit the franchise after *Shelby County*. What Abrams understood, fifteen years before most of us, was that Georgia, like the rest of America, was changing faster than racist voting laws. She arrived on the political scene in 2006 and watched as Georgia Democrats lost almost everything electorally and Republicans won virtually every important office across the state.

But in Abrams's view, Georgia was changing too. The Latino population had doubled; the state was witnessing an explosion in its Asian
American and Pacific Islander population. Abrams was tracking what
she has described as the start of a "reverse migration of African
Americans who had moved to the Midwest and were relocating back
South." At present, according to *The Atlanta Journal-Constitution*, the
population of Georgia is around 10.5 million, and that population
was 57.5 percent white in 2008. It was 54.2 percent white in 2018. It
was 50.1 percent white in 2021. Abrams's take is that if minorities
were poised to become majorities, that should be reflected in who gets
elected to office.

In 2014, after Democrats held on to the seats they had won in 2012,
Abrams was raising millions of dollars from across the country—
earning some blowback from venerable civil rights groups in Georgia
who saw her as an upstart and a newcomer. For her gubernatorial
campaign in 2018, she raised $40 million—more money spent than on
any governor's race in history. Abrams was building and funding and
growing an infrastructure consisting almost wholly of human capital.
As she later explained to Traister, "In 2013, I created the New Georgia
Project, which trained poor folks in South Georgia to be quasi-
navigators, deploying them across 39 counties to help folks sign up for
the Affordable Care Act. Fast-forward: in 2014 it became a voter-
registration project." She said she realized that people didn't recognize
that it wasn't Obama denying them access to Medicaid; "it was the
governor and that Republican state legislator you keep voting for. Vote
him out and maybe things will get better." The message at that point
was simple: "You can't vote him out if you're not registered." Her focus
turned to the 800,000 unregistered Black and brown people in Georgia. After the 2014 election cycle, she created a group called the Voter
Access Institute, "because low-propensity voters are only 20 percent
likely to turn out and vote. We needed to think about how to boost
that number."

The special sauce Abrams added was education and engagement. It wouldn't be enough just to register new voters. They would need a whole tool kit on how and why to vote. As Abrams explained it, "It's the equivalent of giving someone keys to a car but never teaching them how to drive." People needed to learn where to vote, how to vote, and what to do if their attempts to vote were being diminished. In 2020, she told Traister that "having volunteers is great, but having experienced volunteers is vital. So when someone learns how to door-knock, when someone learns how to organize and get other people to work with them, that is *gold*."

Abrams described what she was striving to build as campaign "muscle memory," and her challenge was to create that in places where it hasn't existed before. If you think, then, about the vast communities of women you know who surged into political consciousness after 2016, Stacey Abrams had actually helped set the template for that long before Donald Trump even announced his candidacy. And it was Abrams who was targeting what she called the "New American Majority—people of color, those 18 to 29 years of age, and unmarried women"—as the keys to Georgia's future. Since 2014, the New Georgia Project has registered 500,000 Georgians to vote.

In a book about women lawyers who make change, about fame and not-fame, about insiders and outsiders, and about law versus power, Stacey Abrams struck me as an exemplar of all of the above. What she sought to do, in a political culture driven by cults of fame and personality and by stories of Great Men with marked cowboy leanings, was to decenter the candidate and change the view of an election as a reality show or morality play. It was Abrams who understood that political campaigns must rise and fall less on the charisma and popularity of any one candidate than on the agency and passion of every last voter. It was Abrams who didn't just want voters who swooned for an Obama or knocked on doors for a Hillary. She wanted voters who fully bought into the idea that every part of government needed to work for and respond to the electorate. As she would put it, "For me, the through-line is: If it's entirely based on a single person's personality, or reputation, when that gets hit, everything falls apart."

Abrams explained this in a granular way to Traister: "I don't run Fair Fight. Lauren Groh-Wargo is the CEO of Fair Fight. I don't run Fair Count. Rebecca DeHart is the CEO of Fair Count. I'm always very cognizant of the fact that when we place the focus on a single person instead of on the work, if that person falters, the work becomes invalidated." What Abrams emphasized, both in her run for the Georgia governor's seat in 2018 and as a through line in her elections work, is that if it's about any one individual, no matter how famous or charismatic, the risks of that person screwing up eventually become intolerable. She had found and built the cure for electoral politics as reality show. At minimum, she was helping voters to understand that if electoral politics *are* a reality show, it is the voter herself who is the star. And as I reflected on women and their special connection to law and to justice and to equality, the notion that they would by necessity become some of the primary agents behind the battle to protect voting rights seemed ever more apt. Women had to fight for this very right for decades.

Another element of Abrams's strategy? You campaign in Every. Single. District. You go to the town halls and the meet and greets even in the districts where seven voters show up for events and only four of them will ultimately vote for you. In her 2018 gubernatorial run, Abrams knocked on doors in rural Georgia where the Confederate flag stood at minimum for "southern heritage" if not for overt white supremacy. Again, this comes down to Abrams's broader vision of electoral engagement: you aren't building a cult of personality; you're building a political infrastructure. Abrams campaigned in every county in 2018, even in counties that wouldn't elect a Democrat if she were running against a Muppet. As Jelani Cobb put it in *The New Yorker* in 2019, for Abrams, the point of continuing to try to organize in deep red counties was to create "a cross-racial coalition that can make the state more competitive for Democrats. In that sense, her efforts look less like a Hail Mary than like a pass hurled downfield toward a specific receiver whom no one else has noticed." Abrams eschewed TV ads and knocked on doors, talked to rural voters about issues that really worried them where they lived their lives: health and education and green jobs and a restorative criminal-justice system. As she and her former campaign manager Lauren Groh-Wargo would write in 2021 of their ten-year plan to flip Georgia blue,

> Georgians deserved better, so we devised and began executing a 10-year plan to transform Georgia into a battleground state. As the world knows, President Biden won Georgia's 16 electoral votes in November, and the January runoff elections for two Senate seats secured full congressional control for the Democratic Party. Yet the result wasn't a miracle or truly a surprise, at least not to us. Years of planning, testing, innovating, sustained investment and organizing yielded the record-breaking results we knew they could and should.

So. That 2018 governor's race in Georgia.

Abrams had at this point developed her gigantic war chest, her national reputation, and the strategic plan she'd been working up for years. By her lights, if everything went right, a Black woman really might be elected governor in a southern red state. But Abrams was also running against Brian Kemp, who ran as a "Trump conservative" and bragged during the campaign that he had a pickup truck big enough to "round up criminal illegals." That wasn't the main concern. The deeper problem was that candidate Kemp was also serving as Georgia's secretary of state throughout the race. It was Brian Kemp, then, who was formally tasked with setting the rules for the election he was also running in. Is that weird? Yes. Yes, it is. Former president

Jimmy Carter would later say that this conflict of interest ran "counter to the most fundamental principle of democratic elections—that the electoral process be managed by an independent and impartial election authority."

In some sense, the current obsession with a mythical rash of "vote fraud" that has been deployed to restrict minority voting had been incubating in Georgia for decades. One of the modern forefathers of the voter fraud myth, Hans von Spakovsky, got his start in Georgia, where he was chairman of the Fulton County GOP and a member of the election board in the 1990s. Vote fraud became the basis for Kemp's long-standing efforts to throw voters off the rolls. That means that among other irregularities around the 2018 election, during his time as secretary of state, Kemp had purged 1.5 million voters from Georgia's election rolls. That effort took several forms that have become increasingly familiar. For instance, as Jelani Cobb explained in *The New Yorker*, according to a study by American Public Media, Secretary Kemp's office had canceled 100,000 voter registrations for Georgians who hadn't voted in seven years under a "use it or lose it" policy. Kemp also, in the name of fighting "vote fraud," put in place an "exact match" policy that demanded voter registration applications be a flawless match to the information contained on official government documents. The spelling of a name, a misplaced hyphen, an accent in the wrong place—anything at all could be the basis for rejecting registrations. Somehow, voter registrations of 53,000 voters, of whom 70 percent were Black, were suddenly flagged for review. As the race approached, there were more and more reports of peculiarities: absentee ballots that were requested but never mailed, new citizens told they were ineligible to vote, a report of 4,700 absentee ballot requests that were lost in DeKalb County. In 2020, a House committee studying the 2018 election determined, among other irregularities, that after removing 500,000 voters from rolls—perhaps the largest single cancellation of voter registrations in US history, as reported by *The*

Atlanta Journal-Constitution—Kemp and a campaign staffer shared a Democratic candidate's press release about the threat of systemic voter suppression, annotating it with the word "us" with laughing and smiling emojis.

The historian Carol Anderson, writing in *The Atlantic* in 2018, pointed out that while Kemp was insisting to the media that these tens of thousands of new voter registrations pouring into his office were per se evidence of voter fraud that he was unwilling to tolerate, and launching investigations of Abrams and the New Georgia Project, by at least 2014 he was telling fellow Republicans the truth in private: "Democrats are working hard, and all these stories about them, you know, registering all these minority voters that are out there and others that are sitting on the sidelines, if they can do that, they can win these elections in November."

Four days before the gubernatorial election, a federal district judge ruled that the exact-match policy was a burden for voters, and Common Cause Georgia brought a suit to ensure that provisional ballots were properly counted. Two days before the November election, Kemp's office announced, with little evidence, that it was opening an inquiry into the state Democratic Party after a private citizen reported what was termed "a failed attempt to hack the state's voter registration system." No such hack was ever proven, although the Georgia Bureau of Investigation conducted a thorough investigation. In addition to missing absentee ballots and ballots tossed for failing to exactly match the corresponding registrations, Georgians suffered from shuttered polling places and maddeningly long lines, power failures in minority precincts, precincts with too few voting machines, and polling places with too few provisional ballots. If that sounds like a point-by-point weaponization of the post-*Shelby* strategies, it's because it was. And prior to *Shelby*, Georgia would have been under preclearance, meaning that new voting practices would have required approval. Post-*Shelby*, it was Calvinball.

Kemp was ultimately declared the winner by a margin of less than two percentage points. In her *Brnovich* dissent on the Voting Rights Act in 2021, Justice Kagan emphasized that "elections are often fought and won at the margins" and that Georgia's election was all about the margins. The 2018 governor's race was decided by fifty-five thousand votes, of nearly four million cast, in an election in which hundreds of thousands of voter registrations had been canceled. In November 2018, Abrams gave a speech in which she explained why she found it impossible to concede. "I acknowledge that former Secretary of State Brian Kemp will be certified as the victor of the 2018 gubernatorial election," she announced. "But to watch an elected official—who claims to represent the people of this state—baldly pin his hopes for election on the suppression of the people's democratic right to vote has been truly appalling. So, to be clear, this is not a speech of concession." We may never know for certain what did or did not decide the 2018 Georgia race, but we know without a doubt that the tactic of making it ever more difficult for minorities to vote would only become more prevalent.

When Donald Trump would refuse to concede in 2020, it would be said that Stacey Abrams started it. But of course Abrams could argue, and multiple lawsuits would later show, that her own election was significantly flawed. Despite tens of lawsuits after the 2020 presidential contest, Donald Trump has still failed to prevail in legal claims alleging massive impropriety, stolen ballots, or widespread irregularity. Georgia would come to stand as a dry run for close elections, for voter suppression, and for counterclaims of vote fraud and of "illegal" voters. That Georgia gubernatorial contest, with the vote suppression pitted against claims of fraud and illegal organizing, was the minor-league game that perfectly presaged the 2020 contest to come.

But in one important sense, that 2018 election became a huge win for the principle that every vote must count. In Georgia, the participation rate for nineteen- to twenty-eight-year-old voters increased by

476 percent from the 2014 midterms. African American and Latino turnout in the state went up 165 percent and 571 percent, respectively. The statistic Abrams often cited after the 2018 contest was this one: 925,000 African Americans voted in the 2014 gubernatorial race; in 2018, 1.4 million African Americans voted. And 94 percent of them had voted for Stacey Abrams. That is transformational power, and it was harnessed and helmed at least in part by a female tax lawyer who was still, in 2018, writing romance novels under a pseudonym.

After that election, Stacey Abrams says she went into mourning for ten days and then got back to work. She was soon being courted for the vice presidential nomination in 2020, had her name floated as a prospective Democratic president's Supreme Court nominee, and was also asked to run for the Georgia Senate in 2020. But she did none of the above. In service to her own credo about making electoral change as opposed to building a personal brand, Abrams stayed in Georgia. She scaled up. She raised money. And she continued to evangelize for the proposition that the best cure for rampant voter suppression was rampant voter engagement.

Stacey Abrams never believed she was *owed* the Georgia governorship in 2018, but she maintains that both she and Georgia voters were owed an elections system that functions to count every single vote.

So after the 2018 election was called, Abrams founded Fair Fight Action, a new voting rights organization that advocates against vote suppression, and Fair Count, which sought to get communities of color, rural populations, and other marginalized groups counted in the 2020 census. Together with Care in Action, a group that organizes domestic workers in the state, Abrams also filed a lawsuit seeking to overhaul the entire Georgia elections system. The sixty-six-page complaint, combined with a host of other lawsuits filed statewide to challenge the 2018 election, laid out the ways in which voter purges, suspended registration applications, long lines and other problems at nonwhite

voting precincts, and mishandled absentee and provisional ballots un-
constitutionally burdened the state's voters of color. In addition to
demanding reforms in advance of the 2020 election, the lawsuit asked
that Georgia be placed back under the preclearance requirements of
the Voting Rights Act, meaning that a federal court would need to
preapprove any new voting practices to ensure they didn't violate
minority voting rights. As UC Irvine's voting rights expert Richard
Hasen wrote in *Slate* in November 2018, when the suit was filed, the
scope of this new lawsuit was capacious by design: It attacked the
voter purges and the strict "exact match" policy that kept thousands
of voters off the rolls for discrepancies between voting forms and driving records as minor as a missing hyphen. It went after the state's ancient voter registration database and voting machines, the closing and
moving of polling places, the inaccurate voter registration rolls, the
management of provisional ballots and absentee ballots. "The suit," he
wrote, "alleges these problems together violate the Voting Rights Act,
the Help America Vote Act, and the due process and equal protection
clauses of the 14th Amendment."

Additionally, the suit was filed far in advance of the 2020 election
so that courts would have plenty of time to review claims without running afoul of a legal presumption against changing voting practices
immediately before voting is set to begin. The complaint detailed suppression of lawful Georgia voters, like Carlos del Rio, chair of the
Department of Global Health at the Rollins School of Public Health
at Emory University, who was initially turned away from his voting
precinct on November 6, 2018, because the state database wrongly
listed his last name as being spelled "delRio." Abrams was putting a
face on an abstraction—how seemingly race-neutral tweaks within a
decentralized state elections machinery fall most heavily on people
who are poor, Black, brown, or new immigrants. That litigation became a vehicle for challenging a 2019 purge of twenty-two thousand
voters in Georgia, and while the lawsuit remains unresolved, Donald

Trump still faults his 2020 loss in Georgia on a consent decree that resulted from the litigation.

Election law was fast becoming the sexiest thing a young lawyer could do. And Georgia was just the beginning. Anyone who believed that voter roll purges and shuttered polling places and signature match requirements were limited to Atlanta was missing the fact that it was happening in their own backyard. As Abrams would explain to Traister in 2020, it wasn't just that she scaled up voter engagement, registration, and education. She also nationalized the message that throwing out ballots would be an ongoing strategy in tight elections. The lesson of 2018, she said, was to mitigate "voter suppression *across the country*. Voter suppression existed in '16; it existed in '18. But we had a voter-protection apparatus that covered the country through these battleground states: Wisconsin, Michigan, Pennsylvania, Arizona, Nevada, Minnesota. The work done through Fair Fight to mitigate voter suppression got people to the polls. It's not the only thing, but it is a *huge* thing."

The other lesson of that 2018 gubernatorial election that became crucial in organizing around voting rights in 2020 was that it forced inchoate and unproven claims about widespread vote fraud to be proven. Just as the then secretary of state Brian Kemp had waved vaguely at unfounded claims about "vote fraud" to justify holding on to, throwing out, and refusing to match ballots to voter registrations, the whole country would soon fall prey to false claims about tainted mail-in ballots and elections stolen by foreigners, virtually all of which were proven false in a court of law. The trial run in Georgia afforded proponents of generous voting rights ample time and resources to defend against the imaginary vote fraud that would soon be deployed to try to choke off voting by mail, early registration, drop boxes, and the other expansions of the franchise that would come to define the 2020 election wars.

Let's do this quickly, then: There is no widespread crisis of in-person vote fraud in America. None. There is also no widespread crisis of

mail-in vote fraud or early voting fraud. None. Based on the most generous set of data collected by the Heritage Foundation, the incidence
of voter fraud in the two decades before the 2020 election was about
0.00006 percent of total ballots cast. That's about twelve hundred
cases dating back to the 1980s. The nonpartisan Brennan Center's
massive study from 2007 put that number at somewhere between
0.0003 percent and 0.0025 percent. That same study famously concluded that it's more likely an American "will be struck by lightning
than that he will impersonate another voter at the polls."

Why, then, do we keep hearing about boxes of stolen ballots, guys
who vote once then put on a fake mustache to vote again, corrupt
election workers who steal or damage great quantities of ballots, and
voting machines cunningly programmed by nefarious Italians and
George Soros to rig and steal and damage elections? Because those
claims serve a very deliberate purpose, which is to make voting far
more difficult for far more people. This, too, has been happening for
more than a decade. Anodyne "voter integrity" measures with names
like Kemp's "exact match" system and the infamous Interstate Crosscheck system are cumbersome computerized database-matching programs that toss eligible voters off the rolls based on trivial errors, of
which the burden will fall on spellings of foreign-sounding names.
One team of researchers at Harvard, Yale, Stanford, and the University of Pennsylvania determined that the Crosscheck program once
pressed by Kansas's secretary of state Kris Kobach had an eye-popping
error rate of 99 percent and that for every fraudulent vote it stopped,
it would impede two thousand eligible voters from casting a ballot.
Texas officials were sued after a "review" of their own state voter rolls
led to challenges to the citizenship status of thousands of voters who
turned out largely to be naturalized citizens. Voter suppression, as
Justice Kagan put it in her *Brnovich* dissent, is all a big game of whack-
a-mole, and Stacey Abrams's response was to sign up voters faster than
they were being turned away and to challenge state practices that

burden minority voters disproportionately. More than a lawyer and an organizer, Abrams became a teacher, a roaming constitutional law class on election manipulation.

THE ROBERTS COURT HAS WORKED hand in glove with states trying to turn voting into an obstacle course, and that has been done in response to a nonexistent emergency that has never been proven by way of statistical analysis, political science modeling, or litigation. "The right to vote freely for the candidate of one's choice is of the essence of a democratic society, and any restrictions on that right strike at the heart of representative government," Chief Justice Earl Warren announced in 1964 in *Reynolds v. Sims*—the high-water mark for voting rights at the Supreme Court. That is the message Stacey Abrams carried out of 2018 and it was very much a message Americans needed to hear.

It wasn't just *Shelby County* that opened the floodgates to widespread suppression of minority voting. The high court had signed off on strict voter-ID laws in *Crawford v. Marion County* in 2008, even as it acknowledged that the scourge of so-called vote fraud it was intended to deter was vanishingly rare. In a 2018 case, *Husted v. A. Philip Randolph Institute*, the Supreme Court blessed Ohio's voter purge system, allowing the state to use one's failure to vote to trigger the process of removing someone from the voter rolls. In 2019 in *Rucho v. Common Cause*, the Supreme Court decided that political gerrymandering claims are beyond the reach of federal courts and cannot be litigated because they are not "justiciable." And of course, in 2010, the Supreme Court opened the floodgates to dark, untraceable money in financing political campaigns with the decision in *Citizens United v. FEC*. Georgia in 2018 was running the playbook, but the Roberts Court was writing the plays.

It is a cliché to assert that one of the enduring lessons of the four years Trump held office was that norms that did not have the force of law could collapse so swiftly under the weight of lies and deceptions. One of the norms Trump sought to crush was the conviction that voting is a secure and rational activity in which everyone who is eligible should be allowed to participate. After they were repeatedly told that vote fraud is everywhere and that Trump lost the popular vote to Hillary Clinton in 2016 only because millions of people cast illegal ballots, it was certainly possible that Americans would simply give up on voting. That, more so even than vote suppression, was the existential fear of the Trump attack on voting. The message he would attempt to convey in the 2020 presidential election was not merely that voting systems were rife with cheating but that voting is fundamentally pointless. Nihilism, as much as shuttered polling places and rejected voter registrations, was the real currency in which Trump was trading. Tell enough voters that Democrats, Italians, letter carriers, George Soros, the people who build voting machines, foreign voters, and nonpartisan state election officials are all conspiring to throw the election, and why would anyone vote again? Better to stay at home and root for the insurrection.

Voting in the United States is, at bottom, a fantastical act of trust in complicated, decentralized, and aging election systems operated by humans who make fewer errors than one might expect. Why would *anyone*, amid claims that the media was lying and foreigners were flipping election machines, engage in the monstrously irrational act of standing in endless lines, sometimes for hours and, in 2020, during a global health catastrophe, to do something that's fundamentally just statistically senseless? The nihilism and denialism that swamped so much of American discourse and thought could easily have overmastered anyone's interest in or desire to vote. One 2009 study found that in the states in which any single vote was *most* likely to matter, one vote had an approximate one-in-ten-million chance of determining the national election outcome. On average, the same study concluded, any one voter in America had a one-in-sixty-million chance of being decisive in the presidential election. Voting is mathematically *pointless*. It's a whispered prayer. It's an act of collective hope and activism that feels anachronistic when the temptation to believe that the fix is in is overwhelming. Trump's enduring contribution to America—long before the 2020 contest he still disputes—was to undermine voter trust in the absence of any evidence. It's enduring because, as of this writing, about six in ten Republicans believe that Joe Biden lost the 2020 election, without any evidence to support that view. And that statistic is vital because under cover of "election integrity" claims, voting is being suppressed nationwide.

Even before COVID and a last-minute effort by Trump's attorney general and postmaster general to undermine voting by mail, I was beset by the fear that if I put into writing that voting was under attack, I was inviting my own readers to sit out elections; that just talking and writing about vote suppression and voter intimidation and long lines and court interventions would give prospective voters a reason to give up and stay home. Georgia historian Carol Anderson, author of *One Person, No Vote*, was having none of that. In an interview in February 2020, when I asked her on a podcast why anyone should even bother attempting to vote considering all the barriers faced by minorities, young people, and other vulnerable communities, she reminded me that citizens are personally responsible for shoring up the Fifteenth Amendment, and that when states erect barriers to voting, one's individual responsibility only increases:

> When I talk about putting the responsibility of adhering to the 15th Amendment on the shoulders and on the backs of the individuals, that means checking your voter registration on a consistent basis to make sure you're still registered and to

make sure your voting place is where you know it is, and then making a screenshot of it. So you have evidence of it. It means knowing that the lines are probably going to be really long, if you vote in a minority precinct. So you come prepared. You come with your cellphone. You come with a battery pack. You come with water, you come with snacks, you come with comfortable shoes. Because if we don't do that now, what comes afterwards is something that's going to be absolutely horrific to deal with.

In the face of barriers to voting, you vote, she was urging. You vote in precisely the way most Black people have voted in America for decades, if and when they were permitted to vote at all. Vote for the promise because there is no backup plan. At the Democratic National Convention in August 2020, former president Barack Obama sounded the same uncharacteristically wary note, warning of Trump, "This president and those in power—those who benefit from keeping things the way they are—they are counting on your cynicism. They know they can't win you over with their policies. So they're hoping to make it as hard as possible for you to vote, and to convince you that your vote doesn't matter." Former first lady Michelle Obama, in her own DNC speech, offered a more graphic caution. "Right now," she said, "folks who know they cannot win fair and square at the ballot box are doing everything they can to stop us from voting. They're closing down polling places in minority neighborhoods. They're purging voter rolls. They're sending people out to intimidate voters and they're lying about the security of our ballots. These tactics are not new." The Obamas' final charge in the months before the 2020 election was that in the face of electoral cynicism and fear, making any one vote matter is how you make voting matter, and that long after the founding, long after the Reconstruction Amendments, long after the Voting Rights Act and *Shelby County*, voting when the franchise is under assault is the most patriotic act of all. It was the advice Anita Hill had given in defense of standing up and naming your sexual harasser: you do it because "think about where we would be if nobody was doing it."

As I was finishing this chapter—ostensibly about the events of the 2018 gubernatorial race in Georgia—the Supreme Court handed down an opinion on July 1, 2021, in a voting rights case I mentioned earlier, called *Brnovich v. DNC*. Dissenting in this decision on the last day of the term, Justice Elena Kagan essentially ghostwrote this chapter about the 2018 Georgia governor's race by setting forth the long history of state-sanctioned vote suppression in the United States. It may well become the most important dissenting opinion she ever writes, and she's already penned some doozies.

In a crushing blow to democracy, and voting along 6–3 lines, the high court in *Brnovich* effectively put an end to Section 2 of the Voting Rights Act of 1965. The Supreme Court had already eviscerated Section 5 of the VRA back in 2013 in *Shelby County v. Holder*. Section 2 barred any "voting qualification," any "prerequisite to voting," or any "standard, practice, or procedure" that "results in a denial or abridgement of the right" to "vote on account of race." Section 5 was intended to get around the fact that litigation is slow, expensive, and burdensome by putting jurisdictions with racist voting histories under federal supervision, or preclearance. Gutting Section 5 in 2013, the court soothed itself by noting that vulnerable voters would always be able to rely upon the protections of Section 2 to fight racialized voting practices. In 2021, Section 2 was blown up as well. Justice Kagan, dissenting on behalf of herself, Sonia Sotomayor, and Stephen Breyer in *Brnovich*, wrote what can only be described as an elegy to the American efforts to build a true representational democracy. Her opening passage set forth the history of recent decades:

If a single statute represents the best of America, it is the Voting Rights Act. It marries two great ideals: democracy and racial equality. And it dedicates our country to carrying them out. Section 2, the provision at issue here, guarantees that members of every racial group will have equal voting opportunities. Citizens of every race will have the same shot to participate in the political process and to elect representatives of their choice. They will all own our democracy together—no one more and no one less than any other.

If a single statute reminds us of the worst of America, it is the Voting Rights Act. Because it was—and remains—so necessary. Because a century after the Civil War was fought, at the time of the Act's passage, the promise of political equality remained a distant dream for African American citizens. Because States and localities continually "contriv[ed] new rules," mostly neutral on their face but discriminatory in operation, to keep minority voters from the polls . . . Because "Congress had reason to suppose" that States would "try similar maneuvers in the future"—"pour[ing] old poison into new bottles" to suppress minority votes . . . Because Congress has been proved right.

It is astounding that the world's oldest constitutional democracy continues to be unable to guarantee that every person who wishes to vote can do so. It is astounding that instead of starting from the presumption that everyone should vote, there are state legislatures, state courts, and federal judges who are intent on making it ever harder for people to vote because of a wholly imaginary scourge of fraudulent voting that has never been proven. Most astounding of all is that this is how the country that calls itself the world's oldest constitutional democracy has chosen to embark upon the twenty-first century.

Stacey Abrams's contribution to the seeming doom loop of shrink-ing voting rights, as aided and abetted by the Supreme Court, was to refuse to succumb to the doom. In her view, voting is an act of confi-dence, a choice to be visible, a web of connections, a mechanism to better your condition, and a refusal to be told that you don't belong in the governor's mansion, whether you're a high schooler who arrived via public transport or a Black woman trying to organize uncommit-ted voters. Abrams came out of the 2018 governor's race with no illu-sions about the hazards of voting while Black. She told CBS News in 2021 that this was part of the point: "When you've never had to think about the hardship of voting, then yes, these conversations on voter suppression seem absurd to you. When you have never spent more than seven minutes in line, it is nearly impossible to imagine that there are poor Black people who stand in line for eight hours, miss an entire day's wages, risk losing their jobs simply to cast a ballot in an election that may or may not have any benefit in their lives."

In short, what Stacey Abrams offered Americans was rooted in the transformational force of taking back power and believing in democ-racy in the face of being told nothing matters. But also what she of-fered up was the obligation to take on the extraordinary act of empathy and imagination required to understand what Kagan was saying in *Brnovich* in 2021: that just because *you* have voter ID, and just because *you* have a mailbox up the street, and just because *you* have the last name Smith doesn't make voting simple for everyone. And if thou-sands of people cannot vote because of where they live or how their last name is spelled or because they live on an Indian reservation with a PO box, then nobody is voting in a real democracy. Justice Samuel Alito, writing for the majority in *Brnovich*, failed to even attempt to imagine what voting might be like on a reservation. The only suffer-ing he seemed able to see was his own unfounded fear about rampant vote fraud.

One of the things women bring to the law is the capacity to see outside the hermetically sealed story of the law itself: what I've called the split-screen understanding that the entire edifice of the legal system is a privilege that was for so long denied to so many. It's why it matters that Stacey Abrams writes romance novels and that Pauli Murray wrote poems. Both are acts of imagination and generosity. Abrams didn't just build a machine that would "get out the vote" in Georgia. She told a story that would set the stage for a 2020 election in Georgia, and across the nation, in which millions of Americans who never had the experience of voting while Black could finally both imagine what that was like and prepare themselves to do so.

10

The Elections Long Game: Redistricting and the Census

Nina Perales: The Latino Vote Strategist

N ina Perales, who helms voting rights litigation at MALDEF, the Mexican American Legal Defense and Educational Fund, always starts with the reminder that the right to vote is singular: "The right to vote has been described as fundamental to the exercise of all other rights. Without the ability to have a voice in government, you lose on a lot of other fronts, including public education and immigration policy. Particularly for the Latino community, the ability to translate our demographic growth into a voice in politics is central to our entry into American life."

That battle has been Perales's daily existence for more than two decades. Perales is laugh-out-loud funny and disarmingly frank for a tactician and litigator. She wears her brown hair in a tidy bun and describes the Women's March in DC in 2017 in terms of "these women that went to DC and they wore pink hats with little cat ears on them." But that wasn't her experience of January 2017. She told me she saw photos of the first Women's March, sure, but "that wasn't really necessarily something that was big happening in Texas." Perales was born in New York, and she holds an associate of arts degree from Bard College at Simon's Rock, a bachelor's degree from Brown University, and a JD from Columbia Law School. "I was definitely a student activist," she says. "I went to Brown undergrad and I was a student activist." She went to law school always knowing she wanted to become a civil rights attorney because she was born to it. "My dad," she says, "was also a civil rights lawyer, and he was a founder of the Puerto Rican Legal Defense Fund. Some of the other founders remember me being very small and going to some of those meetings."

After a five-year stint at the Puerto Rican Legal Defense and Education Fund in New York City and having attended the fourth UN World Conference on Women in Beijing in 1995, with a delegation of Latina women, Perales moved with her husband to Texas, where they have lived for twenty-five years. She arrived in Texas, she says, "as a young bride" and applied for a voting rights attorney position at MALDEF in San Antonio. "I must've interviewed when I was nine months pregnant," she told me, "because I looked like a house. . . . In fact, somebody had to drive me to the interview because I couldn't reach the steering wheel anymore. And I got the job, and so I came right off maternity leave and started working at MALDEF and that was twenty-five years ago."

Today, Perales manages all the day-to-day litigation activity of MALDEF's regional offices, and her voting rights work demands more and more attention to redistricting, focusing on how electoral districts are drawn to dilute minority voting. In a 2021 podcast, she explained that "redistricting means that even if everyone has full access to voting, you can dilute the vote even if everyone had the opportunity to register and cast a ballot. Redistricting plans can ensure that the minority voice is still suppressed." In other words, when voter purges and voter ID and onerous registration requirements can't get the job done, redistricting can ensure that even if you manage to vote, you are not heard or represented. That's a simple matter of drawing maps that drown out some voices and amplify others.

Perales started at MALDEF doing voting rights, then, in the 2001 redistricting cycle, she moved onto a Texas case that went all the way to the Supreme Court. In 2006, she argued and won a vote dilution case pressed by Latino voters under the Voting Rights Act, *League of United Latin American Citizens v. Perry.* In that case, the justices found that the Texas legislature had blocked West Texas's Latino voters from electing their preferred candidate by removing 100,000 Latinos from their congressional district. Perales has since been involved in redistricting in Texas, Arizona, and Arkansas, and with the 2020 census just taken, she told me, "we're getting ready to do redistricting all over the map for this upcoming round." Redistricting cases fall to a relatively small group of attorneys, and almost none of them are women.

Asked whether discrimination against Latinos looked different growing up in New York than it does today in Texas, Perales explained, "It was different for me, because my ethnic origin is Puerto Rican. But I moved to Laredo—for the first year my husband was clerking in Laredo—and Laredo is 98 percent Mexican American." In one sense, she told me, she "moved from one Spanish-speaking community to another Spanish-speaking community." But she added that New York once had a literacy test while Texas did not. Perales told me that a good deal of voting rights work done in New York came amid a lot of backlash against arriving immigrants. "That's where the literacy test in New York came from," she said.

"The Puerto Rican experience in New York," Perales added, "the great migration of the '50s and the '60s, involved a lot of pushback against brown folks arriving. And Puerto Ricans are US citizens by birth, so they were eligible to vote, and there were *still* so many barriers put up, particularly for language." Coming from that to Texas, she told me, was very different, "but a lot of the historical trends were the same." Perales explained that the coalition built around redistricting and Latino voting rights first took root after World War II: "One of my clients is the GI Forum. Those are Latino war veterans. And when I did the redistricting in the 2000 round, a lot of my guys were still from World War II. These were the guys that came back from Europe, where they saw integration, to the United States." Returning to the United States, these soldiers "saw the same Jim Crow segregation they were raised with: segregated parks, swimming pools, libraries, schools, restaurants, theaters, where you have to go in a separate entrance and sit in a different area." In some ways, though, they were lucky, she told me: they were young, able to get a good education because of the GI bill. "And these were the guys that really built the legs under the Latino civil rights movement, and they built the legs under MALDEF and many other organizations."

Perales told me that Latino voters don't necessarily skew to the Democrats, who have not always served their interests. "Some of these guys were still around in the 2000s when I was representing the GI Forum, and their memories go deeply into the time when Texas was a Democratic state and deeply racist and segregated." For those voters, she added, "the party label was not as important as the opportunity for the Latino community to be able to cast a ballot." In the last round of redistricting, Perales said, "it was institutional memory of these Latino organizations that were coming together saying, 'We need to get on top of this, or we're just going to end up at the disadvantage we had before.'"

Long before Trump's election in 2016, Perales saw that voting rights were going to be swept up into a larger political discourse that fomented fear of immigrants and communities of color, that "Make America

Great Again" never really envisioned allowing every American to vote, and that this would be about color and immigration, more than who was, strictly speaking, American. That's been her life these past years. In 2018, Perales started defending the federal Deferred Action for Childhood Arrivals program that offered the children of undocumented immigrants who were brought to the States a pathway to citizenship. That same year MALDEF challenged a Texas law requiring counties and cities to enforce federal immigration law against local residents. In 2018, Perales was at the Supreme Court with another racial gerrymandering case in Texas. Because one of the truly enduring legacies of Trumpism has been about making minorities in America invisible.

Trump took office in 2017 with a clear plan to diminish voting rights, and he used the lie of widespread vote fraud to do so. His first attorney general, Jeff Sessions, was notorious for his (botched) efforts as a US attorney in Alabama to convict three African American activists for voter fraud. His overzealous prosecution of those voting rights activists was one of the reasons the Senate rejected Sessions for a federal judgeship in 1986. Over the twenty years Sessions sat in the US Senate, only one Black person was ever appointed to a federal judgeship in Alabama, a state that is 26 percent African American. But what once precluded Sessions from a judicial seat made him doubly attractive as a Trump surrogate on the campaign trail and then as Trump's first attorney general.

When Trump was out campaigning for the presidency in 2016, Sessions was amplifying his false claims about voter ID and mass vote fraud and echoing Trump's insistence that the Democrats were "attempting to rig this election." When it emerged that Trump had lost the popular vote to Hillary Clinton by 2.9 million votes in the 2016 presidential race, Trump refused to accept that those ballots were cast legitimately. He hastily assembled the nominally bipartisan Presidential Advisory Commission on Election Integrity in 2017. That commission was tasked with determining which "laws, rules, policies, activities, strategies, and practices . . . undermine the American people's confidence in the integrity of voting processes used in Federal elections," all in the hopes of further undermining the American people's confidence in the integrity of voting processes. The commission was co-chaired by Vice President Mike Pence and the longtime election fraud enthusiast/fabulist Kris Kobach.

While he was Kansas's secretary of state, Kobach's signature legal intervention had required every new voter to prove citizenship before registering, a measure that had blocked the registrations of more than thirty-five thousand eligible Kansas voters. That requirement was eventually struck down in 2018 by a federal judge, Julie Robinson. Kobach, who argued on behalf of Kansas in court, was fined, sanctioned, and sent to a lawyers' equivalent of traffic school for his misconduct during the trial. Judge Robinson concluded in her 2018 opinion that after scrupulously examining all the statistical evidence put forth by Kobach, "while there is evidence of a small number of noncitizen registrations in Kansas, it is largely explained by administrative error, confusion, or mistake." Kobach, she added, had promised that the fraud he had alleged was just the tip of the iceberg, and yet "the Court draws the more obvious conclusion that there is no iceberg; only an icicle, largely created by confusion and administrative error." In his eight-year crusade to unearth mass vote fraud in Kansas, Kobach ultimately secured nine convictions in a state of nearly two million voters.

Trump's so-called Election Integrity Commission was similarly doomed to fail. In its first official act in 2017, the commission demanded vast quantities of public information from the states about their voters, including names, addresses, dates of birth, political affiliations, voting history, and the last four digits of their Social Security numbers. That triggered outrage from both sides of the political spectrum, as well as multiple lawsuits that eventually led to the disintegration of the commission in 2018. Like Kobach's spectacular flameout in the Kansas fed-eral courts, it was obvious the entire purpose of this commission wasn't to unearth vote fraud but to use the specter of imaginary vote fraud to roll back the vote and to terrorize immigrants and voters of color.

One lesson of the Trump years with respect to voting rights was this: just as there is no single way to choke off the right to vote, there is no one way to defend against it. While there were armies of elec-tion lawyers and lawsuits in the four years Trump was president, there was never *the* voting rights case of the Trump era, and you'd be hard-pressed to name *the* voting rights lawyer. As Vanita Gupta suggested earlier in this book, voting rights wins across the country were achieved by hundreds of organizers and litigators. The ACLU's Dale Ho, with a phalanx of staff attorneys, prevailed in the Kansas lawsuit against Ko-bach's citizenship law. Marc Elias and his colleagues at Perkins Coie beat back dozens of election challenges from Trump and his allies around the 2020 election. Sherrilyn Ifill at the NAACP Legal Defense Fund, Paul Smith at the Campaign Legal Center, Kristen Clarke at the Lawyers' Committee for Civil Rights, and Stacey Abrams in Georgia were all "the lawyer," and they operated in coalitions nationwide, part-nered with private law firms, academic advisors, volunteer lawyers, and law students.

As of this writing, Latinos constitute 18 percent of the US popula-tion and represent half the population growth in the United States over the past ten years. Texas is now home to the second-biggest La-tino population in the country, behind California, and by 2040 it's projected that Latinos will constitute the majority of its citizens. And in Texas, Perales was seeing the trends Abrams had clocked in Georgia. Minorities flexing new electoral muscle. "What happened in 2018," she told me, "in a midterm election where Latinos bumped their vote share up by five percentage points . . . I've never seen that happen before, ever."

What accounted for that massive uptick in Latino engagement?

Perales laughed. "I don't know exactly what was going on in 2018, except Beto O'Rourke, who by the way is not Latino. Beto O'Rourke really caught fire in the young people." As was the case with respect to women voters around the country, young Latinos in 2018 were mobilized and activated, and there was a huge jump in voter turnout. "And I think that was very scary for the people who are in leadership in Texas right now. I think that's why we are seeing so many proposals now that would make it more difficult to vote in Texas."

At the time of its founding, MALDEF was contending with Jim Crow–style discrimination leveled against Mexican Americans in housing, schooling, public accommodations, and employment. MALDEF has since expanded to represent all Latinos, not just in the Southwest but around the country. They litigate around racist and unfair elections, local ordinances, and employment practices. And Perales was quick to point out that while we think of Jim Crow in terms of deliberate discrimination against Black Americans, legal discrimination against Mexican Americans in the Southwest was always pervasive. Texas's long history of voting discrimination against its Latino and African American citizens dates back to 1845. Section 5 of the Voting Rights Act was in fact expanded to include Texas for preclearance of new election rules in 1975.

One reason Perales has been involved in so many voting and redistricting cases around the country is that Texas has been a kind of dark laboratory for years of efforts to suppress Latino votes. Three decades ago, a Republican operative, Thomas Hofeller, infamously said, "I define redistricting as the only legalized form of vote-stealing left in the United States today." The same Hofeller explained gleefully in 2001 that "redistricting is like an election in reverse! It's a great event. . . . Usually the voters get to pick the politicians. In redistricting, the politicians get to pick the voters!"

It was Hofeller who would become the primary architect of the GOP's broad, years-long gerrymandering program that relied on collecting data on race and voting behavior, then crafting maps surgically reverse engineered to dilute the influence of minority voters. It was also Hofeller, even in death, who would become a central part of the Trump administration's attempt to add a citizenship question to the 2020 census. That census would be the basis for new voting maps drawn in 2021 and for distorting the minority count. In 2019, MALDEF was part of a coalition of groups that successfully challenged that effort.

That Trump citizenship census case was not the most important of the big Trump-era lawsuits, but it is quite probably one of the most preposterous. The administration's ham-fisted attempt to rig the 2020 census to dilute and depress the power of minority voters and terrorize noncitizens was emblematic of the ways in which unskilled and sloppy lawyering ultimately blunted the most racist Trump impulses. Had they succeeded, the move would have discouraged minorities from being counted in the census, which would have led to electoral maps that dramatically undercounted them. In tandem with the voter suppression happening nationwide, the effect would have been to ensure that even if Latino voters were able to register and vote, their votes would count for less.

Perales explained that the citizenship census question took aim at a very different population from the groups that organize around voting or redistricting. "The citizenship question," she explains, would have "had a strong deterrent effect on people answering the census." The target was always "newly arrived immigrants." That's a different constituency from her redistricting clients, who are "usually voter-eligible folks that are doing a lot of the advocacy around redistricting," she explains. "People who would identify as Chicano, people who would use that word for themselves, people who are Mexican American and who identify as Mexican American. But the census citizenship question was aimed directly at the heart of the immigrant community."

The census litigation eventually revealed that as early as July 2017,

Kansas's secretary of state, Kris Kobach, had written to Trump's commerce secretary, Wilbur Ross, who oversaw the Census Bureau, urging that a citizenship question be added to the decennial census of 2020. In Kobach's mind, this was "essential" because a failure to confirm citizenship "leads to the problem that aliens who do not actually 'reside' in the United States are still counted for congressional apportionment purposes."

Article 1, section 2, of the Constitution requires an "actual Enumeration" of the population every ten years, "in such Manner as [Congress] shall by Law direct," so that congressional representatives may be "apportioned among the several States." Section 2 of the Fourteenth Amendment further adds that "Representatives shall be apportioned among the several States according to their respective numbers, counting the whole number of persons in each State." "Persons" doesn't mean "citizens" of course. The Constitution mandates that every "person" be counted. And the Census Bureau's official position has long been that asking questions about citizenship would depress the count for "hard to count" groups, including noncitizens and Latinos, because they would be afraid—not unreasonably—that the information would be used against them and their loved ones. The Census Bureau stopped asking about citizenship on the decennial census after 1950.

But anti-immigrant groups have long been pushing the idea that only *citizens* should be counted, because data from the census is used to allocate hundreds of billions of dollars in federal funding each year and to determine redistricting and congressional reapportionment. The effect of counting only citizens would be to push power and funding away from urban areas to less populated rural districts, a move already accomplished by both Senate malapportionment and the Electoral College. The Supreme Court rejected the citizenship argument in 2016, in a case called *Evenwel v. Abbott*, reaffirming that states must draw legislative maps based on their total population and not the number of citizens in a district. Justice Ruth Bader Ginsburg in an 8–0 opinion was clear: "It remains beyond doubt that the principle of representational equality figured prominently in the decision to count people, whether or not they qualify as voters."

Secretary Ross's own Census Bureau didn't want a citizenship question. So he overruled them. Virtually no conservative groups or think tanks supported adding the citizenship question. Oh, well. Six former directors of the Census Bureau wrote to Ross warning that adding the untested question would undermine the accuracy of the census data. It didn't matter. Secretary Ross first announced that he was adding a citizenship question to the census in 2018, and he said it needed to be done in response to a December 2017 request from the Justice Department for information they could use to better enforce Section 2 of the Voting Rights Act. The Trump administration's DOJ had not at that point filed even one case to enforce the Voting Rights Act, so it was not clear why they might feel any urgency to start now. We would eventually learn, through this litigation, that Ross was determined to put the question on the census, that he was pestering DOJ to formally ask him to add the question, and that they kept putting it off until he was forced to go directly to the then attorney general, Jeff Sessions, and pitch a fit. Every lower court judge who ultimately heard this case eventually agreed that Ross's claims about the DOJ's purported need to better enforce the Voting Rights Act were pretextual and that Ross in fact worked backward from the desire to add a citizenship question to cobbling together a rationale that would sound legitimate.

A coalition of blue states, cities, and advocacy groups sued the administration, challenging the decision to add a citizenship question. Six different lawsuits were filed in courts around the country, with MALDEF as one of the litigants. Their case *La Unión del Pueblo Entero v. Ross* was filed in federal court in Maryland in May 2018. Other challenges proceeded in courtrooms around the country. Ross refused to testify—a dispute that itself ended up going all the way to the Supreme Court in October 2018. The high court would ultimately shield him from having to testify. All told, three different federal judges ruled that the citizenship question was improperly added and that Ross was not truthful about the fact that the decision had originated with him and not the Justice Department. It was a spanking for the Trump administration.

After a full trial in Manhattan, the federal district court judge Jesse Furman was the first to find in 2019 that Ross had violated the Administrative Procedure Act's prohibition on "arbitrary and capricious" agency decisions. "The evidence is clear," Furman wrote in his opinion, "that Secretary Ross's rationale was pretextual—that is, that the real reason for his decision was something other than the sole reason he put forward in his Memorandum, namely enhancement of DOJ's VRA enforcement efforts." That was the case that was appealed directly to the Supreme Court and heard on an expedited basis; the clock was now ticking to have the census forms printed that summer.

In March 2019, a federal judge in California found that the administration's decision to add the question violated administrative law. The following month the US district judge George Hazel of Maryland released a 119-page opinion siding with the MALDEF challengers in yet another lawsuit: "The unreasonableness of Defendants' addition of a citizenship question to the Census is underscored by the lack of any genuine need for the citizenship question, the woefully deficient process that led to it, the mysterious and potentially improper political considerations that motivated the decision and the clear pretext offered to the public." Both the California and the Maryland courts also found the census question unconstitutional because, at a time of increased immigration enforcement and anti-immigrant rhetoric, it would hamper the government's ability to count every US person.

While the MALDEF decision headed to the Fourth Circuit Court of Appeals, the US Supreme Court heard arguments in the appeal of the New York lawsuit in April 2019. After that oral argument, the high court appeared poised to hand down a 5–4, conservative/liberal ruling in favor of Ross and the Trump administration, permitting the citizenship question to be printed. But before the decision came down, *The New York Times*, in May 2019, published a bombshell: Thomas Hofeller, the aforementioned Republican voting strategist, had once been asked to craft a mechanism for redistricting that would advantage "Republicans and non-Hispanic whites." His work had been used almost verbatim, and uncredited, to bolster the letter from the Justice Department seeking citizenship data.

Hofeller had been dubbed "the Michelangelo of gerrymandering." He died in August 2018. His estranged daughter found files on his hard drive as she went through his personal effects, revealing that Hofeller had produced a study in 2015 theorizing about new ways to help Texas Republicans create extreme gerrymanders. He'd suggested crafting new rules for redistricting so that legislative districts could be drawn based on the number of voting citizens, not the total number of people living there. Sure, Hofeller acknowledged, this would represent a "radical departure from the federal 'one person, one vote' rule presently used in the United State[s]." But if you *could* count only citizens of voting age, he'd urged, and exclude noncitizens and their children, these new political maps "would be advantageous to Republicans and non-Hispanic whites" while diluting the political power of Texas's Hispanic voters.

Of course, Hofeller's problem in 2015, when he suggested apportionment based on citizenship, was that there was no detailed citizenship information being collected. So, as he put it in his study, "without a question on citizenship being included on the 2020 Decennial Census questionnaire, the use of citizen voting age population is functionally unworkable." (In his study, Hofeller opted to sidestep the question of whether "the gain of GOP voting strength [would] be worth the alienation of Latino voters who will perceive a switch to CVAP [Citizen Voting Age Population] as an attempt to diminish their voting strength.") In other words, in order to be able to draw legislative districts that would advantage Republicans and whites, Hofeller needed an instrument to measure citizenship. That proved to be the engine that drove the census citizenship question.

The discovery of the Hofeller hard drives revealed that Trump officials had lied. The plaintiffs filed a letter with the court while the case was pending, putting the new revelations directly before the justices as they drafted opinions. This made voting for Team Wilbur Ross awkward, at least for Chief Justice John Roberts. The US Supreme Court released its opinion in the New York litigation in late June with a 5–4 split and a majority opinion penned by Roberts. He had joined the court's liberal wing to conclude that Secretary Ross's stated reason for adding the question was pretextual. The court held that Ross was required under the Administrative Procedure Act to provide the true reason for adding the question, and left open the possibility that he could still do so, although time was running out to print the census forms. But the chief justice was unstinting in his criticism of the mountain of dishonesty the census litigation had unearthed:

> Altogether, the evidence tells a story that does not match the explanation the Secretary gave for his decision. In the Secretary's telling, Commerce was simply acting on a routine data request from another agency. Yet the materials before us indicate that Commerce went to great lengths to elicit the request from DOJ (or any other willing agency). And unlike a typical case in which an agency may have both stated and unstated reasons for a decision, here the VRA enforcement rationale— the sole stated reason—seems to have been contrived.

"Contrived" is a sober institutionalist's word for "pants on fire." Roberts concluded, "Our review is deferential, but we are 'not required to exhibit a naivete from which ordinary citizens are free.'" The four conservative justices were outraged that the courts sought to probe Secretary Ross's genuine motivations and desires, with Clarence Thomas writing to question the trial court judge Jesse Furman's personal integrity: "I do not deny that a judge predisposed to distrust the Secretary or the administration could arrange those facts on a corkboard and—with a jar of pins and a spool of string—create an eye-catching conspiracy web."

For a few weeks, it looked as if the administration was going to attempt to craft a new citizenship question rationale that would mollify the high court, and in July 2019, Trump announced that the question was still going to be on the census. "We are absolutely moving forward, as we must, because of the importance of the answer to this question," Trump tweeted, on July 3, 2019, leading Judge Hazel, who was overseeing the MALDEF challenge, to demand an emergency telephone hearing with the administration's lawyers, who had themselves learned of the president's new plans via tweet. Within days, a group of career Justice Department attorneys who had been working on the New York and Maryland cases asked to be removed from the lawsuit altogether. Evidently, even they had seen enough.

In July, Trump signed an executive order barring undocumented immigrants from being counted for congressional apportionment purposes and seeking citizenship data that would be collected by other means. That, too, was challenged in court. Finally, Trump and Ross attempted to shorten the census count by a month, a move *also* challenged in court. Most of these efforts evaporated when Trump left office, but they do shine a light on the myriad ways in which the battle has expanded from overt vote suppression to sneaky apportionment.

Nina Perales continued to litigate the census cases into 2020, and she reflected that the effort to depress minority turnout might well have had the desired effect, even after Trump and Ross failed to get the citizenship question onto the form. "There's a strong sense here among my clients that there was an undercount," she told me. "As the census was happening in the middle of the pandemic, I was talking to one of my clients, the lead plaintiff in the census litigation, LUPE [La Unión del Pueblo Entero], and they were saying, 'We're trying to get people to answer the census, but the self-response rates were far below 50 percent.' So, census questionnaires were going out, and they weren't coming back in really high numbers." She added that "LUPE was doing everything they could to try to get people to return those census forms. And I remember them saying, there's going to be a huge undercount."

Does that mean the Trump administration won, even by losing, in that the depressed noncitizen response rates would lead to an undercount? No, Perales was quick to say. "They did not win. They may have suppressed some of the response on the census, but they didn't win." These victories matter to her clients. "We were able to get that census done without a citizenship question on it, and then we subsequently litigated this issue of whether Trump could try to come up with another citizenship database. And then because of delays in the census, that resolved itself while we were still in court."

Perales told me that when her case went back to the Fourth Circuit Court of Appeals, "our three-judge panel was so happy when we dismissed that case." With a small coda for her. "By the way," she said with a smile. "That was a three-judge panel of all women. And I have to tell you, arguing in front of a three-judge panel on this case was amazing." I asked her why. "I have never, in my years, argued to a three-judge federal panel of only women, as a trial panel, because they're so rare. And it was me and the three judges, and then of course there was a guy representing DOJ. And I was like, 'Yeah, *he's* in the minority this time.'" This was being argued remotely because of COVID. "And it was a Zoom argument, so I had my three judges, I had minimized my Zoom window across the top as close to my camera as I could be. So, he was up there in the tray all by himself over there, the only guy, and I didn't have to deal with anybody making basketball analogies or the usual things that happen to me when I'm in court. Because it's always men, especially in redistricting."

Perales has been litigating for decades and was of a generation in which women and men had reached parity or near parity in law school. The fact that the federal bench remains overwhelmingly white and male goes to some of the systemic barriers to parity across the profession flagged by Anita Hill. It also highlights the ways in which we will live under the dead hand of Donald Trump's judicial selections for decades to come. Of the 816 life-tenured federal judges on the Supreme Court, the thirteen federal appeals courts, and the ninety-four district courts, Trump seated 28 percent in a single term in office. The vast majority of his appointments were white males, and the average age of his appellate judges was forty-seven. (Obama's nominees were on average five years older.) The Federal Judicial Center estimated that Trump judges will serve 270 more years than Obama's judges. Trump's judges have been largely unified in their opposition to LGBTQ rights, women's rights, and immigrants' rights. The notion that lawyers may spend years arguing before panels of all-white, all-male Trump nominees is dispiriting, especially for women lawyers who, like Perales, didn't think they would have to wait twenty years to see an all-female panel. Justice Ruth Bader Ginsburg was often asked how many women would be "enough" at the Supreme Court. Her answer was always "nine," because it had been nine men for so long.

Perales teaches young female law students. It's important that they see that in a field like redistricting, where men still dominate, a woman can rise to the top. When I covered the Sonia Sotomayor confirmation hearings in 2009, I noticed a long line of young Latina women that snaked outside the Senate chamber, with many of them standing for hours to get a seat in the hearing room for a few moments. With that visual, I came to understand that they were all opening a door to a future self they had never imagined. The young Black women who saw themselves in a new light as Judge Ketanji Brown Jackson was confirmed in 2022 had the same experience. Representation isn't just about optics, though. It's about experience and history too.

PERALES SAYS IT'S NOT HAPPENSTANCE that someone like Kansas's Kris Kobach slid from his original anti-immigrant initiatives into attempts at voter suppression and census rigging. In her mind, the two are inextricably linked. "The idea that non-US citizens are registering and voting, which is not true except in very, very, very isolated instances of mistakes, is used as the wedge to bring in all kinds of other vote suppression tactics," she told me. "So when Texas enacted voter ID in 2011, it was promoted as an immigration control measure. Voter ID was *immigration control* in Texas." She added that the websites of some legislators put voter-ID initiatives on their immigration landing page, as an example of what they were doing on immigration, "and it was frequently said that we needed voter ID to prevent non-US citizens from voting."

Perales told me that everywhere she goes she encounters the assumption that if you don't speak English, you can't be American. She described a deposition in one case in which a state representative insisted her client could not possibly be a US citizen because she needed interpretation assistance. In another case she litigated, she questioned someone who insisted that non-US citizens couldn't obtain driver's licenses. "They said voter ID would prevent non-US citizens from voting," she told me, but they were failing to understand that many, many green card holders hold driver's licenses. "Legislators use English as a proxy for citizenship and driver's licenses as a proxy for citizenship, failing to comprehend that the former category is too narrow and the latter is too broad."

This legislative promise that you are merely going after the scourge of foreigners voting is inevitably used to justify vote suppression of naturalized Americans. Perales told me, "They use the anti-immigrant sentiment very effectively to bolster the claim of vote fraud by non-US citizens." And this, she explained, is a very old story that has been told in America for a very long time: "The invading hordes. It's every ethnic group that's ever arrived in the United States. It's anti-Semitism. It's the same stuff over and over. The conspiring people who are coming in to take what's ours—those themes are so old in the US and come back to stoking a sense of grievance." That's the "great replacement theory" that launched the Charlottesville Nazis and is repeated on a loop by Tucker Carlson on Fox News. It's why you have to keep adding new voting restrictions. As Perales stated, "There are groups of people who lack ID; it's not a majority, but there it is. And that's a group of people who won't be able to vote. And then there's going to be this other group of people who can't vote. And then if we scare people so terribly that they don't participate in the census, then we don't have to send resources to that area. And then we can also gain an advantage from redistricting."

Perales is unlike some of the other subjects of this book insofar as she doesn't look at the courts—especially the federal courts—with the grim tolerance of someone forced to dance with the judiciary that brought her. She genuinely believes that most federal judges want to do the right thing, and more often than not actually will do the right thing, when it comes to voting rights. Certainly, the sixty-plus lawsuits pressed by Donald Trump's lawyers seeking to set aside the results of the 2020 election reflect the fact that partisan efforts to sideline voting for the most cynical reasons would not move George Bush appointees, Ronald Reagan appointees, and even in some cases,

Donald Trump appointees. Perales felt strongly that it wasn't politics; it's what the courts are designed to do. "In Texas and in many other places," she told me, "the Latino community turns to the federal court to defend us against racial discrimination. For us, the federal courts stand between us and discrimination. And sometimes it *is* hard to convince a federal judge that racism is happening, and that can be frustrating, but I can point to times when racism was happening and there was not a damn thing the people in that town or wherever could do about it." It's why she is a lawyer, she told me. "And we went to federal court and people took the stand, at personal risk, and a federal judge said, 'Yes, there is racism going on,' and forced the place to fix it. And if we hadn't done it, that bad situation would still be happening."

For Perales, "those are the success stories." Federal judges stepping in where nobody else can help. She cited the redistricting case MALDEF did in 2011, the racial gerrymandering claim she litigated at the Supreme Court, and case after case where, as she says, they could show discrimination. "We did well with the voter purge case where Texas tried to purge ninety-eight thousand newly naturalized citizens off the voter rolls. We did well in Pasadena, when we got the judge to strike down what the city was doing. In the redistricting round of 2011, we were able to get a new congressional district. We got gerrymandering fixed up in Tarrant County."

Perales explained that judges will always prefer to see straight-up evidence of racism, what she called "jump-up-and-slap-you-in-the-face, intentional racial discrimination." She added that it requires skillful litigation to satisfy a judge's desire for that kind of evidence. But, she observed, "that's what we did." In Pasadena, she explained, "we had everything, including the mayor bringing a gun with him to the city council meeting when they were going to talk about redistricting." These are real victories, for Perales, for MALDEF and its coalition members, and for thousands of voters. And just as the law is always inching ahead, she told me, the judges are doing so as well: "Judges also are not in the place where they were before. It used to be that separate and equal was okay under the Constitution because, hey, everybody had it equal! And so the judges have made very, very slow progress, but in the right direction."

Ultimately, these efforts to kill off voting, by what Perales calls a thousand cuts, can be met in the courts by a thousand small acts of repair in the opposite direction: redistricting suits here, voter purge challenges there, Voting Rights Act litigation, even under the tougher new standards. "They push," Perales explained, "and we push back, and they push, we push back." She isn't just litigating. She's also watching. She told me that one of her favorite emails from the 2011 redistricting cycle came when a court released a tranche of emails from members of Congress. "All of those emails from the members of Congress fell into our sweaty little clutches," she said, including an email from a congressman writing of a redistricting effort, 'Well, MALDEF is going to oppose this.' And this congressman wrote back and said, 'What does Nina know that we don't?'" To Perales it was an acknowledgment that "if they were going to try to maneuver to get what they wanted, there was this other presence that was there . . . that was keeping an eye on them, that was going to push back."

Of Kris Kobach and his dozens of failed efforts to frighten immigrants and new citizens, Perales pulls no punches: "[Kobach] started out and he wasn't in the voting world. We first met him when he was doing anti-immigrant ordinances in cities, cities that said if you're undocumented, you can't rent an apartment in the city." She added, "We beat him soundly and consistently. . . . We beat him all over the place, everywhere he went." When he shifted to vote suppression and claims about noncitizen immigrants casting ballots in Kansas, she told me, "the ACLU and my friend Dale Ho went out there and did that trial, and Kris was a disaster in the courtroom and got reprimanded and sanctioned by the judge, and the ACLU won that case." When Kobach turned next to the census citizenship question, she says, "we beat him, too, on this case involving proof of citizenship for voter registration. . . . So you know what? Give me more Kris Kobachs. I'll take a Kris Kobach any day."

Redistricting and the census and gerrymandering might seem hopelessly abstract, but Perales believes this is another area in which organizing and young people have made a massive difference in a short time. "I do think it can be very detailed, it can be very abstract," she told me, "but for the Latino community . . . I'll give you a quote from one of my favorite political scientists, Cardi B. When Cardi B was doing census outreach, she said, 'Participating in the census, being counted, is about three things, money, power, and respect.'" Perales told me that in her work throughout Texas, young people are tuned in to find out how they can advocate for themselves in redistricting.

One of the unanticipated bonuses of four years of Trumpism is that an electorate that couldn't explain the vagaries of the emoluments clause and its prohibitions on gifts, or apportionment or political gerrymandering or the Electoral College, now understands just how much devil lies in these constitutional details. Those four years proved to be a master class in citizenship. "If you don't get an opportunity to elect in a redistricting plan," Perales said, "that inequity is locked in for ten years, and that is a message people understand." She explained how this litigation works, and it proves to be the other side of the Stacey Abrams coin: After their last round of redistricting, there was a lot of growth in South Texas, which is majority Latino, so they tried to get a seat apportioned from the upper part of the state into the lower part of the state. When Texas wouldn't add a seat, they litigated to have it brought down to the Rio Grande valley. She told me, "I put a local person on the stand in Washington, DC, . . . and we had him walk through what it meant to have an additional House seat in the Rio Grande valley. And he talked about infrastructure. He talked about a child who died in a house fire, because the ambulance could not get to where the house was, because the road was not paved, and the road was muddy, and the ambulance got bogged down. The child died in this man's arms."

Perales objected to American pollsters and their tendency to lump all Latino voters into a unified category. She said it's complicated: "We have conservative Latinos; we have progressive Latinos. You get everything from Cubans in Miami, to Puerto Ricans in New York, to Mexican Americans in Phoenix." She described a massive gender gap among Latino Trump voters, both in 2016 and in 2020. "So within the Latino community, we have some people, I think, who didn't want to vote for a woman for president," she explained. "And Trump himself was really overtly misogynistic, and I think that there were some people in the Latino community who found that appealing, who found his unapologetic misogyny spoke to them." On the flip side, she said, "I think Latino women were not at all drawn in by Trump, and I think young Latinos were not drawn in by Trump, but there may have been a certain middle-aged male demographic within the Latino community that thought, 'Yeah, this guy, he doesn't apologize.'"

For Perales, it was always about fostering a sense of male grievance. "He stoked misogyny and made men feel like they wanted to return to a time when men were more powerful." But at least for Perales, the arc of the universe unerringly bends toward inclusion. She told me that often when she speaks on panels, someone will ask plaintively whether anything has gotten any better. She noted that she always says, "Hell yes, things have gotten better. Of course they've gotten better, partly because we're nudging it in that direction. Yes, there are people who are trying to reduce voting and reduce response to the census, and they're getting some of this done, but the tide is in our direction, and that's why I'm always positive. I will spend every day getting up and fighting that stuff, so that natural tide can occur."

For Perales, then, it's not just the law that is slouching slowly in the right direction. And it's not just that the judges and the courts are also inching toward a broader and more inclusive idea about what it means to be American. It's also demographics, and youth, and the inevitability of change that brings progress. Nina Perales likes to talk about her statistics: in Texas, data shows that the Anglo population has grown by less than half a million, while Latinos have grown by more than 2 million, sometimes 2.3 million, sometimes 2.5 million, over the three decades she's been working. "That is a tide that will not be stopped. And they can try to limit the polling place hours and they can try to make it a little more difficult to register to vote, but the tide is rolling in our direction."

The Trump years were, in so many ways, an effort to litigate who was presumptively American and who was "other." As so much of this book has suggested, fights over the Muslim ban, over pregnant migrant teens at the border, over illegal "caravans" of alleged rapists, were only a part of that widespread "othering." This debate about what it meant to be a "real American" had an intramural team as well, and we increasingly heard the language of foreignness and otherness deployed against certain Americans based on geography or language or color or race. That debate about who belonged and who was an invader morphed to take the form of white men marching through southern towns in which they did not reside, chanting, "You will not replace us," and of Fox News peddling the fear of nonwhite "replacement." A willingness to turn on other Americans, as some sort of fifth column invading from within, became part of that. And because you can't build a wall against "other" Americans—you can't easily split up their families and place them in ICE detention facilities; you can't conquer them by might—what's left is to just stop counting them. That is why the census cases and the redistricting efforts and the vote suppression became the hill so many Trump administration officials were prepared to die on.

As this book goes to press, the maps emerging from the 2020 census are revealing that yet again in this new redistricting cycle Republicans in swing states—including Pennsylvania, Wisconsin, Texas, and Georgia—continue to draw highly gerrymandered legislative maps in both state legislative districts and congressional districts. Partisan court rulings add to the chaos, as do Supreme Court interventions that seem to fit partisan patterns as well. Politicians picking their voters instead of vice versa is a system guaranteed to thwart real democracy. Apportionment and redistricting remain the least sexy voting rights work out there, and it's a place where Perales has seen women and young people activated and inspired, because the stakes remain so high. The issue goes to the very heart of the Trumpiest ideas about who belongs in the United States and who is merely tolerated. Perales, like many other women lawyers, rose up to do battle on behalf of those who may not be white, may not speak English, and might not have been born here. She told me that this is systems work; it's not glamorous, and it's data-driven and hyper-technical. It requires coordinating with activists and organizers and affiliate groups on the ground, many of which are also led by women and women of color. It's a persistent, grinding counternarrative to the legal work that gets front-page news coverage and Netflix series. Women are doing this work of democracy building, usually in the shadows, because they are really good at it. They are doing it, too, because without it democracy—with all its legal force and protections—cannot stand.

EPILOGUE

This book opened on the heady oral arguments in *Whole Woman's Health*, the 2016 abortion case where, for the first time in history, three female justices on the US Supreme Court managed to beat back a cynical attempt on the part of Texas to shutter abortion clinics by pretending to protect maternal health. Five and a half years later, it concludes the month the court overturned *Roe* in *Dobbs v. Jackson Women's Health Organization*. The decision in *Dobbs* represents the end of a constitutionally protected right to terminate a pregnancy, the first major precedent overturned in order to deny freedom rather than to expand it. The Mississippi law upheld in *Dobbs* made no exceptions for pregnancies due to rape or incest. As I type these words, a Utah clinic announced it will no longer provide medication abortions to residents of neighboring states with abortion bans and a ten-year-old Ohio rape victim was referred to a doctor in Indianapolis for an abortion. As of this writing, abortion has been unavailable after six weeks of pregnancy in Texas for many, many months, again because the Supreme Court allowed a law that permitted anyone to collect a $10,000 bounty for turning in someone who aided or abetted an abortion to continue, first in an unsigned one-paragraph order in September 2021 and then again after arguments and briefing in December 2021. Copycat vigilante bills have proliferated in other states. In the span of a very few years, American women now face material threats not just to their bodily autonomy and economic equality but to contraception, in vitro fertilization, and surrogacy. As the notion of "fetal personhood" becomes ascendant, maternal personhood is less important by the day. "Lock her up" will likely mean that women who miscarry or endanger their pregnancies will face criminal sanctions. These cases—at the hands of zealous state prosecutors or turbocharged bounty-seekers—have already put women in jail, and frequently the women are Native American, young, poor, or Black. Women's bodies in 2022 are lurid crime scenes; in the *Dobbs* opinion, they are dangerous, unwholesome places in which state actors and random vigilantes must keep watch and level consequences. Women are being turned away from emergency rooms in Alabama. Women may face homicide charges for fetal endangerment in Louisiana. And still we are told we are hysterical and overreacting when we express dismay that for the first time in history, the high court is overturning precedent to restore a notion of "liberty" and "privacy" that dates back to a time in which women were considered property. The law, once again, has become a cudgel to isolate and punish the most vulnerable pregnant people: the young, the Black and brown, and the poor.

A book about women and the law must account, as Anita Hill does, for the fact that law doesn't change the culture and the culture only very slowly shapes the law. One of the reasons the string of wildly thrilling legal victories against Donald Trump, white supremacists, and voter suppression captured so much of our attention over the last six years was that while the former president was a television character, flouting the rule of law and using it to punish his critics, the dusty, pedestrian legal rules just kept tripping him up. In the face of his culture of chaos, the foundations of the legal system, for the most part, held fast. That was a comfort. And perhaps we all learned that the law is always in motion and that if your side isn't engaged with it, you may just be losing.

One of the things Stacey Abrams truly mastered in the 2020 elections was marrying activism in the law to activism in the culture. Building on the historic work she had begun in Georgia, she helped voters understand that their right to vote was under attack. People who never considered that democracy could be hard work were suddenly faced with a lethal pandemic, a Supreme Court that had made voting in primaries during a pandemic ever more difficult in the months before that election, states determined to use whatever tactic they might find at hand to shrink margins, gerrymandered districts that distorted majoritarian will, a post office seemingly disinterested in providing postal services, and a president not only undermining voter confidence but weaponizing his own Justice Department to cast doubt upon the outcomes.

The only cure was to vote.

Abrams would run the 2018 play again, but this time it was not just in Georgia. She told CNN in the winter of 2021 that as she campaigned around the country for Biden and Harris, "I had two messages. One, voter suppression is real and we have to have a plan to fight back. Two, Georgia is real. You've got to have a plan to fight here." In addition to the pandemic, the summer of 2020 was shaped by the brutal murder of George Floyd by a police officer, captured on video. That galvanized the Black Lives Matter movement into a summer of furious protest and organizing and meaningful conversations about police reform. Black voters, and particularly Black women, were excited by the Democratic ticket of Joe Biden and Kamala Harris—who might become the first Black woman elected to the vice presidency. It had long been an article of faith that Black women were the heart of the Trump resistance. Black women had carried Doug Jones to a senatorial victory in Alabama in 2017, and Black women lifted up Biden's lackluster presidential campaign with a victory in South Carolina's Democratic primary. Georgia's Democratic state senator Nikema Williams, elected to succeed the late voting rights warrior John Lewis in the Fifth Congressional District, told CNN that not one thing about this was new: "Black women have always been the backbone of the Democratic Party, but what we are seeing now is people digging into the data and recognizing us for what we have been doing."

Since 2018, Abrams's group the New Georgia Project had been working with the National Coalition on Black Civic Participation, the Georgia Coalition for the People's Agenda, ProGeorgia, the Black Voters Matter Fund, Georgia STAND-UP, and other groups to mobilize Black voters. Those groups were also helmed by Black women. So while voting rights lawyers and Democrats nationwide and the Biden campaign mobilized to educate voters about vote suppression and mail-in ballots, and as election lawyers challenged state voting practices, Abrams and the organizers at Fair Fight and the New Georgia Project were going all in to flip Georgia blue. And nobody thought Abrams was pie-in-the-sky this time around. Georgia seemed gettable. By the time of the 2020 election the New Georgia Project said that it had registered about 500,000 new voters. Abrams later told Stephen Colbert that she had been texting with Fair Fight Action's CEO, Lauren Groh-Wargo, and realized, as the Georgia numbers started coming in, "This is the first time I've woken up in November without curling into the fetal position first." She said, "The numbers got bigger and bigger and we got happier and happier."

Despite the pandemic, 2020 was a historic election with historic turnout. By the time the Georgia ballots were counted, Biden had become the first Democrat to win the state in almost thirty years. According to exit polls, 92 percent of Black women in Georgia had pulled the lever for Biden. He managed to win more than 2.4 million votes in Georgia, beating out the incumbent president by nearly 12,000 votes. Abrams's strategy married law to culture to engagement. Building coalitions of voters who had checked out, or never checked in, who had given up on government, or who didn't see themselves reflected or respected there? That was the silver bullet.

The Georgia Senate race went to a runoff election in January. When the numbers were tallied on January 5, the Reverend Raphael Warnock and Jon Ossoff had scored decisive victories against the incumbents Kelly Loeffler and David Perdue. Georgians had chosen a Black pastor and the thirty-three-year-old son of Jewish immigrants to represent them in the Senate, a callback to a partnership of the voting rights struggle of the 1960s. A record-breaking 4.5 million people voted in those runoff elections, about 88 percent of the number voting in November's contest, and roughly 93 percent of Black voters supported Ossoff and Warnock. Abrams and her coalition had flipped two Senate seats, and Democrats controlled the Senate. As Sherrilyn Ifill of the NAACP Legal Defense Fund explained on my podcast, you cannot understand January 6, 2021, without recognizing the impact of transformational empathy and voting power that took place on January 5.

People were, suddenly, awake. Speaking at an Atlanta conference called Paradigm Shift 2.0: Black Women Confronting HIV, Health, and Social Justice in the spring of 2020, Abrams told a roaring crowd of fans that the 2018 governor's race in Georgia was never for, or about, her. "When I ran for governor, I did not run simply for me. We went around this state to all 159 counties, and everywhere we went we talked about the power of people to make a choice. . . . On November 6, when malfeasance and incompetence and my opponent who was a cartoon villain stole the voices of Georgians when he purged 1.4 million voters and oversaw the shutdown of 214 precincts that left 50,000 to 60,000 people without the ability to vote, when Georgia had the longest lines in the nation and the highest rejection rates of absentee ballots and provisional ballots . . . it was not just about me. He was doing that to Georgians."

It was never about me, she said, and then she delivered her punch line: "And the thing is, if I had fought back and said, 'I am going to contest this election and make myself governor,' then everyone who loved me and stood with me would have thought, 'Well, this is about her fight.' My responsibility was instead to focus on the right to vote and not my right to be governor. I had no right to be governor, but I have an obligation to do the work that I said I would do if I were governor." It's a narrative we don't hear often enough: how democracy is about complex systems, not big personalities. It's about voters, not leaders. The law is about citizens, not lawyers. That was the big idea at the founding and that's the big idea still.

The 2020 election story ended with Americans waking up on the morning of January 6, 2021, to the news that Warnock and Ossoff had won their respective runoff races. But within just a few hours, insurrectionists would be scaling the walls of the US Capitol, attempting to decertify Biden's victory in the Electoral College. People would die. The seat of government would be trashed. Elected members ran for their lives and hid in their offices. Donald Trump would later fete the insurrectionists as peaceful patriots. In time, they would be hailed as freedom fighters.

Within a few short weeks, states like Georgia and Texas were passing the most draconian voter suppression bills in the country. Other states hastily followed suit. Although the amount of in-person vote fraud was negligible in the 2020 election, as it has been for decades—as even Attorney General Bill Barr acknowledged—under cover of "election protection," in the first months of 2021, eighteen states enacted more than thirty laws restricting access to the ballot. Projections suggest around thirty-six million people, or about 15 percent of all eligible voters, will be affected. Under false claims of bolstering voter confidence in election integrity, states would try to cancel souls to the polls Sunday voting and would impose onerous new ID requirements. Georgia would make it illegal to bring food or water to voters standing in long lines. Partisan poll watchers would be empowered to harass voters. In the most dangerous move, new powers to set aside election results are being bestowed on state legislatures, with authority removed from nonpartisan election officials. Some states have arrogated new powers over election administration and certification and authorized election "audits" that will be used to discredit the 2022 and 2024 elections. The GOP has purged moderates or those who question the proposition that Trump won in 2020 from party leadership. Republican senators have filibustered national voting rights legislation from even being debated. And a growing spirit of vigilantism has allowed citizens to take law enforcement into their own hands, from Texas's SB 8 enforcement, to stand your ground laws, to state-sanctioned harassment of school officials.

This is horrible, if largely invisible. In many ways, the rule of law feels more fragile in 2022 than it seemed during the Trump years, but voters, including women, seem to be suffering from what some activists have dubbed the Great Forgetting: an abiding desire to relegate the Trump craziness to the ash heap of history; the blind belief that activism saved the country and will prevail in the future; and the assessment that because "the system held" in 2020, it must be magic. None of that is true. About one-third of all voters (and 78 percent of Republicans) believe the 2020 election was stolen by Joe Biden and that those who stormed the Capitol in January 2021 are heroes. State election officials and politicians are openly campaigning for 2022 and 2024 on The Big Lie.

I am not sure why, in the face of this sort of existential threat to democracy, it feels as if so many of us have fallen asleep. COVID and partisanship have surely exhausted us all. Maybe that's why these women lawyers seem more essential than ever to my mind. Their voices and pleadings play out on a loop in my ears late at night—demanding basic dignity, family autonomy, bodily integrity, and other values enshrined in the Fourteenth Amendment. They hold on to our memories when we all just want to forget and move on. Robbie Kaplan and Karen Dunn kept the Charlottesville torch march of 2017 alive for four years. Stacey Abrams kept the 2018 governor's race in Georgia burning for two. I sometimes cling to the fanciful notion that one of the special points of connection between women and the law is that the law's slow, measured progress allows it to preserve histories that might otherwise be erased. That recasts these Trump resistance attorneys as modern-day Philomelas, weaving the details of long-forgotten crimes into a tapestry so that it may stand as evidence.

Mary Beard opens her book *Women and Power: A Manifesto* with Penelope from *The Odyssey*, whose son, Telemachus, scolds her for speaking out in the great hall of her palace. He tells her to "go back up to your quarters, and take up your own work, the loom and the distaff," and reminds her that "speech will be the business of men, all men, and me most of all; for mine is the power in this household." Penelope, too, scoots off to her loom. Perhaps all of this looming of the truth is an ancient female response to being silenced. But it also leads back to what Vanita Gupta and Stacey Abrams keep saying about women and the accumulation of power. Abrams talks compulsively about power. The paperback Abrams published in 2019 is titled *Lead from the Outside: How to Build Your Future and Make Real Change*, a protracted meditation on power and how to build it and use it: "The questions for those in search of power abound: Who has it? How do we get and wield it? What do we do when we have less than the other guy? What do we do when we lose it?"

Beard writes about why contemporary notions of power still exclude women and why "women are still perceived as belonging outside power." She says we still cling to models (thanks, Telemachus) of power as something "elite, coupled to public prestige, to the individual charisma of so-called 'leadership'" that almost always comes with celebrity. (Thanks, cowboys!) Beard imagines structural changes to how we think about power, "decoupling it from public prestige," and it seems to me that the law has emerged as a system that does exactly

that. Framed in the ways leaders like Gupta, Hill, and Abrams describe it, law and power can blossom and grow, far from the klieg
lights of reality TV.

The women lawyers and organizers who sprang up in opposition
to Trump and Trumpism seem to be a natural experiment in adopt-
ing Beard's broader prescription for power, which demands "thinking about the power of followers, not just of leaders." For Beard, that
means, above all, "thinking about power as an attribute or even a verb
('to power'), not as a possession." The women who used the law to save
democracy since 2016 taught us how "to power." They both modeled
and harnessed the "power of followers," whether it was women protesting the travel ban and family separations or getting out the vote.
Women organizing around halting mass shootings, promoting reproductive freedoms, and opposing white supremacy were also lashing the
power of groups to the power of law; it was the furthest thing from a
president who was announcing whimsical executive orders via Twitter
and fomenting violence through mobs.

We are in a truly frightening moment. Election deniers are laying
the tracks to set aside the 2024 election and the Supreme Court has,
for the first time in history, reversed precedent in order to take away
freedom rather than expand it. Justice Samuel Alito produced an
opinion in *Dobbs* in which women were imaginary and fetal personhood was real. He told us to vote if we didn't like it, even as the court
works ever harder to limit voting rights. Gun massacres of school children seem to continue unabated. Yet in 2022, the Supreme Court expanded gun rights substantially. States punish LGBTQ families and
ban books in schools. The Supreme Court will hear a case affording
state legislatures the right to determine election outcomes; the dis-
credited legal theory deployed to try to set aside the 2020 contest.
This will not be reversed in a year or maybe even a decade. But I don't
believe women sleep through revanchist backsliding any easier than
they sleep through colic. We hear things, we see things. We are awake.

Just as Justice Ginsburg unfailingly name-checked Pauli Murray, Stacey Abrams never fails to mention Helen Butler, Nsé Ufot, Deborah Scott, Tamieka Atkins, Atlanta's mayor Keisha Lance Bottoms, LaTosha Brown, and the women who work alongside her. After Biden was sworn in, Vanita Gupta was chosen and confirmed (by a single vote) as associate attorney general of the United States, overseeing the Justice Department's civil rights litigation as well as its antitrust, civil, and environmental divisions. She, too, is scrupulous in highlighting the communities and organizations that do the work in the trenches. Judge Ketanji Brown Jackson, Biden's nominee to replace retiring Justice Stephen Breyer, told us she stood on the shoulders of Constance Baker Motley, the first Black woman ever seated as a federal judge.

Throughout the Trump years, women who were asking themselves, "What can I do?" learned that whether we notice it or not, the law organizes every part of our lives. Lashing ourselves to legal ideas, movements, and causes gave us power. It organized us. It focused us. It connected us to first principles and lofty ideas. And every step of the way, the wins felt tangible and material and enduring. Women have come so far in a few decades, and the law, even with its flaws and its anachronisms, has been a quiet, persistent source of order and meaning in a world that feels ever more out of our control. It's been a source of power beyond just rage. We have a long way to go, the road will be bumpy, and the destination still feels less than clear. But women plus law equals magic; we prove that every day. And bearing witness to what it can and will achieve has been the great privilege of my lifetime.

ACKNOWLEDGMENTS

When people tell you their stories about Tina Bennett, super agent, believe them. It's all true. This book—and indeed much of my career—has been the result of Tina's infinite patience, delicate cajoling, and occasional hammer-dropping. Words cannot express my gratitude. Ann Godoff at Penguin Press is another publishing legend, and it turns out that is also for good reason. She understood this project better than I did when I pitched it, and she shaped it with a transcendent vision and understanding of why we need heroes in order to have hope. Casey Denis and Victoria Lopez at Penguin Press have been beyond invaluable and gracious. My production editor at Penguin, Megan Gerrity, showed infinite patience and grace. And big, big thanks to Penguin's Gail Brussel and Lauren Lauzon for sorting publicity and marketing in an ever-changing pandemic.

The team at WME, including Erin Malone, Jay Mandel, and their staff have been wonderful. Monica Graham gave me a guesthouse, and my whole family a fairy godmother, when it was time to craft a proposal. The folks at Mesa Refuge offered me a place to breathe and stretch and birth this project thanks to Rebecca Solnit and Marty Krasney. Ramón Castellblanch and Robert Franklin, my first partners in crime at that dreamy spot, gave early support and feedback. Same goes for the amazing writers who comprise the David Greenberg Writers Groups in Manhattan, who helped shape the early chapters.

I've been at *Slate* almost longer than there has been an internet, but this book could never have happened without the support of Jared Hohlt and the phenomenal co-pilot who is Mark Joseph Stern. Jeremy Stahl and Nicole Lewis teach me about legal writing every day. How I lucked into both Susan Matthews, the world's greatest editor, and Sara Burningham, the world's greatest podcast producer, is a mystery of both science and faith.

Robin Rice dreamed this book with me using glittering bits of glass and alchemy; she dragged this project to the starting line every time I balked, and the winged Mikhaila Fogel—amid harps and puffy clouds—helped haul it over the finish line. Along the way I had invaluable readers and boosters in Sonja West, RonNell Andersen Jones, Perry Grossman, Walter Dellinger, Claire Potter, Jennifer Taub, Evelyn Rubin, Siân Gibby, Garrett Epps, and Liv Warren, and from Sandy who asked to be in my acknowledgments. To the subjects of this book who gave me time, answers, friendship, and above all hope, I have probably not done justice to the ways you Do Justice. But you trusted me and inspired me and I am grateful to my bones for you all.

People who think they're too old to make new friends just don't know Michelle Shulman, whom I met in the Siberia that was COVID and who nevertheless read every single word of a manuscript from a frantic stranger in a strange land. My parents, Harvey and Yvonne Lithwick, and in-laws, Marcia and Harold Fein, have been invaluable boosters, as have Alex Lithwick and Carolyn Bickerton and Hillel Lithwick and Jackie Harari. My sons, Coby and Sopher, whose wisdom peeps out of some of these pages, have provided both rocket fuel and ballast every day. This book is for the men they are becoming. And finally, my husband, Aaron, read drafts, designed art, unstuck mental hair balls, cooked dinners, circled wagons, troubleshot tech crises, and believed. This book is for a world he helps me imagine can come true.

NOTES

INTRODUCTION

ix **the last truly great day:** Dahlia Lithwick, "The Women Take Over," *Slate*, March 2, 2016, slate.com/news-and-politics/2016/03/in-oral-arguments -for-the-texas-abortion-case-the-three-female-justices-upend-the -supreme-courts-balance-of-power.html.

x ***Griswold v. Connecticut,* the lawsuit protecting:** Oral argument transcript, *Griswold v. Connecticut*, 381 U.S. 479 (1965), www.oyez.org/cases /1964/496.

xi **women made up only one-third:** Kerry Abrams, "Family, Gender, and Leadership in the Legal Profession," *Women and Law*, Feb. 1, 2020, scholarship.law.duke.edu/womenandlaw/1/.

xi **their interrogation of Scott Keller:** Lithwick, "Women Take Over."

xii **The 5–3 ruling that came down:** Adam Liptak, "Supreme Court Strikes Down Texas Abortion Restrictions," *New York Times*, June 27, 2016, www.nytimes.com/2016/06/28/us/supreme-court-texas-abortion.html.

xiii **The GOP candidate for president:** Suzanne Gamboa, "Donald Trump Announces Presidential Bid by Trashing Mexico, Mexicans," NBC News, June 16, 2015, www.nbcnews.com/news/latino/donald-trump-announces -presidential-bid-trashing-mexico-mexicans-n376521; David A. Fahrenthold, "Trump Recorded Having Extremely Lewd Conversation About Women in 2005," *Washington Post*, Oct. 8, 2016, www.washingtonpost.com/politics /trump-recorded-having-extremely-lewd-conversation-about-women-in -2005/2016/10/07/3b9ce776-8cb4-11e6-bf8a-3d26847eeed4_story.html.

xiii **By November of 2016, we learned that:** Jeanine Santucci, Jim Sergent, and George Petras, "19 Women Have Accused Trump of Sexual Misconduct. Here's What Their Stories Have in Common," *USA Today*, Oct. 21, 2020, www.usatoday.com/in-depth/news/investigations/2020/10/21/trump -sexual-assault-allegations-share-similar-patterns-19-women/5279 155002/.

xvi **Kaplan would later resign:** Jodi Kantor and Michael Gold, "Roberta Kaplan, Who Aided Cuomo, Resigns from Time's Up," *New York Times*, Aug. 9, 2021, www.nytimes.com/2021/08/09/nyregion/roberta-kaplan-times-up-cu omo.html.

CHAPTER 1: THE BEGINNING

1 **"Lock her up!" "Lock her up!":** Nick Gass, "'Lock Her Up' Chant Rules Republican Convention," *Politico*, July 20, 2016, www.politico.com/story /2016/07/rnc-2016-lock-her-up-chant-hillary-clinton-225916; Ryan Teague Beckwith, "Michael Flynn Led a 'Lock Her Up' Chant at the Republican Convention. Now He's Charged with Lying to the FBI," *Time*, Dec. 1, 2017, time.com/5044847/michael-flynn-hillary-clinton-republican-convention -lock-her-up/.

1 **Trump warned Clinton:** Josh Hafner, "Trump: If I Win, I Want Special Prosecutor Looking into Clinton's 'Situation,'" *USA Today*, Oct. 9, 2016, www.usatoday.com/story/news/politics/onpolitics/2016/10/09/trump-if -win-want-special-prosecutor-looking-into-clintons-situation/91839398/.

1 **Jeff Sessions, gave a speech:** Julia Jacobs, "Jeff Sessions Laughs and Echoes 'Lock Her Up' Chant with Conservative High Schoolers," *New York Times*, July 24, 2018, www.nytimes.com/2018/07/24/us/politics/jeff-sessions-lock -her-up-hillary-clinton.html.

2 **"Iron my shirt":** Fernando Suarez, "Hecklers Want Clinton to Iron Their Shirts," CBS News, Jan. 7, 2008, www.cbsnews.com/news/hecklers-want -clinton-to-iron-their-shirts/.

2 **"some form of punishment" for women:** Matt Flegenheimer and Maggie Haberman, "Donald Trump, Abortion Foe, Eyes 'Punishment' for Women, Then Recants," *New York Times*, March 30, 2016, www.nytimes.com /2016/03/31/us/politics/donald-trump-abortion.html.

2 **Trump led adoring crowds to chant "Lock her up":** Matthew Rozsa, "'Lock Her Up': Trump Rally Erupts When the President Attacks Kavanaugh Ac- cuser Christine Blasey Ford," *Salon*, Oct. 3, 2018, www.salon.com/2018 /10/03/lock-her-up-trump-rally-erupts-when-the-president-attacks -kavanaugh-accuser-christine-blasey-ford/; Brett Samuels, "Trump Rally Crowd Chants 'Lock Her Up' About Pelosi," *Hill*, Feb. 20, 2020, thehill. com/homenews/campaign/482427-trump-rally-crowd-chants-lock

-her-up-about-pelosi; Tom McCarthy, "Trump Rally Crowd Chants 'Send Her Back' After President Attacks Ilhan Omar," *Guardian*, July 18, 2019, www.theguardian.com/us-news/2019/jul/17/trump-rally-send-her-back -ilhan-omar.

3 **Which brings me to Pauli Murray:** Brittney Cooper, "Black, Queer, Feminist, Erased from History: Meet the Most Important Legal Scholar You've Likely Never Heard Of," *Salon*, Feb. 18, 2015, www.salon.com/2015/02 /18/black_queer_feminist_erased_from_history_meet_the_most_impor tant_legal_scholar_youve_likely_never_heard_of/; Kathryn Schulz, "The Many Lives of Pauli Murray," *New Yorker*, April 10, 2017, www.newyorker .com/magazine/2017/04/17/the-many-lives-of-pauli-murray.

5 **"It may be that when historians":** Susan Ware, *Notable American Women: A Biographical Dictionary Completing the Twentieth Century* (Cambridge, Mass: Belknap Press, 2004).

6 **film about her that was released in 2021:** Melena Ryzik, "Pauli Murray Should Be a Household Name. A New Film Shows Why," *New York Times*, Sept. 15, 2021, www.nytimes.com/2021/09/15/movies/pauli-murray-doc umentary.html.

6 **In 1977, she became the first:** Lakshmi Varanasi, "Yale Will Name a New Residential College After Awesome Civil Rights Activist Pauli Murray," *Slate*, April 10, 2016, slate.com/human-interest/2016/04/yale-names-new -residential-college-after-pauli-murray.html.

6 **"a dream / haunting as amber wine":** Pauli Murray, *Dark Testament, and Other Poems* (Norwalk, Conn.: Silvermine, 1970).

7 **"are likely to be stories":** Carol Sanger, "Curriculum Vitae (Feminae): Biography and Early American Women Lawyers," *Stanford Law Review* 46, no. 5 (May 1994), wlh.law.stanford.edu/wp-content/uploads/2011/01/sanger -cv-feminae.pdf.

7 **"lived on the edge of history":** Eleanor Holmes Norton, introduction to *Song in a Weary Throat*, by Pauli Murray (New York: Harper & Row, 1987).

9 **"And, by the way," she wrote:** Abigail Adams to John Adams, March 13, 1776, www.masshist.org/digitaladams/archive/doc?id=L17760331aa.

10 **After Myra Bradwell took her quest:** *Bradwell v. The State*, 83 U.S. 130 (1873).

10 **"Female doctors could claim":** Barbara J. Harris, *Beyond Her Sphere: Women and the Professions in American History* (Westport, Conn.: Greenwood Press, 1978).

12 **peopled his administration:** Sam Petulla, "Charts Show How Trump's Cabinet Breaks with Tradition," NBC News, Jan. 20, 2017, www.nbcnews .com/storyline/inauguration-2017/trump-cabinet-breakdown-race -gender-n708986; Jason Lange, "White and Male: Broader Bureaucracy

Mirrors Trump's Cabinet Profile," Reuters, Oct. 20, 2017, www.reuters
.com/article/us-trump-effect-diversity/white-and-male-broader-
bureaucracy-mirrors-trump-cabinets-profile-idUSKBN1CP1D1;   Alana
Wise, "Biden Pledged Historic Cabinet Diversity. Here's How His Nominees
Stack Up," NPR, Feb. 5, 2021, www.npr.org/sections/president-biden-takes
-office/2021/02/05/963837953/biden-pledged-historic-cabinet-diversity
-heres-how-his-nominees-stack-up.

12 **determined to be abusers:** Tim Dickinson, "A History of Sex and Abuse in
the Trump Administration," *Rolling Stone*, Feb. 23, 2018, www.rolling
stone.com/politics/politics-news/a-history-of-sex-and-abuse-in-the
-trump-administration-202833/.

12 **he filled the federal bench:** Matthew Nussbaum, "Trump's Judges, U.S.
Attorneys Overwhelmingly White Men," *Politico*, May 10, 2018, www
.politico.com/story/2018/05/10/trump-judges-attorneys-white-men
-582345.

12 **impetus for the Women's March:** Kaveh Waddell, "The Exhausting Work
of Tallying America's Largest Protest," *Atlantic*, Jan. 23, 2017, www
.theatlantic.com/technology/archive/2017/01/womens-march-protest
-count/514166/.

12 **to resign in protest:** "The Trump Administration Officials Who Resigned
over Capitol Violence," *New York Times*, Jan. 17, 2021, www.nytimes.com
/article/trump-resignations.html.

12 **I interviewed Justice Ruth Bader Ginsburg:** Ginsburg, interview by author, Jan. 2020.

13 **It is not, we learned, self-enforcing:** See, for example, Bob Bauer and Jack
Goldsmith *After Trump: Reconstructing the Presidency* (Washington, DC:
Lawfare Press, 2020).

14 **bringing meritless challenges:** Jeremy W. Peters and Alan Feuer, "How Is
Trump's Lawyer Jenna Ellis 'Elite Strike Force' Material?," *New York
Times*, Dec. 20, 2020, www.nytimes.com/2020/12/03/us/politics/jenna
-ellis-trump.html; Emma Brown et al., "Sidney Powell Group Raised More
Than $14 Million Spreading Election Falsehoods," *Washington Post*, Dec.
6, 2021, www.washingtonpost.com/investigations/sidney-powell-defending
-republic-donations/2021/12/06/61bdb004-53ef-11ec-8769-2f4
ecdf7a2ad_story.html; Dahlia Lithwick, "Real Accountability for Those
Responsible for Jan. 6 Is Actually Starting to Pile Up," *Slate*, Aug. 26, 2021,
slate.com/news-and-politics/2021/08/sidney-powell-sanctions
-jan-6-insurrection.html; Brennan Center for Justice and Bipartisan Policy
Center, "Election Officials Under Attack," June 16, 2021, www.brennan
center.org/our-work/policy-solutions/election-officials-under-attack.

15 **"We like our lone and exceptional heroes":** Rebecca Solnit, "When the Hero
Is the Problem," *LitHub*, April 2, 2019, lithub.com/rebecca-solnit-when-the
-hero-is-the-problem.

CHAPTER 2: THE FIRST NO

17 **signed into law an executive order:** Evan Perez, Pamela Brown, and Kevin Liptak, "Inside the Confusion of the Trump Executive Order and Travel Ban," CNN, Jan. 30, 2017, www.cnn.com/2017/01/28/politics/donald -trump-travel-ban/index.html; Benjamin Wittes, "Malevolence Tempered by Incompetence: Trump's Horrifying Executive Order on Refugees and Visas," *Lawfare*, Jan. 28, 2017, www.lawfareblog.com/malevolence -tempered-incompetence-trumps-horrifying-executive-order-refugees-and -visas.

18 **that it was intended for Muslim travelers:** Zainab Ramahi, "The Muslim Ban Cases: A Lost Opportunity for the Court and a Lesson for the Future," *California Law Review* 108, no. 2 (April 2020), www.californialawreview .org/print/muslim-ban-cases.

19 **Yates once told *The New Yorker's* Ryan Lizza:** Ryan Lizza, "Why Sally Yates Stood Up to Trump," *New Yorker*, May 22, 2017, www.newyorker .com/magazine/2017/05/29/why-sally-yates-stood-up-to-trump.

19 **"She would have been a heck of a lawyer":** Henry Unger, "U.S. Attorney Sally Yates: 'Nobody Is a Success on Their Own,'" *Atlanta Journal-Constitution*, Sept. 14, 2013, www.ajc.com/business/attorney-sally-yates-no body-success-their-own/douXrIvSM94UcGacc2pbdM.

20 **"I didn't go for the right reasons":** "Recode Decode: Sally Yates," *Recode Decode*, Nov. 12, 2018, www.vox.com/2018/11/12/18086580/sally-yates -attorney-general-justice-department-doj-donald-trump-corruption-kara -swisher-podcast.

22 **Yates was grilled by Senate Republicans:** Euan McKirdy, "Jeff Sessions Grilled Sally Yates on Constitutional Duty During Confirmation Hearing," CNN, Jan. 31, 2017, www.cnn.com/2017/01/31/politics/sally-yates -jeff-sessions-deputy-attorney-general-hearing/index.html; Josh Gerstein, "Sally Yates Confirmed as No. 2 at Justice Department," *Politico*, May 13, 2015, www.politico.com/blogs/under-the-radar/2015/05/sally-yates -confirmed-as-no-2-at-justice-department-207069.

22 **Obama's point person on prison reform:** Sari Horwitz, "Obama to Commute Hundreds of Federal Drug Sentences in Final Grants of Clemency," *Washington Post*, Jan. 17, 2017, www.washingtonpost.com/world/national -security/obama-to-commute-hundreds-of-federal-drug-sentences -in-final-grants-of-clemency/2017/01/16/c99b4ba6-da5e-11e6-b8b2 -cb5164beba6b_story.html; "Deputy Attorney General Sally Q. Yates Delivers Remarks at Harvard Law School on Sentencing and Prison Reform," Jan. 9, 2017, www.justice.gov/opa/speech/deputy-attorney-general-sally-q -yates-delivers-remarks-harvard-law-school-sentencing-and.

25 **As she later testified, his response:** Matt Apuzzo and Emmarie Huetteman, "Sally Yates Tells Senators She Warned Trump About Mike Flynn,"

New York Times, May 8, 2017, www.nytimes.com/2017/05/08/us/politics/michael-flynn-sally-yates-hearing.html.

26 **her deputy at the Justice Department:** Nicole Sganga, "Sally Yates Talks About Her 10 Days as Acting Attorney General," CBS News, May 20, 2018, www.cbsnews.com/news/sally-yates-talks-about-her-10-days-as-acting-attorney-general.

28 **former ACLU director Burt Neuborne:** Burt Neuborne, *Madison's Music: On Reading the First Amendment* (New York: New Press, 2015).

29 **for a "total and complete shutdown":** Jessica Taylor, "Trump Calls for 'Total and Complete Shutdown of Muslims Entering' U.S.," NPR, Dec. 7, 2015, www.npr.org/2015/12/07/458836388/trump-calls-for-total-and-complete-shutdown-of-muslims-entering-u-s.

29 **an entire team of DOJ lawyers:** Michael Wines, Katie Benner, and Adam Liptak, "Justice Dept. to Replace Lawyers in Census Citizenship Question Case," *New York Times*, July 7, 2019, www.nytimes.com/2019/07/07/us/politics/census-citizenship-question-justice-department.html.

30 **Yates wrote up a statement:** Josh Gerstein, "Trump Fires Defiant Acting Attorney General," *Politico*, Jan. 30, 2017, www.politico.com/story/2017/01/trump-immigration-executive-order-234401.

31 **in 2018, in *Trump v. Hawaii*:** *Trump v. Hawaii*, 17-965, 585 U.S. __ (2018).

31 **fire her via email:** Erica Orden, "Sally Yates, Preet Bharara Stress High Bar for Criminal Charges in the Russia Probe," *Wall Street Journal*, Oct. 4, 2017, www.wsj.com/articles/sally-yates-preet-bharara-stress-high-bar-for-criminal-charges-in-russia-probe-1507158408.

31 **"Monday Night Massacre":** Derek Hawkins, "'Monday Night Massacre'? After Firing of Yates, Nixon's Sordid Moment Has Been Repurposed for Trump," *Washington Post*, Jan. 31, 2017, www.washingtonpost.com/news/morning-mix/wp/2017/01/31/monday-night-massacre-after-firing-of-yates-nixons-sordid-moment-has-been-repurposed-for-trump.

32 **tweeted out a threat:** Devlin Barrett and Sari Horwitz, "Sally Yates to Testify About Her Discussions with the White House on Russia," *Washington Post*, May 8, 2017, www.washingtonpost.com/world/national-security/yates-to-testify-about-her-discussions-with-the-white-house-on-russia/2017/05/05/02a33032-31dd-11e7-9534-00e4656c22aa_story.html.

32 **Senator Ted Cruz (R-Tex.) peered down:** "Ted Cruz Gets into a Heated Exchange with Sally Yates, Prompting Laughter and Groans," *Boston Globe*, May 8, 2017, www.bostonglobe.com/news/politics/2017/05/08/ted-cruz-gets-into-heated-legal-exchange-with-sally-yates-prompting-laughter-and-groans/9Wf3FkwoG4TWPar6iQPapO/story.html.

33 **Leon Neyfakh noted at the time:** Leon Neyfakh, "Slayer of Ted Cruz, Defender of Justice," *Slate*, May 9, 2017, slate.com/news-and-politics/2017/05/sally-yates-walked-out-of-an-aaron-sorkin-script-and-into-liberals-hearts.html.

33 **The blogger Yashar Ali posted:** Yashar Ali (@yashar), "WATCH: Here's
    who Sally Yates reminds me of. . . . . wait for it," Twitter, May 8, 2017,
    5:11 p.m., twitter.com/yashar/status/861690012412366848.

34 **his second attorney general, Bill Barr:** Jen Kirby, "Attorney General Bill Barr
    Contradicted Trump on Voter Fraud. Now He's Resigning," *Vox*, Dec. 14,
    2020, www.vox.com/2020/12/14/22175221/bill-barr-resigns-trump-attorney
    -general.

34 **many lawyers chose to cut ties:** Tom McCarthy and Jon Swaine, "Don
    McGahn: White House Counsel to Resign, Trump Confirms," *Guardian*,
    Aug, 29, 2018, www.theguardian.com/us-news/2018/aug/29/don-mcgahn
    -resign-trump-white-house-counsel; Betsy Woodruff Swan and Nicholas
    Wu, "Top DOJ Official Drafted Resignation Email amid Trump Election
    Pressure," *Politico*, Aug. 4, 2021, www.politico.com/news/2021/08/04/doj
    -official-resignation-trump-election-pressure-502413; Bloomberg Industry
    Group, "Current Employment of Top Trump Lawyers," *Flourish*, June 14,
    2021, public.flourish.studio/visualisation/6368569.

34 **The Mueller report itself is replete:** Special Counsel Robert S. Mueller III,
    "Report on the Investigation into Russian Interference in the 2016 Presi-
    dential Election," U.S. Department of Justice, March 2019, www.justice
    .gov/archives/sco/file/1373816/download.

34 **Chuck Park resigned:** Chuck Park, "I Can No Longer Justify Being a Part of
    Trump's 'Complacent State.' So I'm Resigning," *Washington Post*, Aug. 8,
    2019, www.washingtonpost.com/opinions/i-can-no-longer-justify-being-a
    -part-of-trumps-complacent-state-so-im-resigning/2019/08/08
    /fed849e4-af14-11e9-8e77-03b30bc29f64_story.html.

35 **famously rebuffed public pressure:** "The Public Servant (with Sally Yates),"
    Stay Tuned with Preet, Dec. 12, 2019, cafe.com/stay-tuned/the-public-servant
    -with-sally-yates.

35 **her father's suicide:** Sally Yates, "Sally Yates: When Darkness Falls—My
    Dad's Battle with Depression," CNN, June 11, 2018, www.cnn.com/2018
    /06/11/opinions/when-my-dad-lost-his-struggle-with-depression-sally
    -yates/index.html.

CHAPTER 3: THE AIRPORT REVOLUTION

39 **Trump's executive order barring:** Michael D. Shear, Nicholas Kulish, and
    Alan Feuer, "Judge Blocks Trump Order on Refugees amid Chaos and
    Outcry Worldwide," *New York Times*, Jan. 28, 2017, www.nytimes.com
    /2017/01/28/us/refugees-detained-at-us-airports-prompting-legal
    -challenges-to-trumps-immigration-order.html.

40 **travel ban electrified the rifts:** Ashley Parker, Philip Rucker, and Robert
    Costa, "From Order to Disorder: How Trump's Immigration Directive Ex-
    posed GOP Rifts," *Washington Post*, Jan. 30, 2017, www.washingtonpost

.com/politics/from-order-to-disorder-how-trumps-immigration
-directive-exposed-gop-rifts/2017/01/30/b4e42044-e70f-11e6-b82f
-687d6e6a3e7c_story.html.

40 **In the hours following the launch:** Lyric Lewin, "These Are the Faces of
Trump's Travel Ban," CNN, Jan. 2017, www.cnn.com/interactive/2017/01
/politics/immigration-ban-stories; Claudia Koerner, "Trump's Travel Ban Is
Keeping Sick Kids from Medical Care, So Canada Is Stepping In," *BuzzFeed
News*, Feb. 3, 2017, www.buzzfeednews.com/article/claudiakoerner/trumps
-travel-ban-is-keeping-sick-kids-from-medical-care-so; Yeganeh Torbati, Jeff
Mason, and Mica Rosenberg, "Chaos, Anger as Trump Order Halts Some
Muslim Immigrants," Reuters, Jan. 28, 2017, www.reuters.com/article/us-usa
-trump-immigration-chaos-idUSKBN15C0LD; Jerry Markon, Emma Brown,
and Katherine Shaver, "Judge Halts Deportations as Refugee Ban Causes
Worldwide Furor," *Washington Post*, Jan. 29, 2017, www.washingtonpost
.com/local/social-issues/refugees-detained-at-us-airports-challenge
-trumps-executive-order/2017/01/28/e69501a2-e562-11e6-a547-5fb9411
d332c_story.html.

40 **"like Tom Hanks at the airport":** Adam Liptak, "3 Judges Weigh Trump's
Revised Travel Ban, but Keep Their Poker Faces," *New York Times*, May 15,
2017, www.nytimes.com/2017/05/15/us/politics/trump-travel-ban-appeals
-court.html.

40 **Two such travelers:** Rachel Weiner and Gregory S. Schneider, "Yemeni
Brothers Deported at Dulles Will Probably Be Allowed Back into U.S.,"
Washington Post, Feb. 2, 2017, www.washingtonpost.com/local/public-safe
ty/yemenese-brothers-deported-at-dulles-will-likely-be-allowed-back
-into-us/2017/02/02/7daa044c-e94c-11e6-bf6f-301b6b443624_story
.html.

41 **Another stranded traveler:** Hameed Darweesh, "I Risked My Life for the
U.S. Army in Iraq. But When I Came Here, I Was Nearly Sent Back,"
Washington Post, Feb. 10, 2017, www.washingtonpost.com/posteverything
/wp/2017/02/10/i-worked-for-the-u-s-army-in-iraq-but-when-i
-landed-in-america-i-was-detained.

42 **In Philadelphia, two Syrian families:** Brian X. McCrone, John Taylor, and
David Chang, "Two Syrian Families Detained at Philadelphia International
Airport, Then Put on Return Flight Home, Family Member Says," NBC
Philadelphia, Jan. 29, 2017, www.nbcphiladelphia.com/news/local/two-syrian
-families-detained-at-philadelphia-international-airport-told-to-fly-back-fa
mily-member-says/26565.

42 **being held in Chicago:** Elyssa Cherney, Nereida Moreno, and Tony Briscoe, "Chicagoans Decry Travel Restrictions as Family, Friends Held at
O'Hare," *Chicago Tribune*, Jan. 30, 2017, www.chicagotribune.com/news
/breaking/ct-ohare-immigration-met-20170129-story.html.

42 **Fifty other travelers were detained:** Dianne Solis et al., "U.S. Judge Blocks

Deportations Under Trump Order as Protesters Flock to DFW, Other Airports Nationwide," *Dallas Morning News*, Jan. 29, 2017, www.dallasnews.com/news/politics/2017/01/29/u-s-judge-blocks-deportations-under-trump-order-as-protesters-flock-to-dfw-other-airports-nationwide.

42 **A recent Clemson PhD:** Martha Waggoner, "South Carolina Tech Worker Visiting Iran Can't Return to US," Associated Press, Jan. 29, 2017, apnews.com/article/29c5163604c14d618e8d7e877dd1735e.

42 **A Syrian family of six:** Sarah Jorgensen, "Syrian Christian Family, Visas in Hand, Turned Back at Airport," CNN, Jan. 29, 2017, www.cnn.com/2017/01/28/us/syrian-family-trump-travel-ban/index.html.

42 **Overall, the ACLU estimated:** Javier E. David and Jacob Pramuk, "Judge Blocks US from Deporting Visa Holders Detained After Trump's Refugee Order," CNBC, Jan. 31, 2017, www.cnbc.com/2017/01/28/aclu-mounts-legal-challenge-to-trumps-refugee-ban-calling-it-unlawful.html.

42 **Department of Homeland Security (DHS) put out a statement:** "Department of Homeland Security Response to Recent Litigation," Department of Homeland Security, Jan. 29, 2017, www.dhs.gov/news/2017/01/29/department-homeland-security-response-recent-litigation.

42 **Haider Sameer Abdulkhaleq Alshawi:** Manny Fernandez, "Refugee Ban Injects Chaos into Iraqi Family's Reunion," *New York Times*, Jan. 28, 2017, www.nytimes.com/2017/01/28/us/refugee-ban-injects-chaos-into-iraqi-familys-reunion.html.

43 **"most likely to debate with a teacher":** Miriam Jordan, "A Travel Ban's Foe: A Young Firebrand and Her Pro Bono Brigade," *New York Times*, May 7, 2017, www.nytimes.com/2017/05/07/us/travel-ban-lawyer.html.

43 **"I'd worked on a range of different issues":** Becca Heller, interview by author, Feb. 2019.

51 **as I reported out the story:** Dahlia Lithwick, "The Lawyers Showed Up," *Slate*, Jan. 28, 2017, slate.com/news-and-politics/2017/01/lawyers-take-on-donald-trumps-muslim-ban.html.

51 **three thousand lawyers had volunteered:** Reeves Wiedeman, "24 Hours at JFK: The Hour-by-Hour Account of Two Iraqis' Detainment and Release," *New York*, Jan. 31, 2017, nymag.com/intelligencer/2017/01/24-hours-at-jfk-two-iraqi-refugees-detainment-and-release.html.

52 **New York Taxi Workers Alliance:** Eli Blumenthal, "The Scene at JFK as Taxi Drivers Strike Following Trump's Immigration Ban," *USA Today*, Jan. 28, 2017, www.usatoday.com/story/news/2017/01/28/taxi-drivers-strike-jfk-airport-following-trumps-immigration-ban/97198818.

52 **Thirty thousand people turned up:** Daniel Altschuler (@altochulo), "The march was utterly endless. Our final count is 30,000 beautiful NYers. #NoBanNoWall," Twitter, Jan. 29, 2017, 6:06 p.m., twitter.com/altochulo/status/825842703342649346.

52 **"By the end of the day":** Eli Rosenberg, "Protests Grow 'Out of Nowhere'

at Kennedy Airport After Iraqis Are Detained," *New York Times*, Jan. 28, 2017, www.nytimes.com/2017/01/28/nyregion/jfk-protests-trump-refugee -ban.html.

52 **By 3:00 p.m. Saturday:** Chas Danner, "Protests Against Trump's Travel Ban Break Out Across America," *New York*, Jan. 29, 2017, nymag.com /intelligencer/2017/01/protests-against-trumps-travel-ban-break-out -across-america.html.

53 **attorneys were hunched on the floor:** Jonah Engel Bromwich, "Lawyers Mobilize at Nation's Airports After Trump's Order," *New York Times*, Jan. 29, 2017, www.nytimes.com/2017/01/29/us/lawyers-trump-muslim-ban -immigration.html.

53 **As Jennifer Rubin put it:** Jennifer Rubin, *Resistance: How Women Saved Democracy from Donald Trump* (New York: HarperCollins, 2021).

56 **The first emergency hearing happened:** Muneer I. Ahmad and Michael J. Wishnie, "Call Air Traffic Control! Confronting Crisis as Lawyers and Teachers," in *Crisis Lawyering: Effective Legal Advocacy in Emergency Situations*, ed. Ray Brescia and Eric K. Stern (New York: New York University Press, 2021); Raya Jalabi and Alan Yuhas, "Federal Judge Stays Deportations Under Trump Muslim Country Travel Ban," *Guardian*, Jan. 28, 2017, www.theguardian.com/us-news/2017/jan/28/federal-judge-stays -deportations-trump-muslim-executive-order; Georgett Roberts, Jennifer Bain, and Kathianne Boniello, "Federal Judge Grants Stay for Those Detained Under Trump's Travel Ban," *New York Post*, Jan. 28, 2017, nypost .com/2017/01/28/federal-judge-grants-emergency-stay-for-those -detained-under-trumps-travel-ban.

56 **Donnelly, a former federal prosecutor:** Christopher Mele, "Judge Who Blocked Trump's Refugee Order Praised for 'Firm Moral Compass,'" *New York Times*, Jan. 29, 2017, www.nytimes.com/2017/01/29/us/judge-trump -refugee-order-ann-donnelly.html.

58 **She ordered the Trump administration to refrain:** Timothy B. Lee and Dara Lind, "Read: Full Text of the New Stay Halting Deportations Under Trump's Immigration Order," *Vox*, Jan. 28, 2017, www.vox.com/2017/1 /28/14427846/trump-muslim-ban-order.

59 **two federal judges in Boston:** Daniel A. Gross, "In Boston, a Late-Night Victory Against Trump's Immigration Ban," *New Yorker*, Jan. 29, 2017, www.newyorker.com/news/news-desk/in-boston-a-late-night-victory -against-trumps-immigration-ban.

59 **Researchers have been studying the data:** Jennifer L. Peresie, "Female Judges Matter: Gender and Collegial Decisionmaking in the Federal Appellate Courts," *Yale Law Journal* 114, no. 7 (May 2005), www.yalelaw journal.org/note/female-judges-matter-gender-and-collegial -decisionmaking-in-the-federal-appellate-courts.

59 **Justice Sandra Day O'Connor famously rejected:** Sandra Day O'Connor, "James Madison Lecture: Portia's Progress," *NYU Law Journal* 66 (Dec. 1991), www.law.nyu.edu/sites/default/files/ECM_PRO_059255.pdf.

60 **while Justice Sonia Sotomayor:** Sonia Sotomayor, "A Latina Judge's Voice," *Berkeley La Raza Law Journal* 13, no. 1 (March 2002), lawcat.berkeley.edu/record/1118136.

60 **Those numbers matter whether or not:** John Gramlich, "How Trump Compares with Other Recent Presidents in Appointing Federal Judges," Pew Research Center, Jan. 13, 2021, www.pewresearch.org/fact-tank/2021/01/13/how-trump-compares-with-other-recent-presidents-in-appointing-federal-judges/.

60 **"massive success story":** Josh Gerstein, "Homeland Security Deployed 'Crisis Action Team' to Enforce First Trump Travel Ban," *Politico*, Jan. 2, 2018, www.politico.com/blogs/under-the-radar/2018/01/02/trump-travel-ban-dhs-crisis-team-319894.

60 **"It's not a Muslim ban":** Roberts, Bain, and Boniello, "Federal Judge Grants Stay for Those Detained Under Trump's Travel Ban."

60 **A week after a raft:** Joanna Walters, "Four States Sue Trump Administration over 'Un-American' Travel Ban," *Guardian*, Feb. 1, 2017, www.theguardian.com/us-news/2017/jan/31/trump-travel-ban-state-lawsuits; Nausheen Husain, "Timeline: Legal Fight over Trump's 'Muslim Ban' and the Supreme Court Ruling," *Chicago Tribune*, June 26, 2018, www.chicagotribune.com/data/ct-travel-ban-ruling-timeline-htmlstory.html; Steve Almasy and Darran Simon, "A Timeline of President Trump's Travel Bans," CNN, March 30, 2017, www.cnn.com/2017/02/10/us/trump-travel-ban-timeline/index.html.

61 **a *third* version was unfurled:** *Trump v. Hawaii*, 17-965, 585 U.S. __ (2018).

62 **He would cite this victory:** Olivia Paschal, "Read President Trump's Speech Declaring a National Emergency," *Atlantic*, Feb. 15, 2019, www.theatlantic.com/politics/archive/2019/02/trumps-declaration-national-emergency-full-text/582928.

CHAPTER 4: CHARLOTTESVILLE NAZIS

67 **Nazis marched in Charlottesville:** Phil McCausland, "White Nationalist Leads Torch-Bearing Protesters Against Removal of Confederate Statue," NBC News, May 14, 2017, www.nbcnews.com/news/us-news/white-nationalist-leads-torch-bearing-protesters-against-removal-confederate-statue-n759266.

67 **"It has a population":** Richard C. Schragger, "When White Supremacists Invade a City," *Virginia Law Review* 104 (Jan. 2018), www.virginialawreview.org/articles/when-white-supremacists-invade-city.

68 **Jason Kessler, a local white supremacist:** Natasha Bertrand, "Here's What
We Know About the 'Pro-white' Organizer of 'Unite the Right,' Who Was
Chased Out of His Own Press Conference," *Business Insider,* Aug. 14, 2017,
www.businessinsider.com/who-is-jason-kessler-unite-the-right
-charlottesville-2017-8.

68 **"the Harvard of the Confederacy":** Amiri Baraka, *The Autobiography of
LeRoi Jones* (Chicago: Lawrence Hill Books, 1984).

68 **Monticello, home of Thomas Jefferson:** Annette Gordon-Reed, *The Heming-
ses of Monticello: An American Family* (New York: W. W. Norton, 2008).

68 **"Blood and soil" (or the original:** David Neiwert, "When White Nationalists Chant Their Weird Slogans, What Do They Mean?," Southern Poverty Law Center, Oct. 10, 2017, www.splcenter.org/hatewatch/2017/10
/10/when-white-nationalists-chant-their-weird-slogans-what-do-they
-mean.

69 **"a beautiful aesthetic":** Oliver Laughland, "White Nationalist Richard
Spencer at Rally over Confederate Statue's Removal," *Guardian,* May 14,
2017,   www.theguardian.com/world/2017/may/14/richard-spencer-white
-nationalist-virginia-confederate-statue.

69 **the KKK decided to get in on:** Hawes Spencer and Matt Stevens, "23
Arrested and Tear Gas Deployed After a K.K.K. Rally in Virginia,"
New York Times, July 8, 2017, www.nytimes.com/2017/07/08/us/kkk-rally
-charlottesville-robert-e-lee-statue.html; Sarah Toy, "KKK Rally in Charlottesville Met with Throng of Protesters," *USA Today,* July 8, 2017, www
.usatoday.com/story/news/nation-now/2017/07/08/kkk-holds-rally
-virginia-and-met-protesters/462146001.

70 **so-called Unite the Right rally:** Adam Bhala Lough, *Alt-Right: Age of Rage*
(Netflix, 2018); Ellie Silverman, "Neo-Nazi Told Leader of Group at
Deadly 2017 Charlottesville Rally: 'We're All Doing It Together,'" *Washington Post,* Nov. 4, 2021, www.washingtonpost.com/dc-md-va/2021/11/04
/charlottesville-lawsuit-nazis-heimbach-trial/; Dara Lind, "Unite the Right,
the Violent White Supremacist Rally in Charlottesville, Explained," *Vox,*
Aug. 14, 2017, www.vox.com/2017/8/12/16138246/charlottesville-nazi-rally
-right-uva.

70 **David Duke would attend:** Libby Nelson, "'Why We Voted for Donald
Trump': David Duke Explains the White Supremacist Charlottesville Protests," *Vox,* Aug. 12, 2017, www.vox.com/2017/8/12/16138358/charlottes
ville-protests-david-duke-kkk.

70 **Trump had initially refused to condemn:** Danielle Kurtzleben, "Trump's
Fuzzy History of Denouncing White Nationalism," GBH News, Aug. 15,
2017, www.wgbh.org/news/2017/08/15/politics-government/trumps-fuzzy
-history-denouncing-white-nationalism.

70 **a Twitter account called WhiteGenocideTM:** Nolan D. McCaskill, "Trump
Retweets Another White Supremacist," *Politico,* Feb. 27, 2016, www.politico

.com/blogs/2016-gop-primary-live-updates-and-results/2016/02/donald
-trump-white-supremacist-retweet-219915.

71 **the most speech-protective court:** Joel Gora, "Free Speech Matters: The
Roberts Court and the First Amendment," *Journal of Law and Policy* 25,
no. 1 (2016), brooklynworks.brooklaw.edu/jlp/vol25/iss1/4.

71 **A vast array of sketchy:** *Terminiello v. City of Chicago,* 337 U.S. 1 (1949);
Manual Enterprises Inc. v. Day, 370 U.S. 478 (1962); *R.A.V. v. City of St.
Paul,* 505 U.S. 377 (1992); *United States v. Playboy Entertainment Group,*
529 U.S. 803 (2000); *Snyder v. Phelps,* 562 U.S. 443 (2011).

72 **Skokie, Illinois, had a population:** *National Socialist Party of America v.
Village of Skokie,* 432 U.S. 43 (1977).

72 **counterprotesters "drowned out":** Douglas E. Kneeland, "2,000 Protesters
Drown Out Nazis at Chicago Rally," *New York Times,* June 25, 1978, www
.nytimes.com/1978/06/25/archives/2000-protesters-drown-out
-nazis-at-chicago-rally.html.

73 **"unspectacular end after 10 minutes":** James Yuenger and Ronald Koziol,
"Fear, Loathing, but Little Else, at Nazi Rally," *Chicago Tribune,* June 25,
1978.

73 **tapped a Jewish attorney—David Goldberger:** Associated Press, "Lawyer
Who Aided Illinois Nazis Recalls a 'Very Difficult Odyssey,'" *New York
Times,* April 29, 1979, www.nytimes.com/1979/04/29/archives/lawyer-who
-aided-illinois-nazis-recalls-a-very-difficult-odyssey.html.

73 **ACLU members resigned:** Douglas E. Kneeland, "Nazi Defense by
A.C.L.U. Has Cost 2,000 Members," *New York Times,* Sept. 6, 1977, www
.nytimes.com/1977/09/06/archives/nazi-defense-by-aclu-has-cost-2000
-members.html.

73 **"if we don't believe in freedom of expression":** "MIT Libraries Receive Papers of Distinguished Linguist, Philosopher, and Activist Noam Chomsky,"
MIT Libraries, Feb. 9, 2012, citing *The Guardian,* Nov. 23, 1992, libraries
.mit.edu/news/libraries-receive-papers/7765/.

74 **sued the City of Charlottesville:** Claire Guthrie Gastañaga and Steve
Levinson, "Why We Represented the Alt-Right in Charlottesville," *Rich-
mond Times-Dispatch,* Aug. 26, 2017, richmond.com/opinion/their-opinion
/guest-columnists/gasta-aga-and-levinson-column-why-we-represented
-the-alt/article_15d8a11b-bddf-54af-9a1a-17f21fdae7e4.html.

75 **Hawes Spencer described it:** Hawes Spencer, "A Far-Right Gathering
Bursts into Brawls," *New York Times,* Aug. 13, 2017, www.nytimes.com
/2017/08/13/us/charlottesville-protests-unite-the-right.html.

75 **in his 2018 book, *Summer of Hate*:** Hawes Spencer, *Summer of Hate:
Charlottesville, USA* (Charlottesville: University of Virginia Press, 2018).

75 **political commentator Larry Sabato:** Terry McAuliffe, *Beyond Charlottesville: Taking a Stand Against White Nationalism* (New York: St. Martin's
Press, 2019).

76 **"we'd still do you"**: Terry McAuliffe, "The Inside Story of Charlottesville—and How the Violence Could Have Been Avoided," *Newsweek*, July 30, 2019, www.newsweek.com/2019/08/09/what-happened-charlottesville-virginia-terry-mcauliffe-book-1451608.html.

76 **"first f——g boat home"**: Joel Gunter, "A Reckoning in Charlottesville," BBC, Aug. 13, 2017, www.bbc.com/news/world-us-canada-40914748.

76 **DeAndre Harris, was brutally beaten**: Ian Shapira, "The Parking Garage Beating Lasted 10 Seconds. DeAndre Harris Still Lives with the Damage," *Washington Post*, Sept. 16, 2019, www.washingtonpost.com/local/the-parking-garage-beating-lasted-10-seconds-deandre-harris-still-lives-with-the-damage/2019/09/16/ca6daa48-cfbf-11e9-87fa-8501a456c003_story.html.

76 **David Duke offered up**: Hilary Hanson, "Ex-KKK Leader David Duke Says White Supremacists Will 'Fulfill' Trump's Promises," *Huffington Post*, Aug. 12, 2017, www.huffpost.com/entry/david-duke-charlottesville-rally-trump_n_598f3ca8e4b0909642974a10 (video recorded and uploaded by Mykal McEldowney of *The Indianapolis Star*).

77 **a Dodge Challenger driven by James Alex Fields Jr.**: Complaint in *Sines et al. v. Kessler et al.*, 324 F.Supp.3d 765 (W.D. Va. 2018).

77 **The trauma didn't end**: Complaint in *Sines et al. v. Kessler et al.*, 324 F.Supp.3d 765 (W.D. Va. 2018).

77 **Activists and antiracist protesters**: Ian Shapira, "Finding the White Supremacists Who Beat a Black Man in Charlottesville," *Washington Post*, Aug. 31, 2017, www.washingtonpost.com/local/finding-the-white-supremacists-who-beat-a-black-man-in-charlottesville/2017/08/31/9f36e762-8cfb-11e7-84c0-02cc069f2c37_story.html.

78 **A profile in *The Washington Post***: Karen Heller, "Attorney Roberta Kaplan Is About to Make Trump's Life Extremely Difficult," *Washington Post*, Jan. 18, 2021, www.washingtonpost.com/lifestyle/style/roberta-kaplan-lawyer-attorney-trump/2021/01/17/ae8890f2-50f8-11eb-bda4-615aaefd0555_story.html.

78 **Edie Windsor, the eighty-three-year-old widow**: *United States v. Windsor*, 570 U.S. 744 (2013).

78 **Kaplan was an outsider**: Roberta Kaplan, interview by author, July 2019.

79 **Kaplan had lost a big ACLU suit**: *Samuels v. New York State Department of Health*, 4 N.Y.3d 825 (2005).

79 **Windsor's victory in 2013 would become**: *Obergefell v. Hodges*, 576 U.S. 644 (2015).

80 **she and Edie were gay women**: Roberta Kaplan, *Then Comes Marriage: United States v. Windsor and the Defeat of DOMA*, with Lisa Dickey (New York: W. W. Norton, 2015).

82 **"we condemn in the strongest possible terms"**: Dan Merica, "Trump Condemns 'Hatred, Bigotry, and Violence on Many Sides' in Charlottesville,"

CNN, Aug. 13, 2017, www.cnn.com/2017/08/12/politics/trump-statement
-alt-right-protests/index.html.

82 **The neo-Nazi Andrew Anglin:** Complaint in *Sines et al. v. Kessler et al.*,
324 F.Supp.3d 765 (W.D. Va. 2018).

82 **"You had some very bad people":** Rosie Gray, "Trump Defends White-
Nationalist Protesters: 'Some Very Fine People on Both Sides,'" *Atlantic*, Aug. 15, 2017, www.theatlantic.com/politics/archive/2017/08/trump
-defends-white-nationalist-protesters-some-very-fine-people-on-both
-sides/537012.

82 **In later years, he would claim:** David Jackson, "Trump Defends Response
to Charlottesville Violence, Says He Put It 'Perfectly' with 'Both Sides' Remark," *USA Today*, April 26, 2019, www.usatoday.com/story/news/politics
/2019/04/26/trump-says-both-sides-charlottesville-remark-said
-perfectly/3586024002.

84 **never went to the Supreme Court:** *Planned Parenthood of Columbia/
Willamette Inc. v. American Coalition of Life Activists*, 290 F.3d 1058 (9th
Cir. 2002).

85 **Ku Klux Klan Act of 1871:** 42 U.S.C. §§ 1983–86.

85 **Kaplan and Dunn filed their suit:** Complaint in *Sines et al. v. Kessler et al.*,
324 F.Supp.3d 765 (W.D. Va. 2018).

85 **"The trauma will never go away":** Neil MacFarquhar, "The Charlottesville
Rally Civil Trial, Explained," *New York Times*, Oct. 25, 2019, www.nytimes
.com/live/2021/charlottesville-rally-trial-explained.

86 **Julie Fink is the managing partner:** Julie Fink, interview by author, July
2019.

89 **James E. Kolenich, a civil rights attorney:** Monroe Trombly, "In a Suburban
Cincinnati Office Park, White Nationalists Have Found Their Lawyer—
and an Ally," *Cincinnati Inquirer*, Feb. 26, 2018, www.cincinnati.com/story
/news/2018/02/26/suburban-cincinnati-office-park-white-nationalists
-have-found-their-lawyer-and-ally/338365002.

90 **in a sixty-two-page ruling:** *Sines et al. v. Kessler et al.*, 324 F. Supp.3d 765
(W.D. Va. 2018).

91 **Unite the Right's anniversary:** Richard Fausset, Serge F. Kovaleski, and
Alan Feuer, "A Year After Charlottesville, Disarray in the White Supremacist Movement," *New York Times*, Aug. 13, 2018, www.nytimes.com/2018
/08/13/us/charlottesville-unite-the-right-white-supremacists.html; Joe Heim
et al., "White-Supremacist Rally near White House Dwarfed by Thousands of Anti-hate Protesters," *Washington Post*, Aug. 12, 2018, www.wash
ingtonpost.com/local/washington-readies-for-todays-planned-white-supre
macist-rally-near-white-house/2018/08/12/551720c4-9c28-11e8-8d5e-c6c
594024954_story.html.

91 **Nathan Damigo, another defendant:** Aaron Katersky, "Charlottesville
Rally Lawsuit to Proceed Despite Nathan Damigo's Bankruptcy Filing,"

ABC News, Feb. 19, 2019, abcnews.go.com/US/charlottesville-rally-lawsuit
-proceed-nathan-damigos-bankruptcy-filing/story?id=61149383.

91 **James Fields Jr. was sentenced:** CBS/Associated Press, "Man Gets Life Plus
419 Years in Deadly Charlottesville Car Attack," CBS News, July 15, 2019,
www.cbsnews.com/news/james-alex-fields-jr-charlottesville-car-attack
-sentenced-life-plus-419-years-today-2019-07-15.

91 **Matthew Heimbach was arrested:** Marwa Eltagouri and Avi Selk, "How a
White Nationalist's Family Came to Blows over a Trailer Tryst," *Washington Post*, March 14, 2018, www.washingtonpost.com/news/post-nation/wp
/2018/03/13/white-nationalist-leader-matthew-heimbach-arrested
-for-domestic-battery.

91 **canceled a speaking tour:** Susan Svrluga, "'Antifa Is Winning': Richard
Spencer Rethinks His College Tour After Violent Protests," *Washington
Post*, March 12, 2018, www.washingtonpost.com/news/grade-point/wp
/2018/03/12/antifa-is-winning-richard-spencer-rethinks-his-college-tour
-after-violent-protests/.

91 **Emails released as part of the suit:** Brett Barrouquere, "'Let's Just Ghost
Him': Alt-Right Leaders Were Leery of Jason Kessler Before 'Unite the
Right.' Text Messages Show They Wanted Him Out of the Movement,"
Southern Poverty Law Center, Oct. 17, 2018, www.splcenter.org/hate
watch/2018/10/17/alt-right-leaders-were-leery-jason-kessler.

91 **Kessler was caught on video:** Isaac Stanley-Becker, "Jason Kessler's Anti-
Jewish Screed Was Interrupted by His Father: 'Hey, You Get Out of My
Room,'" *Washington Post*, Aug. 16, 2018, www.washingtonpost.com/news
/morning-mix/wp/2018/08/16/jason-kesslers-anti-jewish-screed-was
-interrupted-by-his-father-hey-get-out-of-my-room.

91 **two prominent clients:** Kelly Weill, "'Crying Nazi' Christopher Cantwell
Allegedly Threatened Charlottesville Lawyer Suing Him," *Daily Beast*,
July 2, 2019, www.thedailybeast.com/crying-nazi-christopher-cantwell
-allegedly-threatened-charlottesville-lawyer-suing-him; Kelly Weill, "Charlottesville Lawyers Dump Nazi Clients," *Daily Beast*, July 29, 2019, www
.thedailybeast.com/charlottesville-lawyers-dump-nazi-clients-chris-the
-crying-nazi-cantwell-and-robert-azzmador-ray.

92 **dropped in toilets:** "Trial of White Nationalists Behind the 2017 Charlottesville Rally Is Set to Begin," *PBS NewsHour*, Oct. 24, 2021, www.pbs
.org/newshour/show/trial-of-the-white-nationalists-behind-the-2017
-charlottesville-rally-is-set-to-begin.

92 **The trial was delayed:** Roberta Kaplan and Karen Dunn, interviews by
author, July 2019.

94 **"for all the women in the country":** Heller, "Attorney Roberta Kaplan Is
About to Make Trump's Life Extremely Difficult."

97 **the Charlottesville jury:** Ellie Silverman et al., "Spencer, Kessler, Cantwell,
and Other White Supremacists Found Liable in Deadly Unite the Right

Rally," *Washington Post*, Nov. 23, 2021, www.washingtonpost.com/dc-md -va/2021/11/23/charlottesville-verdict-live-updates; Neil MacFarquhar, "Jury Finds Rally Organizers Responsible for Charlottesville Violence," *New York Times*, Nov. 23, 2021, www.nytimes.com/2021/11/23/us/char lottesville-rally-verdict.html.

97 **"Once they are in government":** David Cesarani, *Final Solution: The Fate of the Jews, 1933–1949* (New York: St. Martin's Press, 2016).

CHAPTER 5: ABORTION AT THE BORDER

99 **Margaret Atwood's dystopic novel *The Handmaid's Tale*:** Margaret Atwood, *The Handmaid's Tale* (New York: Houghton Mifflin, 1986).

99 **Brigitte Amiri knows all about:** Brigitte Amiri, interview by author, May 2019.

99 **"Jane Doe" was the name given:** Complaint for Injunctive Relief and Damages in *Garza v. Hargan*, Oct. 13, 2017, www.aclu.org/legal-document /garza-v-hargan-complaint-injunctive-relief-and-damages.

100 **Marie Christine Cortez, an attorney from Jane's Due Process:** Cristian Farias, "Meet the Texas Lawyer Who Helped an Undocumented Teen Fight for an Abortion," *New York*, Nov. 3, 2017, www.thecut.com/2017 /11/this-lawyer-helped-undocumented-teen-fight-for-an-abortion.html.

100 **As *Politico* noted in 2018:** Adam Cancryn and Renuka Rayasam, "Meet the Anti-abortion Trump Appointee Taking Care of Separated Kids," *Politico*, June 21, 2018, www.politico.com/story/2018/06/21/scott-lloyd-anti -abortion-separated-kids-642094.

101 **The threat of sexual violence is pervasive:** Manny Fernandez, "'You Have to Pay with Your Body': The Hidden Nightmare of Sexual Violence on the Border," *New York Times*, March 3, 2019, www.nytimes.com/2019/03/03/us /border-rapes-migrant-women.html; Kejal Vyas, "Rapes of U.S.-Bound Migrants Make a Treacherous Route Even More Dangerous," *Wall Street Journal*, Sept. 6, 2021, www.wsj.com/articles/rapes-of-u-s-bound-migrants-make -a-treacherous-route-even-more-dangerous-11630956539; Julia Lurie, "Beatings, Kidnappings, and Rape: Sobering New Data Shows Just How Much Violence Migrants Through Mexico Endure," *Mother Jones*, Aug. 21, 2019, www .motherjones.com/politics/2019/08/beatings-kidnappings-and-rape-sober ing-new-data-shows-just-how-much-violence-migrants-through-mexico -endure.

101 **The ACLU had been investigating:** Brigitte Amiri, "The Obama Administration Is Allowing Religious Organizations to Restrict Health Care for the Most Vulnerable, but We Just Won the First Round," ACLU, Dec. 5, 2016, www.aclu.org/blog/reproductive-freedom/religion-and-reproductive -rights/obama-administration-allowing-religious; Complaint for Injunctive and Declaratory Relief, *RILR v. Johnson*, Dec. 16, 2014, www.aclu.org

/legal-document/rilr-v-johnson-complaint?redirect=immigrants-rights
/rilr-v-johnson-complaint; Shoshanna J. Ehrlich, "The Body as Borderland:
The Abortion (Non)Rights of Unaccompanied Teens in Federal Immigration Custody in the Trump-Pence Era," *UCLA Women's Law Journal* 28,
no. 1 (2021), escholarship.org/uc/item/797961p3.

101 **Lloyd put a new policy into effect:** Complaint for Injunctive Relief and
Damages in *Garza v. Hargan.*

102 **Lloyd wrote in an email:** Jennifer Wright, "The U.S. Is Tracking Migrant
Girls' Periods to Stop Them from Getting Abortions," *Harper's Bazaar,*
April 2, 2019, www.harpersbazaar.com/culture/politics/a26985261/trump
-administration-abortion-period-tracking-migrant-women; Rachel Siegel,
"The Trump Official Who Tried to Stop a Detained Immigrant from Getting an Abortion," *Washington Post,* Oct. 26, 2017, www.washingtonpost
.com/news/post-nation/wp/2017/10/26/the-trump-official-who
-tried-to-stop-a-detained-immigrant-from-getting-an-abortion.

102 **Lloyd's new ORR policy:** Second Amended Complaint for Injunctive Relief, *Garza v. Hargan,* Nov. 11, 2018, www.acludc.org/sites/default/files
/field_documents/garza_v_hargan_2nd_amended_complaint_1-11-2018
.pdf; Michelle Goldberg, "The Trump Administration's Power over a Pregnant Girl," *New York Times,* Oct. 20, 2017, www.nytimes.com/2017/10/20
/opinion/trump-pregnancy-abortion-.html; Ehrlich, "Body as Borderland."

103 **"to be an advocate for people":** Farias, "Meet the Texas Lawyer Who
Helped an Undocumented Teen Fight for an Abortion."

103 **"I'm the daughter of an Iranian immigrant":** Brigitte Amiri, interview by
author, May 2019.

105 **just secured a huge victory:** *Whole Woman's Health v. Hellerstedt,* 579
U.S. 582 (2016).

106 **a 7–2 opinion in *Roe v. Wade*:** *Roe v. Wade,* 410 U.S. 113 (1973).

106 **replacement with Amy Coney Barrett:** Nicholas Fandos, "Senate Confirms
Barrett, Delivering for Trump and Reshaping the Court," *New York Times,*
Oct. 26, 2020, www.nytimes.com/2020/10/26/us/politics/senate-confirms
-barrett.html.

107 **In 1992, in *Planned Parenthood v. Casey*:** *Planned Parenthood v. Casey,*
505 U.S. 833 (1992).

107 **But in 2016, in *Whole Woman's Health v. Hellerstedt*:** *Whole Woman's
Health v. Hellerstedt,* 579 U.S. 582 (2016).

107 **Mitch McConnell's unprecedented blockade:** Ron Elving, "What Happened with Merrick Garland in 2016 and Why It Matters Now," NPR,
June 29, 2018, www.npr.org/2018/06/29/624467256/what-happened-with
-merrick-garland-in-2016-and-why-it-matters-now.

107 **ambivalent evangelical voters:** Olga Khazan, "Why Christians Overwhelm
ingly Backed Trump," *Atlantic,* Nov. 9, 2016, www.theatlantic.com/health
/archive/2016/11/why-women-and-christians-backed-trump/507176.

108 **should suffer "some form of punishment":** Matt Flegenheimer and Maggie Haberman, "Donald Trump, Abortion Foe, Eyes 'Punishment' for Women, Then Recants," *New York Times*, March 30, 2016, www.nytimes.com/2016 /03/31/us/politics/donald-trump-abortion.html.

108 **He even published a list:** Alan Rappeport and Charlie Savage, "Donald Trump Releases List of Possible Supreme Court Picks," *New York Times*, March 18, 2016, www.nytimes.com/2016/05/19/us/politics/donald-trump -supreme-court-nominees.html; Nina Totenberg, "Donald Trump Unveils New, More Diverse Supreme Court Short List," NPR, Sept. 23, 2016, www.npr.org/2016/09/23/495216645/donald-trump-unveils-new-more -diverse-supreme-court-short-list.

108 **Trump won a higher percentage:** Jessica Martínez and Gregory A. Smith, "How the Faithful Voted: A Preliminary 2016 Analysis," Pew Research Center, Nov. 9, 2016, www.pewresearch.org/fact-tank/2016/11/09/how -the-faithful-voted-a-preliminary-2016-analysis.

108 **a critical factor in their vote:** Myriam Renaud, "Myths Debunked: Why Did White Evangelical Christians Vote for Trump?," *Sightings*, Jan. 19, 2017, divinity.uchicago.edu/sightings/articles/myths-debunked-why-did-white -evangelical-christians-vote-trump.

108 **Tony Perkins, who helms the anti-LGBTQ group:** "Family Research Council," Southern Poverty Law Center, www.splcenter.org/fighting-hate /extremist-files/group/family-research-council.

108 **"First, he chose a pro-life conservative":** Katherine Stewart, "Eighty-one Percent of White Evangelicals Voted for Donald Trump. Why?," *Nation*, Nov. 17, 2016, www.thenation.com/article/archive/eighty-one-percent-of -white-evangelicals-voted-for-donald-trump-why.

108 **the most antiabortion US president:** Gabby Orr, "Trumps Sets a New GOP Standard in the Abortion Fight," *Politico*, Jan. 24, 2020, www.politico .com/news/2020/01/24/march-for-life-trump-abortion-speech-103994; Ryan Lucas, "New Documents Reveal How Trump, Cohen, Aides Worked to Seal Hush Money Deals," NPR, Jan. 18, 2019, www.npr.org/2019/07/18 /743112028/trump-spoke-with-cohen-as-they-aides-sealed-hush-money -deals-in-2016; Shane Goldmacher, "F.E.C. Drops Case Reviewing Trump Hush-Money Payments to Women," *New York Times*, May 6, 2021, www .nytimes.com/2021/05/06/us/politics/trump-michael-cohen-fec.html.

108 **States emboldened by Trump's:** Mark Sherman and Jessica Gresko, "Justices Signal They'll OK New Abortion Limits, May Toss Roe," Associated Press, Dec. 1, 2021, apnews.com/article/abortion-donald-trump-us-supreme-court -health-amy-coney-barrett-a3b5cf9621315e6c623dc80a790842d8; Elyssa Spitzer and Nora Ellmann, "State Abortion Legislation in 2021," Center for American Progress, Sept. 21, 2021, www.americanprogress.org/article/state -abortion-legislation-2021/; Zoe Tillman, "Trump's Judges Are Playing a Huge Role in Upholding Anti-abortion Laws Across the Country," *BuzzFeed News*,

Sept. 12, 2012, www.buzzfeednews.com/article/zoetillman/trump-judges
-abortion-access-legal-challenge; Scott S. Greenberger, "Trump-Appointed
Judges Fuel Abortion Debate in the States," *Pew Trusts: Stateline*, Jan. 25,
2021, www.pewtrusts.org/en/research-and-analysis/blogs/stateline/2021/01
/25/trump-appointed-judges-fuel-abortion-debate-in-the-states; Nora Ell-
man, "State Actions Undermining Abortion Rights in 2020," Center for
American Progress, Aug. 27, 2020, www.americanprogress.org/article/state
-actions-undermining-abortion-rights-2020/; What if Roe Fell? (New York:
Center for Reproductive Rights, 2019), reproductiverights.org/sites/default
/files/2019-11/USP-2019-WIRF-Report-Web.pdf.

109 **moves to defund Planned Parenthood:** Pam Belluck, "Trump Administration Blocks Funds for Planned Parenthood and Others over Abortion Re-
ferrals," *New York Times*, Feb. 22, 2019, www.nytimes.com/2019/02/22
/health/trump-defunds-planned-parenthood.html.

109 **employers to deny contraception to employees:** Devin Dwyer, "Supreme
Court Allows Trump to Exempt Employers from Obamacare Birth Control Mandate," ABC News, July 9, 2020, abcnews.go.com/Politics/supreme
-court-trump-exempt-employers-obamacare-birth-control/story?id
=71254754.

109 **"executing babies AFTER birth":** Denise Grady, "'Executing Babies': Here
Are the Facts Behind Trump's Misleading Abortion Tweet," *New York
Times*, Feb. 26, 2019, www.nytimes.com/2019/02/26/health/abortion-bill
-trump.html.

109 **Efforts to pack the federal courts:** Stacy Hawkins, "Trump's Dangerous
Judicial Legacy," *UCLA Law Review*, June 13, 2019, www.uclalawreview
.org/trumps-dangerous-judicial-legacy; Mark Sherman, Kevin Freking,
and Matthew Daly, "Trump's Impact on Courts Likely to Last Long
Beyond His Term," Associated Press, Dec. 26, 2020, apnews.com/article
/joe-biden-donald-trump-mitch-mcconnell-elections-judiciary-d5807340
e86d05fbc78ed50fb43c1c46; Carrie Johnson, "Legal Opinions or Political
Commentary? A New Judge Exemplifies the Trump Era," NPR, July 26,
2018.

110 **ambulance drivers refusing to treat:** Steven Kreytak, "Bus Driver Says Religious Views Led to Firing," *Austin American-Statesman*, Sept. 1, 2012,
www.statesman.com/story/news/local/2012/09/01/bus-driver-says
-religious-views-led-to-firing/9849616007.

110 **refusing to fill prescriptions:** Minyvonne Burke, "A Woman's Doctor Pre-
scribed a Morning-After Pill. Pharmacists Refused to Fill It, Suit Says,"
NBC News, Dec. 13, 2019, www.nbcnews.com/news/us-news/woman-s
-doctor-prescribed-morning-after-pill-pharmacists-refused-fill-n1101586.

110 **craft stores named Hobby Lobby:** *Burwell v. Hobby Lobby*, 573 U.S. 682
(2014).

110 **"After failing to prohibit abortion":** Reva Siegel and Douglas NeJaime, "Conscience and the Culture Wars," *American Prospect*, June 29, 2015, prospect.org/labor/conscience-culture-wars.

110 **hospital ownership became consolidated:** Shamane Mills, "With Hospital Consolidation, Abortion and Tubal Ligation Rates Drop," Wisconsin Public Radio, Jan. 1, 2018, www.wpr.org/hospital-consolidation-abortion-and-tu bal-ligation-rates-drop; Rikha Sharma Rani, "Worried About Abortion Laws? Catholic Hospital Mergers Also Seen as Threat to Women's Health Care," *USA Today*, Dec. 27, 2019, www.usatoday.com/story/news/2019 /12/27/worried-abortion-laws-more-catholic-hospitals-also-seen-threat /4269242002.

110 **Faith-based foster care:** Associated Press and Tim Fitzsimmons, "S.C. Group Can Reject Gays and Jews as Foster Parents, Trump Admin Says," NBC News, Jan. 24, 2019, www.nbcnews.com/feature/nbc-out/s-c-group -can-reject-gays-jews-foster-parents-trump-n962306.

110 **exemptions to the COVID vaccine:** Hayley Fowler, "Religious Exemptions to COVID Vaccine: What Counts, What Doesn't, and How It Works," *Miami Herald*, Nov. 23, 2021, www.miamiherald.com/news/coronavirus/article 255509366.html; Deepa Shivaram, "1 in 10 Americans Say the COVID-19 Vaccine Conflicts with Their Religious Beliefs," NPR, Dec. 9, 2021, www .npr.org/2021/12/09/1062655300/survey-religion-vaccine-hesitancy-exemp tions.

110 **Amiri was working:** Amiri, interview by author, May 2019.

111 **the judge felt it was the wrong venue:** Order Denying Motion for Leave to Amend and a Temporary Restraining Order, *American Civil Liberties Union of Northern California v. Burwell* (N.D. Cal., June 24, 2016) (on file with author).

111 **Amiri filed an emergency petition:** Complaint for Injunctive Relief and Damages in *Garza v. Hargan*, Oct. 13, 2017.

111 **Judge Chutkan ordered HHS:** Temporary Restraining Order in *Garza v. Hargan*, Oct. 18, 2017, www.acludc.org/sites/default/files/garza_v_har gan_tro_order_10-18-2017.pdf.

112 **The panel Amiri drew for oral argument:** Amiri, interview by author, May 2019; "*Garza v. Hargan* Oral Argument (AUDIO ONLY)," C-SPAN, Oct. 20, 2017, www.c-span.org/video/?436060-1/dc-circuit-court-hears-undocu mented-teen-detainee-abortion-case-audio-only.

115 **The new order set a new deadline:** Order in *Garza v. Hargan*, Oct. 20, 2017, www.acludc.org/sites/default/files/field_documents/garza_v_hargan _appeals_ct_decision_10-20-2017.pdf.

115 **judge Patricia Millett dissented:** Order (attached statement of Judge Mil lett), Oct. 20, 2017, www.acludc.org/sites/default/files/field_documents /garza_v_hargan_appeals_ct_millett_dissent_10-20-2017.pdf.

116 **As Amiri had put it to me:** Dahlia Lithwick, "The Trump Administration Gets Religion," *Slate*, Oct. 24, 2017, slate.com/news-and-politics/2017/10/the-connection-between-hobby-lobby-and-the-jane-doe-abortion-case.html.

117 **the court voted by a 6–3 margin:** Order from the Rehearing En Banc of the U.S. Circuit Court of Appeals for the District of Columbia in *Garza v. Hargan*, Oct. 24, 2017, www.acludc.org/sites/default/files/field_documents/garza_v_hargan_full_appeals_ct_order_10-24-2017.pdf.

117 **Kavanaugh penned a bitter dissent:** Order from the Rehearing En Banc of the U.S. Circuit Court of Appeals for the District of Columbia in *Garza v. Hargan*, Oct. 24, 2017.

117 **auditioning in part:** Robert Barnes and Ann E. Marimow, "In Major Abortion Ruling, Kavanaugh Offers Clues of How He Might Handle Divisive Issue on the Supreme Court," *Washington Post*, July 11, 2018, www.washingtonpost.com/politics/courts_law/in-major-abortion-ruling-kavanaugh-offers-clues-of-how-he-might-handle-divisive-issue-on-the-supreme-court/2018/07/11/1acd980a-8515-11e8-9e80-403a221946a7_story.html.

117 **Amy Hagstrom Miller is CEO and founder:** Hagstrom Miller, interview by author, Aug. 2019.

118 **On October 24, the lower court judge:** Amended Temporary Restraining Order, *Garza v. Hargan*, Oct. 24, 2017 (on file with the author).

119 **interview with *Vice News*:** Antonia Hylton, "EXCLUSIVE: 'Jane Doe' Talks About Her Abortion Battle with Trump's DOJ," *Vice News*, Oct. 25, 2017, www.vice.com/en/article/7xweag/exclusive-jane-doe-talks-about-her-abortion-battle-with-trumps-doj.

120 **Noel Francisco filed an appeal:** Petition for a Writ of Certiorari, *Garza v. Hargan*, 183 S.Ct. 1790 (2018).

122 **Internal ORR documents:** E. Scott Lloyd, "Letter from E. Scott Lloyd to Jonathan White re: Use of Federal Funds to Terminate a Pregnancy for [redacted]—DECISION," Dec. 6, 2017, www.acludc.org/sites/default/files/field_documents/garza_v_hargan_orr_letter_12-22-2017.pdf.

122 **On June 4, 2018, the justices did grant:** *Azar v. Garza*, 138 S.Ct. 1790 (2018).

122 **filed a separate class action:** Plaintiff's Renewed Motion for Class Certification and a Preliminary Injunction Based on New Facts Demonstrating Continued Need for Urgent Relief, *Garza v. Hargan*, March 2, 2018 (on file with author).

123 **barred DHS from denying:** Memorandum and Order, *Garza v. Hargan*, March 30, 2018, www.acludc.org/sites/default/files/field_documents/garza_v_hargan_memo_opinion_and_order_3-30-2018.pdf.

123 **certified the ACLU's class-action:** Order Granting Class Certification, *Garza v. Hargan*, March 20, 2018, www.acludc.org/sites/default/files/field_documents/garza_v_hargan_order_granting_class_cert_3-30-2018.pdf.

123 **issued a new policy:** Joint Stipulation of Dismissal Without Prejudice (Ex-hibit A), *Garza v. Hargan*, Sept. 29, 2020, www.acludc.org/sites/default /files/field_documents/garza.168.stipulation_of_dismissal_without _prejudice.pdf.

123 **drop their class action:** Joint Stipulation of Dismissal Without Prejudice, *Garza v. Hargan*, Sept. 29, 2020.

123 **"There is some book by John Irving":** John Irving, *A Prayer for Owen Meany* (New York: HarperCollins, 1989).

124 **Lloyd admitted under oath:** Christina Cauterucci, "Trump Official Con-sidered Forcing Undocumented Minor into Untested 'Abortion Rever-sal' Procedure," *Slate*, Jan. 31, 2018, slate.com/news-and-politics/2018/01 /trump-official-considered-forcing-undocumented-minor-into-untested -abortion-reversal-procedure.html.

124 **In another deposition, taken in February:** Mark Joseph Stern, "Scott Lloyd Tells All," *Slate*, Aug. 5, 2018, slate.com/news-and-politics/2018/04/aclu -deposition-shows-scott-lloyd-abused-power-to-prevent-undocumented -minors-from-getting-abortions.html.

124 **further said under oath:** Stern, "Scott Lloyd Tells All."

125 **calling, visiting, and otherwise micromanaging:** Renuka Rayasam, "Trump Official Halts Abortions Among Undocumented, Pregnant Teens," *Polit-ico*, Oct. 16, 2017, www.politico.com/story/2017/10/16/undocumented-preg nant-girl-trump-abortion-texas-243844.

125 **meticulous track of the menstrual cycles:** Rachel Maddow, "Trump Admin Tracked Individual Migrant Girls' Pregnancies," MSNBC, March 15, 2019, www.msnbc.com/rachel-maddow/watch/trump-admin-tracked-individual -migrant-girls-pregnancies-1459294787849?cid=sm_tw_maddow.

125 *The Handmaid's Tale* **designation:** Wright, "U.S. Is Tracking Migrant Girls' Periods to Stop Them from Getting Abortions."

125 **at least partly responsible:** Dan Diamond, "Trump Appointee Under Scrutiny for Handling of Child Separations," *Politico*, Feb. 26, 2019, www .politico.com/story/2019/02/26/trump-refugee-director-family -separations-1211032.

125 **he had failed to alert HHS officials:** Dan Diamond, "Former Trump Refu-gee Director Says He Never Warned Higher-Ups About Family Separa-tions," *Politico*, Feb. 26, 2019, www.politico.com/story/2019/02/26/scott -lloyd-migrant-family-separations-1216323.

125 **mental health catastrophe:** Dan Diamond, "Federal Health Official Warned of Risk of Separating Migrant Children," *Politico*, Feb. 7, 2019, www.politico.com/story/2019/02/07/democrats-migrant-family -separations-1155524.

125 **stop keeping spreadsheets:** Dan Diamond, "HHS Reviews Refugee Opera-tions as Trump Calls for Border Crackdown," *Politico*, Oct. 23, 2018, www .politico.com/story/2018/10/23/trump-caravan-border-hhs-873152.

125 **eventual review of the case files:** Diamond, "HHS Reviews Refugee Operations as Trump Calls for Border Crackdown."

125 **In lawsuits, federal judges ordered:** Lance Williams and Matt Smith, "Judge Orders Government to Release Immigrant Kids from Troubled Texas Shelter," *Texas Tribune*, July 31, 2018, www.texastribune.org/2018/07/31/judge -orders-government-release-immigrant-kids-texas-shelter.

126 **allegations surfaced that staff:** Associated Press, "Teens Kept at Virginia Center Say They Were Cuffed, Beaten," ABC8 News, June 21, 2018, www .wric.com/news/virginia-news/teens-kept-at-virginia-center-say-they-were -cuffed-beaten.

126 **Amy Hagstrom Miller said:** Hagstrom Miller, interview by author, Aug. 2019.

126 **"Three federal courts have rebuked":** Hannah Levintova, "The Trump Official Who Failed to Reunify Dozens of Separated Children Is Getting a New Role," *Mother Jones*, Jan./Feb. 2019, www.motherjones.com/politics /2018/11/scott-lloyd-abortion-child-migrants-office-of-refugee-resettle ment.

126 **One month later he published a novel:** E. Scott Lloyd, *The Undergraduate* (n.p.: Liberty Island, 2018).

127 **Lloyd quietly left:** Diamond, "Former Trump Refugee Director to Depart HHS."

127 **imperative work of rolling back:** Maggie Astor, "What Is the Hyde Amendment? A Look at Its Impact as Biden Reverses His Stance," *New York Times*, June 7, 2019, www.nytimes.com/2019/06/07/us/politics/what-is-the-hyde -amendment.html.

128 **attack moved rapidly from banning abortion:** Wynne Davis, "As the Supreme Court Weighs the Future of 'Roe v. Wade,' Experts Look Beyond Abortion," NPR, Dec. 10, 2021, www.npr.org/2021/12/10/1062702221 /supreme-court-weighs-mississippi-abortion-law-experts-look-further; David H. Gans, "The Mississippi Abortion Case Threatens the Right to Use Birth Control, Marry, and Even Make Choices About Sex," *Slate*, Oct. 12, 2021, slate.com/news-and-politics/2021/10/mississippi-abortion-birth -control-lgbtq-scotus.html; Marisa Endicott, "A New Federal Judge Appointed by Trump Has Fought Against Abortion, Fertility Treatments, and Surrogacy," *Mother Jones*, Dec. 4, 2019, www.motherjones.com/politics/2019 /12/a-new-federal-judge-appointed-by-trump-has-fought-against-abortion -fertility-treatments-and-surrogacy.

128 **second most populous state:** Adam Liptak, "Supreme Court Allows Challenge to Texas Abortion Law but Leaves It in Effect," *New York Times*, Dec. 10, 2021, www.nytimes.com/2021/12/10/us/politics/texas-abortion -supreme-court.html.

128 **that sign that became familiar:** Joseph Hurley, "I Can't Believe I'm Still Protesting This Shit Sign, Women's March on Washington, 2017-01-21,"

Jan. 21, 2017, Georgia State University Library Exhibits, exhibits.library
.gsu.edu/current/items/show/3221.

128 **listeners tuned in en masse:** "Huge Numbers Tune In to Listen to Court
on Trump Travel Ban," Associated Press, Feb. 7, 2017, apnews.com/article
/6dc42276c3044cb8a9d891466eb95f08.

128 **Institute for Policy Integrity:** Bethany A. Davis Noll, "'Tired of Winning':
Judicial Review of Regulatory Policy in the Trump Administration," *Administrative Law Review* 73, no. 2 (2021), www.law.nyu.edu/sites/default
/files/DavisNoll-TiredofWinning_0.pdf.

CHAPTER 6: THE CIVIL RIGHTS LAWYER

133 **And nobody was more surprised by:** Vanita Gupta, interview by author,
Aug. 2019.

134 **"There was a series of incidents":** Zoe Carpenter, "The Woman Leading a
'Strategic Hub of the Resistance' in the Age of Trump," *Rolling Stone*,
March 8, 2019, www.rollingstone.com/politics/politics-features/vanita-gupta
-leadership-council-civil-rights-802158.

134 **"I became an activist in high school":** Mattie Kahn, "'Despair Is the Enemy
of Justice': Vanita Gupta on Voting, Marching, and Staying in the Fight,"
Glamour, Aug. 26, 2020, www.glamour.com/story/vanita-gupta-on-voting
-marching-and-staying-in-the-fight.

135 **The *Tulia Herald* feted Tulia's law enforcement:** Vanita Gupta, "Critical
Race Lawyering in Tulia, Texas," *Fordham Law Review* 73, no. 5 (2005),
ir.lawnet.fordham.edu/cgi/viewcontent.cgi?article=4071&context=flr.

136 **Bob Herbert, helped publicize:** Bob Herbert, "Kafka in Tulia," *New York
Times*, July 29, 2002, www.nytimes.com/2002/07/29/opinion/kafka-in-tu
lia.html; Bob Herbert, "'Lawman of the Year,'" *New York Times*, Aug. 1,
2002, www.nytimes.com/2002/08/01/opinion/lawman-of-the-year.html;
Bob Herbert, "Tulia's Shattered Lives," *New York Times*, Aug. 5, 2002,
www.nytimes.com/2002/08/05/opinion/tulia-s-shattered-lives.html; Bob
Herbert, "Railroaded in Texas," *New York Times*, Aug. 8, 2002, www.ny
times.com/2002/08/08/opinion/railroaded-in-texas.html; Bob Herbert,
"Justice Goes into Hiding," *New York Times*, Aug. 12, 2002, www.nytimes
.com/2002/08/12/opinion/justice-goes-into-hiding.html; Bob Herbert, "A
Confused Inquiry," *New York Times*, Aug. 22, 2002, www.nytimes.com
/2002/08/22/opinion/a-confused-inquiry.html; Bob Herbert, "The Latest
from Tulia," *New York Times*, Dec. 26, 2002, www.nytimes.com/2002/08
/22/opinion/a-confused-inquiry.html; Bob Herbert, "Mugging the Needy,"
New York Times, April 2, 2003, www.nytimes.com/2003/04/03/opinion
/mugging-the-needy.html; Bob Herbert, "The Tulia Story Isn't Over," *New
York Times*, April 28, 2003, www.nytimes.com/2003/04/28/opinion/the
-tulia-story-isn-t-over.html; Bob Herbert, "Partway to Freedom," *New York*

Times, June 16, 2003, www.nytimes.com/2003/06/16/opinion/partway-to
-freedom.html; Bob Herbert, "A Good Day," *New York Times*, June 19,
2003, www.nytimes.com/by/bob-herbert.

136 **To those who hold the Tulia victory:** Gupta, "Critical Race Lawyering in
Tulia, Texas."

138 **winning a landmark settlement:** "Landmark Settlement Announced in Federal Lawsuit Challenging Conditions at Immigrant Detention Center in
Texas," ACLU, Aug. 27, 2007, www.aclu.org/press-releases/landmark-settle
ment-announced-federal-lawsuit-challenging-conditions-immigrant.

138 **"I am not naïve":** Vanita Gupta, "How to Really End Mass Incarceration,"
New York Times, Aug. 14, 2013, www.nytimes.com/2013/08/15/opinion
/how-to-really-end-mass-incarceration.html.

139 **massive report on the Ferguson Police:** "Investigation of the Ferguson
Police Department," U.S. Department of Justice Civil Rights Division,
March 4, 2015, www.justice.gov/sites/default/files/opa/press-releases/attach
ments/2015/03/04/ferguson_police_department_report.pdf.

140 **Gupta told me on my podcast:** "Race, Police, and the Law," *Amicus
with Dahlia Lithwick*, June 6, 2020, slate.com/podcasts/amicus/2020/06
/americas-overpolicing-problem.

141 **"I served a president":** Kahn, "'Despair Is the Enemy of Justice'."

141 **In a *New Yorker* profile:** Jennifer Gonnerman, "Last Day at the Civil
Rights Division," *New Yorker*, Jan. 21, 2017, www.newyorker.com/news
/news-desk/last-day-at-the-civil-rights-division.

142 **In 2019, a *Vice* investigation:** Rob Arthur, "EXCLUSIVE: Trump's Justice
Department Is Investigating 60% Fewer Civil Rights Cases Than Obama's,"
Vice News, March 6, 2019, www.vice.com/en/article/bjq37m/exclusive
-trumps-justice-department-is-investigating-60-fewer-civil-rights-cases
-than-obamas.

142 **what she characterized as:** Vanita Gupta, interview by author, Aug. 2019.

145 **"In just the last few years":** Kahn, "'Despair Is the Enemy of Justice'."

145 **into a strategic hub of the resistance:** Vanita Gupta, interview by author,
Aug. 2019.

146 **to support a platform:** "Civil Rights Coalition Letter on Federal Police Priorities," Leadership Conference on Civil and Human Rights, June 1, 2020,
civilrights.org/resource/civil-rights-coalition-letter-on-federal
-policing-priorities/#; "How We're Fighting for Police Reform and Systemic
Change in America," Leadership Conference on Civil and Human Rights,
June 12, 2020, civilrights.org/blog/how-were-fighting-for-police-reform
-and-systemic-change-in-america/#.

147 **in seven hundred cities across the country:** Jen Kirby and Emily Stewart,
"Families Belong Together Protest Underway in More Than 700 Cities,"
Vox, June 30, 2018, www.vox.com/2018/6/18/17477376/families-belong
-together-march-june-30; Phil McCausland, Patricia Guadalupe, and Kalhan

Rosenblatt, "Thousands Across U.S. Join 'Keep Families Together' March to Protest Family Separation," NBC News, June 30, 2018, www .nbcnews.com/news/us-news/thousands-across-u-s-join-keep-families -together-march-protest-n888006; Joe Mahr, Tony Briscoe, and Ese Olumhense, "Demonstrators Rally in the Loop Against Separation of Immigrant Families," *Chicago Tribune*, June 30, 2018, www.chicagotribune.com/news /breaking/ct-met-loop-immigration-family-separation-rally-20180630 -story.html; Dino-Rey Ramos, "Hollywood Shows Up in Full Force to Support 'Families Belong Together' Immigration Rallies Across the Nation," *Deadline*, June 30, 2018, deadline.com/2018/06/families-belong-together -immigration-protest-rally-john-legend-chrissy-teigen-laura-dern-lin -manuel-miranda-kerry-washington-america-ferrera-donald-trump -1202420138/; Alexandra Yoon-Hendricks and Zoe Greenberg, "Protests Across U.S. Call for an End to Migrant Family Separation," *New York Times*, June 30, 2018, www.nytimes.com/2018/06/30/us/politics/trump-protests -family-separation.html; Alan Taylor, "Photos from the Nationwide 'Families Belong Together' Marches," *Atlantic*, July 1, 2018, www.theatlantic .com/photo/2018/07/photos-from-the-nationwide-families-belong -together-marches/564251.

148   **Sarah Palin got a big laugh:** Linton Weeks, "A Small-Town Mayor vs. a Community Organizer," NPR, Sept. 12, 2008, www.npr.org/templates/story /story.php?storyId=94526145.

148   **question could not be added:** *Department of Commerce v. New York*, 18-966, 588 U.S. __ (2019).

150   **Gupta co-wrote an op-ed:** Vanita Gupta and Fatima Goss Graves, "We Mobilized to Oppose Kavanaugh. Let's Corral That Same Energy to Protect Our Democracy Now," Morning Consult, Oct. 23, 2019, morningconsult .com/opinions/we-mobilized-to-oppose-kavanaugh-lets-corral-that-same -energy-to-protect-our-democracy-now.

151   **The Kavanaugh nomination was a watershed moment:** Jennifer Rubin, *Resistance: How Women Saved Democracy from Donald Trump* (New York: HarperCollins, 2021); Opheli Garcia Lawler, "The Collective Wail of Women," *New York*, Oct. 6, 2018, www.thecut.com/2018/10/women-react-to-brett-kavana ughs-supreme-court-confirmation.html; David Bauder, "More Than 20 Million People Watched the Kavanaugh Hearing," Associated Press, Sept. 28, 2018, apnews.com/article/ap-top-news-jeff-flake-judiciary-sexual-assault -supreme-courts-caa510f21dcd4c569a4c8ea91f587a44; Jennifer Wright, "With Kavanaugh Confirmed, It's Time to Burn It Down," *Harper's Bazaar*, Oct. 6, 2018, www.harpersbazaar.com/culture/politics/a23509937/brett-ka vanaugh-confirmation-rebellion; Editorial Board, "Women on Watching," *New York Times*, Sept. 28, 2018, www.nytimes.com/2018/09/28/opinion /brett-kavanaugh-jeff-flake-gop-women.html; Kelly Virella, "We Asked Women What the Kavanaugh Vote Means for the Next Generation. 40,000

Responded," *New York Times*, Oct. 9, 2018, www.nytimes.com/2018/10/09 /reader-center/women-kavanaugh-confirmation.html.

152   **testified in support of H.R. 1:** Peter Overby, "House Democrats Introduce Anti-corruption Bill as Symbolic 1st Act," NPR, Jan. 5, 2019, www.npr .org/2019/01/05/682286587/house-democrats-introduce-anti-corruption -bill-as-symbolic-first-act; Ella Nilsen, "House Democrats Just Passed a Slate of Significant Reforms to Get Money Out of Politics," *Vox*, March 8, 2019, www.vox.com/2019/3/8/18253609/hr-1-pelosi-house-democrats -anti-corruption-mcconnell.

152   **In congressional testimony before the Judiciary Committee:** Vanita Gupta, "Statement of Vanita Gupta, President and CEO, the Leadership Confer- ence on Civil and Human Rights," U.S. House Committee on the Judiciary, Jan. 29, 2019, civilrightsdocs.info/pdf/testimony/HJC-hearing-on-HR1-VG -written-testimony-1.29.19-FINAL.pdf.

153   **testifying in both the House of Representatives:** Vanita Gupta, "Statement of Vanita Gupta, President and CEO, the Leadership Conference on Civil and Human Rights," U.S. Senate Committee on the Judiciary, June 16, 2020, www.judiciary.senate.gov/imo/media/doc/Gupta%20Testmony1.pdf; Vanita Gupta, "Statement of Vanita Gupta, President and CEO, the Lead- ership Conference on Civil and Human Rights," U.S. House Committee on the Judiciary, June 10, 2016, docs.house.gov/meetings/JU/JU00/20200610 /110775/HHRG-116-JU00-Wstate-GuptaV-20200610.pdf.

153   **a claim that has been debunked:** Robert Farley, "Cruz Distorts Nominees' Defund Police Positions," FactCheck.org, May 18, 2021, www.factcheck .org/2021/05/cruz-distorts-nominees-defund-police-positions.

153   **voted against certifying:** Jenny Gross and Luke Broadwater, "Here Are the Republicans Who Objected to Certifying the Election Results," *New York Times*, Jan. 8, 2021, www.nytimes.com/2021/01/07/us/politics/republicans -against-certification.html.

153   **every major national law enforcement:** Matt Zapotosky, "Law Enforce- ment Groups Dispute GOP Senator's Insinuation They Were Coerced to Support Biden Justice Dept. Nominee," *Washington Post*, March 12, 2021, www.washingtonpost.com/national-security/vanita-gupta-tom-cotton /2021/03/12/8999eae2-8344-11eb-9ca6-54e187ee4939_story.html.

157   **Toni Morrison argues that the critical function:** Toni Morrison, "A Human- ist View" (speech delivered at Portland State University, May 30, 1975), www.mackenzian.com/wp-content/uploads/2014/07/Transcript_Portland State_TMorrison.pdf.

CHAPTER 7: #METOO

159   **"You testified this morning":** Michael S. Rosenwald, "No Women Served on the Senate Judiciary Committee in 1991. The Ugly Anita Hill Hearings

Changed That," *Washington Post*, Sept. 18, 2018, www.washingtonpost
.com/history/2018/09/18/no-women-served-senate-judiciary-committee
-ugly-anita-hill-hearings-changed-that.

159 **"Now, in trying to determine":** Grace Segers, "Here Are Some of the Questions Anita Hill Answered in 1991," CBS News, Sept. 19, 2018, www.cbs
news.com/news/here-are-some-of-the-questions-anita-hill-fielded-in-1991.

160 **one empirical study after another:** See, for example, Anne E. Martin and
Teresa R. Fisher-Ari, "'If We Don't Have Diversity, There's No Future to
See': High-School Students' Perceptions of Race and Gender Representation in STEM," *Science Education*, Aug. 13, 2021, doi-org.ezp-prod1.hul
.harvard.edu/10.1002/sce.21677; Dasia Simpson, Abby Beatty, and Cissy
Ballen, "Teaching Between the Lines: Representation in Science Textbooks," *Trends in Ecology and Evolution*, Jan. 2021, doi.org/10.1016/j.tree
.2020.10.010; Morgan E. Ellithrope and Amy Bleakley, "Wanting to See
People Like Me? Racial and Gender Diversity in Popular Adolescent Television," *Journal of Youth and Adolescence* 45 (2016), doi.org/10.1007/s109
64-016-0415-4; Fabrizio Gilardi, "The Temporary Importance of Role
Models for Women's Political Representation," *American Journal of Political Science* 59, no. 4 (Oct. 2015), www.jstor.org/stable/24582959; Toni
Schmader, Katharia Block, and Brian Lickel, "Social Identity Threat in
Response to Stereotypic Film Portrayals: Effects on Self-Conscious Emotion and Implicit Ingroup Attitudes," *Journal of Social Issues* 71, no. 1 (2015),
doi.org/10.1111/josi.12096; Tyler Johnson, "Equality, Morality, and the Impact of Media Framing: Explaining Opposition to Same-Sex Marriage and
Civil Unions," *Politics and Policy* 40, no. 6 (Dec. 2012), doi.org/10.1111/j.1747
-1346.2012.00398.x; Marc Bühlmann and Lisa Schädel, "Representation
Matters: The Impact of Descriptive Women's Representation on the Political
Involvement of Women," *Representation* 48, no. 1 (2012), doi.org/10.1080
/00344893.2012.653246; Monique L. Ward, "Wading Through the Stereotypes: Positive and Negative Associations Between Media Use and Black Adolescents' Conceptions of Self," *Developmental Psychology* 40, no. 2 (2004), doi
.org/10.1037/0012-1649.40.2.284.

161 **$400,000 signing bonus:** Adam Liptak, "Law Firms Pay Supreme Court
Clerks $400,000 Bonuses. What Are They Buying?," *New York Times*,
Sept. 21, 2020, www.nytimes.com/2020/09/21/us/politics/supreme-court
-clerk-bonuses.html.

161 **One legendary feeder judge:** Claire Madill, "Blind Justices," *Slate*, Dec. 15,
2017, slate.com/news-and-politics/2017/12/how-the-supreme-court-justices
-abetted-judge-alex-kozinskis-inappropriate-behavior.html; Ryan J. Foley and
Curt Anderson, "Kavanaugh's Ties to Disgraced Mentor Loom over Confirmation," Associated Press, Aug. 29, 2018, apnews.com/article/donald-trump
-confirmation-hearings-us-supreme-court-judiciary-courts-e37ba9bc11014
b72a5db6f926f80eb42.

161   **when Kennedy gave up his seat:** Ruth Marcus, *Supreme Ambition: Brett Kavanaugh and the Conservative Takeover* (New York: Simon & Schuster, 2019).

162   **Supreme Court reporter Tony Mauro:** Tony Mauro, "Supreme Court Clerks Are Overwhelmingly White and Male. Just Like 20 Years Ago," *USA Today*, Jan. 8, 2018, www.usatoday.com/story/opinion/2018/01/08 /supreme-court-clerks-overwhelmingly-white-male-just-like-20-years -ago-tony-mauro-column/965945001.

162   **As of August 2019, 73 percent:** Danielle Root, Jake Faleschini, and Grace Oyenubi, "Building a More Inclusive Federal Judiciary," Center for American Progress, Oct. 2019, www.americanprogress.org/article/building-inclu sive-federal-judiciary.

162   **Alex Kozinski was universally acknowledged:** Matt Zapotosky, "Prominent Appeals Court Judge Alex Kozinski Accused of Sexual Misconduct," *Washington Post*, Dec. 8, 2017, www.washingtonpost.com/world/national -security/prominent-appeals-court-judge-alex-kozinski-accused-of-sexual -misconduct/2017/12/08/1763e2b8-d913-11e7-a841-2066faf731ef_story .html; John R. Vile, "Alex Kozinski," in *The First Amendment Encyclopedia*, Nov. 2018, www.mtsu.edu/first-amendment/article/1342/alex-kozinski.

162   **the Senate confirmed a thirty-three-year-old woman:** Jamal Thalji, "Senate Confirms Trump's Youngest Federal Judge to Serve in Tampa," *Tampa Bay Times*, Nov. 18, 2020, www.tampabay.com/news/breaking-news/2020/11 /18/senate-confirms-trumps-youngest-federal-judge-to-serve-in-tampa.

162   **Kavanaugh, back in 1985:** Howard Kurtz, "Senate Committee to Reconsider Judicial Nominee," *Washington Post*, Nov. 1, 1985, www.washington post.com/archive/politics/1985/11/01/senate-committee-to-reconsider-judi cial-nominee/da4e4e3a-2a50-41b4-975f-445ba4301737/; Ben A. Franklin, "Senate Confirms Appellate Judge," *New York Times*, Nov. 8, 1985, www.nytimes.com/1985/11/08/us/senate-confirms-appellate-judge.html.

162   **Kozinski famously shared:** Alex Kozinski, "Diary: Day Two," *Slate*, July 22, 1996, slate.com/human-interest/1996/07/alex-kozinski-10.html.

162   **link to a video of himself:** "9th Circuit's Kozinski Admonished but Not Disciplined for Online Pornography," Law.com, July 6, 2009, www.law .com/almID/1202431991121.

163   ***The Dating Game,* where he planted:** Zapotosky, "Prominent Appeals Court Judge Alex Kozinski Accused of Sexual Misconduct."

163   **In a Second Amendment opinion:** *Silveira v. Lockyer,* 328 F.3d 567 (9th Cir. 2003) (Kozinski, J., dissenting).

163   **over a trademark dispute:** *Mattel Inc. v. MCA Records Inc.,* 296 F.3d 894 (9th Cir. 2002).

163   **a return to the firing squad:** *Wood v. Ryan,* 759 F.3d 1076 (9th Cir. 2014) (Kozinski, J., dissenting).

163	**2004 profile of the judge:** Emily Bazelon, "The Big Kozinski," *Legal Affairs*, Jan. 2004, www.legalaffairs.org/issues/January-February-2004/feature_baz elon_janfeb04.msp.

164	**jerry-rigged an internet security system:** Stephanie Kirschgaessner, "Kavanaugh Clerk Hire Casts Light on Link to Judge Forced to Quit in #MeToo Era," *Guardian*, Oct. 1, 2018, www.theguardian.com/us-news/2018/oct /01/kavanaugh-clerk-hire-casts-light-on-link-to-judge-forced-to-resign -in-metoo-era.

164	**"naked women on all fours":** Scott Glover, "9th Circuit's Chief Judge Posted Sexually Explicit Matter on His Website," *Los Angeles Times*, June 11, 2008, www.latimes.com/local/la-me-kozinski12-2008jun12-story .html.

164	**maintained an email list:** Scott Glover, "Judge Alex Kozinski Apologizes for Distributing Crude Jokes," *Los Angeles Times*, Oct. 28, 2009, www .latimes.com/archives/la-xpm-2009-oct-28-me-kozinksi28-story.html.

164	**handed down its findings:** "Memorandum Opinion In re: Complaint of Judicial Misconduct," Judicial Council of the Third Circuit, June 5, 2009, www2.ca3.uscourts.gov/opinarch/089050p.pdf.

165	**reporter Lise Olsen pointed out:** Lise Olsen, *Code of Silence: Sexual Misconduct by Federal Judges, the Secret System That Protects Them, and the Women Who Blew the Whistle* (Boston: Beacon Press, 2021).

165	**two women, Heidi Bond and Emily Murphy:** Zapotosky, "Prominent Appeals Court Judge Alex Kozinski Accused of Sexual Misconduct."

165	**posted her firsthand account:** Courtney Milan, "Judge Kozinski," CourtneyMilan.com, Dec. 8, 2017, www.courtneymilan.com/metoo/kozinski.html.

167	**"I have been a judge for 35 years":** Zapotosky, "Prominent Appeals Court Judge Alex Kozinski Accused of Sexual Misconduct."

168	**Kozinski went on the offense:** Maura Dolan, "9th Circuit Judge Alex Kozinski Is Accused by Former Clerks of Making Sexual Comments," *Los Angeles Times*, Dec. 8, 2017, www.latimes.com/local/lanow/la-me-ln-kozinski -sexual-misconduct-20171208-story.html.

168	**in 2018 by CNN's Joan Biskupic:** Joan Biskupic, "CNN Investigation: Sexual Misconduct by Judges Kept Under Wraps," CNN, Jan. 26, 2018, www.cnn .com/2018/01/25/politics/courts-judges-sexual-harassment/index.html.

169	**her contracts class at UC Hastings:** Olsen, *Code of Silence*.

169	**Joanna Grossman, now a law professor:** Joanna Grossman (@JoannaGrossman), "When I clerked on the Ninth Circuit, Kozinski sent a memo to all the judges suggesting that a rule prohibiting female attorneys from wearing push-up bras would be more effective than the newly convened Gender Bias Task Force. His disrespect for women is legendary." Twitter, Dec. 9, 2017, 12:09 p.m., twitter.com/joannagrossman/status/939542418 638147584.

170 **Alexandra Brodsky, a civil rights attorney:** Kathryn Rubino, "More Women
     Speak Out About Judge Kozinski's Behavior; Say It Was an 'Open Secret,'"
     Above the Law, Dec. 11, 2017, abovethelaw.com/2017/12/more-women
     -acknowledge-judge-kozinskis-behavior-was-an-open-secret.

170 **Nancy Rapoport, special counsel:** Rubino, "More Women Speak Out
     About Judge Kozinski's Behavior."

170 **The piece I wrote about the judge:** Dahlia Lithwick, "He Made Us All
     Victims and Accomplices," *Slate*, Dec. 13, 2017, slate.com/news-and
     -politics/2017/12/judge-alex-kozinski-made-us-all-victims-and
     -accomplices.html.

174 **nine *more* women came forward:** Matt Zapotosky, "Nine More Women
     Say Judge Subjected Them to Inappropriate Behavior, Including Four
     Who Say He Touched or Kissed Them," *Washington Post*, Dec. 15, 2017,
     www.washingtonpost.com/world/national-security/nine-more-women
     -say-judge-subjected-them-to-inappropriate-behavior-including-four-who
     -say-he-touched-or-kissed-them/2017/12/15/8729b736-e105-11e7-8679-a97
     28984779c_story.html.

175 **all three of his clerks:** Kathryn Rubino and Elie Mystal, "Sources Report 3
     Kozinski Clerks Are Out," *Above the Law*, Dec. 14, 2017, abovethelaw.com
     /2017/12/sources-report-3-kozinski-clerks-are-out.

175 **Judge Kozinski stepped down on:** Cristiano Lima, "Federal Appeals Court
     Judge Steps Down amid Sexual Misconduct Probe," *Politico*, Dec. 18, 2017,
     www.politico.com/story/2017/12/18/alex-kozinski-retire-sexual
     -misconduct-allegations-302251.

175 **The Second Circuit Judicial Council announced:** "In re Complaint of Ju-
     dicial Misconduct," Judicial Council of the Second Circuit, Feb. 5, 2018,
     cdn.cnn.com/cnn/2018/images/02/05/doc020218.pdf.

176 **Lise Olsen later reported:** Olsen, *Code of Silence*.

176 **"With his immediate retirement":** Katherine Ku, "Pressuring Harassers to
     Quit Can End Up Protecting Them," *Washington Post*, Jan. 5, 2018, www
     .washingtonpost.com/outlook/pressuring-harassers-to-quit-can-end
     -up-protecting-them/2018/01/05/0d44aeba-ea5d-11e7-8a6a-80acf
     0774e64_story.html.

176 **Within six months, Kozinski was writing:** Matt Zapotosky, "Judge Who
     Quit over Harassment Allegations Reemerges, Dismaying Those Who Ac-
     cused Him," *Washington Post*, July 24, 2018, https://www.washingtonpost
     .com/world/national-security/judge-who-quit-over-harassment-allegations
     -reemerges-dismaying-those-who-accused-him/2018/07/23/750a02f2-89
     db-11e8-a345-a1bf7847b375_story.html.

177 **write an op-ed in *The New York Times:*** Leah Litman, Emily Murphy,
     and Katherine H. Ku, "A Comeback but No Reckoning," *New York Times*,
     Aug. 2, 2018, www.nytimes.com/2018/08/02/opinion/sunday/alex-kozin
     ski-harassment-allegations-comeback.html.

178 **would come to publicly corroborate:** Zapotosky, "Nine More Women Say
     Judge Subjected Them to Inappropriate Behavior."

178 **his 2017 year-end report:** Chief Justice John Roberts, "2017 Year-End Re-
     port on the Federal Judiciary," U.S. Supreme Court, Dec. 31, 2017, www
     .supremecourt.gov/publicinfo/year-end/2017year-endreport.pdf.

178 **amended its Code of Conduct:** Renee Knake Jefferson, "Judicial Ethics
     in the #MeToo World," *Fordham Law Review* 89, no. 4 (2020), ir.lawnet
     .fordham.edu/cgi/viewcontent.cgi?article=5800&context=flr.

179 **"kicking the can down the road":** Olsen, *Code of Silence*, 224.

179 **The legal journalist Irin Carmon:** Irin Carmon, "What Did Brett Kavanaugh
     Know About His Former Boss's Sexual Misconduct?," *New York*, Sept. 4,
     2018, www.thecut.com/2018/09/kavanaugh-confirmation-kozinski-sexual
     -assault.html.

179 **Kavanaugh had phoned Kozinski:** Sophie Tatum, "Kavanaugh Contacted
     Kozinski After Resignation Because He Was 'Concerned About His Men-
     tal Health,'" CNN, Sept. 13, 2018, www.cnn.com/2018/09/13/politics/ka
     vanaugh-kozinski/index.html; Susan Matthews, "Brett Kavanaugh Failed
     the Alex Kozinski Test," *Slate*, Sept. 6, 2018, slate.com/news-and-politics
     /2018/09/kavanaugh-confirmation-hearing-alex-kozinski-sexual-harass
     ment.html.

179 **Senator Mazie Hirono of Hawaii:** "Sen. Hirono & Judge Kavanaugh Have
     Heated Exchange on Sexual Harassment in Judicial Branch," C-SPAN,
     Sept. 5, 2018, www.c-span.org/video/?c4747547/sen-hirono-judge-kavana
     ugh-heated-exchange-sexual-harassment-judicial-branch.

180 **Olivia Warren, who had clerked:** Olivia Warren, "Protecting Federal Judi-
     ciary Employees from Sexual Harassment, Discrimination, and Other Work-
     place Misconduct," U.S. House Committee on the Judiciary, Subcommittee
     on Courts, Intellectual Property, and the Internet, Feb. 13, 2020, www.cong
     ress.gov/116/meeting/house/110505/witnesses/HHRG-116-JU03-Wstate
     -WarrenO-20200213-U2.pdf.

181 **corroborated one part:** Mark Sherman, "Former Law Clerk Alleges Harass-
     ment by Late Prominent Judge," ABC News/Associated Press, Feb. 13, 2020,
     abcnews.go.com/Politics/wireStory/law-clerk-alleges-harassment-late
     -prominent-judge-68962969.

181 **confirmed on Twitter:** Catie Edmondson, "Former Clerk Alleges Sexual
     Harassment by Appellate Judge," *New York Times*, Feb. 13, 2020, www
     .nytimes.com/2020/02/13/us/politics/judge-reinhardt-sexual
     -harassment.html.

181 **A letter signed by more than seventy:** Debra Cassens Weiss, "Over 70
     Former Reinhardt Clerks Urge Judiciary to Change Reporting Procedures
     and Training," *ABA Journal*, Feb. 21, 2020, www.abajournal.com/news
     /article/former-reinhardt-clerks-urge-judiciary-to-change-reporting
     -procedures-and-training.

181 **in a 2021 podcast with Anita Hill:** "The Conversation: Prof. Anita Hill and Dr. Christine Blasey Ford," *Because of Anita*, Oct. 11, 2021, pineapple.fm /because-of-anita-ep-3.

181 **Leah Litman tweeted:** Edmondson, "Former Clerk Alleges Sexual Harassment by Appellate Judge."

182 **I testified alongside Warren:** Dahlia Lithwick, "Written Statement of Dahlia Lithwick: Protecting Federal Judiciary Employees from Sexual Harassment, Discrimination, and Other Workplace Misconduct," U.S. House Committee on the Judiciary, Subcommittee on Courts, Intellectual Property, and the Internet, Feb. 13, 2020, docs.house.gov/meetings/JU/JU03 /20200213/110505/HHRG-116-JU03-Wstate-LithwickD-20200213.pdf.

183 **"there is virtue in screaming":** Olivia Warren, "Enough Is Not Enough: Reflections on Sexual Harassment in the Federal Judiciary," *Harvard Law Review* 134 (2021), harvardlawreview.org/wp-content/uploads/2021/06 /134-Harv.-L.-Rev.-F.-446.pdf.

183 **When we delegate the issue:** Leah M. Litman and Deeva Shah, "On Sexual Harassment in the Judiciary," *Northwestern University Law Review* 115, no. 2 (2020), scholarlycommons.law.northwestern.edu/nulr/vol115/iss2/5.

185 **she told NPR in September:** Mary Louise Kelly and Maureen Pao, "Anita Hill on Sexual Harassment in Hollywood and Beyond," NPR, Sept. 29, 2020, www.npr.org/2020/09/29/918262089/anita-hill-on-sexual-harassment -in-hollywood-and-beyond.

185 **accepting a Mirror Award:** Dade Hayes, "Mirror Awards Go to Probes of Charlie Rose, Harvey Weinstein; Honoree Confronts 'the System in This Room,'" *Yahoo News*, June 14, 2018, www.yahoo.com/news/mirror-awards -probes-charlie-rose-191908576.html.

CHAPTER 8: #HERTOO

189 **the transcript used "Question":** "U.S. Supreme Court Oral Argument Transcripts," Cornell University Law Library, updated July 28, 2021, guides.library.cornell.edu/SupCourtOralArguments.

190 **the press corps colluded a bit:** David Margolick, "Meet the Supremes," *New York Times*, Sept. 23, 2007, www.nytimes.com/2007/09/23/books /review/Margolick-t.html.

191 **oral arguments in *Bush v. Gore*:** Bush v. Gore, 531 U.S. 98 (2000).

191 **seminal cases like *Obergefell v. Hodges*:** Obergefell v. Hodges, 576 U.S. 644 (2015).

191 ***District of Columbia v. Heller,* finding a right:** District of Columbia v. Heller, 554 U.S. 570 (2008).

191 **like the 2016 abortion case:** Whole Woman's Health v. Hellerstedt, 579 U.S. 582 (2016).

191 **audience of more than twenty million:** Helen Coster, "Factbox: Trump
      Impeachment Hearings Likely to Draw High Ratings in New Era of Polit-
      ical TV," Reuters, Nov. 8, 2019, www.reuters.com/article/uk-usa-trump
      -impeachment-tv-factbox-idUKKBN1XI1AK.

191 **Thomas famously and furiously denied:** Michael S. Rosenwald, "'A High-
      Tech Lynching': How Brett Kavanaugh Took a Page from the Clarence
      Thomas Playbook," *Washington Post*, Sept. 27, 2018, www.washingtonpost
      .com/history/2018/09/25/high-tech-lynching-how-clarence-thomass
      -fury-saved-his-supreme-court-nomination.

192 **As Jill Abramson and Jane Mayer reported:** Jill Abramson and Jane Mayer,
      Strange Justice (Boston: Houghton Mifflin, 1994).

192 **Senator Alan Simpson, a Republican:** "Thomas Second Hearing Day 2,
      Part 3," C-SPAN, Oct. 12, 1991, www.c-span.org/video/?22218-1/thomas
      -hearing-day-2-part-3#!.

192 **Hatch also insisted:** "Thomas Second Hearing Day 2, Part 1," C-SPAN,
      Oct. 12, 1991, www.c-span.org/video/?c1043.

192 **only 29 percent of Americans:** Grace Sparks, "Anita Hill's Accusations
      Did Not Hurt Public Support for Clarence Thomas in '91," CNN, Sept. 17,
      2018, www.cnn.com/2018/09/17/politics/hill-thomas-kavanaugh-sexual
      -assault/index.html.

193 **Cynthia Hogan, one of the lawyers:** Elise Viebeck, "Joe Biden Was in
      Charge of the Anita Hill Hearing. Even He Says It Wasn't Fair," *Washing-
      ton Post*, April 26, 2019, www.washingtonpost.com/politics/joe-biden-was
      -in-charge-of-the-anita-hill-hearing-even-he-says-it-wasnt-fair/2019/04
      /26/a9a6f384-6500-11e9-82ba-fcfeff232e8f_story.html.

193 **Elise Viebeck concluded:** Viebeck, "Joe Biden Was in Charge of the Anita
      Hill Hearing."

194 **When I first interviewed her:** Dahlia Lithwick, "'All These Issues Are
      Still with Us,'" *Slate*, March 21, 2014, slate.com/human-interest/2014/03
      /talking-to-anita-hill-at-57-the-woman-who-stood-up-to-clarence
      -thomas-is-as-truthful-as-ever.html.

194 **As she noted at the time:** Annys Shin and Libby Casey, "Anita Hill and
      Her 1991 Congressional Defenders to Joe Biden: You Were Part of the
      Problem," *Washington Post*, Nov. 22, 2017, www.washingtonpost.com/life
      style/magazine/anita-hill-and-her-1991-congressional-defenders-to-joe
      -biden-you-were-part-of-the-problem/2017/11/21/2303ba8a-ce69-11e7
      -a1a3-0d1e45a6de3d_story.html.

195 **holding forth on how appalling:** Sen. Chuck Grassley, "Judicial Employ-
      ees Deserve Protection from Sexual Harassment, Misconduct," Prepared
      Statement, Senate Judiciary Committee, June 13, 2018, www.grassley
      .senate.gov/news/news-releases/grassley-judicial-employees-deserve
      -protection-sexual-harassment-misconduct.

195 **appeal of a pregnant migrant teen:** Robert Barnes and Ann E. Marimow, "In Major Abortion Ruling, Kavanaugh Offers Clues of How He Might Handle Divisive Issue on the Supreme Court," *Washington Post*, July 11, 2018, www.washingtonpost.com/politics/courts_law/in-major-abortion-ru ling-kavanaugh-offers-clues-of-how-he-might-handle-divisive-is sue-on-the-supreme-court/2018/07/11/1acd980a-8515-11e8-9e80-403 a221946a7_story.html.

195 **ultimately drafting a memo:** Brett M. Kavanaugh, "Memorandum to Judge Starr, All Attorneys re 'Slack for the President?,'" Office of the Independent Counsel, Aug. 15, 1998, www.archives.gov/files/research/kavanaugh /releases/kavanaugh8.15.98.pdf.

196 **reportedly been less than completely candid:** David A. Graham, "How Kavanaugh's Last Confirmation Hearing Could Haunt Him," *Atlantic*, July 17, 2018, www.theatlantic.com/politics/archive/2018/07/how-kavanaughs -last-confirmation-hearing-could-haunt-him/565304.

196 **Jane Mayer and Ronan Farrow reported:** Ronan Farrow and Jane Mayer, "A Sexual-Misconduct Allegation Against the Supreme Court Nominee Brett Kavanaugh Stirs Tension Among Democrats in Congress," *New Yorker*, Sept. 14, 2018, www.newyorker.com/news/news-desk/a-sexual-mis conduct-allegation-against-the-supreme-court-nominee-brett-kavanaugh -stirs-tension-among-democrats-in-congress.

196 **another accuser, Deborah Ramirez:** Ronan Farrow and Jane Mayer, "Senate Democrats Investigate a New Allegation of Sexual Misconduct, from Brett Kavanaugh's College Years," *New Yorker*, Sept. 23, 2018, www .newyorker.com/news/news-desk/senate-democrats-investigate-a-new -allegation-of-sexual-misconduct-from-the-supreme-court-nominee -brett-kavanaughs-college-years-deborah-ramirez.

196 **A third came forward:** Steve Eder, Jim Rutenberg, and Rebecca R. Ruiz, "Julie Swetnick Is Third Woman to Accuse Brett Kavanaugh of Sexual Misconduct," *New York Times*, Sept. 26, 2018, www.nytimes.com/2018 /09/26/us/politics/julie-swetnick-avenatti-kavenaugh.html.

196 **Heidi Bond would later write:** Heidi Bond, "I Received Some of Kozinski's Infamous Gag List Emails. I'm Baffled by Kavanaugh's Responses to Questions About Them," *Slate*, Sept. 14, 2018, slate.com/news-and-politics /2018/09/kavanaugh-kozinski-gag-list-emails-senate-hearings.html.

196 **Kavanaugh told a group of students:** Pema Levy, "Brett Kavanaugh Gave a Speech About Binge Drinking in Law School," *Mother Jones*, Sept. 17, 2018, www.motherjones.com/politics/2018/09/brett-kavanaugh-gave -a-speech-about-binge-drinking-in-law-school.

197 **say under oath:** Dr. Christine Blasey Ford, "Written Testimony of Dr. Christine Blasey Ford," U.S. Senate Judiciary Committee, Sept. 26, 2018, www.npr.org/2018/09/26/651941113/read-christine-blasey-fords -opening-statement-for-senate-hearing.

197 **authored a book in 1997:** Amanda Arnold, "Everything to Know About Mark Judge, Brett Kavanaugh's Alleged Accomplice," *New York*, Oct. 2, 2018, www.thecut.com/2018/10/mark-judge-kavanaughs-alleged-accomplice -what-to-know.html.

197 **One of Judge's former girlfriends:** Farrow and Mayer, "Senate Democrats Investigate a New Allegation of Sexual Misconduct, from Brett Kavanaugh's College Years."

197 **declined to speak publicly:** Ledyard King, "Kavanaugh Classmate Mark Judge Says He Can't Talk Publicly Despite Publisher's Promotion," *USA Today*, Sept. 28, 2018, www.usatoday.com/story/news/politics/onpolitics /2018/09/28/brett-kavanaugh-mark-judge/1456286002.

197 **friend's beach house in Delaware:** Adam Serwer, "What Mark Judge's Absence Reveals," *Atlantic*, Sept. 27, 2018, www.theatlantic.com/ideas/ar chive/2018/09/kavanaugh-ford-mark-judge/571540.

197 **In *The Education of Brett Kavanaugh*:** Robin Pogrebin and Kate Kelly, *The Education of Brett Kavanaugh* (New York: Portfolio/Penguin, 2019).

198 **measured and lawyerly opinion piece:** Anita Hill, "How to Get the Kavanaugh Hearings Right," *New York Times*, Sept. 18, 2018, www.nytimes .com/2018/09/18/opinion/anita-hill-brett-kavanaugh-clarence-thomas .html.

198 **hired Rachel Mitchell:** Camila Domonoske, "Sex Crimes Prosecutor Picked for Kavanaugh Hearing Brings Decades of Experience," NPR, Sept. 26, 2018, www.npr.org/2018/09/26/651735137/sex-crimes-prosecutor -picked-for-kavanaugh-hearing-brings-decades-of-experience.

198 **"Indelible in the hippocampus is the laughter":** Maeve Reston, "'I Will Never Forget': Christine Blasey Ford Recounts Her Trauma in Raw Testimony," CNN, Sept. 27, 2018, www.cnn.com/2018/09/27/politics/christine -blasey-ford-raw-testimony/index.html.

199 **Republican majority also declined:** Lauren Fox et al., "Yale Classmates Remember Very Different Images of Brett Kavanaugh," CNN, Sept. 26, 2018, www.cnn.com/2018/09/26/politics/yale-kavanaugh/index.html.

199 **Senator Klobuchar asked Kavanaugh:** Dan Merica, "Kavanaugh Gets Combative with Democratic Senator over Questions About Drinking," CNN, Sept. 27, 2018, www.cnn.com/2018/09/27/politics/kavanaugh-klobuchar -questions-about-drinking/index.html.

199 **controlled by the same entities:** Dareh Gregorian, "Democrats Blast FBI as New Details of Kavanaugh Inquiry Emerge," NBC News, July 22, 2021, www.nbcnews.com/politics/justice-department/democrats-blast-fbi -new-details-kavanaugh-inquiry-emerge-n1274766.

199 **he had been exculpated:** Calvin Woodward and Chloe Kim, "AP FACT CHECK: Kavanaugh's Claim of Exoneration," AP News, Sept. 27, 2018, apnews.com/article/north-america-us-supreme-court-christine-blasey -ford-dc-wire-ca-state-wire-883321a1030c4854bf502e08c187d334.

199 **threaten revenge on the groups:** Aaron Blake, "Brett Kavanaugh Just Got Remarkably Angry—and Political—for a Supreme Court Nominee," *Washington Post*, Sept. 27, 2018, www.washingtonpost.com/politics/2018 /09/27/brett-kavanaugh-just-got-remarkably-angry-political-supreme -court-nominee.

200 **Fox News's Chris Wallace:** Summer Meza, "Fox News' Chris Wallace Calls Christine Blasey Ford's Hearing a 'Disaster for the Republicans,'" *Week*, Sept. 27, 2018, theweek.com/speedreads/798545/fox-news-chris -wallace-calls-christine-blasey-fords-hearing-disaster-republicans.

200 **Thirty-five percent said the Senate:** Kate Kelly and Robin Pogrebin, "We Spent 10 Months Investigating Kavanaugh. Here's What We Found," *Atlantic*, Sept. 17, 2019, www.theatlantic.com/ideas/archive/2019/09/pog rebin-kelly-kavanaugh/598159.

200 **"This is not tolerable":** Haley Sweetland Edwards, "How Christine Blasey Ford's Testimony Changed America," *Time*, Oct. 4, 2018, time.com/maga zine/us/5415016/october-15th-2018-vol-192-no-15-u-s.

200 **Dr. Ford had described:** Ford, "Written Testimony of Dr. Christine Blasey Ford."

201 **"Judge Kavanaugh showed America":** Reuters Staff, "Trump Calls Kava- naugh Testimony Powerful, Calls for Senate Vote," Reuters, Sept. 27, 2018, www.reuters.com/article/uk-usa-court-kavanaugh-trump/trump-calls -kavanaugh-testimony-powerful-calls-for-senate-vote-idUKKCN1M8022.

201 **"Those who chanted 'Lock her up!'":** Serwer, "What Mark Judge's Ab- sence Reveals."

201 **rally in October in Mississippi:** John Wagner, "Trump Says It's a 'Very Scary Time' for Young Men Who Can Be Falsely Accused of Bad Behav- ior," *Washington Post*, Oct. 2, 2018, www.washingtonpost.com/politics /trump-says-its-a-very-scary-time-for-young-men-who-can-be-falsely -accused-of-bad-behavior/2018/10/02/5c45af34-c629-11e8-9b1c-a90 f1daae309_story.html.

201 **He began mocking Dr. Ford:** Jonathan Allen, "Trump Mocks Kavanaugh Accuser Christine Blasey Ford at Campaign Rally," NBC News, Oct. 2, 2018, www.nbcnews.com/politics/politics-news/trump-mocks-christine -blasey-ford-mississippi-campaign-rally-n916061.

201 **The legal philosopher Martha Nussbaum:** Martha Nussbaum, *Citadels of Pride: Sexual Abuse, Accountability, and Reconciliation* (New York: W. W. Norton, 2021).

202 **"they should've had a process":** *New York Times* Staff, "How History Changed Anita Hill," *New York Times*, June 17, 2019, www.nytimes.com /2019/06/17/us/anita-hill-women-power.html.

202 **In a podcast done in 2021:** "The Conversation: Prof. Anita Hill and Dr. Christine Blasey Ford," *Because of Anita*, Oct. 11, 2021, pineapple.fm /because-of-anita-ep-3.

203 **"Can you imagine that we are putting judges":** Anita Hill, interview by author, May 2021.

203 **"complaints against a judge":** Ariane de Vogue, "Judicial Conduct Panel Dismisses Ethics Complaints Against Brett Kavanaugh," CNN, Aug. 2, 2019, www.cnn.com/2019/08/02/politics/kavanaugh-ethics-complaints-dismissed/index.html.

203 **Susan Collins, the Republican senator:** Sen. Susan Collins, "Read Susan Collins's Speech Declaring Support for Brett Kavanaugh," *New York Times*, Oct. 5, 2018, www.nytimes.com/2018/10/05/us/politics/susan-collins-speech-brett-kavanaugh.html.

204 **presidential candidate Joe Biden telephoned:** Sheryl Gay Stolberg and Carl Hulse, "Joe Biden Expresses Regret to Anita Hill, but She Says 'I'm Sorry' Is Not Enough," *New York Times*, April 25, 2019, www.nytimes.com/2019/04/25/us/politics/joe-biden-anita-hill.html.

204 **"After Dr. Blasey's courageous testimony":** Anita Hill, "Let's Talk About How to End Sexual Violence," *New York Times*, May 9, 2019, www.nytimes.com/2019/05/09/opinion/anita-hill-sexual-violence.html.

205 **between Hill and Ford:** "Conversation: Prof. Anita Hill and Dr. Christine Blasey Ford," *Because of Anita*.

206 **harassment and assault in the military:** Patricia Kime, "Despite Efforts, Sexual Assaults Up Nearly 40% in US Military," Military.com, May 2, 2019, www.military.com/daily-news/2019/05/02/despite-efforts-sexual-assaults-nearly-40-us-military.html.

206 **CDC reports that one in three women:** "Preventing Sexual Violence," Centers for Disease Control and Prevention, last updated Feb. 5, 2021, www.cdc.gov/violenceprevention/sexualviolence/fastfact.html.

206 **According to the EEOC:** "Charges Alleging Sex-Based Harassment (Charges Filed with EEOC) FY 2010–FY 2020," U.S. Equal Employment Opportunity Commission, www.eeoc.gov/statistics/charges-alleging-sex-based-harassment-charges-filed-eeoc-fy-2010-fy-2020.

206 **"Part of the reason I think":** Hill, interview by author, May 2021.

208 **as a "bounty" system:** Peter Holley and Dan Solomon, "Your Questions About Texas's New Abortion Law, Answered," *Texas Monthly*, Oct. 7, 2021, www.texasmonthly.com/news-politics/texas-abortion-law-explained.

208 **The day after the law went into effect:** *Whole Woman's Health v. Jackson*, 21-463, 595 U.S. __ (2021).

209 **allowed the law to stand:** *Whole Woman's Health v. Jackson*, 21-463, 595 U.S. __ (2021) (slip opinion).

210 **wrote an article explaining:** Dahlia Lithwick, "Why I Haven't Gone Back to SCOTUS Since Kavanaugh," *Slate*, Oct. 30, 2019, slate.com/news-and-politics/2019/10/year-after-kavanaugh-cant-go-back-to-scotus.html.

211 **concluded in that piece:** Lithwick, "Why I Haven't Gone Back to SCOTUS Since Kavanaugh."

211 **anthology about the Kavanaugh hearings:** Dahlia Lithwick, "The Room Where It Happened," in *Believe Me: How Trusting Women Can Change the World*, ed. Jessica Valenti and Jaclyn Friedman (New York: Seal Press, 2020).

211 **"Without law it's chaos":** Hill, interview by author, May 2021.

214 **Rebecca Traister and Brittney Cooper:** Hill, interview by author, May 2021.

216 **"I think at one point":** Hill, interview by author, May 2021.

CHAPTER 9: ELECTIONS PART 1—VOTING GEORGIA 2018

218 **My parents and I arrived on the MARTA bus:** CBS News Staff, "Stacey Abrams on Writing Herself into the Story—and History," CBS News, May 9, 2021, www.cbsnews.com/news/stacey-abrams-on-writing-herself-into -the-story-and-history.

218 **Abrams was a voracious reader:** Kevin Powell, "The Power of Stacey Abrams," *Washington Post*, May 14, 2020, www.washingtonpost.com /magazine/2020/05/14/stacey-abrams-political-power.

219 **she became a tax lawyer:** Powell, "The Power of Stacey Abrams."

219 **"The writing. I've been writing":** Cori Murray, "Say Her Name: Stacey Abrams Steps Out of the Shadows into Her New Title, 'Author,'" *Essence*, May 10, 2021, www.essence.com/feature/stacey-abrams-balancing-fiction -writing-politics-new-book.

219 **"It's important that we enjoy":** Rebecca Traister, "Stacey Abrams on Finishing the Job in Georgia: 'It Can Be Undone Just as Quickly and as Effectively as We Did It,'" *New York*, Nov. 19, 2020, www.thecut.com/2020 /11/stacey-abrams-on-flipping-georgia-blue.html.

220 **Abrams said she wants:** Traister, "Stacey Abrams on Finishing the Job in Georgia."

220 **"I grew up not only writing":** CBS News Staff, "Stacey Abrams on Writing Herself into the Story."

220 **"one of the most detail-oriented":** Traister, "Stacey Abrams on Finishing the Job in Georgia."

221 **"Please pay attention to Georgia":** Traister, "Stacey Abrams on Finishing the Job in Georgia."

221 **Her big idea was simply:** Carol Anderson, "Brian Kemp's Lead in Georgia Needs an Asterisk," *Atlantic*, Nov. 7, 2018, www.theatlantic.com/ideas /archive/2018/11/georgia-governor-kemp-abrams/575095.

221 **"people were skeptical but willing to meet":** Traister, "Stacey Abrams on Finishing the Job in Georgia."

221 **She gathered a fleet:** Astead W. Herndon, "Georgia Was a Big Win for Democrats. Black Women Did the Groundwork," *New York Times*, Dec. 3, 2020, www.nytimes.com/2020/12/03/us/politics/georgia-democrats-black -women.html.

222 **the highest voter-participation rates:** Vanessa Williams, "Black Women Vow to Be a Powerful Voting Force Again This Year," *Washington Post*, Jan. 10, 2016, www.washingtonpost.com/politics/black-women-vow-to-be -a-powerful-voting-force-again-this-year/2016/01/10/f0c290fc-b324 -11e5-a842-0feb51d1d124_story.html.

223 **Justice Elena Kagan characterized it:** *Brnovich v. Democratic National Committee*, 19-1257, 594 U.S. __ (2021).

223 **That number stood at 4.3 percent:** Timothy Smith, "How Voter Suppression Threatens Our Democracy," *Washington Post*, Sept. 20, 2018, www.wash ingtonpost.com/outlook/how-voter-suppression-threatens-our-democracy /2018/09/20/c1dd3b8a-aad3-11e8-b1da-ff7faa680710_story.html.

223 **again dissenting in *Brnovich*:** *Brnovich*, 19-1257, 594 U.S. __ (2021).

224 **"Following the dramatic rise":** Michael J. Pitts, "Section 5 of the Voting Rights Act: A Once and Future Remedy," *Denver Law Review* 81, no. 2 (2003), digitalcommons.du.edu/cgi/viewcontent.cgi?article=1624&context =dlr.

225 **Lee Atwater's classic formulation:** Rick Perlstein, "Exclusive: Lee Atwater's Infamous 1981 Interview on the Southern Strategy," *Nation*, Nov. 13, 2012, www.thenation.com/article/archive/exclusive-lee-atwaters-infamous -1981-interview-southern-strategy.

225 **in *Shelby County v. Holder*, under:** *Shelby County v. Holder*, 570 U.S. 529 (2013).

225 **reauthorized the preclearance formula:** "Voting Rights Act Reauthoriza- tion 2006," NAACP Legal Defense Fund, Feb. 16, 2018, www.naacpldf .org/case-issue/voting-rights-act-reauthorization-2006.

225 **her dissent in *Shelby County*:** *Shelby County*, 570 U.S.

226 **But in Roberts's view, by 2013:** *Shelby County*, 570 U.S.

226 **Texas voter-ID law:** Jim Malewitz, "Texas Voter ID Law Violates Voting Rights Act, Court Rules," *Texas Tribune*, July 20, 2016, www.texastribune .org/2016/07/20/appeals-court-rules-texas-voter-id.

226 **mayor of Pasadena, Texas:** Manny Fernandez, "In Texas, a Test of Whether the Voting Rights Act Still Has Teeth," *New York Times*, Jan. 15, 2017, www.nytimes.com/2017/01/15/us/in-texas-a-test-of-whether-the-voting -rights-act-still-has-teeth.html.

227 **That law was eventually deemed:** Christopher Ingraham, "The 'Smoking Gun' Proving North Carolina Republicans Tried to Disenfranchise Black Voters," *Washington Post*, July 29, 2016, www.washingtonpost.com/news /wonk/wp/2016/07/29/the-smoking-gun-proving-north-carolina -republicans-tried-to-disenfranchise-black-voters.

227 *Vice* **reported in 2018:** Allison McCann, "How the Gutting of the Voting Rights Act Led to Hundreds of Closed Polls," *Vice News*, Oct. 16, 2018, www.vice.com/en/article/kz58qx/how-the-gutting-of-the-voting-rights -act-led-to-closed-polls.

227 **Ari Berman, the voting rights columnist:** Ari Berman, "Voting Rights in the Age of Trump," *New York Times*, Nov. 19, 2016, www.nytimes.com/2016 /11/22/opinion/voting-rights-in-the-age-of-trump.html.

227 **"Jim Crow in a suit and tie":** Nicole Hemmer, "What Jim Crow Looks Like in 2021," CNN, March 25, 2021, www.cnn.com/2021/03/25/opinions/vot ing-rights-suppression-is-jim-crow-suit-and-tie-hemmer/index.html.

228 **harder to vote with false claims:** Aaron Blake, "The Trump Team and Fox News Alleged Dead Voters. Most Cases Were Either Debunked or Actually Involved Republicans," *Washington Post*, Oct. 25, 2021, www.washing tonpost.com/politics/2021/10/25/trump-team-fox-news-alleged -dead-voters-most-cases-were-either-debunked-or-actually-involved -republicans.

228 **Abrams unfailingly references herself:** Traister, "Stacey Abrams on Finishing the Job in Georgia."

229 **"reverse migration of African Americans":** Traister, "Stacey Abrams on Finishing the Job in Georgia."

229 **It was 54.2 percent white in 2018:** Jelani Cobb, "Stacey Abrams's Fight for a Fair Vote," *New Yorker*, Aug. 19, 2019, www.newyorker.com/magazine /2019/08/19/stacey-abrams-fight-for-a-fair-vote.

229 **It was 50.1 percent white in 2021:** Patricia Murphy, Greg Bluestein, and Tia Mitchell, "The Jolt: For the First Time, Metro Atlanta Is Now Majority-Nonwhite," *Atlanta Journal-Constitution*, Aug. 13, 2021, www.ajc.com /politics/politics-blog/the-jolt-for-the-first-time-metro-atlanta-is-now -majority-nonwhite/VRYNX467VBHQBAPLUDDMK4RK5U.

229 **she raised $40 million:** Traister, "Stacey Abrams on Finishing the Job in Georgia."

230 **"having volunteers is great":** Traister, "Stacey Abrams on Finishing the Job in Georgia."

230 **"New American Majority":** Katanga Johnson and Heather Timmons, "How Stacey Abrams Paved the Way for a Democratic Victory in 'New Georgia,'" Reuters, Nov. 9, 2020, www.reuters.com/article/usa-election -georgia-idUSKBN27P197.

231 **"For me, the through-line is":** Traister, "Stacey Abrams on Finishing the Job in Georgia."

231 **"I don't run Fair Fight":** Traister, "Stacey Abrams on Finishing the Job in Georgia."

232 **"a cross-racial coalition":** Cobb, "Stacey Abrams's Fight for a Fair Vote."

232 **Georgians deserved better, so we devised:** Stacey Abrams and Lauren Groh-Wargo, "How to Turn Your Red State Blue," *New York Times*, Feb. 11, 2021, www.nytimes.com/2021/02/11/opinion/stacey-abrams-georgia -election.html.

232 **"round up criminal illegals":** Alan Blinder and Richard Fausset, "Stacey Abrams Ends Fight for Georgia Governor with Harsh Words for Her

Rival," *New York Times*, Nov. 16, 2018, www.nytimes.com/2018/11/16/us /elections/georgia-governor-race-kemp-abrams.html.

233 **"counter to the most fundamental principle":** Anderson, "Brian Kemp's Lead in Georgia Needs an Asterisk."

233 **Hans von Spakovsky, got his start in Georgia:** Dan Eggen, "Official's Article on Voting Law Spurs Outcry," *Washington Post*, April 13, 2006, www .washingtonpost.com/archive/politics/2006/04/13/officials-article-on -voting-law-spurs-outcry/77a7617a-ad6a-48e8-9e76-a2826b4d8942.

233 **Kemp had purged 1.5 million voters:** Anderson, "Brian Kemp's Lead in Georgia Needs an Asterisk."

233 **as Jelani Cobb explained in *The New Yorker*:** Cobb, "Stacey Abrams's Fight for a Fair Vote."

233 **voter registrations of 53,000 voters:** Eli Watkins, "Stacey Abrams: Voter Suppression 'About Terrifying People' from Voting," CNN, Oct. 14, 2018, www.cnn.com/2018/10/14/politics/stacey-abrams-brian-kemp-georgia -cnntv/index.html.

233 **more reports of peculiarities:** Cobb, "Stacey Abrams's Fight for a Fair Vote."

233 **largest single cancellation of voter registrations:** Alan Judd, "Georgia's Strict Laws Lead to Large Purge of Voters," *Atlanta Journal-Constitution*, Oct. 27, 2018, www.ajc.com/news/state--regional-govt politics/voter-pur ge-begs-question-what-the-matter-with-georgia/YAFvuk3Bu95kJIMa DiDFqJ.

234 **laughing and smiling emojis:** Ella Lee, "Fact Check: Post Online About Stacey Abrams' 2018 Run for Georgia Governor Is Partly False," *USA Today*, Nov. 18, 2020, www.usatoday.com/story/news/factcheck/2020/11/18/fact -check-partly-false-claim-stacey-abrams-2018-race/6318836002.

234 **"Democrats are working hard":** Anderson, "Brian Kemp's Lead in Georgia Needs an Asterisk."

234 **exact-match policy was a burden:** Cobb, "Stacey Abrams's Fight for a Fair Vote."

234 **it was opening an inquiry:** Gregory Krieg et al., "Kemp's Office Launches Probe of Georgia Democratic Party Ahead of Historic Election," CNN, Nov. 5, 2018, www.cnn.com/2018/11/04/politics/georgia-voter-registration -hacking-attempt-investigation/index.html.

234 **Georgians suffered from shuttered polling:** Cobb, "Stacey Abrams's Fight for a Fair Vote."

235 **"elections are often fought":** *Brnovich v. Democratic National Committee*, 19-1257, 594 U.S. __ (2021).

235 **nearly four million cast:** Cobb, "Stacey Abrams's Fight for a Fair Vote."

235 **"I acknowledge that former Secretary of State":** Cobb, "Stacey Abrams's Fight for a Fair Vote."

235 **her own election was significantly flawed:** Richard L. Hasen, "Stacey Abrams' New Lawsuit Against Georgia's Broken Voting System Is Incred-

ibly Smart," *Slate*, Nov. 27, 2018, slate.com/news-and-politics/2018/11
/stacey-abrams-georgia-voting-rights-lawsuit.html.

235 **has still failed to prevail:** William Cummings, Joey Garrison, and Jim Sergent, "By the Numbers: President Donald Trump's Failed Efforts to Overturn the Election," *USA Today*, Jan. 6, 2021, www.usatoday.com/in-depth
/news/politics/elections/2021/01/06/trumps-failed-efforts-overturn
-election-numbers/4130307001.

235 **In Georgia, the participation rate:** Anderson, "Brian Kemp's Lead in Georgia Needs an Asterisk."

236 **And 94 percent of them had voted:** Cobb, "Stacey Abrams's Fight for a Fair
Vote."

236 **The sixty-six-page complaint:** Complaint in *Fair Fight Action et al. v. Crit-
tenden*, Nov. 27, 2018 (on file with author).

237 **"The suit,"** **he wrote:** Hasen, "Stacey Abrams' New Lawsuit Against
Georgia's Broken Voting System Is Incredibly Smart."

237 **as being spelled "delRio":** P. R. Lockhart, "The Lawsuit Challenging Georgia's Entire Elections System, Explained," *Vox*, May 30, 2019, www.vox
.com/policy-and-politics/2018/11/30/18118264/georgia-election-lawsuit
-voter-suppression-abrams-kemp-race.

237 **That litigation became a vehicle:** "AP FACT CHECK: Trump Wrong on
Georgia Voter Signature Checks," Associated Press, Nov. 15, 2020, apnews
.com/article/ap-fact-check-donald-trump-georgia-elections-voter
-registration-40bb602e6f0facf8eecc331e83ab36e0.

238 **As Abrams would explain to Traister:** Traister, "Stacey Abrams on Finishing the Job in Georgia."

238 **There is no widespread crisis:** Jesse Wegman, "Surprise! There's No Voter
Fraud. Again," *New York Times*, Dec. 17, 2021, www.nytimes.com/2021
/12/17/opinion/election-vote-fraud-data.html.

239 **was about 0.00006 percent of total ballots cast:** Amber McReynolds and
Charles Stewart III, "Let's Put the Vote-by-Mail 'Fraud' Myth to Rest,"
Hill, April 28, 2020, thehill.com/opinion/campaign/494189-lets-put-the
-vote-by-mail-fraud-myth-to-rest.

239 **The nonpartisan Brennan Center's massive study:** Justin Levitt, "The
Truth About Voter Fraud," Brennan Center for Justice, Nov. 9, 2007,
www.brennancenter.org/our-work/research-reports/truth-about
-voter-fraud.

239 **impede two thousand eligible voters:** Sharad Goel et al., "One Person, One
Vote: Estimating the Prevalence of Double Voting in U.S. Presidential Elections," *American Political Science Review* 114, no. 2 (2020), 5harad.com
/papers/1p1v.pdf.

240 **in 1964 in *Reynolds v. Sims*:** *Reynolds v. Sims*, 377 U.S. 533 (1964).

240 **strict voter-ID laws in *Crawford*:** *Crawford* v. *Marion County Election
Board*, 553 U.S. 181 (2008).

240 **In a 2018 case, *Husted v. A. Philip Randolph Institute*:** Husted v. A. Philip
Randolph Institute, 16-980, 584 U.S. __ (2018).
240 **In 2019 in *Rucho v. Common Cause*:** Rucho v. Common Cause, 18-422,
588 U.S. __ (2019).
240 **the decision in *Citizens United v. FEC*:** Citizens United v. FEC, 558 U.S.
310 (2010).
241 **Trump lost the popular vote:** Tom LoBianco, "Trump Falsely Claims
'Millions of People Who Voted Illegally' Cost Him Popular Vote," CNN,
Nov. 28, 2016, www.cnn.com/2016/11/27/politics/donald-trump-voter-fra
ud-popular-vote/index.html.
241 **One 2009 study found that in the states:** Andrew Gelman, Nate Silver,
and Aaron Edlin, "What Is the Probability Your Vote Will Make a Difference?," *Economic Inquiry* 50, no. 2 (2009), www.researchgate.net/publica
tion/227372262_What_Is_the_Probability_Your_Vote_Will_Make_a
_Difference.
242 **six in ten Republicans:** Susan Page and Sarah Elbeshbishi, "A Year After
Jan. 6, Americans Say Democracy Is in Peril but Disagree on Why: USA
TODAY/Suffolk Poll," *USA Today*, Jan. 4, 2022, www.usatoday.com/story
/news/politics/2022/01/04/jan-6-democracy-danger-usa-today-suffolk
-poll-finds/9023578002.
242 **When I talk about putting:** Dahlia Lithwick, "Voting Is Broken. It's the
Only Way Out," *Slate*, Aug. 21, 2020, slate.com/news-and-politics/2020
/08/obamas-dnc-voting-only-hope.html.
243 **At the Democratic National Convention:** Lithwick, "Voting Is Broken. It's
the Only Way Out."
244 **called *Brnovich v. DNC*:** Brnovich v. Democratic National Committee, 19-
1257, 594 U.S. __ (2021).
245 **If a single statute represents:** Brnovich, 19-1257, 594 U.S. __ (2021).
246 **"When you've never had to think":** CBS News Staff, "Stacey Abrams on
Writing Herself into the Story."

CHAPTER 10: ELECTIONS PART 2—THE ELECTIONS
LONG GAME: REDISTRICTING AND THE CENSUS

249 **"The right to vote has been described":** Samantha Neal, "Nina Perales
on Latinx Voting Rights," *Taking Liberties*, episode 16, April 26, 2021,
harvardcrcl.org/taking-liberties-episode-16-nina-perales-of-maldef.
249 **That battle has been Perales's daily existence:** Perales, interview by author,
June 2021.
250 **In a 2021 podcast, she explained:** Neal, "Nina Perales on Latinx Voting
Rights."
251 **In 2006, she argued and won:** *League of United Latin American Citizens v.
Perry*, 548 U.S. 399 (2006).

253 **MALDEF challenged a Texas law:** Krystina Martinez, "MALDEF Vows to Fight 'Vigilante Justice Bill' After Texas Sues over SB 4," KERA News, May 26, 2017, www.keranews.org/politics/2017-05-26/maldef-vows-to-fi ght-vigilante-justice-bill-after-texas-sues-over-sb-4.

253 **to convict three African American activists:** Ari Berman, "Jeff Sessions Claims to Be a Champion of Voting Rights, but His Record Suggests Otherwise," *Nation*, Jan. 11, 2017, www.thenation.com/article/archive /jeff-sessions-claims-to-be-a-champion-of-voting-rights-but-his-record -suggests-otherwise.

253 **the Senate rejected Sessions:** Emily Bazelon, "The Voter Fraud Case Jeff Sessions Lost and Can't Escape," *New York Times*, Jan. 9, 2017, www.ny times.com/2017/01/09/magazine/the-voter-fraud-case-jeff-sessions-lost -and-cant-escape.html.

253 **Sessions sat in the US Senate:** Hank Sanders, "Sessions Cannot Do Justice as Head of Justice Dept.," *Selma Times-Journal*, Dec. 13, 2016, www.selma timesjournal.com/2016/12/13/sessions-cannot-do-justice-as-head-of -justice-dept.

253 **"attempting to rig this election":** Rebecca Morin, "Trump, Sessions Draw Heat for 'Rigged' Election Claim," *Politico*, Oct. 15, 2016, www.politico .com/story/2016/10/republicans-react-to-trumps-rigged-election-229 845.

253 **Trump refused to accept:** Tom LoBianco, "Trump Falsely Claims 'Millions of People Who Voted Illegally' Cost Him Popular Vote," CNN, Nov. 28, 2016, www.cnn.com/2016/11/27/politics/donald-trump-voter-fraud-popular -vote/index.html.

253 **Presidential Advisory Commission on Election Integrity:** "Background on Trump's 'Voter Fraud' Commission," Brennan Center for Justice, July 18, 2017, www.brennancenter.org/our-work/analysis-opinion/background -trumps-voter-fraud-commission.

254 **That requirement was eventually struck:** Jessica Huseman, "How the Case for Voter Fraud Was Tested—and Utterly Failed," ProPublica, June 19, 2018, www.propublica.org/article/kris-kobach-voter-fraud-kansas-trial.

254 **argued on behalf of Kansas:** Emily Bazelon, "A Crusader Against Voter Fraud Fails to Prove His Case," *New York Times*, June 19, 2018, www .nytimes.com/2018/06/19/opinion/a-crusader-against-voter-fraud -fails-to-prove-his-case.html.

254 **lawyers' equivalent of traffic school:** Huseman, "How the Case for Voter Fraud Was Tested."

254 **Judge Robinson concluded:** Findings of Facts and Conclusions of Law, *Fish v. Kobach*, 309 F. Supp. 3d 1048 (D. Kans. 2018), www.aclu.org/legal -document/fish-v-kobach-findings-fact-and-conclusions-law.

254 **the commission demanded vast quantities:** Christopher Ingraham, "Trump's Voter-Fraud Commission Wants to Know Voting History, Party ID, and

Address of Every Voter in the U.S.," *Washington Post*, June 29, 2017, www .washingtonpost.com/news/wonk/wp/2017/06/29/trumps-voter -fraud-commission-wants-to-know-the-voting-history-party-id-and -address-of-every-voter-in-america.

254 **That triggered outrage from both sides:** Liz Stark and Grace Hauck, "Forty-four States and DC Have Refused to Give Certain Voter Informa- tion to Trump Commission," CNN, July 5, 2017, www.cnn.com/2017/07 /03/politics/kris-kobach-letter-voter-fraud-commission-information /index.html.

255 **Latinos constitute 18 percent of the US population:** Nicholas Jones et al., "2020 Census Illuminates Racial and Ethnic Composition of the Country," U.S. Census Bureau, Aug. 12, 2021, www.census.gov/library/stories/2021 /08/improved-race-ethnicity-measures-reveal-united-states-population -much-more-multiracial.html.

256 **expanded to include Texas for preclearance:** "About Section 5 of the Vot- ing Rights Acts," U.S. Department of Justice, updated Nov. 29, 2021, www.justice.gov/crt/about-section-5-voting-rights-act.

256 **"I define redistricting as the only":** "Impact of Census on Congres- sional Elections," C-SPAN, April 2, 1991, www.c-span.org/video/?18139 -1/impact-census-congressional-elections&start=2454.

256 **explained gleefully in 2001:** "User Clip: Hofeller on Redistricting," C-SPAN, June 20, 2019, https://www.c-span.org/video/?c4804050/hofeller -redistricing.

258 **Kris Kobach, had written:** Hansi Lo Wang, "Kris Kobach Discussed Census Citizenship Question with 2016 Trump Campaign," NPR, June 7, 2019, www.npr.org/2019/06/07/730756245/kris-kobach-discussed-census -citizenship-question-with-2016-trump-campaign.

258 **stopped asking about citizenship:** Edith Honan, "Citizenship Question Dropped from Census, but Advocates Fear 'Damage Has Been Done,'" ABC News, July 12, 2019, abcnews.go.com/Politics/citizenship-question -dropped-census-advocates-fear-damage/story?id=64225417.

258 **in a case called *Evenwel v. Abbott*:** *Evenwel v. Abbott*, 578 U.S. 54 (2016).

259 **So he overruled them:** Richard Wolf, "Inside Trump Administration's Mysterious Plan to Secure a 2020 Census Citizenship Question," *USA Today*, April 13, 2019, www.usatoday.com/story/news/politics/2019/04 /13/wilbur-ross-pushed-census-citizenship-question-2020-trump -administration/3412922002.

259 **Six former directors:** Vincent P. Barabba et al., "Letter from Former Di- rectors of the U.S. Census Bureau to Sec. Wilbur Ross," Jan. 26, 2018, available through *Washington Post*, www.washingtonpost.com/r/2010 -2019/WashingtonPost/2018/03/27/Editorial-Opinion/Graphics/DOJ _census_ques_request_Former_Directors_ltr_to_Ross.pdf.

259 **Secretary Ross first announced:** Emily Baumgaertner, "Despite Concerns, Census Will Ask Respondents if They Are U.S. Citizens," *New York Times*, March 26, 2018, www.nytimes.com/2018/03/26/us/politics/census -citizenship-question-trump.html.

259 **December 2017 request:** Salvador Rizzo, "Wilbur Ross's False Claim to Congress That the Census Citizenship Question Was DOJ's Idea," *Washington Post*, July 30, 2018, www.washingtonpost.com/news/fact-checker /wp/2018/07/30/wilbur-rosss-false-claim-to-congress-that-the-census -citizenship-question-was-dojs-idea.

259 **Every lower court judge:** Andrew Prokop, "Trump's Census Citizenship Question Fiasco, Explained," *Vox*, July 11, 2019, www.vox.com/2019/7/11 /20689015/census-citizenship-question-trump-executive-order.

260 **to the Supreme Court in October 2018:** Josh Gerstein, "Supreme Court Halts Wilbur Ross Deposition," *Politico*, Oct. 22, 2018, www.politico.com /story/2018/10/22/supreme-court-wilbur-ross-929497.

260 **violated the Administrative Procedure Act's prohibition:** *New York v. Department of Commerce*, 351 F. Supp. 3d 502 (S.D.N.Y.), s3.documentcloud .org/documents/5684702/Findings-of-Fact-Conclusions-of-Law.pdf.

260 **"The unreasonableness of Defendants' addition":** *Kravitz v. Department of Commerce*, 366 F. Supp. 3d 681 (D. Md. 2019), www.washingtonpost.com /context/maryland-judge-s-ruling-on-census-citizenship-question/?no teId=56929fc2-acea-4720-9053-18ff2c50e262&questionId=abe6aabb -3cbf-4e9a-86d0-59ba41cb0ce5&utm_term=.7711c635d803&itid=lk _interstitial_manual_8.

261 **published a bombshell:** Michael Wines, "Deceased G.O.P. Strategist's Hard Drives Reveal New Details on the Census Citizenship Question," *New York Times*, May 30, 2019, www.nytimes.com/2019/05/30/us/census -citizenship-question-hofeller.html.

262 **The plaintiffs filed a letter:** Lawrence Hurley, "Advocacy Groups Ask Supreme Court to Delay Ruling on Census Citizenship Question," Reuters, June 12, 2019, www.reuters.com/article/us-usa-court-census-idUSKCN1 TE00U.

262 **opinion in the New York litigation:** *Department of Commerce v. New York*, 18-966, 588 U.S. __ (2019).

263 **Trump tweeted, on July 3:** Kevin Breuninger and Dan Mangan, "Trump Says He Is 'Absolutely Moving Forward' with Census Citizenship Question, Contradicting His Own Administration," CNBC, July 4, 2019, www .cnbc.com/2019/07/03/trump-says-absolutely-moving-forward-with -census-citizenship-question.html.

263 **asked to be removed:** Michael Wines, Katie Benner, and Adam Liptak, "Justice Dept. to Replace Lawyers in Census Citizenship Question Case," *New York Times*, July 7, 2019, www.nytimes.com/2019/07/07/us/politics /census-citizenship-question-justice-department.html.

265 **Trump seated 28 percent:** John Gramlich, "How Trump Compares with Other Recent Presidents in Appointing Federal Judges," Pew Research Center, Jan. 13, 2021, www.pewresearch.org/fact-tank/2021/01/13/how -trump-compares-with-other-recent-presidents-in-appointing-federal -judges.

265 **average age of his appellate judges:** Erin Snodgrass and Madison Hall, "How Donald Trump Hurt Female Representation in Federal Courts," *Business Insider*, March 31, 2021, www.businessinsider.com/trump-appointed -way-more-male-judges-than-female-2021-3.

265 **The Federal Judicial Center estimated:** Micah Schwartzman and David Fontana, "Trump Picked the Youngest Judges to Sit on the Federal Bench. Your Move, Biden," *Washington Post*, Feb. 16, 2021, www.washingtonpost.com /outlook/2021/02/16/court-appointments-age-biden-trump-judges-age.

265 **Ginsburg was often asked how many:** Nina Totenberg, "Justice Ginsburg: 'I Am Very Much Alive,'" NPR, July 24, 2019, www.npr.org/2019/07/24 /744633713/justice-ginsburg-i-am-very-much-alive.

267 **"great replacement theory":** Aaron Blake, "How Republicans Learned to Stop Worrying and Embrace 'Replacement Theory'—by Name," *Washington Post*, Sept. 27, 2021, www.washingtonpost.com/politics/2021/09/27 /how-republicans-learned-stop-worrying-embrace-replacement-theory -by-name.

267 **the sixty-plus lawsuits:** William Cummings, Joey Garrison, and Jim Sergent, "By the Numbers: President Donald Trump's Failed Efforts to Overturn the Election," *USA Today*, Jan. 6, 2021, www.usatoday.com/in-depth /news/politics/elections/2021/01/06/trumps-failed-efforts-overturn -election-numbers/4130307001.

273 **highly gerrymandered legislative maps:** Paul LeBlanc and Kelly Mena, "Obama Says GOP Gerrymandering Is 'Not How Democracy Is Supposed to Work,'" CNN, Dec. 8, 2021, www.cnn.com/2021/12/08/politics/obama -redistricting-democracy-voting/index.html.

EPILOGUE

275 **heady oral arguments in *Whole Woman's Health*:** *Whole Woman's Health v. Hellerstedt*, 579 U.S. 582 (2016).

276 **unsigned one-paragraph order in September 2021:** *Whole Woman's Health v. Jackson*, 21-463, 595 U.S. __ (2021).

276 **after arguments and briefing:** *Whole Woman's Health v. Jackson*, 21-463, 595 U.S. __ (2021) (slip opinion), www.supremecourt.gov/opinions/21pdf /21-463_3ebh.pdf.

276 **American women now face material threats:** Wynne Davis, "As the Supreme Court Weighs the Future of 'Roe v. Wade,' Experts Look Beyond Abortion," NPR, Dec. 10, 2021, www.npr.org/2021/12/10/1062702221

/supreme-court-weighs-mississippi-abortion-law-experts-look-further; David H. Gans, "The Mississippi Abortion Case Threatens the Right to Use Birth Control, Marry, and Even Make Choices About Sex," *Slate*, Oct. 12, 2021, slate.com/news-and-politics/2021/10/mississippi-abortion-birth -control-lgbtq-scotus.html; Marisa Endicott, "A New Federal Judge Appointed by Trump Has Fought Against Abortion, Fertility Treatments, and Surrogacy," *Mother Jones*, Dec. 4, 2019, www.motherjones.com/politics /2019/12/a-new-federal-judge-appointed-by-trump-has-fought-against -abortion-fertility-treatments-and-surrogacy.

276 **pregnancies will face criminal sanctions:** Dahlia Lithwick, "We're Not Going Back to 'Before *Roe*,'" *Slate*, Dec. 8, 2021, slate.com/news-and -politics/2021/12/not-going-back-to-before-roe-religion.html.

277 **primaries during a pandemic:** Linda Greenhouse, "The Supreme Court Fails Us," *New York Times*, April 9, 2020, www.nytimes.com/2020/04/09 /opinion/wisconsin-primary-supreme-court.html.

277 **She told CNN in the winter:** Faith Karimi, "For Stacey Abrams, Revenge Is a Dish Best Served Blue," CNN, Jan. 6, 2021, www.cnn.com/2020/11 /07/us/stacey-abrams-georgia-voter-suppression-trnd/index.html.

278 **"Black women have always been the backbone":** Nicquel Terry Ellis, "Black Women Helped Push Democrats to the Finish Line in Georgia. Here's How They Can Do It Again," CNN, Nov. 21, 2020, www.cnn.com/2020 /11/21/politics/black-women-crucial-georgia-democrats/index.html.

278 **Abrams later told Stephen Colbert:** Jazz Tangcay, "Stacey Abrams Hailed as a 'Game-Changer' by Documentarians Who Chronicled Her," *Variety*, Nov. 9, 2020, variety.com/2020/politics/news/stacey-abrams-2020-election -all-in-documentaries-1234826048.

279 **4.5 million people voted:** Kenya Evelyn, "How Black Voters Lifted Georgia Democrats to Senate Runoff Victories," *Guardian*, Jan. 7, 2021, www .theguardian.com/us-news/2021/jan/07/georgia-senate-runoff-black -voters-stacey-abrams.

279 **Abrams told a roaring crowd:** Kevin Powell, "The Power of Stacey Abrams," *Washington Post*, May 14, 2020, www.washingtonpost.com/mag azine/2020/05/14/stacey-abrams-political-power.

280 **insurrectionists would be scaling:** *New York Times* Staff, "At the Capitol on Jan. 6, a Day of Remembrance and Division," *New York Times*, Jan. 6, 2022, www.nytimes.com/live/2022/01/06/us/jan-6-capitol-riot.

280 **eighteen states enacted more than thirty laws:** "Voting Laws Roundup: July 2021," Brennan Center for Justice, July 22, 2021, www.brennancen ter.org/our-work/research-reports/voting-laws-roundup-july-2021.

281 **powers to set aside election results:** Ari Berman, "14 GOP-Controlled States Have Passed Laws to Impede Free Elections," *Mother Jones*, June 10, 2021, www.motherjones.com/politics/2021/06/14-gop-controlled-states -have-passed-laws-to-impede-free-elections.

281 **The GOP has purged moderates:** James Oliphant and Nathan Layne, "Georgia Republicans Purge Black Democrats from County Election Boards," Reuters, Dec. 9, 2021, www.reuters.com/world/us/georgia-repub licans-purge-black-democrats-county-election-boards-2021-12-09.

281 **growing spirit of vigilantism:** Dahlia Lithwick, "The Vigilante Next Door," *Slate*, Jan. 4, 2022, slate.com/news-and-politics/2022/01/jan-6-ushered-in-an -new-era-of-political-vigilantism.html.

281 **the Great Forgetting:** Renée Graham, "History Won't Hold Trump Accountable Either," *Boston Globe*, Feb. 16, 2021, www.bostonglobe.com /2021/02/16/opinion/history-wont-hold-trump-accountable-either /?event=event12.

281 **believe the 2020 election was stolen:** Melissa Block, "The Clear and Present Danger of Trump's Enduring 'Big Lie,'" NPR, Dec. 23, 2021, www.npr .org/2021/12/23/1065277246/trump-big-lie-jan-6-election.

282 **Mary Beard opens her book:** Mary Beard, *Women and Power: A Manifesto* (New York: W. W. Norton, 2017).

282 **The paperback Abrams published in 2019:** Stacey Abrams, *Lead from the Outside: How to Build Your Future and Make Real Change* (New York: Picador, 2019).

INDEX